THAT OTHER WORLD

being
the proceedings of the conference entitled
'"That Other World": The Supernatural and the Fantastic in
Irish Literature and its Contexts'
held at the Princess Grace Irish Library in Monaco
from 29th May to 1st June 1998

THE PRINCESS GRACE IRISH LIBRARY SERIES
(ISSN 0269-2619)

1. *Assessing the 1984* Ulysses. C. George Sandulescu and Clive Hart (editors)
2. *Irishness in a Changing Society.* The Princess Grace Irish Library (editor)
3. *Yeats the European.* A. Norman Jeffares (editor)
4. Ulysses: *a Review of Three Texts.* Philip Gaskell and Clive Hart
5. *The Literary Works of Jack B. Yeats.* John W. Purser
6. *The Celtic Connection.* Glanville Price (editor)
7. *Vertue Rewarded or The Irish Princess.* Anon. Hubert McDermott (editor)
8. *Rediscovering Oscar Wilde.* C. George Sandulescu (editor)
9. *Beckett and Beyond.*
10. *Oscar Wilde's* The Importance of Being Earnest: *The First Production.* Joseph Donohue (editor) with Ruth Berggren
11. *Images of Joyce.* 2 volumes. Clive Hart, C. George Sandulescu, Bonnie K. Scott, Fritz Senn (editors)
12. *That Other World.* 2 volumes. Bruce Stewart (editor)

THE PRINCESS GRACE IRISH LIBRARY LECTURES
(ISSN 0950-5121)

1. *Parameters of Irish Literature in English.* A. N. Jeffares
2. *Language and Structure in Beckett's Plays.* Clive Hart, with *A Beckett Synopsis.* C. George Sandulescu
3. *Jonathan Swift and the Art of Raillery.* Charles Peake
4. *Ireland and the Celtic Connection.* Glanville Price with *A Celtic Bibliography.* Morfydd E. Owen
5. *Joyce, Huston, and the Making of* The Dead. Clive Hart
6. *Joyce, the Artist Manqué, and Indeterminacy.* Morris Beja
7. *Flann O'Brien, Myles from Dublin.* Monique Gallagher with *Bernard Shaw & the Comedy of Approval* Marc Poitou
8. *Synge's* The Aran Islands: '*A World of Grey*'. Arnold Goldman with *Joyce & Vico & Linguistic Theory.* C. George Sandulescu
9. *Who Says What,* and *The Question of Voice.* Denis Donoghue

THAT OTHER WORLD
The Supernatural and the Fantastic
in Irish Literature and its Contexts

Volume Two

edited by
Bruce Stewart

PRINCESS GRACE IRISH LIBRARY: 12

COLIN SMYTHE
Gerrards Cross, 1998

This collection copyright © 1998 by
The Princess Grace Irish Library, Monaco

Contributions copyright © 1998 by the individual contributors
as listed on the Contents pages and their rights to be identified
as authors of their articles are hereby asserted in accordance
with the Copyright, Designs and Patents Act, 1988

First published in 1998 by Colin Smythe Limited, Gerrards Cross,
Buckinghamshire SL9 8XA, UK

Distributed in North America by Oxford University Press
198 Madison Avenue, New York, NY 10016, USA

British Library Cataloguing in Publication Data
A catalogue record for this book is available
from the British Library

Volume 1 ISBN 0-86140-417-3
Volume 2 ISBN 0-86140-418-1
the pair ISBN 0-86140-419-X

All rights reserved. Apart from any fair dealing for the purposes of
research or private study, or criticism or review, as permitted under the
Copyright, Designs and Patents Act, 1988, this publication may be
reproduced, stored or transmitted, in any forms or by any means, only
with the prior permission in writing of the publishers, or in the case of
reprographic reproduction in accordance with the terms of licences
issued by the Copyright Licensing Agency. Enquiries concerning
reproduction outside these terms should be sent to the publishers at the
above-mentioned address.

Appropriate acknowledgments have been given to the publishers of the
quotations printed in this volume, all of which come within the
meaning of the term 'fair dealing' as defined by the Copyright, Design
and Patents Act, 1988. If any holders of rights in works quoted herein
consider this interpretation to be incorrect, they should get in touch
with this company.

Produced in Great Britain
Printed and bound by T. J. International Ltd.,
Trecerus Industrial Estate, Padstow, Cornwall PL28 8RW

CONTENTS

KEYNOTE LECTURE 2
Peter Kuch: WRITING "EASTER 1916"   1

BRAM STOKER
Antonio Ballesteros Gonzales: PORTRAITS, RATS AND OTHER DANGEROUS THINGS: BRAM STOKER'S "THE JUDGE'S HOUSE"   18
Colin Graham: A LATE POLITICS OF IRISH GOTHIC: BRAM STOKER'S "THE LADY OF THE SHROUD"   30
Nicholas Daly: THE COLONIAL ROOTS OF *DRACULA*   40
William Hughes: 'IT MUST BE SOMETHING MENTAL': VICTORIAN MEDICINE AND CLINICAL HYSTERIA IN BRAM STOKER'S *DRACULA*   52
Bruce Stewart: BRAM STOKER'S *DRACULA*: POSSESSED BY THE SPIRIT OF THE NATION?   65

20TH CENTURY WRITERS
Gilles Menegaldo: FABULATION, ONEIRISM, AND IRONIC DISTANCE IN LORD DUNSANY'S SHORT FICTION   84
Bernard McKenna: 'GREEN FIRE INTO THE FROZEN BRANCH'—VIOLENCE AND THE RECOVERY OF IDENTITY IN VINCENT WOODS'S *AT THE BLACK PIG'S DYKE* AND SEAMUS HEANEY'S *THE CURE AT TROY*   97
Csilla Bertha: 'THAT OTHER WORLD': THE MYTHIC AND THE FANTASTIC IN CONTEMPORARY IRISH DRAMA   120
Alexander G. Gonzalez: DANIEL CORKERY AND THE GROTESQUE   136
Michael Faherty: TREATING THE WORLD AS A TRAMPOLINE: THE ALTERNATIVE REALISM OF MATTHEW SWEENEY   144

BECKETT AND FLANN O'BRIEN

Anthony Easthope: IRISH FANTASY, ENGLISH
   FANTASY: BECKETT AND LEWIS CARROLL — 158
Irene Eynat-Confino: YEATS AND BECKETT:
   FANTASTIC DISCOURSES ON THE STAGE — 167
Mark Harman: TERMINAL FANTASIES:
   BECKETT AND KAFKA — 177
Joseph M. Hassett: FLANN O'BRIEN'S OTHER
   WORLD OF FANTASY — 188
Monique Gallagher: *THE THIRD POLICEMAN*:
   A GRAVE YARN — 196

KEYNOTE LECTURE 3

Terence Brown: MAGIC AND REVOLUTION:
   YEATS'S "EASTER 1916" — 208

WILDE AND OTHERS

Maria Pilar Pulido: THE INCURSION OF THE WILDES
   INTO TÍR-NA-NÓG — 219
Neil Sammells: OSCAR WILDE, THE FAIRY TALE,
   AND THE CRITICS — 228
Paul Murray: LAFCADIO HEARN AND THE IRISH
   HORROR TRADITION — 238
Jerry C. M. Nolan: READING AND DREAMING IN
   MORGANTE THE LESSER (1890): A PLEA FOR
   RECLAIMING AN ABANDONED TEXT — 255
Donald Morse: MAKING THE FAMILIAR UNFAMILIAR:
   THE FANTASTIC IN FOUR TWENTIETH-CENTURY
   IRISH NOVELS — 267

W. B. YEATS

Elizabeth Heine: YEATS AND ASTROLOGY:
   "SUPERNATURAL SONGS" — 282
Deirdre Toomey: STRANGE EXPERIENCES IN
   PEMBROKE ROAD — 303
Matthew M. DeForrest: THE OTHERWORLDLY DEBTS
   OF W. B. YEATS'S *A VISION* (1937) — 319
Warwick Gould: STRANGER THAN FICTION: YEATS
   AND THE *VISIONS* NOTEBOOK, 1898-1901 — 331

Contents

Stanley Galloway: NIAMH: A SYMBOL OF DESIRE
   IN THE POETRY OF WILLIAM BUTLER YEATS   351
Bruce Stewart: "OUR PROPER DARK":
   A CHAPTER OF CONCLUSIONS   365

POETRY READING
Medbh McGuckian: "CAPTAIN HEAVEN"   386

INDEX   388

Contents - Volume 1:
Introduction; Opening Addresses; Inaugural Lecture; General Themes;
Keynote Lecture 1; Women's Studies; Gothic Fiction;
Joseph Sheridan Le Fanu; Poetry Reading

Keynote Lecture 2

WRITING "EASTER 1916"

Peter Kuch

> 'The Light from that consuming fire
> Which is the end of all desire.' *AE*

In this paper I would like to explore some of the points of intersection between the 'supernatural', the 'fantastic', and the 1916 Easter Uprising—particularly within the framework of a cultural history of the period, pivoted on Yeats's and Russell's literary associations, a cultural history that I have been working on for several years.

That the 'supernatural' and the 'fantastic' intersect has been posited by Tzvetan Todorov in *The Fantastic: A Structural Approach to a Literary Genre* (1970) where he defines the 'fantastic' as 'that hesitation experienced by a person who knows only the laws of nature, confronting an apparently supernatural event'.[1] Such a 'person' might be either a 'reader' or a 'character' who must decide whether what they perceive derives from "reality" as 'it exists in the common opinion', or whether their conception of "reality" must be changed.[2] Once that decision is made, Todorov argues, the 'fantastic' evaporates.

> If [that person] decides that the laws of reality remain intact and permit an explanation of the phenomena described, we say that the work belongs to another genre: the uncanny. If, on the contrary, [he] decides that new laws of nature must be entertained to account for the phenomena, we enter the genre of the marvelous.[3]

Thus, the fantastic can be conceived as a mode of speaking or writing which, having been obliged to admit what it considers to be the supernatural, neither explains it nor explains it away.

What interests me here is the idea that a literary genre can be thought of as a space where other modes of speaking and writing, such as clarification or explanation, do not proceed. Once the supernatural is explained in terms of existing paradigms, Todorov argues, we enter the uncanny or, once new paradigms are devised, we enter the marvellous. The fantastic then is characterised by a hesitation that derives from either an inability or a refusal to explain the supernatural. The inability might lie in the person or in language; the refusal might be self-imposed or imposed from without.

Whether it is an inability or a refusal, linguistic determinism is involved—the idea that perhaps language both discloses and encloses experience, that words though necessary even for conceiving whatever it is we have felt or thought might also circumscribe such thoughts and feelings. What then are the relationships between language and experience? Does language augment experience and thereby accommodate the supernatural? Or does the experience of what is thought to be the supernatural generate language? Either way, the supernatural might be considered as hovering on the cusp of language as the fantastic hesitates before the uncanny and the marvellous.[4]

And because I am interested in a hesitation as an experience rather than the fantastic as a literary genre—in other words a process rather than a structure, a gap, a silence, a refusal, an interstice, a prohibition, a hiatus—I would like to read Todorov's investigation of the fantastic in terms of Foucault's theories of discourse. What Foucault meant by discourse is difficult to establish. He admits, in *The Archaeology of Knowledge*, to using the term indiscriminately.[5] It could mean a self-regulating corpus of knowledge that informs a certain praxis—such as the discourse of 'traditional medicine', a 'profession' which seems to need perpetually to defend itself from a range of 'alternative medicines' that constellate around it and threaten its hegemony. Or it could mean a self-regulating system of language that constitutes a specific ideology, such as the discourse of Imperialism. Or it could mean a distinctive way of speaking and writing about something such as the way a particular religion speaks or writes about the supernatural. Underpinning all of these uses, however, is the idea that discourse, which is derived from the Latin *discurrere* meaning to 'run to and fro, to traverse', at once enables and determines what can and what cannot be said.[6]

Of course the simultaneous refusal to explain or to explain away the supernatural that constitutes the fantastic, as many literary historians have pointed out, was seized by Ernest Renan and Matthew Arnold around the middle of the nineteenth century as one of the defining characteristics of the 'Celt'. Arnold, in particular, believed that such a stance was a necessary corrective to the ills of late Victorian society, with the result that the 'fantastic', as a discourse of resistance to English philistinism, was utilised—albeit indiscriminately—in the Pan-

Celticism of the eighteen-nineties; only to experience an identity crisis in Yeats's turn of the century negotiations with cultural stereotypes; come clamorously under attack from D. P. Moran's 'Irish Ireland' and the Gaelic League as simply another Imperial fraud perpetrated on the Irish people; and finally be sent packing by Joyce's contemptuous dismissal of all such stereotypes as so much 'cultic twalette'.[7] All this is preliminary to saying that I would like towards the end of this paper to read Russell's autobiographical fragment, "The Sunset of Fantasy", for what it can add to our understanding of the 'fantastic' as a discourse of resistance and for what it can tell us about the 'fantastic' in terms of the 'supernatural' and the ethos of the 1916 Easter Uprising.

Finally, as discourses of resistance are dialogic,[8] the refusal either to explain or to explain away the supernatural can be seen as either a deliberate choice—as a politically considered act of resistance, or as an imposed prohibition—as one of the political realities of having been colonised. It might be that the subject decides not to speak. Or it might be that the subject is unable to speak because either the language to express what they want to say is unavailable to them or is being used by somebody else in such a way that it is saturated with inappropriate meaning. But what if revolutionaries like Connolly and Pearse, and poets like Yeats and Russell, needed recourse to a language of the supernatural to legitimate their vision of Ireland? Did their conception of independence require a validating discourse of the supernatural to counter the hegemonic power of the Catholic Church and the hegemonic power of the British Empire, both of which claimed a prerogative on the supernatural? And what if Connolly and Pearse and Yeats and Russell wanted to push beyond the fantastic as a discourse of resistance into discourses of self-determination and liberation, to transform resistance into revolution? How then could they speak about the supernatural—if they could speak about it at all? And who or what, to raise the fundamental issue of agency, would empower them to speak?

Much of the recent debate about a causal relationship between literature and the Easter Uprising has been generated by post-colonial readings of early Modern Ireland, particularly those advanced in Declan Kiberd's *Inventing Ireland* (1995). His basic argument is that the Irish were so in thrall to the master discourse of British Imperialism that liberation could only be achieved through a concerted effort to recapture and scrutinise the self. In conceiving of liberation as a national program of 'self' recovery, Kiberd has acknowledged his debt to writers like Franz Fanon, who affirmed: 'I am my own foundation. And it is by going beyond the historical, instrumental hypothesis that I will initiate the cycle of my freedom.'[9] The agency for such a programme, Kiberd argues with great wit and considerable ingenuity, is literature—particularly in the way it offers, explores and interrogates images of the self.

But this is a view of agency derived from liberal humanism, from the belief that self-engendered self-exploration promotes self-improvement, and that self-improvement eventually results in self-realisation, a state that is equated with freedom. Such a view of agency is questionable on two counts. Firstly it assumes that, despite the hegemony of the imperial discourse, despite its intrusiveness and power, the self retains the capacity to reconstitute itself within a perpetual cycle of self-reflexivity—or, to use Fanon's phrase, that it is possible merely by self-assertion and self-realisation to escape the 'historical, instrumental hypothesis'. Secondly it assumes that, in promoting self-realisation, literary discourses function largely free of interference from other discourses. Such a view of agency leaves little room for the 'fantastic'—for a form of exploring experience predicated not on progression but on hesitation, not on licence but on self-prohibition, not on coherence but on discontinuity.

James Connolly is an interesting case in point. It is well-known that from his return to Ireland in 1910 until his execution in 1916 Connolly found it progressively difficult and yet increasingly necessary to find some way of accommodating various aspects of the cultural and political nationalisms of his day to his own passionate commitment to Socialism.[10] The complex history of this debate with himself, and whether or not it was ever resolved, is subject to dispute[11]—though it is generally agreed that, towards the end of his life, his Socialism had become aligned with a form of quasi-mystical nationalism most likely derived from Pearse.[12] As his political biographer has pointed out, 'on the evidence of the last twenty months of Connolly's life, it is very difficult to associate Easter 1916 solely with international proletarian revolution'.[13] Furthermore, as many commentators have pointed out, in the declaration read from the steps of the Post-Office, a declaration that Connolly himself had helped to draft—there is almost no evidence of the Socialist Republic that he had devoted his life to advocating.

It is unlikely that we will resolve the question easily as to whether James Connolly died a Socialist or a mystical-nationalist, or some combination of the two, or whether he remained an 'unaccommodated man' to the end.[14] What I would like to explore briefly in this paper is the tension, particularly during his latter years in Ireland, between his public commitment to Socialism and his private religious faith. Connolly became a fervent Socialist in his early youth and was a passionate propagandist for the cause all his life, but he was born into an avowedly Catholic family. The prenuptial guarantee required by the Bishop before his parents were permitted to marry was intended to ensure that he was at least raised in the faith.[15] He sent his children to Catholic schools, though as an adult he rarely attended mass.[16] Yet he was accompanied to his execution by two priests; after which a Capuchin anointed his body.[17]

For Connolly, the problem of how to accommodate his personal faith to his Socialism was particularly complex. On the one hand Engels' historical respect for religion, particularly his work on primitive Christianity, licensed Socialists to speak about religion. And Connolly seems to have acquired his Socialism from Engels, Hyndman, and Marx mediated by Leslie.[18] Yet, on the other hand, Marx had declared that organised religion was merely a pernicious instrument of Capitalism, that, in popular parlance, it was an 'opiate', and consequently a major impediment to revolution. For their part, the Catholic Church, alarmed at the growth of Socialism throughout the 1890s, attacked it with growing vehemence, with the result that Connolly found himself increasingly obliged not only to declare himself either for Socialism or Catholicism but also to defend one against the other.[19] To do so he adopted a number of strategies, all of which incorporated some form of hesitation or prohibition, and all of which conceived of the supernatural, not as a personal experience, but as that power which the Church claimed validated its universal authority.

His most frequently employed strategy was to anchor Socialism in the public world and relegate religious faith to a private world, and insist that the two should clearly remain separate from one another. In an article for the *Workers' Republic* in 1899 and later reprinted in *The New Evangel* (1901) Connolly went beyond current Socialist thinking as advocated by Engels—who, in support of the Erfurt declaration of the SDP in 1891, had affirmed that religion was 'a private matter'[20]—to advocate the right of individual Irish Socialists to consult their own consciences and hold their own religious beliefs.

> The Socialist Party of Ireland prohibits the discussion of theological or antitheological questions at its meetings, public or private. This is in

conformity with the practice of the chief Socialist parties of the world, which have frequently, in Germany for example, declared Religion to be a private matter, and outside the scope of Socialist action. Modern Socialism, in fact, as it exists in the minds of its leading exponents, and as it is held and worked for by an increasing number of enthusiastic adherents throughout the civilised world, has an essentially material, matter-of-fact foundation. We do not mean that its supporters are necessarily materialists in the vulgar, and merely anti-theological, sense of the term, but that they do not base their Socialism upon any interpretation of the language or meaning of Scripture, nor upon the real or supposed intentions of a beneficent Deity. They as a party neither affirm or deny those things, but leave it to the individual conscience of each member to determine what beliefs on such questions they shall hold.[21]

A decade later, he wrote:

> [...] Socialists are bound as Socialists only to the acceptance of one great principle—*the ownership and control of the wealth-producing power by the state*, and that therefore totally antagonistic interpretations of the Bible or of prophecy and revelation, theories of marriage, and of history, may be held by Socialists without in the slightest degree interfering with their activities as such, or their proper classification as supporters of Socialist doctrine.[22]

Dialectical materialism and economic theory, it would appear, were free to range the public world of political discussion and party-room debate, while spiritual beliefs, whether or not they were inimical to Socialism, must remain private and in quarantine. The supernatural, whether experiential or discursive, was prohibited. The desire to explain or to explain away must not merely be checked by a hesitation; it must be held in suspense and perhaps held in suspense for a long time.

It is not that Connolly himself did not ponder such matters. Shortly before he 'played his part' in the Easter Uprising he wrote:

> I realise that human nature is a wonderful thing, that the soul of man gives expression to strange and complex phenomena and that no man knows what powers or possibilities for good or evil lie in humanity. [...] I try to preserve my receptivity to new ideas, my tolerance towards all manifestations of social activity.[23]

Yet, as a Socialist under attack from the Church, he seems to have been bereft of 'new ideas'. His second most common strategy in trying to accommodate his faith to his Socialism was to reply point by point to attacks from the Catholic Church. Consequently, what he wrote was often merely a denial or simply a counter-attack made up of accusations marked 'return to sender'. This is true of his reaction to the

1891 Papal Encyclical *Rerum Novarum*; and his reply to the 1901 attack on Socialism in *Father Finlay, S.J., and Socialism: An Exposition of Social Evolution* (1901). And it is also true of *Labour, Nationality and Religion* (1910), Connolly's reply to Father Kane, the Jesuit who delivered the Lenten pastorals at Gardiner Street in 1909. In all, Connolly simply denied what had been alleged or argued that Socialism was fundamentally more Christian than the political and religious systems attacking it.

In part this was due to a firm conviction, derived perhaps from Engels, that primitive Christianity and Socialism were based on similar principles. 'How, then', he wrote in *Labour, Nationality and Religion* (1910), 'can that doctrine which is high and holy in theory on the lips of a Catholic become a hissing and a blasphemy when practised by a Socialist?'[24] Thus, the language he employed for the purposes of achieving liberation remained saturated with meanings associated with the very system he was trying to discredit. For example, writing for *The Harp* in January 1909, he proclaimed:

> Religion, I hope, is not bound up with a system founded on buying human labour in the cheapest market, and selling its product in the dearest; when the organized Socialist working class tramples upon the capitalist class it will not be trampling upon a pillar of God's Church but upon a blasphemous defiler of the Sanctuary, it will be *rescuing the Faith* from the impious vermin who make it noisome to the really religious men and women. [My emphasis.][25]

A post-colonial theorist might argue that in this passage Connolly was simply appropriating the language of the Church for the purposes of liberating its believers, that he was strategically placing old words in new contexts and thereby infusing them with revolutionary meaning. But there is a fundamental problem with this. 'Words' cannot be so readily detached from discourse. Even if they are given new contexts, traces of old meanings remain. For example, the phrase 'rescuing the Faith' might be seen not as a rallying call to a broad-church Socialism (as I suspect was Connolly's intention) but as a call to reform the Catholic Church, to restore it to its original purity. The image which structures the passage is the image of Christ cleansing the temple in Jerusalem in order to usher in the Kingdom of God; the argument of the passage is that the Christian Church will be restored to its original purity once Capitalism is expelled from society in the same way that Christ cleansed the Temple by driving out the money-changers. At least in this passage, Connolly seems to be writing more as a left-wing Catholic than as a Socialist.[26]

But what is more important for my argument is Connolly's conviction that religion can only function as it should after the Socialist revolution has taken place. In other words, the issue of whether or not the supernatural ought to be explained in terms of existing paradigms, or whether or not new paradigms ought to be devised should not be taken up until the 'organised Socialist working class' had trampled 'upon the capitalist class'. Until then the supernatural should remain within the Fantastic.

Thus, in terms of Connolly's beliefs, the 1916 Easter Uprising can be seen both as a radical act of conservation and as a conservative act of revolution. An Irish Socialist Republic would of itself prevent the Irish working class from becoming irredeemably corrupted by the rampant capitalism unleashed by World War I—a war of imperial aggression that even by 1916, as many Socialist feared, had irreparably damaged the international solidarity of the working class. Moreover, an Irish Socialist Republic would challenge the hegemonic power of the British Empire and the Catholic Church, both of which claimed a prerogative on the supernatural. In such a society, Connolly believed, Socialism, political and cultural nationalism and religious faith could reinforce one another for the greater good of all Irish people. The soap-box, ballot-box, meeting, pamphlet, book, rally, and strike having failed, Connolly reached impatiently for a gun.

It is worth pausing here to emphasise the way events have come a full circle. In his Presidential address to the reconvened Ard Fheis on Sunday, 10 May 1998 supporting a "Yes" vote for the Good Friday Peace Agreement, Gerry Adams declared:

> This is the day that James Connolly was executed in this city eighty-two years ago. It is a good day for us to recommit ourselves to our republican ideals and the struggles which lie ahead of us. In one of my first presidential address I quoted from Connolly's *Sinn Fein and Socialism*. He wrote: 'Sinn Féin. That is a good name for the new Irish movement of which we hear so much nowadays. Sinn Féin, or in English, "Ourselves".'[27]

Having exchanged politics for the gun it now seems time for the reverse to take place, and the gun to be exchanged for politics.

For Padraic Pearse, the most notable point of intersection between a commitment to revolutionary violence, the supernatural and the fantastic seems to have occurred barely a year before the Uprising.

Though many critics have attempted to fix the time when Pearse first pledged himself wholly to an armed insurrection, Ruth Dudley Edwards has persuasively argued in her biography, *The Triumph of Failure*, that it was not until 'from mid-1915 onwards that Pearse felt secure and had no more fears about the righteousness of his cause. There was no looking back.'[28] In part, as Roy Foster has pointed out, this had to do with the ethos of fideism and self-annihilation that drove millions of young men to slaughter one another on the battle fields of Europe.[29] And in part it had to do with the way Pearse's intensely religious temperament found expression through a commitment to a doctrine of blood sacrifice derived as much from Christ as from Cuchullain. Pearse's Christ is the crucified Christ of baroque Catholicism, whose ignominious death fully discharged the divine mandate that 'without the shedding of blood there could be no remission of sin'. His Cuchullain is the gloriously bloodied Cuchullain, who, though haunted by premonitions of fate, nevertheless plunged into battle crying: 'I care not though I were to live but one day and one night provided my fame and my deeds live after me', only to be treacherously slain by a Fool and a Blind Man.[30]

But what Pearse appears not to have fully realised until early 1915 was that a commitment to heroic self-sacrifice was not something that could be striven for; it had to be supernaturally revealed, and it had to be accepted in an act of simple faith.

This realisation is evident in a play he wrote and staged in 1915 in the Hardwicke Street Hall, Dublin, as part of his St Enda's School annual pageant. Set in pre-Christian Ireland, *The Master* dramatises the conflict between Ciaran, the Christian master of a small forest school, and Daire, a King who comes to challenge the school master about the alleged power and superiority of the new religion. Before his arrival, Ciaran is shown tortured by guilt about his inability to commit himself to a decisive course of action. But when the King does arrive, he threatens to kill Iollann Beg, Ciaran's favourite pupil, unless Heaven intervenes, at which point, such is the strength of the child's faith, the archangel Michael instantly manifests himself in a blaze of apocalyptic glory. Daire immediately kneels in an act of submission. Ciaran briefly salutes the Archangel as a harbinger of the supernatural in a two line speech, and promptly falls dead, thus bringing the play to an abrupt end.

> DAIRE (*To Iollann*) [...] Come hither, child. (*Iollann Beag approaches.*) He is daintily fashioned, Ciaran, this last little pupil of

yours. I swear to you that he shall die unless your God sends down an angel to rescue him. Kneel boy. (*Iollann Baeg kneels.*) Speak now, if God has ears to hear.
He raises his sword.
CIARAN (aside) I dare not speak. My God, my God, why hast Thou forsaken me?
IOLLANN BEAG. Fear not, little Master, I remember the word you taught me [...]. Young Michael, stand near me!
The figure of a mighty Warrior, winged, and clothed in light, seems to stand beside the boy.
Ciaran bends on one knee.
DAIRE. Who art thou, O Soldier?
MICHAEL. I am he that waiteth at the portal. I am he that hasteneth. I am he that rideth before the squadron. I am he that holdeth a shield over the retreat of man's host when Satan cometh in war. I am he that turneth and smiteth. I am he that is Captain of the Host of God.
Daire bends slowly on one knee.
CIARAN. The Seraphim and the Cherubim stand horsed. I hear the thunder of their coming. [...] O Splendour!
He falls forward, dead.
CURTAIN [31]

To revert to Todorov's typology, Pearse's play exemplifies the fantastic in that the manifestation of the supernatural, which occurs moments before the final curtain, is neither explained nor explained away. But what is equally if not more noteworthy for my purposes is that in *The Master* Pearse is not simply appropriating the iconography of Christianity to his own messianic brand of revolutionary politics as some post-colonial critics have claimed. His strategy is at once more vital and more complex. Rather than simply seize various images and symbols and use them for his own purposes, Pearse had come to realise by 1915 that all he needed to do was inhabit them.

Inhabiting rather than simply appropriating the iconography of heroic blood sacrifice enabled Pearse to solve the complex problem of the relationship between agency and the supernatural. *The Bible* and *The Tain* simply assert that Christ and Cuchullain embody, enact, and are empowered by the supernatural. No explanation is given. The reader of both texts must accept that this is the case. As Eric Auerbach has argued in the opening chapter of *Mimesis: The Representation of Reality in Western Literature* (1946), where he compares the Old Testament story of the sacrifice of Isaac with that episode in *The Odyssey* where the faithful Euryclea recognises Odysseus from a scar as she washes his feet at his return to Ithaca, the reader accepts the claim that the Isaac story is divinely inspired because it makes no attempt whatsoever to explain the intervention of the supernatural.[32] It simply asserts, as does Pearse's play, that the supernatural manifests itself to set injustice to rights.

Similarly, Pearse's play, which appears indebted to the Isaac story, at the very least in the way it associates blood sacrifice with a test of unquestioning obedience as evidence of faith, neither attempts to explain or to explain away the supernatural intervention of the archangel Michael. Heroism, *The Master* suggests, is not about knowing, but about being. Triumph attends affirmation, not deliberation. In the final moments of the play the archangel, symbolic of the great apocalyptic battle of Armageddon, is instantly summoned by the act of child-like faith. His very manifestation defeats the Imperial power. In other words, the issue of whether or not the supernatural ought to be explained in terms of existing paradigms, or whether or not new paradigms ought to be devised, is not relevant. Pearse's play advances the radical proposition that the supernatural will be evoked once the faithful revolutionaries commit themselves unquestioningly to their righteous cause. Thus, for Pearse, the supernatural—particularly in terms of agency—remains lodged in the fantastic.[33]

The argument I have advanced for Connolly and Pearse could also be advanced for Joseph Plunkett and Thomas MacDonagh, and, I suspect, for several of the other key revolutionaries who took part in the Easter Uprising. To assert that they had by this time come to inhabit the fantastic is not to denigrate them, but simply to point out that by the 24th of April 1916, the day they abandoned themselves to the Uprising, their desire for an Irish Republic had reached such a pitch that it was being inexorably driven by an unquestioning faith in the transforming power of the supernatural.

George William Russell ("AE"), believed the fantastic was quintessential to the Irish character. In *The Sunset of Fantasy*, the working title of his autobiography which had been commissioned by Macmillan to complement the autobiographical writings of Yeats and several of the other leading writers of the Irish Literary Renaissance (but which was never in fact completed),[34] Russell declared:

> We of the Anglo-Irish have a dual character partly quickened by the aged thought of the world and partly inherited from an Irish ancestry. Ireland was never part of the ancient Roman Empire, and the imagination of its people had never been disciplined by philosophy or dialectic or science as other European peoples had been in whose minds something of the thought [of] Plato or Aristotle had incarnated. Our Irish ancestors continued for long centuries to live by imagination

which was I think the culture of the world before the Grecian mind became dominant. I think imagination has its own truth, a relation of image, myth or symbol to deep inner being, the truth which is in religion or poetry or the relations the drama of dream may have to our waking desires or to being in the world beyond dream. When imagination does not fly so high as the spirit it indulges in fantasy. [... N]o literature is fuller of imagination or fantasy undisciplined by philosophy than the Irish [...].[35]

The last sentence of this paragraph is the most significant for my purposes—the idea that intimations from the 'world beyond dream', if undisciplined by philosophy, remain lodged in the fantastic. And though this conception of the fantastic is not as rigidly systematic as Todorov's schema, and though it seems to derive something from the distinction Coleridge draws in the *Biographia Literaria* between imagination and fantasy, the insistence that the fantastic is characterised by a refusal to explain the experience of the supernatural is common to both Todorov and Russell.

This refusal to explain goes some way itself towards elucidating the particular nature of Russell's attempts to understand the Rising as an expression of something inherent in the Irish character. In his long poem "Michael", for example, a poem justly admired by J. B. Yeats, the narrator's refusal to explain the supernatural experience that initiates Michael into revolutionary politics works against the reader's expectations of explanations generated by the narrative structure of the poem. At a key point in the narrative, the narrator intervenes with a rhetorical question, which has the effect of suspending or postponing the explanation of Michael's vision of Ildathach, The Many-Coloured Land of ancient Irish myth, the land which Russell believed was the source of every impulse to restore the Irish to their ancient heritage. The vision simply takes place. Existing paradigms are not invoked nor are new paradigms devised.

The poem opens with the eponymous protagonist wandering through the countryside, receiving spiritual strength from Nature, until he reaches the rocky coast:

>   The salt air stung,
> From crag to crag did Michael leap
> Until he overhung the deep;
> Saw in vast caves the waters roam,
> The ceaseless ecstasy of foam,
> Whirlpools of opal, lace of light
> Strewn over quivering malachite,
> Ice-tinted mounds of water rise,
> Glinting as with a million eyes,

> Reel in and out of light and shade,
> Show depths of ivory or jade,
> New broidery every instant wear
> Spun by the magic weaver, Air.
>
> Then Michael's gaze was turned from these
> Unto the far, rejoicing seas
> Whose twilight legions onward rolled
> A turbulence of dusky gold,
> A dim magnificence of froth,
> A thunder tone which was not wrath,
> But such a speech as earth might cry
> Unto far kinsmen in the sky.
> The spray was tossed aloft in air:
> A bird was flying here and there.
> Foam, bird and twilight to the boy
> Seemed to be but a single joy.
> He closed his eyes that he might be
> Alone with all that ecstasy.
>
> What was it unto Michael gave
> This joy, the life of earth and wave?
> Or did his candle shine so bright
> But by its own and natural light?
> Ah, who can answer for what powers
> Are with us in the secret hours![36]

Fired by his vision, Michael joins a band of revolutionaries and, like the men of Easter 1916, sacrifices his life for an ideal. The narrator concludes:

> So it may be that Michael died
> For some far other countryside
> Than that grey Ireland he had known,
> Yet on his dream of it was thrown
> Some light from that consuming Fire
> Which is the end of all desire.[37]

While "The Sunset of Fantasy" reveals Russell's belief that the quintessence of Irishness expresses itself in the fantastic, "Michael" derives from a discourse of resistance in which violence, desire and the supernatural meet at the inexplicable.[38]

Yeats, perhaps more than any of his contemporaries, came to acknowledge the role of the fantastic in the Easter Uprising and to understand the way the fantastic intersected with desire, violence and the supernatural. In "The Stare's Nest by My Window" in *Meditations in Time of Civil War* he declared, his imagination ranging over at least a quarter of a century's celebration of an Irish identity constructed from an amalgam of primitive Christianity, pagan folk-lore and heroic myth:

> We had fed the heart on fantasies,
> The heart's grown brutal from the fare;
> More substance in our enmities
> Than in our love; O honey-bees,
> Come build in the empty house of the stare.[39]

Towards the end of his life, in "The Man and the Echo", in that frequently quoted interrogative debate with himself, Yeats speculated:

> And did that play of mine send out
> Certain men the English shot? (*VP*, p.632.)

As is now well known, that 'play of mine', *Cathleen ni Houlihan*, was in fact for the most part written by Lady Gregory. First staged in 1902, it was revived shortly before the Uprising. And though Yeats's claim that the play influenced some to participate cannot be conclusively substantiated, *Cathleen ni Houlihan* nevertheless was seminal in the literary history of the Uprising in that it was remarkably prescient. Many of its principal themes re-emerged in the issues that eventually gave rise to 1916—such as the conflict of the generations; the need to validate republicanism through armed struggle, perhaps in alliance with a foreign power; the suspicion that heroism might be nothing more than the 'delirium of the brave' (*VP*, p.290); and the insistence that nativism was inextricably allied with and could only express itself through the genuine ownership of land.[40]

But it is the closing scene of the play, which juxtaposes several discourses of desire with imminent violence and a supernatural transformation, that anchors *Cathleen ni Houlihan* in the fantastic. Peter Gillane, who has seen his eldest son Michael fall under the spell of the *Shan van Vocht* and turn his back on a strenuously bargained marriage settlement that would consolidate the family's holdings of land, asks his younger son if he saw his brother depart in thrall to an 'old woman'. 'I did not', the twelve year old Patrick replies, 'but I saw a young girl and she had the walk of a queen.'[41] And at that the curtain closes. *Cathleen ni Houlihan* exemplifies the fantastic because it refuses to explain the supernatural as anything other than self-evident.

The extent to which the supernatural resists explanation, escapes systems, Yeats speculates in "The Man and the Echo" as he returns to ponder the possible influence of *Cathleen ni Houlihan* on the men of Easter 1916 perhaps owes as much to external forces as to internal. On the one hand MAN would like relentlessly to pursue 'The spiritual intellect's great work' to achieve an ordering of experience where 'all's arranged in one clear view'. On the other, the sheer enormity of the task, and the random incursions of that casual violence that daily plays itself out in the everyday world oblige MAN to confront one of the most simple but also one of the most fundamental of all questions:

> What do we know but that we face
> One another in this place? (*VP*, pp.632-33.)

NOTES

1 *The Fantastic: A Structural Approach to a Literary Genre* [1970], trans. Robert Howard (NY: Cornell UP 1975), p.25. For critiques of Todorov see Rosemary Jackson, *Fantasy: The Literature of Subversion* [1981] (London: Methuen 1988) which explores the cultural construction of the fantastic in terms of Marxist cultural politics and psychoanalytic theory; and Kathryn Hume, *Fantasy and Mimesis: Responses to Reality in Western Literature* (NY: Methuen 1984), which proposes that all literature is comprised of the mimetic and the fantastic.
2 ibid., p.41.
3 idem. Fredric Jameson holds that the modern fantastic presents 'an object world forever suspended on the point of meaning, forever disposed to receive a revelation, whether of evil or of grace, that never takes place'. (Jameson, 'Magical Narratives: Romance as Genre', in *New Literary History*, VII, 1, Autumn 1975, p.146; cited in Jackson, op. cit., 1988, p.159.) Hume, op. cit. (1984), p.14, claims that 'one inescapable drawback of Todorov's definition is that many works conform to it up until their last pages, at which point they either explain the mystery (thus becoming merely uncanny) or affirm the reality of the supernatural event and thus become examples of the marvelous' (op cit., 1988, p.14).
4 Jackson argues that the fantastic is predicated on a type of oxymoron holding together contradictions even while sustaining them 'in an impossible unity, without progressing towards synthesis' (op. cit., 1988, p.21); also, '[t]he fantastic traces the unsaid and the unseen of culture, that which has been silenced, made invisible, covered over and made "absent".' (ibid., p.26).
5 *The Archaeology of Knowledge* [1972], trans. Sheridan Smith (London: Routledge 1994), p.31.
6 ibid., pp.27, 49, 55, 74, 80, 107, 117, 125, 150, 169, 210-11.
7 *Finnegans Wake* (London: Faber 1939), p.344 [344.12]. See Peter Kuch, *Yeats and AE: 'The Antagonism that Unites Dear Friends'* (Gerrards Cross: Colin Smythe; NY: Barnes & Noble 1986), pp.128-71.
8 Note however Todorov's caution regarding the 'dialogic hypothesis' in his review of C. Emerson, *The First Hundred Years of Mikhail Bakhtin* (New Jersey: Princeton UP 1998) in *Times Literary Supplement,* 31 March 1998, p.7: 'The most serious objections made against the dialogic hypothesis have to do with its exemplary manifestations in the work of Dostoevsky, as Bakhtin describes them. If we examine them carefully, we can see in reality, rather than true dialogue—that is to say, a relationship that preserves the freedom of the other—these examples display an authoritarian integration of the other's point of view into one's own consciousness.'

9   *Black Skin, White Masks*, trans. Charles Lam Markmann [1986] (London: Pluto Press 1991), p.231. See Declan Kiberd, *Inventing Ireland: The Literature of a Modern Nation* (London: Jonathan Cape 1995), pp.5, et passim.
10 Not that this problem was encountered only by Connolly. Austen Morgan has pointed out that in 1907 the Socialist Party of Ireland wrote to the Socialist Parties of Hungary, Finland, and Poland for guidance about nationalism. (*James Connolly: A Political Biography*, Manchester UP 1988, p.92.) This should however be set against a contemporary newspaper's wry observation that the Irish Socialist Republican Party had more syllables in its name than members on its list. (Quoted in Desmond Greaves, *The Life and Times of James Connolly*, London: Lawrence & Wishart 1961, p.65.)
11 See Morgan, op. cit. (1988), p.45; Greaves, op. cit. (1961), p.60. The most frequently cited source for the thesis of 'complementarity' is Connolly's pamphlet *Erin's Hope: The End and the Means* (1897), p.25: '[W]e will have based our revolutionary movement upon a correct appreciation of the needs of the hour, as well as upon the vital principles of economic justice and uncompromising nationality.'
12 Compare Connolly's article, 'Why the Citizen Army Honours Rossa', of 1 August 1915, with his pronouncing Pearse a 'blithering idiot' when the latter claimed in December 1915 that 'the old heart of the earth needed to be warmed with the red wine of the battlefields [...].' (Cited in Beresford Ellis, ed., *James Connolly: Selected Writings*, London: Monthly Review Press 1973, pp.44-45.)
13 Morgan, op. cit. (1988), p.45.
14 See Morgan, further: 'By 30 August 1914 Socialism had ceased to be his guiding ideology [...] But Connolly was still a trade union official in Belfast who was ignorant of the internal politics of the Irish Volunteers and had no responsibility for the Irish Citizen Army.' (ibid., pp.134-35.)
15 Greaves, op. cit. (1961), p.25.
16 ibid., p.110. Greaves also mentions the way Connolly's religion was used against him in his first election campaign. (ibid., p.51.)
17 See Father Aloysius, OFM, 'Easter Week 1916: Personal Recollections', *Capuchin Annual* (1942), p.220. See also Greaves, op. cit. (1961), pp.15, 65.
18 Greaves, op. cit. (1961), pp.42-44. Marx's *Das Capital* was first translated into English in 1887; *The Communist Manifesto* was first translated in 1888; Engels' *Socialisms: Utopian and Scientific* was first translated in 1892. According to Morgan, Hyndman's *Socialism Made Plain* (1883) was used extensively in framing the Manifesto of the Irish Socialist Republican Party (op. cit., 1988, pp.28-29). Note however Connolly's attack on Hyndman quoted in Ellis, op. cit. (1973), pp.134-35.
19 Greaves quotes John Leslie, who took issue in *The Present Position of the Irish Question* (1894) with the most widely-circulated of the priestly denunciations that 'Hell is not hot enough or eternity long enough to punish the wretches who are endeavouring to root Continental Socialism in the soil of Holy Ireland.' (op. cit., 1961, p.42.)
20 Morgan, op. cit. (1988), pp.44, 57. Note that Engels' argument that Socialists should press for the separation of Church and State ... only became known in 1901.

21 James Connolly, *The New Evangel* in *Erin's Hope: The End and the Means* [1897] *and The New Evangel: Preached to Irish Toilers* [1901], intro. Joseph Deasy (Dublin & Belfast: New Books Publications 1968), p.33.
22 Ellis (1973), p.68.
23 Quoted in Greaves, op. cit. (1961), p.279.
24 Ellis., op. cit. (1973), p.105.
25 ibid., p.41.
26 See Greaves, op. cit. (1961), p.83, and Morgan (1988), pp.59-60 for similar assessments of Connolly's *The Rights of Life and the Rights of Property* (1898) and *Labour, Nationality and Religion* (1910) respectively.
27 'Address to the reconvened Ard Fheis', Sunday, 10 May 1998, copied from http://www.irlnet.com/rmlist at 10 May 1998.
28 *Patrick Pearse: The Triumph of Failure* (1977; London: Faber 1979), p.233.
29 *Modern Ireland 1600-1972* (London: Allen Lane 1988), pp.461-84.
30 Quoted in Edwards, op. cit. (1977), p.117.
31 [Anon., ed.,] *The Collected Works of Padraic H. Pearse: Plays, Stories, Poems* (Dublin & London: Maunsel 1917), pp.99-100.
32 *Mimesis: The Representation of Reality in Western Literature* [1946] (NJ: Princeton UP 1974), pp.3-23.
33 Jackson argues that a death-wish is in fact inherent in the fantastic (op. cit., 1988, p.156).
34 Peter Kuch, ed., '"The Sunset of Fantasy" by AE', in *Yeats Annual*, No. 10 (London: Macmillan 1993), pp.188-203.
35 ibid., p.195.
36 "Michael", in *Selected Poems* (London: Macmillan 1935), pp.130-31.
37 ibid., p.139.
38 Cf. Jackson's contention that 'the fantastic images the possibility of radical cultural transformation through attempting to shatter the boundary lines between the imaginary and the symbolic' (op. cit., 1988, p.178.)
39 Peter Allt and Russell K. Alspach, eds., *The Variorum Edition of the Poems of W. B. Yeats* [corrected 3rd edn.,] (London: Macmillan 1966), p.425; henceforth *VP*.
40 Connolly, Pearse, and Russell all subscribed to the mistaken belief that land was communally held in ancient Irish society.
41 Russell K. Alspach and Catharine C. Alspach, eds., *The Variorum Edition of the Plays of W. B. Yeats* (London: Macmillan 1966), p.231.

PORTRAITS, RATS AND OTHER DANGEROUS THINGS: BRAM STOKER'S "THE JUDGE'S HOUSE"

Antonio Ballesteros González

The popularity of Bram Stoker as the configurator of one of the most fruitful contemporary myths, and the subsequent consideration of Dracula as an influential cornerstone in the evolution of fantasy and horror literature, have been inversely proportional to the critical attention generally paid to the rest of his works. Academic interest in the writer and his literary production has been usually limited to his famous masterpiece, especially in the context of the centenary of the novel in 1997. However, the widespread opinion from a canonical perspective that Stoker was a careless and second-rate writer should not obscure the evidence of literary genius discernible in his works. An effort should be made in order to get rid of traditional *a-prioristic* prejudices concerning Stoker's miscellaneous writings, and scholars ought to focus more objectively on the global parameters of Stoker's career. This brief study aims at analysing, from a literary and ideological perspective, one of Stoker's most anthologised short stories, although, paradoxically, one which has attracted hardly any critical attention. "The Judge's House" provides a good example of Stoker's gifts as a horror writer and deserves some critical response, like many other instances of his short fiction (which, on the whole, clarify and contribute to our understanding of the delimitation of the intrinsic development of Victorian fantasy).

"The Judge's House", as is well known, was posthumously published in 1914 by the writer's widow, Florence Balcombe, together with other short stories, under the general title of *Dracula's Guest*, a volume which includes the homonymous tale which some critics have interpreted as an episode originally intended for inclusion in *Dracula* but later discarded, as Christopher Frayling has sufficiently proved.[1] The collection attempted at taking advantage of the popularity of the figure of Count Dracula. It is important to note the indebtedness of "Dracula's Guest" to Sheridan Le Fanu's "Carmilla", one of the most disturbing vampire stories ever written. This intertextual relationship is relevant to the background of our study, for "The Judge's House" was also heavily influenced by two short stories written by Le Fanu: "Mr Justice Harbottle" (1872), and "An Account of Some Strange Disturbances in Aungier Street" (1923) where many coincidences in the treatment of symbols, images and structure are linked to the corresponding devices used by Stoker in his tale, as will be briefly discussed later in this article.[2]

Like many other stories whose origins are to be found in the development of Gothic patterns, the structure of "The Judge's House" can be schematically described as entailing the threefold division of transgression, encounter with the numinous, and retribution. These elements constitute the seminal foundations and the skeleton of the short story. The main character is a student of mathematics who is extremely worried about an examination on this subject, a situation with slight biographical connotations, for Stoker graduated with honours in science (pure mathematics) from Trinity College, Dublin.[3] Mathematics is the evident referent of logical reasoning, and there are certain similarities between Malcolm Malcolmson—the emphatic maintenance of what Lacan termed *Nom de Père* cannot be coincidental in a story with strong patriarchal connotations—to other well-known "students of unhallowed arts", punning on Mary Shelley's description of the very epitome of the transgressor: Victor Frankenstein. Knowledge—Gothic and Biblical readers are always aware—is dangerous. Mathematics, as the weapon of pure logic, are useless against the domains of 'that other world'. Reason will once again be defeated by powers which escape scientific control and explanation.

Although to a lesser extent, it could be argued that the dichotomous struggle between science and folklore (i.e., popular imagination) remains a valid consideration in interpreting "The Judge's House", as it was in *Dracula*. 'There are more things [...]': Hamlet's intriguing sentence can constitute a reminder of the perpetual warning against transgressors. Malcolm Malcolmson is—it should be admitted—a very modest parallel of Victor Frankenstein, Dr Jekyll or Dr Moreau. But, like all these characters, inserted in an intertextual male world of Gothic echoes, patriarchal solipsism and narcissism (generally leading to irresponsibility against the rules of a maternal and nurturing Nature), he also shares the ominous expectations of punishment. The

Promethean spark in Malcolm is very feeble: he is just a student of mathematics who wants to find a quiet place in order to study an examination. However, from a symbolic perspective, some relationships can be established between this young man and his illustrious predecessors: Malcolm's transgression suggests a desire for isolation and the implicit rejection of the folkloric community and the bourgeois family that did so much to sustain the Victorian ideal of an egalitarian society, an ideal replete with no little contradictions in a period of English history so beset by such unlikely dualisms. Malcolm 'wished to avoid friends', and when he arrives at the little town of Benchurch he rejoices at the impression that the place is 'as attractive as a desert'.[4] However, his longing for utter isolation makes him exchange the motherly cares of Mrs Witham, the landlady of the hospitable inn 'The Good Traveller', for an old Jacobean edifice, the symbol of the past and the uncanny, for the house is, as can be expected, haunted. The description of this place leaves no doubt about its Gothic connotations: it is the representation of the 'closed space', the domain of evil and otherness:[5]

> It was an old rambling, *heavy-built* house of the Jacobean style, with *heavy* gables and windows, *unusually small*, and set higher than was customary in such houses, and was surrounded *with a high brick wall massively built*. Indeed, on examination, it looked *more like a fortified house* than an ordinary dwelling. *But all these things pleased Malcolm.* (*TJH*, pp.151-52; [my emphasis.])

The feeling of oppression implied by Stoker's choice of vocabulary is apparently counterpointed by the last sentence, which symbolically emphasises Malcolm's disdain for communal values in the same way as prior folkloric referents, like 'Fearless John'.

The reason/superstition dichotomy provides a context to the tale similar to that of a morality play, for there are people in Benchurch like Dr Thornhill and Mrs Witham who warn him against dwelling in the house (which used to be 'the abode of a judge who was held in great terror on account of his harsh sentences and his hostility to prisoners at Assizes'), whereas others like Mr Carnford, the local lawyer and agent, and Mrs Dempster, the charwoman, side with Malcolm's sceptical position. However, the latters' opinions are obviously motivated by their economic profit, for both take advantage of, respectively, the main character's renting the house and need of a maidservant to keep it clean. This fact would probably make the contemporary reader distrust their less superstitious behaviour.

The elements relating this world and the 'other world' of the uncanny, in contrast to Malcolm's youthful pride in his mathematical knowledge, consist of the big rat, the oak chair, the portrait, and the rope tied to the alarm bell. These elements reflect the semantic mechanism of horror propitiated by non-human 'ITs'. All of these 'somethings' (as they are ambiguously referred to in the story) are connected with the evil Judge, and—with the exception of the chair and the coil of rope, which fulfils the function of the magic object of the folktale as a means of help for Malcolm, but also as a means of danger and aggression which in the end destroys him—both the rat and the portrait are dual projections of the Magistrate. The animal image, a representation of the numinous, is more complex and will need further explanation; with respect to the picture representing the Judge, Ziolkowski has convincingly analysed the iconological values of the enchanted portrait as the mirror image of a literary character.[6] It should be remembered that, in this particular case, the figure of the Judge was hidden under a layer of dirt and dust until Malcolm has Mrs Dempster clean the surface of the portrait to see what it represents—a recurrent device which can be traced in Le Fanu's fiction ("Harbottle", "Aungier Street", "Carmilla", &c.). If the enchanted picture stands for an outer projection of the soul (like in Poe's *The Oval Portrait* or Wilde's *Dorian Gray*), Malcolm's instruction—together with other causes—unleashes the evil powers of the dual object, returning the Judge to the 'real world'.

The three nights in which the plot is developed link the story with the prototypical structure of many folktales. The unbalancing effect of the number three underlines the desire (whether conscious or unconscious) on the part of Stoker to unfold the plot in a coherent way with regards to a thematic structure where the presence of folkloric values and superstitions—which in the event turn out to be only too well founded—are so significant. The events taking place during the three nights correspond to the scheme of rhetorical *amplificatio* and culmination. Stoker's inspired use of this neat parallelism contributes to the cyclical feeling of oppression and suspense in the reader's mind.

Malcolm's joy in his isolation is unexpectedly interrupted on the first night—the alternation of nocturnal gloom and optimistic daylight is undoubtedly important for the *chiaroscuro* effect of the tale—by the noise made by the rats inhabiting the old place. Stoker's use of the onomatopoeia in the description of the rats is striking:

How busy they were! and hark to the strange noises! Up and down behind the old wainscot, over the ceiling and under the floor they raced, and gnawed, and scratched! (*TJH*, p.155.)

The writer, like Le Fanu, was evidently fond of the uncanny associations of the image of the rat, which he reproduced in several other tales—"The Burial of the Rats" being the most significant example.

Malcolm is aware of the proverbial, chiastic words of the sceptical Mrs Dempster: 'Bogies is rats, and rats is bogies' (*TJH*, p.155). But the noise, together with the tea-induced alertness, makes him explore parts of the room not hitherto noticed accompanied by his lamp, an obvious 'Enlightenment' symbol of reason facing the realm of darkness. It is then that he discovers the old pictures on the walls, coated with dust and dirt, and the rope of the great alarm bell hanging from the roof. Although he goes back to his research, concentrating on mathematical problems, he is soon interrupted by the presence of the enormous rat, which, as a dual representation of the evil Judge, is sitting on the great high-backed carved oak chair. The appearance is related to the ceasing of the noise produced by the other rats. It may be that the 'real' rats function as doubles of the community of Benchurch; just as the human group used to be frightened by the imposing Judge, so these ordinary rodents are intimidated by this unnatural specimen. The rats also serve Malcolm as a reminder of the danger he is exposing himself to in staying alone in the haunted house.

The descriptions of the big rat—an epitome of 'otherness' and the numinous, as can be seen in the recurrent re-ification of the pronoun 'it' as applied to the rodent—invariably includes references to its cruel, baleful eyes: the same eyes as the protagonist will later discover in the portrait of the Judge. Malcolm tries to kill the rodent, and throws at it the poker from the hearth, which proves to be useless, for the animal runs up the rope of the alarm bell and disappears. When the youth relates these events to Mrs Witham next morning, he is more emphatically warned by the landlady about the risk he runs in living in the old house in complete isolation.

On the second night, when the horrifying rat again appears in the suffocating atmosphere created by the frightful silence of the other fellow rodents, Malcolm flings a book of logarithms at it. The action is of course deeply symbolic, resembling that in the first chapter of *Wuthering Heights* where Lockwood, when Catherine's ghost appears to him in a nightmare, piles up a heap of books to prevent the apparition from entering the room. Both the books and the logarithms represent culture and reason as opposed to uncanny forces which menace sanity. As mathematical works prove to be ineffectual, Malcolm uses the poker on the second occasion, and so the process is repeated: the rat flees up the rope of the alarm bell, the Judge's instrument of torture and death. Ironically, the youth foresees his own fate when he reflects of the rope, '[y]ou could hang a man with it' (*TJH*, p.159).

Sitting on the great carved oak chair that used to belong to the Judge, Malcolm ties the end of the rope to his lamp shortly before the rat returns to interrupt once more his eager study. Persisting with the ritual, he now throws several books at the malignant creature. His scientific work is in abeyance. Suddenly a change takes place:

> At last, as he stood with a book poised in his hand to throw, the rat squeaked and seemed afraid. This made Malcolmson more than ever eager to strike, and the book flew and struck the rat a resounding blow. It gave a terrified squeak, and turning on its pursuer a look of terrible malevolence, ran up the chair-back and made a great jump to the rope of the alarm bell and ran up like lightning [...] disappear[ing] through a hole in one of the great pictures which hanged on the wall, obscured and invisible through its coating of dirt and dust (*TJH*, p.160).

The picture, the third (again the number three) from the fireplace—its light providing an image of domestic ease and comfort—is, of course, the Judge's portrait, as Malcolm will discover after he has Mrs Dempster wash it the following night. It can come as no surprise to the habitual reader of Gothic fiction that the book which eventually strikes the rat is a Bible that his mother had given him: 'What an odd coincidence' (*TJH*, p.160), thinks Malcolm, but we know otherwise. The sacred book given by the protective mother has proved far more useful in this context than the *Conic Sections*, the *Cycloidal Oscillations*, the *Principia Mathematica*, the *Quaternions* or the *Thermodynamics*, the scientific defenders of the surprised student and a linguistic means of alienating the reader.

The Bible is connected, no doubt, with the ancestral powers of religion and folklore, the only forces capable of overcoming evil influences. Van Helsing's transformation in *Dracula* from a scientist using obscure jargon and techniques into the paladin of the bourgeois Victorian family is caused by his awareness of the fact that it is impossible to destroy the malignant creations of folkloric minds solely by means of the heterogeneous weapons of science and conventional reasoning. Dr Thornhill's role in the story mirrors, with obvious limitations, Van Helsing's position as a benevolent agent. His name is composed of two elements of nature, underlining the beneficent capabilities of the nurturing mother. (The allusion to *thorns* symbolically prefigures Malcolm's ultimate ritual sacrifice.) Thornhill's patronising behaviour towards Malcolm includes medical advice—not to take so much tea—and warning against the ominous forces of the past haunting the present. The Doctor informs Malcolm that the rope was the one that the hangman used for all the victims of the Judge's 'judicial rancour'. The oppressive atmosphere is interrupted by Mrs Witham fainting twice, a detail of anti-climactic humour. Thornhill is taking 'reasonable explanations' into consideration when thinking about Malcolm's account of the strange facts, and he interprets the latter's experiences as 'some strange fright or hallucination'. He is the one to provide a possible solution in case of danger, suggesting Malcolm's pulling the rope (implying, in other words, that the evil link between the framework of reality and that of the other world—the magic object—be used for a pragmatic purpose). In general terms, Thornhill seems to stand for the positive representation of the 'humanistic scientist', a label connecting him with Van Helsing, the defender of Victorian social values and order.

The third night brings with it the story's dénouement. Symbolically enough, 'The reading-lamp only was lit and its green shade kept the ceiling and the upper part of the room in darkness'. Once again, we can observe the metaphorical struggle between light and shade, between reason and the domain of the irrational. The youth's former desire of solitude and isolation is now weaker, for he is glad to hear the noise of the rats—the 'real' rats—while he is studying. This passage is full of positive adjectives ('glad', 'cheerful', 'warm', 'cheery', 'buoyant', [...] &c.) and a general tone of tense calmness. This optimistic interval heightens the reader's suspense by delaying the tragic end of the story. As he promised Dr Thornhill, he does not drink tea: the reader is thus persuaded that what follows is not brought about by Malcolm's overtiredness or a possible hallucination.

In the usual Gothic fashion, Malcolm's gradually disturbed feelings are related to the storm which takes place during the night. The alliterative and onomatopoeic passage, with the evocative recurrence of /r/, where Stoker describes the atmospheric phenomenon, is a good example of his command of frightening rhetoric:

> By this time the wind had become a gale, and the gale a storm. The old house, solid though it was, seemed to shake to its foundations, and the storm roared and raged through its many chimneys and its queer old gables, producing strange, unearthly sounds in the empty rooms and corridors. Even the great alarm bell on the roof must have felt the force of the wind, for the rope rose and fell slightly, as though the bell were moved a little from time to time, and the limber rope fell on the oak floor with a hard and hollow sound. (*TJH*, p.164.)

Malcolm cannot avoid taking Thornhill's advice and warning into consideration, and his eyes are intent on the rope. Coinciding as usual with the silence of the 'real' rats, the big messenger of the supernatural appears again. When immediately after this event he glances at the clean portrait of the wicked Judge, Malcolm loses all his scientific self-confidence and, for the first time, experiences all the ancestral horror of folkloric superstition. The description of the evil Judge's eyes reminds Malcolm of the eyes of the great rat, this physical feature underlining their dual nature. This duality becomes even clearer when he sees 'the rat with its baleful eyes peering out through the hole in the corner of the picture'.

What Malcolm sees in the portrait is a mirror image of the room where he is standing, with a discordant element: himself, for he has usurped the space formerly inhabited by the owner of the old house, the Judge:

> The Judge was seated in a great high-backed carved oak chair, on the right-hand side of a great stone fireplace where, in the corner, a rope hung down from the ceiling, its end lying coiled on the floor. With a feeling of something like horror, Malcolmson recognised the scene of the room as it stood, and gazed around him in an awe-struck manner as though he expected to find some strange presence behind him. (*TJH*, p.165.)

The presence is, of course, the *great* rat, sitting on the Judge's armchair. The repetition of the adjective 'great', used to excellent effect by Stoker throughout the story, is significant. It is evident now that the rodent has the Judge's baleful eyes, 'intensified and with a fiendish leer'. While he picks up the fallen lamp (the symbol of reason which is now submitted to the powers of darkness), Malcolm tries to think again in logical terms, going back to his work, to the unambiguous study of mathematics. He intends to recover his sense of reality, the world of facts that could separate him from the sphere of the unknown and the ineffable in which he has become caught up.

An hour later, the big rat appears for the third time on the same night, but now it has completed its dreadful task: gnawed through, the rope falls on the floor. Malcolm has lost his only possibility of assistance from the Benchurch community, and he is a prisoner in the closed Gothic space of the old house. The beneficent magic object has become the very representation of menace, at the same time that the scary image of the rat swaying to and fro at the end of the rope foreshadows Malcolm's tragic end. The recurrent effort of hurling a book at the animal—it is difficult to see why Malcolm does not use his mother's Bible again for this purpose—is vain; and, as usual, the rat disappears into darkness. When Malcolm lights up the shadows, he is shocked by the change he perceives in the enchanted portrait:

> In the centre of the picture was a great irregular patch of brown canvas, as fresh as when it was stretched on the frame. The background was as before, with chair and chimney-corner and rope, but the figure of the Judge had disappeared. (*TJH*, pp.166-67.)

Malcolm has at this stage integrated fear and horror in his self-confident routine of the solitary student of mathematics. Incapable of action or movement, he can only see and hear. From his semantic position as an experiencer he has now metamorphosed into a patient.[7] The Judge, in his human appearance and the role of agent, with his baleful eyes and cruel mouth, claims back his place in the sphere of reality. The only referent of the world outside the house for Malcolm is the noise of the storm, while he remains as still as a statue, the paralysed prey of a bloody predator. To this extent, the Judge is similar to the vampire, the devil, or Coleridge's Ancient Mariner, among other figures. The victim cannot avoid his fascination with the features of the aggressor.

At midnight—for the tale adheres remorselessly to all the conventions of the archetypal horror story—when time seems to come to a halt in contravention of the laws of common experience, Malcolm makes a mighty effort and tries to break free from the Judge's spell. The student experiences the sensation of relief when he becomes aware of the comforting presence of the eyes of perfectly ordinary rats at the rat-holes. A sense of solidarity and the desire for company seems responsible for the magical effect whereby the rodents try to make the bell toll, thus turning themselves into the symbolic doubles of the Benchurch community once more.

Unfortunately for Malcolm it is too late. With the disproportionate retribution conventional in Gothic fiction, the transgressor—weak overreacher here—is punished in an ending that reverses the conclusion of Le Fanu's "Aungier Street". The Judge's action of grasping and shaking the rope makes the rats flee. As members of the 'real' world, they also show in this way their atavistic fear of this disturbing representative of 'that other world'. Malcolm's anguish takes the form of paralysing horror at the prospect of the Judge's well-practised procedure—as a professional who knows only too well how to execute the gruesome sentence. When the Benchurch crowd reaches the house in a scene that suggests the cyclical battle between folkloric agencies for good and the menace of supernatural forces—a conflict often embodied in episodes of film versions of *Frankenstein* and *Dracula*—they are in time to meet with the hanged body of the student and to witness a suitably malignant smile on the lips of the Judge framed in the picture.

Unlike *Dracula*, "The Judge's House"—which is on the whole a Gothic fable where an inexorable 'fate' disproportionately punishes an apparently slight transgression—contains a deterministic and negative victory of the forces of evil over those of good. Here Stoker follows more straightforwardly a Victorian transformation of the Gothic pattern where the integration into the social nucleus on the part of the transgressor is contemplated as imperfect or impossible. On the other hand, the fact that the representative of evil is a Judge involves significant ideological implications, connecting this short story with such other Gothic instances of political and social injustice as William Godwin's *Caleb Williams* (1794). Taking her father's novel as the main source, Mary Shelley's *Frankenstein* (1818; revised edn. 1831) also shows the degree of injustice generated by an inhuman and Machiavellian judicial apparatus, which seems to be recurrent not only in the evolution of the Gothic and horror genre, but also in realist and 'bourgeois' fiction throughout the nineteenth century (Dickens deserving mention in this context). As an essentially divided period of English social history, the Victorian Age embodies the dichotomy of a puritanical society where the appearance of social order belies a state of affairs in which the seeds of injustice and political corruption actually impregnated every layer of the social framework. (Many examples might be furnished in a longer article.)

"The Judge's House" undoubtedly shares the same preoccupations as its main sources, Le Fanu's stories "Mr Justice Harbottle" and "An

Account of Some Strange Disturbances in Aungier Street", written at the apogee of the Victorian Age by another Irish author.[8] That Stoker based his tale on Le Fanu's more complex allegories of injustice and wickedness, is evident if attention is paid to the many points of similarity between them apart from the role of evil judges as the protagonists of each—ruthless individuals who terrorise the community by their arbitrary exercise of law—we find in Le Fanu's narratives a past haunting the present, occasioning an incursion from 'that other world' upon it. This intrusion is generally embodied as a setting by the haunted building in the form of an old Jacobean family mansion of the kind so easily associated with the 'hanging judges' of an earlier period. Indeed, Chapter I of Le Fanu's "Mr Justice Harbottle" is actually entitled "The Judge's House", thus providing the title of Stoker's later story.

Indeed, "Mr Justice Harbottle" displays a greater concentration of features germane to Stoker's tale than "Aungier Street", including such semiotic furnishings as the coil of rope (*MJH*, pp.100, 114), pictures on the wall, standing for the past (*MJH*, pp.96, 112), even the sedan-chair (*MJH*, pp.112)—as well as the symbolic 'ferocity of eye and visage' with which the Judge is always described. There is also a conventional development of the *Doppelgänger* motif, implicit in the dual projections of Lewis Pyneweck and that even more evident of Chief Justice Twofold (the otherworldly 'judge' who tries Harbottle), as his surname seems to indicate. Although "Mr Justice Harbottle" contains more moral undertones and oneirical and allegorical associations, and though the punishment is more justified in moral and social terms than in "The Judge's House", it involves a basically identical conception of Gothic retribution meted out to the transgressor. Fate plays an important role in both stories. On the other hand, the ending of "Aungier Street" presents a more optimistic *dénouement*, and the protagonist—yet another medical student—ultimately overcomes the forces of the supernatural by moving to different lodgings before it is too late. Some fatal implications of contact with the demonic remain however, since his fellow-student—who has an overt encounter contact with the uncanny Judge (here expressively called 'Horrocks'), dies young in the exercise of his clerical duties.

Le Fanu's "Mr Justice Harbottle" suggests deeper ideological relations than Stoker's story—most evidently in its more strongly suggested critique of the English legal system. At the same time, the rivetting portrait of evil judge in Le Fanu's tale may be regarded as the model for Stoker's answering narrative:

> The Judge was at that time a man of some sixty-seven years. He had a great mulberry-coloured face, a big carbuncled nose, fierce eyes, and a grim and brutal mouth. My father, who was young at the time, thought it the most formidable face he had ever seen [...]. This old gentleman has the reputation of being about the wickedest man in England. Even on the bench he now and then showed his scorn of opinion. He had carried cases his own way, it was said, in spite of counsel, authorities, and even of juries, by a sort of cajolery, violence, and bamboozling, that somehow confused and overpowered resistance. He had never actually committed himself; he was too cunning to do that. He had the character of being, however, a dangerous and unscrupulous judge [...].
> (*MJH*, p.88.)

Against the force of that description, the greater sense of isolation of the central character in Stoker's story, together with the profound atmosphere of suspense surrounding his fate, create a strong feeling of sympathy for him in the reader. Despite such minor stylistic flaws as occasional careless repetitions, "The Judge's House" is a powerful example of Stoker's skill in horror fiction and well deserves its place in the best anthologies of the genre.

NOTES
1. *Vampires: Lord Byron to Count Dracula* (London: Faber & Faber 1991), pp.351-53.
2. Collected in M. R. James, ed., *Madame Crowl's Ghost and Other Stories* [1923] (Hertfordshire: Wordsworth Classics 1994).
3. Clive Leatherdale, *Dracula: The Novel and the Legend* (Brighton: Desert Island Books 1993), p.58.
4. *The Judge's House*, in Leslie Shepard, ed., *The Dracula Book of Great Horror Stories* (Avenel: Wings Books 1991); henceforth *TJH*.
5. See Manuel Aguirre, *The Closed Space* (Manchester UP 1989).
6. Theodore Ziolkowski, *Disenchanted Images A Literary Iconology* (Princeton UP 1977)
7. See Talmy Givón, *Mind, Code and Context. Essays in Pragmatics* (Hillsdale & London: Lawrence Erlbaum 1989).
8. *Mr Justice Harbottle*, rep. in *In a Glass Darkly* (Gloucester: Alan Sutton 1990); henceforth *MJH*.

A LATE POLITICS OF IRISH GOTHIC: BRAM STOKER'S *THE LADY OF THE SHROUD* (1909)

Colin Graham

Like most critical and theoretical concepts in literary studies, the Gothic seems to suffer a degree of adaptation or contortion when it is moved into the Irish context as it competes with existing politicised notions of the 'Irish' and settles, however uncomfortably, into a co-existence with current practices and trends in readings of Irish literature. That there is the potential for a tradition of Irish Gothic seems indisputable; Charles Maturin, Sheridan Le Fanu and Bram Stoker, along with some of the writings of Maria Edgeworth, William Carleton, W. B. Yeats and Oscar Wilde, can be placed in a relatively logical linear progression of literary history.[1] How these texts are read in an Irish context will always be less stable than the tradition they suggest; if the Gothic is a literature of class alienation, repression, sexuality, guilt and the fear of the 'barbaric'—characteristics common to most contemporary definitions of the Gothic[2]—then a series of Irish texts embodying these themes and written almost exclusively by Protestant Ascendancy writers will initially be forced into inevitable political meanings and allegories. It is how such thematics are to be critically and theoretically shaped in Irish Gothic that is still somewhat unclear. In this essay I hope to discuss the prospects (and some of the difficulties) of understanding Irish Gothic from a theoretical view-point that assumes a particular post-colonial critical perspective on Irish literature, before going on to discuss Bram Stoker's novel *The Lady of the Shroud* (1909) in an attempt to clarify a potential post-colonial critique of the unstable and complex political nature of interpreting Irish Gothic.

A helpfully exemplary political reading of the Gothic in Irish literature is implied in Julian Moynahan's essay on 'The Politics of Anglo-Irish Gothic',[3] where he writes:

Gothic literature often carries a heavily political or meta-political charge. The Gothic seems to flourish in disrupted societies, to give a voice to the powerless and unenfranchised [sic], and even at times to subvert or contradict the overt best intentions of the author.[4]

Moynahan avoids the explicit formulation of a theory of Irish Gothic, but the political implications of this summary of the Gothic are relatively clear: Irish Gothic texts will disrupt the official Protestant Ascendancy discourse of their authors, articulating their fear of the 'repressed' and 'powerless', expressing the ambiguities of their position as simultaneously Anglo- and Irish, and pointing towards the final political undermining of this class. This is certainly an attractive basis for reading Irish Gothic, and allows for a theory of the sub-genre which is born out by and in specific texts. The major objection to this way of reading Irish Gothic is perhaps anticipated in Moynahan's careful wording when suggesting that the Gothic 'carries a heavily political *or meta-political* charge', since it becomes apparent on reading the most prominent texts which could be classed as Irish Gothic (viz., *In a Glass Darkly, Uncle Silas, Dracula, The Picture of Dorian Gray*) that these are not always specifically Irish in their context. They do not deal with Ireland directly, and any slippages revealing an anxiety of the dominant in these texts must be on some level metaphorical if not allegorical. As the embarrassed and anti-superstitious priest in Bram Stoker's *The Snake's Pass* (1891) says to the narrator, explaining local legends: 'It is a queer thing that men must always be putting abstract ideas into concrete shape.'[5] Irish Gothic, if it exists at all, seems to displace itself to a position which is not fully encapsulated by either the abstract or the concrete, the meta-political or the political.

Differences in the reading of Irish Gothic tend not to dispute the 'return of the repressed' model which Moynahan hints at.[6] The castle, the aristocratic house, superstition, religion, an obsession with the landscape and environment, and inheritance all have political resonances in an Irish context, and a 'theory' of Irish Gothic can quickly emerge in which all metaphors tend to match these expectations. Reading Stoker's *Dracula* (1897), for example, Andrew Parkin says:

> The rhythms of the Count are that of an Irish speaker of English rather than a European one; they fit with the image of Dracula as a nobleman with a 'Gothic' castle, and a country house, as well as a London town house to which he periodically withdraws.[7]

Dracula here is representative of his author, as his author is representative of his class; simply put, Dracula is an Irish landlord, preying on the blood of the peasantry. Seamus Deane ingeniously extends this reading when he says that *Dracula*

> tells the story of an absentee landlord who is dependent in his London residence on the maintenance of a supply of soil in which he might coffin himself before the dawn comes [...]. Landlord that he is, with all his enslaved victims, his Celtic twilight is endangered by the approach of a nationalist dawn, a Home Rule sun inexorably rising behind the old Irish Parliament.[8]

There is a neatness to such readings of *Dracula*, and they can easily be transferred methodologically to other Irish Gothic texts. But an Irish Gothic criticism which allows such readings as its limits denies both the impact a text such as *Dracula* has in other critical contexts and unnecessarily demarcates a restricted field for the meaning of Irish Gothic itself. Parkin and Deane, for example, imply a very static notion of Dracula as 'landed' in every sense; tied to his land or absent from it in England, he is a figure of the relationship between an Irish peasantry and the Ascendancy which is waiting to be overturned. The colonial anxiety here is apparent, but latent and monologic, made quiet by the lack of a necessity to defend itself; the colonial relationship in the text reflects the apparently silenced nature of the colonised, because in this version Dracula is metaphorically a coloniser while his English victims are more literally colonial in terms of their relationship to Ireland.

Thus, while this is a potentially satisfying account of the text as Irish Gothic, it produces a reading in which the 'repressed' can only 'return' through the relatively untroubled dominance of the coloniser, and then in near silence and non-representation.[9] This runs against the grain of recent Gothic criticism in general and *Dracula* criticism in particular. (It also contradicts more recent writings in post-colonial theory which stress a more active, subverting role for the colonised voice speaking back through colonial textuality.) Stephen Arata, Thomas Richards and Ken Gelder, for example—critics who are not interested primarily in the Irishness of Stoker—read *Dracula* in terms of imperialism and colonialism; but for them the text is dynamic in its representation of colonial inter-relations. Arata's 'The Occidental Tourist: *Dracula* and the Anxiety of Reverse Colonisation'[10] sees the Count as a colonial figure, but in terms which overturn Parkin and Deane. For Arata, Dracula signifies rather than suffers the return of the colonial repressed; Dracula is the colonised speaking back through the anxieties of the coloniser; he 'invades' from the East and the empire bites back. As Thomas Richards suggests, 'in [*Dracula*] the periphery attempts to colonize the centre'.[11] For Gelder, Transylvania is 'a region which lies under the shadow of—but is still, for the moment, *outside*— colonisation [my emphasis];[12] and here again Dracula figures the colonised in subverting ways rather than being the coloniser who is subverted. Where Parkin and Deane use language and soil as their guiding thematics in constructing a reading of *Dracula*, Gelder, Richards, and Arata, aware of the wider ethnographic and potentially post-colonial context of Gothic, can read *Dracula* in more open ways, less fettered by the need for allegories and fitting metaphors.

This suggests that an Irish Gothic criticism could usefully be opened up to a post-colonial theory which emphasises the possibilities of finding faultlines within colonial discourse. Ireland's liminal colonial position as simultaneous coloniser and colonised, centre and periphery, makes it uniquely suitable to such readings. As a result hybridity, ambiguity, and contradiction are arguably inherent tropes of Irish colonial cultural interaction, the impact of which is denied by the allegorising impulse driving much criticism of Irish Gothic texts.[13] This means, for example, that the critic of Irish Gothic should sit up when Gelder argues that *Dracula* deliberately confuses, and makes a spectacle of, the issues of race and nationality that underpin imperialism:

> Diversity means instability: it invites contestation: identities become confused: one can no longer tell 'who was who'. In short diversity means the *loss* of one's nationality—hardly appropriate for an imperialist ideology which depends upon a stable identification between nation and self.[14]

So the poverty of a theory of Irish Gothic which sees Irish Gothic texts as always representative of a fixed colonial power structure in which textuality is always and without complication on the side of the coloniser (and thus excludes the colonised) simplifies unnecessarily the ambiguities of both the Irish context and the nature of Gothic itself. Judie Newman succinctly describes post-colonial Gothic thus, in terms that can usefully be translated into the liminal space of colonial Irish culture:

> At its heart lies the unresolved conflict between the imperial power and the [...] colony, which the mystery at the centre of its plot both figures and conceals. Its discourse therefore establishes a dynamic between the unspoken and the 'spoken for' [...].[15]

In reading Stoker's *The Lady of the Shroud* (1909), I want to suggest that this text not only benefits from a post-colonial critical basis for understanding Irish Gothic, and a warning about the over-anxious search for fixed and predetermined allegory in the text, but that we can use the text to make clearer how it might be possible to proceed in formulating an alternative notion of the textual politics of Irish Gothic. Indeed it may be possible to suggest that Stoker uses *The Lady of the Shroud*—in some ways a 'late' Irish Gothic text—to examine his own difficulties with the politics and the political capabilities of Gothic and, further, that these difficulties eventually led Stoker to an Anglo-Irish assertion of hierarchy within Ireland while projecting fears of the impetus of nationalism moving towards independence. *The Lady of the Shroud* then becomes an apparently contradictory site of both the coloniser's assertion of dominance and a prefiguration of the end of colonialism itself: coloniser and colonised, imperialism and emergent nationalism overlap in the text, so undermining the very allegories which support these distinctions and the nostalgias of identification upon which they call.

The Lady of the Shroud reads initially like an obvious attempt on Stoker's part to follow up the popular success of *Dracula*.[16] The novel opens with an extract from *The Journal of Occultism*, telling the story of a white lady who floats in a coffin in the Adriatic just off the coast of the Land of the Blue Mountains. The novel then switches to a *Dracula*-like mode of narration, using documents, memoirs and letters to piece together its story. Rupert St. Leger inherits a vast fortune from his uncle Roger Melton on condition that he goes to live in the Castle of Vissarion, in the Land of the Blue Mountains, for a period of at least six months. While Rupert, seven feet tall and an experienced adventurer, is in the Blue Mountains, having accepted the conditions of the will, he becomes involved in two parallel plots: he attempts to take up the cause of nationalism in the Land of the Blue Mountains—a nation which feels itself to be under threat from its Balkan neighbours. He also sights several times, and is visited by, the 'Lady of the Shroud' as he calls her (the ghost-like figure referred to in the opening journal extract). Rupert assumes that she is a vampire, having discovered her glass-covered coffin in a cave, and that his love for her will at best be unrequited and may even lead to his death. The two storylines come together however, when it becomes clear that the Lady is not one of the undead but in fact the Princess of the Blue Mountains forced to pose as a vampire to create a legend which will avoid splitting the nation.

A Late Politics of Irish Gothic: Stoker's The Lady of the Shroud 35

Rupert marries her (while he still believes she is a vampire), then saves her from kidnappers and eventually goes about arming the warriors of the Blue Mountains with weapons and technology (including aeroplanes) bought with his inheritance, thus allowing the nation to at last assert its independence.

The novel offers several possible interpretations in the light of my discussion of Irish Gothic above. Perhaps the most significant fissure in this text—which will always be read in the shadow of *Dracula*—is the use of the vampire story and the way in which it appears to lure the reader into reading in the mode of *Dracula*, only to find that the novel rejects the theme of vampirism, using it as a political ploy in narrative terms instead. The vampire in *Dracula* was a submerged political figure who can be seen to have acted either as landlord or as a returning repressed coloniser's conscience; in *The Lady of the Shroud* the vampiric is deliberately exposed in an explicit political realm and as part of a struggle for national assertion. W. J. McCormack argues that Stoker, along with Yeats, 'found a place for the expiring gothic note';[17] in *The Lady of the Shroud* Irish Gothic may be fading but the novel also reveals that Irish Gothic is crucially underwritten by a politics of empire, nationality, and violence.

If the novel then uses *Dracula* as a way into an alternative narrative, what are we to make of the differences between *The Lady of the Shroud* and *Dracula* in terms of a putative post-colonial Irish Gothic? As was apparent from Irish critics reading *Dracula*, there is a consensus that in Irish Gothic the politics of the Ascendancy psyche are unsettled; what is debated is the extent to which the Irish Gothic text attempts, or is able, to resubmerge the supernatural. It is tempting to see *The Lady of the Shroud* as an overturning of the politics of *Dracula*; if Stoker's most famous vampire is a figure of reverse colonisation, as Arata suggests, then *The Lady of the Shroud* redirects the reversal of colonialism in *Dracula* to face the 'appropriate' way, dispensing with the supernatural in order to return to colonial stability. Thus because Rupert represents the West and goes to the East to bring order, control, and power through wealth and technology, he appears to be recolonising that area which *Dracula*/Dracula forfeited. However such shifts, overturnings, and ambiguities in the colonial semantics of the text strain a politicised reading of it, they are nevertheless essential to an understanding of Irish Gothic since they reflect the unsettled, often unfixed nature of colonialism in an Irish context. That the roles of the coloniser and colonised should merge, separate and exist in contradiction is entirely in keeping with both the potentially paranoid nature of Gothic and the split position of the 'colonial' in Ireland.

To further untangle the complexities of Irish Gothic in this text we can go back to one of the most basic elements of Gothic itself: inheritance. As Fred Botting points out, the Gothic novel often involves characters who 'usurp rightful heirs, rob reputable families of property';[18] Le Fanu's *Uncle Silas* unfolds such themes, while *Dracula* transforms them into metaphors of various potential meanings. *The Lady of the Shroud* begins with a controversy over a will. Rupert's cousin, Ernest Melton, believes himself to be due the fortune which Roger Melton leaves Rupert. Indeed this part of the novel prepares us for the narrative disjunction in the vampire story—at the beginning Ernest Melton appears to be the central figure in the novel, but there is an early switch in the narration which moves Rupert to the centre of the plot. The issue of inheritance is (for Ernest at least) linked to ancestry, family, and class. For Ernest, his branch of the family, the Meltons proper, are far superior to Rupert's, the St. Legers. Underlying Ernest's belief that he has been 'disinherited' by his uncle's will in favour of Rupert is a family history which seems to point us in the direction of the potential 'Irishness' of the text.

Ernest traces his own branch of the Melton family to his great-great-grandfather who changed the spelling of the family name from 'Milton' to 'Melton':

> [He] was a practical man not given to sentiment, and feared lest he should in the public eye be confused with others belonging to the family of a Radical person called Milton, who wrote poetry and was some sort of official in the time of Cromwell, whilst we are Conservatives. (*LOS*, p.31.)

Against this branch of the family, who regard themselves explicitly as 'landowners' (*LOS*, p.15) and believe in the 'honour of bearing our Name' (*LOS*, p.18), are set the St. Legers. Information on this family line is disseminated through the snobbery of Ernest Melton. This name (St. Leger) has entered the Melton family through marriage to an 'Irishman of the name of Sellenger' (*LOS*, p.4). Like the Meltons, the St. Legers have had their name altered for the sake of propriety. St. Leger is seen by Ernest as a more acceptable, de-Irishised form of the name, and these changes alerts us to the dichotomies we are meant to see between the decent, honourable, adventurous, liberal, 'poverty-stricken' and (questionably) Irish Rupert and the snobbish, objectionable, wealthy, conservative (manifestly English) Ernest.

There is a potential neatness here, then. It is now possible to argue that Rupert, as a figure of the Anglo-Irish, rediscovers his Irishness in the battle to free the Land of the Blue Mountains. The novel would thus be symbolic (perhaps inadvertently) of the shaking off of the shadow of Ascendancy Gothic traumas (the rejection of the vampiric in the plot) in a newly regenerated Ireland.[19] But this is perhaps too simplistic: Rupert St. Leger is, after all, never going to be 'purely' Irish. Indeed one key to his identity might lie in a possible source for Stoker's use of the name St. Leger. The most prominent St. Leger in Irish history is Sir Anthony St. Leger, Lord Deputy of Ireland in the sixteenth century, who suggested that Henry VIII 'change his title from Lord of Ireland to King of Ireland' in order to persuade 'the Gaelic lords and their people [... to] become more loyal to the Crown and abide by English law'.[20] Rupert St. Leger is, at the end of *The Lady of the Shroud*, made King of the Land of the Blue Mountains. His acceptance of the crown is described in an extract from the 'Record of the First Meeting of the National Council' at which Rupert says:

> 'Hereby I swear to be honest and just—to be, God helping me, such a King as you would wish [...].'
> [...] This ended the business of the Session, and the Council showed unmeasured delight. Again and again the handjars flashed, as the cheers rose 'three times three' in British fashion. (*LOS*, p.225.)

Rupert's nationality is thus ambiguous, hybridised and confused—his family's Irishness (more properly Anglo-Irishness) appears to resurface, yet the resonances of the family name are changed to accord with an act of imperialism and possession. Henry's kingship is doubled by Rupert's kingship. Rupert's inability to be *of* the Blue Mountains whilst attaining possession and power in the Blue Mountains, is only emphasised by the clause in his uncle's will, often referred to throughout the text, which denies him the right to change his British citizenship without the assent of the Privy Council. Rupert's inheritance is thus genealogically Anglo-Irish while legally British, and the overlaying of these two allows him only to rule rather than 'belong in' the Blue Mountains.

And yet still the novel asserts the rights of freedom of this small nation at a time when, in Ireland, 'home rule seemed to be assured'.[21] Rupert's double role as liberator and ruler can be seen then in its historical context and in its Irish Gothic context. Rupert's national identity represses his Anglo-Irishness, and reinforces his Britishness by legality and obligation. His apparent contradictions are in the nature of the Anglo-Irish themselves, their hybridity placelessness placing them precariously over the already liminal space of colonialism in Ireland. As a fantasy of the Protestant Ascendancy, *The Lady of the Shroud* expresses the desire to retain Britishness, to be Irish and yet to assert the current class and social hierarchy. It is only by allowing Irish Gothic to constitute a potential opening up of the marginal spaces of colonial theory in an Irish context that we can begin to arrive at such a reading. To allegorise, to pull the text back to certainty, would be to see Rupert as either a metaphor for a suppressed Irish identity or as a symbol of what Phyllis A. Roth calls Stoker's 'Anglo-Irish chauvinism'[22]—assuming that 'he' (Rupert/Stoker as Anglo-Irish) should 'rule' the Irish. *The Lady of the Shroud* converts Gothic tropes of inheritance, the castle, the land, and identity into a potentially Irish context; it explicitly politicises itself by jettisoning the vampire narrative in favour of a story of technology, power, and resurgent nationality; and it allows the trauma of the Gothic to encompass the awkward, unsettled, and doubled cultural identities which the process of colonialism and colonisation in Ireland engendered. The repressed both returns in *The Lady of the Shroud* and is in turn repressed— perhaps at this late point in Irish Gothic the dialectic play between the two became closer to equivalence than it had been previously.[23] As a late Irish Gothic text *The Lady of the Shroud* may be more open— semantically and allegorically—than earlier Irish Gothic texts, and thus more useful in moving towards a theorisation of the politics of nineteenth-century Irish Gothic.

NOTES

1. For a version of this history—which can of course be extended into the twentieth century—see W. J. McCormack, 'Irish Gothic and After', in Seamus Deane, gen. ed., *The Field Day Anthology of Irish Literature* (Derry: Field Day 1991), Vol. 2, pp.831-54.
2. See, for instance, David Punter, *The Literature of Terror: A History of Gothic Fictions from 1765 to the Present Day* (London: Longman 1980).
3. Julian Moynahan, 'The Politics of Anglo-Irish Gothic: Maturin, Le Fanu and 'The Return of the Repressed'', in Heinz Kosok, ed., *Studies in Anglo-Irish Literature* (Bonn: Bouvier Verlag Herbert Grundmann 1982), pp.43-53.
4. Moynahan, op. cit. (1982), p.44
5. Stoker, *The Snake's Pass* (Dingle: Brandon 1990 [1891]), p.28
6. See however McCormack's *Field Day Anthology* editorial essay, in which he tends to doubt the existence of a coherent tradition of Irish Gothic while paradoxically canonising it (op. cit., 1991, espec. p.832f.)
7. Andrew Parkin, 'Shadows of Destruction: The Big House in Contemporary Irish Fiction' in Michael Kenneally, ed., *Cultural Contexts and Literary*

Idioms in Contemporary Irish Literature (Gerrards Cross: Colin Smythe 1988), pp.307-08.
8   Seamus Deane, 'Land and Soil: A Territorial Rhetoric', in *History Ireland* (Spring 1994), p.33; later incorporated into and extended in *Strange Country: Modernity and Nationhood in Irish Writing Since 1790* (Oxford: Clarendon 1997).
9   This allegorising tendency is discussed in a different context by Luke Gibbons. See 'Identity Without a Centre: Allegory, History and Irish Nationalism' in *Transformations in Irish Culture* [Critical Conditions] (Field Day/Cork UP 1996).
10 Stephen Arata, 'The Occidental Tourist: *Dracula* and the Anxiety of Reverse Colonisation', *Victorian Studies*, 33, 4 (1990), pp.621-45.
11 Thomas Richards, *The Imperial Archive: Knowledge and the Fantasy of Empire* (London: Verso 1993), p.61
12 Ken Gelder, *Reading the Vampire* (London: Routledge 1994), p.1
13 For an expanded version of this notion of Irish post-coloniality see my 'Liminal Spaces: Post-Colonial Theories and Irish Culture', in *The Irish Review*, 16 (1994), pp.29-43.
14 op. cit. (1994), pp.11-12.
15 Judie Newman, *The Ballistic Bard: Postcolonial Fictions* (London: Edward Arnold 1995), p.70.
16 Bram Stoker, *The Lady of the Shroud* [1909] (Stroud: Alan Sutton 1994); henceforth *LOS*.
17 McCormack, op. cit. (1991), p.831.
18 Fred Botting, *The Gothic* (London: Routledge 1996), p.4.
19 Numerous commentators have pointed out Stoker's avowed support for Home Rule. See, for instance, William Hughes, '"For Ireland's Good": The Reconstruction of Rural Ireland in Bram Stoker's *The Snake's Pass*', in *Irish Studies Review*, 12 (Autumn 1995), p.17ff.
20 Jonathan Bardon, *A History of Ulster* (Belfast: Blackstaff 1992), p.71.
21 George Boyce, *Nationalism in Ireland* [3rd. edn.] (London: Routledge 1995), p.280.
22 Phyllis A. Roth, *Bram Stoker* (Boston: Twayne 1982), p.80.
23 David Glover suggests a similar kind of reading of *The Lady of the Shroud*, though his is perhaps a more optimistic vision of Stoker's authorial/cultural imagination: 'At a new peak of imperialist enthusiasm, yet at a moment when the question of British imperialism in Ireland had temporarily stalled, Stoker imagines the most impossible of utopias, a benevolent colonialism of near-equals in which two marginalised peoples come together to create a new world.' See Glover, *Vampires, Mummies and Liberals: Bram Stoker and the Politics of Popular Fiction* (Duke UP 1996), p.57.

THE COLONIAL ROOTS OF *DRACULA*

Nicholas Daly

By now no particular novelty attaches to attempts to link the nineteenth-century English novel to the history of England's overseas possessions and interests. Books like Patrick Brantlinger's *Rule of Darkness* have shown us that empire is an important component of novels that appear at first glance to be English to the backbone: the England of *Great Expectations* is inextricably linked to the 'other world' of Australia; that of *Vanity Fair* to India; and even *Cranford* suggests the dependence of the vision of English pastoral on an imperial elsewhere.[1] Edward Said has gone further and argued that—there is a complex web uniting imperial authority and the narrative authority constituted in the novel itself as a genre: 'without empire', he claims 'there is no European novel as we know it'.[2] Thus at some level of generality, Said seems to suggest, *all* European novels are about empire—though at this level of generality one might also, perhaps, claim that all European novels are about modernity, or about subjectivity.

In the specific context of Anglo-Irish relations, Terry Eagleton has argued that *Wuthering Heights*—which, with a handful of other novels, like *Jane Eyre, Bleak House*, and *Middlemarch*, might claim to be the archetypal nineteenth-century English novel—is partly built of Irish colonial bricks, reading the character of Heathcliff as the mark of offstage Irish history.[3] (Eagleton assumes, as do I, that Ireland can be considered in terms of colonialism, although the country was never formally know as a colony. This is not to suggest that nineteenth-century Ireland can be unproblematically equated with India, or the African colonies, but nor does it mean that it cannot be profitably compared with those.)[4]

Of course with the Brontës one has biographical material from which to forge such links between metropolis and colony—their father was born in an Irish cabin. There are much more direct links in the case of Bram Stoker, who was born in Ireland and didn't move to London until he was in his thirties. One might even claim that despite its English and eastern European setting, the novel that I wish to discuss here, *Dracula* (1897), is first and foremost an Irish novel, and that it is the merest sleight of hand, literary history as *léger de main*, to say that *Dracula* is an English novel at all, more dramatically to show its Irish roots.

However, I think that simply to reascribe *Dracula* to another national literature, to see it as first and foremost an Irish novel rather than an English novel, may be to miss the point rather. There are some good theoretical reasons for resisting the ascription of novels to any national literature. If one believes Benedict Anderson, for example, the novel is one of the cornerstones of national identity—it makes possible the imagining of the nation as a community—so there is a certain circularity in any unreflective labelling of novels as English, or Irish, or whatever.[5] Here, though, I would adduce a more straightforward reason for leaving the nation-novel question open in the case of *Dracula,* and that is that I see Stoker's novel as being quite literally inter-national. This is not to say, with Said, that the English novel, like Englishness itself, is constituted by what lies outside it, rather it is to question the extent to which the category 'English novel' makes any sense in this case. But if *Dracula* is not simply an English novel, it is not simply an Irish novel either. In terms of its origins, I would describe *Dracula* as a colonial novel, a syncretic cultural artefact whose textual origins lie somewhere between Holyhead and Dun Laoghaire. In part—though not exclusively—because of this, I think that *Dracula* is a novel that is preoccupied with questions of national boundaries and national identity. To read such a text historically we need, in the words of Paul Gilroy in *The Black Atlantic,* to be 'less intimidated by and respectful of the boundaries and integrity of modern nation states', and to think more about the fantasies—of wholeness, harmony and union, but also of violation and impurity—through which nations define their boundaries.[6]

Intercultural penetration inscribes itself in *Dracula's* thematics: the definition of the limits of the nation, both at the level of national borders and at the level of the individual bodies of national subjects, is one of the novel's central projects. Here, as is indeed generally the case, the narrative delineates national limits by imagining their transgression. In this respect *Dracula* is close kin to the 'invasion narratives' that began to appear in England in the last quarter of the nineteenth century, and that remained popular at least up to

World War I.[7] Many of these were explicitly political fantasies of Britain's military subjugation at the hands of the continental powers— e.g., Sir George Chesney's *The Battle of Dorking* (1871), H. F. Lester's *The Taking of Dover* (1888), and even H. G. Wells's *The War of the Worlds* (1898). But other stories—closer kin to *Dracula*—develop fantasies of a less tangible intrusion, and suggest that it is the nature of British identity, and not just pre-war political rivalry, that is at stake in this literature of invasion. In this category belong stories of imperial haunting, like Conan Doyle's "The Brown Hand" (1899), where empire, but also supernatural forces banished by scientific positivism, come home to roost. Other sorts of threats to the national boundaries were also current. As Britain began to cede its place as the 'workshop of the world', the popular press imagined the national territory invaded by an army of foreign commodities rather than soldiers—these are the years of the protectionist cry 'Made in Germany'.

Linking empire, the supernatural and the commodity invasion was a whole generation of mummy stories from the 1880s on, in many of which imported mummies from ancient Egypt come to life in modern England. These include Conan Doyle's "Lot No. 249" (1892), H. D. Everett's *Iras, A Mystery* (1896), and indeed Bram Stoker's own *The Jewel of Seven Stars* (1903).[8] Recalling Marx's theory of commodity fetishism, in these stories unruly objects refuse to bow down to the world of subjects. But that such stories are not only to be read as emplotting fears of an influx of foreign goods is suggested by the fact that in the 1890s Britain was also troubled by visions of a tide of immigration that would, it was feared, alter the very character of the nation. The violent persecution of Jews following the assassination of Tsar Alexander II led to a considerable increase in the number of Ashkenazi Jews entering Britain (and to a lesser extent Ireland) from Russia, the Austrian empire and Rumania, generating anxieties about the composition of Britain that eventually led to the Aliens Act of 1905.[9]

Dracula too, of course, rehearses this fantasy of a cargo come to life (you will remember that the Count is imported in a cargo of mould) but Dracula is a much more threatening import than the mummy. Conceived of as a commodity, Dracula is an import who threatens to consume this nation of emergent consumers. In this way his penetration of the fragile bodies of his English victims mimics *in parvo* his earlier penetration of the national boundaries. Conceived of as an immigrant, he threatens to make the people of England part of *his* nation by the laws of vampirism. But the very diversity of the other invasion stories—military, supernatural, consumerist, xenophobic—would seem to warn us that we should not be too quick to allegorise *Dracula*, to point to the 'real' threat that stands behind the vampiric count. What we can say about *Dracula*, and indeed about all these stories, is that they suggest a widespread sensitivity to questions of national definition at the end of the nineteenth century.

At the time of writing, the connection between fantasies about cargoes of goods that turn out to be human and immigration is, perhaps, particularly obvious. While the European Union is lowering its internal barriers to movement and trade, and indeed at a time when Ireland itself is to some extent attempting to soften its national carapace, some people are still condemned to do their international travelling disguised as freight.[10] Indeed *Dracula* looks forward to an important strain within late twentieth-century fiction and cinema, those tales of colonial and postcolonial recoil that deal with the circuits of global mobility (what Arjun Appadurai has called 'global ethnocapes'), with *Gastarbeiter*, refugees, and with immigration into the imperial 'mother' countries.[11] Thus the Count's secret journey across Europe, aided by corrupt officials and by the nomadic Gypsies or Sziganys looks forward to a later diasporic moment of border crossings, faked documents, of being a perpetual 'stranger in a strange land'.[12] The Count worries about the quality of his English, and urges Jonathan Harker to help him improve his grasp of the vernacular: 'I am content if I am like the rest, so that no man stops if he sees me, or pause in his speaking if he hear my words to say, 'Ha, ha! a stranger!''[13] Despite his will to mastery, then, the Count begins to appear from this perspective as the distant ancestor of the tragicomic immigrant protagonist of Franco Brusati's film, *Bread and Chocolate* (1973). More specifically, however, *Dracula* prefigures a novel like Tayeb Salih's *Season of Migration to the North*.[14] In Salih's text, which is also in many ways a programmatic rewriting of another famous *fin de siècle* story, Joseph Conrad's *Heart of Darkness*, the protagonist, Mustafa Sa'eed, leaves his Sudanese home to study in England where, Kurtz-like, he becomes murderously deranged. The link between this story and Stoker's is not so much the element of inter-cultural violence (though that is crucial, I think) but rather the connection between colonialism, the crossing of national boundaries, and questions of identity. But where *Season of Migration to the North*, like *Heart of Darkness*, tells of the dissolution of identity in a foreign environment, the vampire in *Dracula* represents a force that can assimilate the host country, rather than vice versa. In this respect all by himself he seems to figure a sort of portable, hyper-incorporative nation, or counter-nation.

Identity in *Dracula* is closely connected to orality—after all, vampires are what they eat/drink.[15] When the Count tells us that in his veins and in the veins of his people, 'flows the blood of many brave races' (*D*, p.41), we infer that this blood may have gotten there by other routes than heredity. The thematics of border-crossing, of what the nation can safely contain, metamorphoses here into what the body's own boundaries can legitimately contain without a change of substance. This *Blud/Boden* link is further stressed early in the novel in the local history lesson that the Count gives to Harker: 'there is hardly a foot of soil in all this region that has not been enriched by the blood of men, patriots or invaders' (*D*, p.33). Having absorbed as much Englishness as he can from books, the Count now plans to take it orally, to 'share its life' (*D*, p.31), as he rather coyly puts it.

Prefiguring this dimension of the Count's English tour, Harker gives us detailed descriptions of some of the toothsome national dishes that he eats in Transylvania, like the good tourist that he is: 'I had for dinner, or rather supper, a chicken done up some way with red pepper, which was very good but thirsty. *(Mem.,* get recipe for Mina)' (*D*, p.9), and, 'I had for breakfast more paprika, and a sort of porridge of maize flour which they said was "*mamaliga*", and eggplant stuffed with forcemeat, a very excellent dish, which they call "*impletata*". (*Mem.,* get recipe for this also)' (*D*, p.10). These scenes of culinary tourism, where you can have the world on your plate without loss of your own national identity, find their grisly mirror image later in the novel, when Dracula's 'dining out' in Whitby and London is also recorded in detail. But if the count can incorporate other races into his bloodstream without the loss of his own identity, this is not the way it works for Mina Harker, who becomes self-estranged when she is forced to drink Dracula's blood. *Losing* blood is equally alienating for Lucy Westenra, the Count's first English victim, who becomes herself a vampire. To incorporate or to be incorporated—both seem equally dangerous for the English characters; either way one risks becoming a foreign body.

In this respect too, of course, the novel anticipates—albeit in a rather grisly fashion—another major thematics of the postcolonial novel. Food, its preparation and its consumption frequently preoccupy recent novels that thematicize postcolonial hybridity (e.g., Timothy Mo's *Sour Sweet,* Jessica Hagedom's *Dogeaters,* and Ameena Meer's

Bombay Talkie) providing a rich metaphorics of cultural interpenetration. In *Sour Sweet,* for example, the competing pulls of cultural affiliation on a group of Chinese immigrants in Britain find their objective correlative in the food they prepare for themselves and others. The hybrid Anglo-Chinese cuisine that they come to sell in their takeaway restaurant represents a compromise between assimilation— being swallowed up by England and Englishness—and cultural separatism.

Such contemporary narratives of global ethnoscapes also have their more phobic, metropolitan versions, of course, and these more closely resemble *Dracula* than late twentieth-century 'coming to America', or 'coming to England' novels. US popular culture in particular has generated such narratives, where the fear and desire of the potentially unassimilable other appears not in the language of that which it is good to eat, but that which generates false appetites, that which ultimately poisons the national body: drugs. As exercises in what Fredric Jameson calls cognitive mapping these narratives project a map of the world with the US at its centre, defending its borders against substances (and the individuals who carry them) which threaten the nation's health and wealth. Thus Brian de Palma's 1983 reworking of Howard Hawks's *Scarface* (1932, aka *The Shame of a Nation)* links immigration and crime, as did the original, but makes the immigrant gangsters into drug-dealers.[16] In the phobic national imaginary drug-users—like immigrants—appear as a secret and unassimilable internal counter-nation, secreting poison into the national bloodstream. And like vampires, of course, they are always expanding their territory. (Closer in date to *Dracula,* Oscar Wilde's *The Picture of Dorian Gray* [1891] uses addiction to figure another internal nation—that of male homosexuality.)

Nineteenth-century England has its own version of such fantasies of national alienation through addiction. Opium in Wilkie Collins's *The Moonstone* (1868) and Charles Dickens's unfinished *The Mystery of Edwin Drood* (1870) occupies a similar symbolic role to that which cocaine or heroin does in the late twentieth-century national imaginary of the US. In *Drood,* in particular, the taint of empire seeps into England through the opium dens of the East End of London, and finds its way even to remote Cloisterham. Jasper's Orientalist opium visions of omnipotence issue in the (we assume) actual murder of Edwin, which Dickens appears to have envisaged as a species of Thuggee strangling. But even before this England appears to have become transformed to the point of self-estrangement through its imperial ties: Cloisterham is represented as a sort of home-counties Memphis, with its culture of death and monumental memory; the arranged marriage of Edwin and Rosa is distinctly un-English; even the eating of Turkish delight takes on a sinister aspect. Everywhere in *Drood* one has the distinct sense that—through empire—England has bitten off more than it can chew. Just as individual opium addicts, like jasper, lose their self-possession, so does the empire-addicted nation lose its sense of self.

Dracula's particular oral figuration of the problems of national identity and national boundaries is by no means unique, then. At the same time there is something quite distinctive about vampirism as a way of imagining a counter-nation. I want to finish by suggesting that we can to some extent trace this distinctness to Anglo-Irish relations, and to Stoker's own positioning as a member of an increasingly marginalised Anglo-Irish middle class. While the novel is not cut entirely from Irish colonial cloth, its phobic narrative echoing dozens of English stories from the same period, some of its most crimson threads can be traced back to colonial history. The Anglo-Irish roots of the novel lie in two directions. One set can be traced back, of course, to Joseph Sheridan Le Fanu's memorable vampire story, "Carmilla", which seems to recast the predicament of the Anglo-Irish as a class in remote Styria (the original setting, indeed, of *Dracula)*. A proper account of the way in which Le Fanu's seductive female vampire is transmogrified into Stoker's hubristic Count lies outside the ambit of this paper, unfortunately.

The other major pre-text for *Dracula,* in which the logic of incorporation is most fully explored, is Stoker's own first novel, *The Snake's Pass* (1890), a tale of love, land, and buried treasure in the West of Ireland.[17] One of the most intriguing aspects of this novel, though, is the amount of space it devotes to describing a peculiar shifting bog, which (quite literally) dominates the landscape, and which is the only force in the text analogous to the threat of Dracula in the later novel. The bog is as murderous as the vampire Count, as the following dialogue between the hero and his old schoolfriend shows:

A body suddenly immersed [in the bog] would, when the air of the lungs had escaped and the *rigor mortis* had set in, probably sink a considerable distance; then it would rise after nine days, when decomposition began to generate gases [...]. Not succeeding in this, it would ultimately waste away, and the bones would become *incorporated* with the existing vegetation somewhere about the roots, or would lie among the slime at the bottom.[18]

The bog, like the vampire, has the capacity to assimilate foreign bodies, to incorporate matter into its own substance. To be drained by the vampire is to have your blood circulate with his, to have your essence preserved, yet to be personally destroyed; in the case of the victim of the shifting bog, 'the bones [...] become incorporated with the existing vegetation somewhere about the roots.'

The earlier novel allows us to see how the figure of the vampire is a more portable and internationalised version of a figure that originally belongs to a specifically Anglo-Irish demonology. Both 'vampire' and 'bog' are loan-words in English, and both seem to set a limit to the project of empire while also appearing as its mirror image. The vampire lies outside the borders of modern science, just as the bog seems to have somehow fallen through the grids of (imperial) knowledge. As the protagonist's engineer friend tells us,

> 'the special authorities are scant indeed. Some day, when you want occupation, just you try to find in any library, in any city of the world, any works of a scientific character devoted to the subject [...]. You can imagine how devoid of knowledge we are, when I tell you that even the last edition of the 'Encyclopaedia Britannica' does not contain the heading 'bog' (*TSP*, p.55).

It is easy enough, I think, to see how both vampire and bog could be folded into a by now familiar Foucauldian reading of that which resists and thus solicits the operation of power/knowledge. Or, on a different interpretative paradigm, one could read the bog or the vampire as the figure of *différence* itself, threatening the dissolution of all binary opposites. Here though, I would like to suggest a more local, less global, reading of this recurring figure of incorporation, of the dissolution of identity.[19]

Perhaps the most obvious threat condensed in the figure of the bog relates to the marriage plot of *The Snake's Pass,* which involves the novel's English hero, Arthur Severn, and the Irish 'peasant' heroine, Nora Joyce. Where marriage seems to figure a healing, co-operative alliance between Irish and English culture (or, perhaps, between Anglo-Irish and a more 'native' Irish culture), the bog figures a nightmarish form of alliance in which individual identity is swallowed up. To put it crudely, the veiled political fantasy of the novel seems to be that the grafting of Anglo-Irish culture onto a more 'Irish' strain (figured by Nora, but also by the bog, the two twinned by a series of jokes in the text) will result in the annihilation of the former. Ireland is not so much envisaged as a melting-pot but as a stew-pot, the contents of which will always taste the same.

Paradoxically, the other fear encoded in the figure of the bog is not of the dissolution of identity, but of historical preservation, an anxious vision of history itself as that which will not go away; the forging of healing cross-class alliances that the novel's marriage plot envisages appears impossible when historical conflicts are somehow still 'there'. Marking this problem of political *rapprochement*, the moving bog of *The Snake's Pass* preserves its incorporated bodies more-or-less whole. The treasure that it conceals and eventually gives up was left behind by the French expeditionary force in 1798, and the skeletons of the men who carried the treasure are also concealed in the bog, 'the fleshless fingers grasping the metal handle' (*TSP*, p.239). In this respect the bog behaves differently to the vampire: whatever it has swallowed up, the traces of violent colonial history, lurk in its depths and may be delivered up again. Such images of the past's *presence* are of course also a part of the cultural imaginary of late nineteenth-century Irish nationalism. Nationalism, as Homi Bhabha has pointed out, is Janus-faced, looking back for authenticating folk-roots as well as looking forward to some future coalescence of the people-nation and the state, its 'teleology of progress tipping over into the "timeless" discourse of irrationality'.[20] The bog, I would suggest, figures the *danger* of the backward look for an Anglo-Irish group whose Irish roots were in blood-soaked soil.

The shift from the dissolving/preserving bog of *The Snake's Pass* to the vampire of *Dracula* turns this fantasy of Anglo-Irish national identity into a fantasy of the anxieties attendant upon *English* national identity—fears that have less to do with national origins than with the fragility of the borders of the nation and the self in a modern global economy. And yet Stoker's Transylvanian aristocrat preserves some features of his Irish origins. This is partly visible in the form of total incorporation that the vampire represents (the vampire as counter nation, as portable melting-pot). This, though, as I have suggested is not unique to Bram Stoker's novel, and elsewhere appears under the sign of addiction. Perhaps a more striking survival from the earlier novel is that despite his Eastern European trappings Dracula remains a frozen dialectical image of the Janus-faced aspect of Irish nationalism. Not only does the vampiric Count, like the bog, preserve the past, he also has an eye to the future. He lives in a ruined medieval castle, but he plans to conquer London, the other capital of the nineteenth century. His rooms may be decorated with centuries-old brocade, but he reads there 'of all things in the world, an English Bradshaw's [Railway] Guide' (D, p.34). Moreover, while Dracula appears at times like a nightmare vision of the feudal past, the lord of the manor as lord of life and death, at other times he mirrors the very-up-to-date Harker, who notes that 'he certainly left me under the impression that he would have made a wonderful solicitor' (D, p.44).

This same imbrication of the past and the present, of the archaic and the modern, is evident in Jonathan Harker's experience of Transylvania. The opening chapters of the novel constantly collate Harker's time-consciousness with the sense of Transylvania as beyond time, or as governed by some kind of ritual time quite distinct from the 'homogeneous empty time' of modernity, the time of railways and telegrams.[21] Harker's modern sense of the punctual collides with the very different temporality of 'the eve of St George's Day' (D, p.13); the time appealed to in the phrase 'the train started a little before eight' (D, p.10) meets the time of 'when the clock strikes midnight, all the evil things in the world will have full sway' (D, p.13). Here indeed we are in the uncannily 'disjunctive time of the nation's modernity', in Bhabha's phrase.[22] I will finish by noting that the imaginary repertoire of nationalism was also inherited by writers who were even more anxious to escape its terms than was Stoker, albeit for different reasons. The incorporating bog/vampire seems to look forward to Stephen Dedalus's vision of Ireland as an old sow that eats her own farrow. But there is also less distance than one might at first imagine between the ultra-modern Stephen's resentment of (nationalist) history as a nightmare from which he must awake, and Jonathan Harker's sense that though it may be 'nineteenth century up-to-date with a vengeance—the old centuries had, and have, powers of their own which mere "modernity" cannot kill' (D, p.49).

NOTES

1   Patrick Brantlinger, *Rule of Darkness: British Literature and Imperialism, 1830-1914* (Cornell UP 1988).
2   Edward Said, *Culture and Imperialism* (NY: Alfred A. Knopf 1993), p.69.
3   See 'Emily Brontë and the Great Hunger', *Irish Review*, No.12 (1992) and *Heathcliff and the Great Hunger* (London: Verso 1995).
4   On the question of the specificity of colonial situations and colonial texts, and the theoretical problems of 'colonial discourse' approaches, see Nicholas Thomas, *Colonialism's Culture: Anthropology, Travel and Government* (Princeton UP 1994), Chap. 2.

5   See Benedict Anderson, *Imagined Communities: Reflections on the Origin and Spread of Nationalism* (London: New Left Books 1983).
6   Paul Gilroy, *The Black Atlantic: Modernity and Double Consciousness* (London and NY: Verso 1993), p.4.
7   See Brantlinger, *Rule of Darkness*, pp.233-36.
8   For a discussion of these stories see my 'That Obscure Object of Desire: Victorian Commodity Culture and Fictions of the Mummy', *Novel* 28, 1 (1994), pp.24-51.
9   On the connections between anti-semitism and *Dracula* see Jules Zanger, 'A Sympathetic Vibration: Dracula and the Jews', *English Literature in Transition* 34, 1 (1991), pp.33-44, and Judith Halberstam, 'Technologies of Monstrosity: Bram Stoker's *Dracula*', in Sally Ledger and Scott McCracken, eds., *Cultural Politics at the Fin de Siècle* (Cambridge UP 1995), pp.248-66.
10 According to a recent story in the *Irish Times*, Romanian refugees are being smuggled into sealed freight containers at French ports and thus brought illegally into Britain and Ireland. See *The Irish Times*, 19 May 1998, p.6, and see the front page report in the same paper on 22 non-nationals who were detained at Rosslare while attempting to enter Ireland from France in freight containers.
11 See Arjun Appadurai, 'Disjuncture and Difference in the Global Cultural Economy', in Bruce Robbins, ed., *The Phantom Public Sphere* (Minnesota UP 1993), pp.269-95.
12 See for example Ghassan Kanafani's tale of smuggling migrant workers into Kuwait, "Men in the Sun", in *Men in the Sun and other Palestinian Stories*, trans. Hilary Kilpatrick (London: Heinemann 1978).
13 *Dracula* (Harmondsworth: Penguin 1985), p.31; henceforth cited as *D*.
14 Tayeb Salih, *Season of Migration to the North* (Portsmouth, New Hampshire: Heinemann 1969). On *Dracula* as a story of 'reverse colonisation' see Stephen D. Arata, 'The Occidental Tourist: *Dracula* and the Anxiety of Reverse Colonisation', in *Victorian Studies* (1990), pp.621-45.
15 On eating and identity see, for example, Pasi Falk, *The Consuming Body* (London: Sage 1994).
16 Cf. the rather more complex treatment of nations, borders, and narcotics in Orson Welles's *Touch of Evil* (1958). In public discourse the language of the invasion narratives reappears during the 1980s as the 'war on drugs' under Ronald Reagan's drug 'Czar', William Bennett.
17 For a detailed treatment of the novel, see David Glover's excellent *Vampires, Mummies and Liberals: Bram Stoker and the Politics of Popular Fiction* (Durham and London: Duke UP 1996) and his '"Dark enough for any man": Bram Stoker's Sexual Ethnology and the Question of Irish Nationalism', in *Late Imperial Culture*, eds., Roman de la Campa, E. Ann Kaplan and Michael Sprinker (London: Verso 1994). For recent commentary on this long-forgotten novel see also Chris Morash, '"Ever Under Some Unnatural Condition": Bram Stoker and the Colonial Fantastic', in Brian Cosgrove, ed., *Literature and the Supernatural: Essays for the Maynooth Bicentenary* (Dublin: Columba Press 1995), pp.95-119, and Luke Gibbons, '"Some Hysterical Hatred": History, Hysteria and the Literary Revival', in *Irish University Review* 27, 1 (1997), pp.7-23, espec. p.14. My own essay on the novel, 'Irish Roots: The Romance of History in Bram Stoker's *The Snake's Pass*', in *Literature and History* 4, 2 (1995),

pp.42-70, deals with the connections between the English 'revival of romance' and Stoker's political fantasies.
18 *The Snake's Pass* (1890; Dingle: Brandon Press 1990), p.59; henceforth cited as *TSP*.
19 The rhetoric of undecidability is certainly part of the discourse of Irish national identity. 'Everywhere in the mentality of Irish people are flux and uncertainty. Our national consciousness may be described, in a native phrase, as a *quaking sod*. It gives no footing. It is not English, nor Irish, nor Anglo-Irish (my emphasis). Quoted in David Lloyd, *Anomalous States: Irish Writing and the Post-Colonial Moment* (Durham: Duke UP 1993), p.43. A similar thematics of undecidability is pervasive in Anglo-Irish fiction. For example, Elizabeth Bowen's subtle account of belonging and estrangement, *The Last September*, maps the principal character, Lois's, adolescent sense of being an outsider onto a more historically rooted in-betweenness, or instability. Having been kissed by her English army officer boyfriend, Gerald, the Anglo-Irish Lois sees no prospect of a happy future: 'She shut her eyes and tried—as sometimes when she was seasick, locked in misery between Holyhead and Kingstown—to be enclosed in nonentity, in some ideal no-place, perfect and clear as a bubble.' *The Last September* (1929; Harmondsworth: Penguin 1987), p.89.
20 Homi Bhabha, *The Location of Culture* (London and NY: Routledge 1994), p.142.
21 The phrase is Walter Benjamin's. See *Illuminations*, ed., Hannah Arendt, trans., Edmund Jephcott (NY: Schocken 1969) pp.261-64. See also Anderson, *Imagined Communities*, pp.22-36.
22 Bhabha, op. cit. (1994), p.142.

'IT MUST BE SOMETHING MENTAL': VICTORIAN MEDICINE AND CLINICAL HYSTERIA IN BRAM STOKER'S *DRACULA*

William Hughes

The critical response to *Dracula* has for many years been dominated by readings premised upon Freudian or post-Freudian psychology.[1] Some recent studies of Stoker's 1897 novel, however, have addressed the text's apparent psychoanalytical content in a historical rather than diagnostic manner. Such readings regard *Dracula* as a text supported by a recognisable methodology and a series of concepts, rather than as a mere discharge through symbolism of the neuroses of the author. Writing in 1994, for example, Ken Gelder argues that '*Dracula* itself draws liberally on psychoanalytical concepts, trading on their growing prominence in the popular mind'.[2] Gelder is somewhat reticent regarding the background to this 'growing prominence', and advances only the basic information that *Dracula* was published two years later than Freud and Breuer's *Studies on Hysteria* and one year after the term 'psychoanalysis' itself was coined.[3] Nina Auerbach, similarly, argues that 'Stoker might conceivably have known of Freud's work', where Rebecca Stott in *The Fabrication of the Late-Victorian Femme Fatale* (1992) advances the view that Van Helsing's practice is informed by 'hypnotism as it is used in psychoanalysis and confession, the 'talking cure'.[4]

Such readings arguably demonstrate the residual power still associated with the Freudian approach to *Dracula*. Apparently discarded as an interpretative tool, psychoanalysis becomes a 'hidden' content to be revealed through criticism, a textual feature as pervasive and subtle as the novel's epistolary style or its technological allusions. Attractive though they may be in critical terms, however, such attempts to configure *Dracula* as an early participant in the discourse of Freudian psychology can only prove specious. Freud and Breuer's *Studien über Hysterie*—a work written in German for a specialist medical audience—was not published in English translation until 1909.[5] Though Stoker visited Germany in 1885, it is not known whether he had a reading knowledge of the language.[6] The clinical theory of cathartic treatment, developed as a result of Freud's collaboration with Breuer, is similarly not identical with the psychoanalytical practices subsequently associated with Freud's name. Freud, significantly, suggested that he had 'gone beyond that theory' by 1901.[7] Freud—the Freud of *The Psychopathology of Everyday Life* or *The Interpretation of Dreams*—is quite simply not the psychological key to *Dracula*, just as *Dracula* is arguably not the key to the psyche of Bram Stoker.

If the persistence of the Freudian discourse is in part dependent upon its historical utility as a critical tool, its alleged presence in *Dracula* is equally supported by the novel's brief references to the work of Jean-Martin Charcot, Freud's tutor at the Salpêtrière in Paris for four and a half months in the mid-eighteen eighties. In criticism of *Dracula*, Freud's presence is effectively read *through* Charcot in the sense that Charcot's work on hysteria forms part of the experimental context of the case histories of Freud and Breuer.

The concept of hysteria is frequently acknowledged though seldom satisfactorily explained in critical writings on *Dracula*: it is enough, for example, for Elaine Showalter to simply observe that the portrayal of 'mental breakdowns in *Dracula* [...] drew on popular myths of the hysterical personality'.[8] Closer examination of any one of these 'mental breakdowns'—those experienced by Lucy Westenra, Mina Harker, Jonathan Harker and, in Seward's opinion, Van Helsing—however, reveals a consistent pattern of mental deterioration which, while accessible by a non-specialist audience familiar with the symptomatologies of popular medical guides, remains dependent upon clinical models representative of British and Irish diagnostic practice in the mid- to late-nineteenth century.[9] Indeed, the influence of Charcot may be discerned more fully in *Dracula* through the French physician's contribution to the ethical and gender debates surrounding the mental conditions of hysteria, trance and hypnotism rather than in the novel's depiction of diagnosis and therapeutic practice. The medical script of *Dracula* is thus an exercise in the problematics, as well as the consequences, associated with the application of the pre-Freudian concept 'hysteria' at the *fin de siècle*.

The fictional pathology of Lucy Westenra, the first person to be attacked by the vampire on English soil, is the pivot upon which the medical script of *Dracula* turns. Lucy becomes the subject of what is effectively a medical case study approximately one month after her initial encounter with Dracula at the Yorkshire health resort of Whitby. Her progressive debilitation following the attack is rendered in terms of conventional disease. John Seward, the physician in attendance, initially attributes her decline to an unknown though apparently conventional physiological disorder. Seward's report confides:

> I could easily see that she is somewhat bloodless, but I could not see the usual anaemic signs, and by a chance I was actually able to test the quality of her blood, for in opening a window which was stiff a cord gave way, and she cut her hand slightly with broken glass [...] I secured a few drops of the blood and have analysed them. The qualitative analysis gives quite a normal condition, and shows, I should infer, in itself a vigorous state of health.[10]

Rather surprisingly, Seward fails to undertake the *quantitative* analysis which would reveal that Lucy's bloodless appearance and sensation of feeling 'horribly weak' is a conventional consequence of sustained blood loss. As one nursing manual from the period confirms: 'Considerable loss of blood usually produces faintness, indicated by pallor and temporary loss of consciousness, accompanied by a feeble pulse.' [11]

Seward, however, is not so much guilty of misdiagnosis here as of moving too quickly from an incomplete physical examination towards what appears an obvious diagnostic conclusion. Discarding a physiological causality, Seward moves rapidly to the consideration of Lucy's condition as being a consequence of a hitherto unsuspected mental illness. The report continues:

> In other physical matters I was quite satisfied that there is no need for anxiety; but as there must be a cause somewhere, I have come to the conclusion that it must be something mental [...] I am in doubt, and so have done the best thing I know of: I have written to my old friend and master, Professor Van Helsing of Amsterdam, who knows as much about obscure diseases as anyone in the world. (*D*, p.111.)

Seward's admission that he is 'in doubt' betrays that he has already formulated a hypothesis requiring a specialist second opinion. His invitation to Van Helsing, rather than to a British or Irish practitioner, suggests further that Seward looks for expertise in the treatment of the neurosis not from within England but from the medical schools of continental Europe.[12]

Victorian Medicine and Clinical Hysteria in Dracula 55

Seward's diagnosis, it may be argued, is based upon a recognition of what appear to be some of the conventional symptoms of hysteria within the physical and mental consequences of the vampire's attack. These symptoms are clearly marked in *Dracula*. Seward's report, for example, notes blandly that Lucy 'complains of difficulty in breathing satisfactorily at times' (*D*, p.110). Mina Harker's recollection of Lucy's respiratory difficulties and constricted throat in a diary entry made twenty-two days earlier is, however, considerably more explicit. Mina recalls that Lucy 'was breathing—not softly, as usual with her, but in long, heavy gasps, as though striving to get her lungs full at every breath' (*D*, p.91, cf. *D*, p.95). Lucy's symptoms here correspond closely to the consequences of the movement of the so-called *globus hystericus* in the hysterical patient. A contemporary account describes the symptoms as 'the sensation of a ball rising apparently from the lower portion of the abdomen, and proceeding upwards, with various convolutions, to the stomach; and thence to the throat, causing an intense sense of suffocation'. In physical terms, 'the respiration is slow and laborious, owing to spasms about the pharynx and glottis causing the patient to grasp the neck and throat'.[13] These spasms are recalled in *Dracula* through Lucy's habit of 'holding her hand to her throat, as though to protect it from cold' after the vampire's attack (*D*, p.94).

Lucy's flirtatiousness—which the reader may access through her narrative of the three marriage proposals—and her anticipation of her forthcoming marriage to Arthur Holmwood are also factors which may function within Seward's diagnosis. Robert Brudenell Carter, one of the major Victorian theorists of the complaint noted that 'the sexual emotions are those most concerned in the production of the disease'.[14] Beyond this, the very absence of a physical lesion in the case, as noted by Seward, above, may be treated as evidence in favour of the hysterical hypothesis. *Cassell's Family Doctor*, published like *Dracula* in 1897, notes that:

> It is quite true that no visible diseased condition is discovered in any particular organ; the brain and nervous system generally show no evident changes in their structure, and the disease must therefore be classed amongst those which we have described as functional diseases, the functions of the nervous system being those chiefly at fault.[15]

For an empirical and orthodox thinker such as Seward (*D*, p.191), the diagnosis would appear almost conclusive. The symptoms of one disorder are here clearly being interpreted as those of another. The unprecedented pathology of vampirism is thus ironically read as if it were conventional hysteria. The connection between Seward and Lucy, based on a rejected marriage proposal between the two, coupled with his long-standing friendship with her eventual fiancé—the recipient of Seward's medical report—compels the doctor, again, to refrain from naming what he believes to be her disorder. Quite simply, the cultural association of hysteria with sexuality compromises the explicit signifiers of 'sweetness and purity' (*D*, p.217) through which the chivalric males in the novel construct their female counterparts.

The construction of Lucy's illness is, however, a complex gesture which has implications beyond its proclamation of Seward's restricted and conventional empiricism. Nineteenth-century medical writers consistently portrayed hysteria as a protean complaint whose symptoms were direct emulations of those associated with physical rather than purely mental disorders.[16] Vampirism, the alternative pathology of *Dracula*, thus might be said to emulate in the novel not merely a series of disorders associated with the throat and circulation, but through them the imitative nature of hysteria itself. Indeed, the aetiology and progress of Lucy's supposed disorder is sufficiently detailed to permit an identification of the specific model of hysteria upon which Seward's misdiagnosis is based. Despite Seward's apparent familiarity with the work of Charcot (*D*, p.191), this model is firmly grounded in British rather than continental medical practice.

The British physician Robert Brudenell Carter posits three main factors in the aetiology of hysteria: the temperament of the patient; the occurrence which triggers the initial attack; and the degree to which the patient is compelled to repress this latter event, the so-called 'exciting cause' of the neurosis.[17] These factors are replicated without parody or comment in *Dracula*. The genetic inheritance which Lucy receives from her valetudinarian mother—'who has been more than usually ill lately', as Mina euphemistically puts it—and somnambulistic father, should, according to Carter's thesis, predispose her through temperament to hysteria (*D*, p.89). There is a tacit reference to this in an entry in Mina's private journal: 'I greatly fear that she is of too supersensitive a nature to go through the world without trouble' (*D*, p.87). Again, the impending marriage of the patient, with the threat to the effecting of the nuptials posed by the approaching death of the groom's terminally-ill father, are a factor in Lucy's state of mind at the time of her involvement with the vampire. Mina, again, acknowledges that this disturbs Lucy at least mentally when it first arises:

Victorian Medicine and Clinical Hysteria in Dracula 57

Mr Holmwood has been suddenly called to Ring to see his father, who has been taken seriously ill. Lucy frets at the postponement of seeing him, but it does not touch her looks [...] I pray it will all last. (*D*, p.72.)

The unspoken sub-text of Mina's prayer is the fear on her part that any protracted delay in the lovers' meeting will provoke a physical manifestation of Lucy's interior tension. The name of Holmwood's country estate, *Ring*, mentioned here for the first time, would seem also to confirm symbolically the importance of the forthcoming marriage.

The novel's rendering of the initial attack, Carter's second factor, may be appreciated only in retrospect. Two passages are crucial here, the latter placing the former in context. Mina recalls an incident which occurs four days after Lucy is first bitten by the Count in a Whitby churchyard:

[...] We were silent for a while, and suddenly Lucy murmured as if to herself:-
'His red eyes again! They are just the same.' It was such an odd expression, coming *apropos* of nothing, that it quite startled me. I slewed round a little, so as to see Lucy well without seeming to stare at her, and saw that she was in a half-dreamy state, with an odd look on her face that I could not quite make out; so I said nothing but followed her eyes. She appeared to be looking over at our seat, whereon was a dark figure seated alone. I was a little startled myself, for it seemed for an instant as if the stranger had great eyes like burning flames; but a second look dispelled the illusion. The red sunlight was shining on the windows of St. Mary's Church behind our seat, and as the sun dipped there was just sufficient change in the refraction and reflection to make it appear as if the light moved. (*D*, pp.93-94)

Four days later, Lucy herself describes to Mina the sensations which accompanied the initial attack by the vampire:

[...] I have a vague memory of something long and dark with red eyes, just as we saw in the sunset, and something very sweet and very bitter all around me at once; and then I seemed sinking into the deep green water, and there was a singing in my ears, as I have heard there is to drowning men [...]. (*D*, p.98.)

Again, the vampiric pathology follows Carter's model. The red eyes of Count Dracula, which are observed by Mina herself when she disrupts the vampire's first attack on Lucy, are the central component of the latter's vampiric neurosis (*D*, p.90). Viewed here on the same seat where the initial attack took place, the vampire's eyes become what Carter termed the 'exciting cause' or catalyst that triggers each of a series of hysteroid fits experienced by Lucy. Their uncanny redness, it may be argued, is associated in Lucy's mind with the turbulent emotions and consequent prostration which characterise the initial attack. To recall or to re-encounter anything resembling them is thus to risk a relapse.[18] As Carter suggests, 'the recollection of a certain event, or a train of thought, is usually followed by the fit'.[19] Hence, Lucy's distraction at the red sunlight which accompanies the figure viewed at St Mary's Church signifies the first of a series of 'secondary' hysteroid attacks, as proposed by Carter in the course of conventional hysteria. In this way, Lucy's symptoms remain, perversely, significant in both the conventional and occult diagnoses of her present state of ill health.

The representation of vampirism through Carter's third factor—the repression of the memory and expression of the initial attack by the hysterical patient—is, again, closely linked to Lucy's attempt to recall the incident for Mina's benefit. When describing the sensations felt during the initial attack Lucy appears unable—or unwilling—to recall directly the physical experiences that accompanied the act of self-perception. The signification of Lucy's symptoms within both occult and conventional pathologies combines easily here with the popular reading of the vampiric act as coded sexuality.[20] There is, indeed, an expression of attraction alternating with repulsion in the bittersweet experience, which transforms easily into a symbolic alternation of pleasure and pain.[21]

If the subsequent experience of Mina Harker is to be relied upon, there is also an element of guilt associated with the eventual cognition of personal participation in the act of being drained by the vampire (*D*, pp.28, 296). Mina, like Lucy, is reluctant to speak of her induction into vampirism (*D*, p.288) because the act of giving or receiving blood is capable of being read symbolically as fornication or sexual infidelity. Faced with experiences which are seemingly communicable only through the language of shame and reluctance, it is easy to read such transformations as the vampire effects as being simply part of the production of what Phyllis Roth calls the 'suddenly sexual woman'.[22]

To read the vampirised (or hysterical) woman as a released libido is in effect to concur with Seward's misdiagnosis. Such a reading, though, fails to take account of the contextual medico-legal debate on the culpability of patients suffering from abnormal mental conditions who are drawn into crime or apparent sexual promiscuity. Seward, who is scripted both as an asylum-keeper and a medico-jurist—an expert medical witness who may be called upon to give evidence in criminal trials—should certainly be aware of how this debate relates to his patients.

Significantly, Seward regards the experimental work of Charcot as being sufficient authority for the effective existence of hypnotism as a demonstrable phenomenon (*D*, p.191). It must be noted, however, that Charcot regarded susceptibility to hypnotism as a sign of latent or actual hysteria within the subject.[23] Lucy and Mina both display a susceptibility to hypnoid states. The vampire controls both women from a distance, instructing Lucy to destroy the paper upon which her account of the death of her mother is written (*D*, p.152) and utilising Mina as an unwilling spy within the camp of his opponents (*D*, p.327).[24] Both women are thus, to recall Charcot's terms of reference, 'capable of becoming hysterical, if not actually hysterical at the beginning of the experiments'.[25]

The implicit illness of Lucy and Mina is, however, the factor by which the moral closure which *should* disqualify the vampire's apparently sexualised victims is evaded. In an article for the journal *Forum*, Charcot noted that, though a hypnotised patient might retain the capability of 'withstanding suggestions of a certain class', the power of a hypnotist may be sufficient to overcome 'the moral force of resistance'.[26] In a discussion of the mental pathology of hypnotic somnambulism, Charcot states:

> The somnambule can, as I have said, withstand a suggestion; but I must add that by the very fact of the somnambulism there arises a quite special state of 'affectivity' between the hypnotiser and the hypnotised. Thus, a woman who in the waking state would have been chaste, may during the somnambulism give herself up to the one who has hypnotised her, especially if the hypnosis has been repeated many times.[27]

Read in this context, the sexual burden of guilt shifts back to Count Dracula, who becomes a rapist rather than a seducer or demon lover.[28] Lucy and Mina, by contrast, may be read as passive victims rather than unequivocal temptresses.

Both women remain innocent of sexual guilt in the literal sense: they are victims of vampirism, not of seduction or indeed of conventional hysteria. Their active participation in the vampiric act is further disarmed by the circumstances of their initiation into the company of the Un-Dead. Lucy is attacked whilst sleepwalking (*D*, p.201)—a condition which was regarded by some nineteenth-century medical commentators as being analogous to hypnotic trance.[29] Mina, similarly, is attacked when physically exhausted and on one occasion whilst under sedation (*D*, pp.256, 260). Neither, therefore, is in a state of mind that reflects the conventional morality of their public lives. Yet, simultaneously, the two express the symptoms and the guilt of sexual transgression through their participation in what has come to be regarded as coded sexuality. Hence their guilt and self-abasement is at once both a sign of their modesty, and a reminder of the quasi-sexual exposure to which they have been subjected in the vampiric attacks (*D*, pp.216, 281-82). Perversely, then both women are subject to hysteria, yet in the final assessment remain free from its cultural and moral associations of salaciousness.

The representation of hysterical symptoms in *Dracula* is not, however, confined to the descriptions of the two main female characters. Lucy's fiancé, Arthur Holmwood, is prostrated by hysteria following his participation in the ritual exorcism of Lucy's vampiric body. His breakdown occurs when he meets Mina Harker on the day following the exorcism. She recalls:

> In an instant the poor fellow was overwhelmed with grief. It seemed to me that all he had of late been suffering in silence found a vent at once. He grew quite hysterical, and raising his open hands, beat his palms together in a perfect agony of grief. He stood up and then sat down again, and the tears rained down his cheeks. I felt an infinite pity for him, and opened my arms unthinkingly. With a sob he laid his head on my shoulder and cried like a weary child, whilst he shook with emotion. (*D*, p.230.)

The physical setting of Holmwood's collapse betrays the 'exciting cause' that has revived his neurosis. The nobleman's hysteria is associated with the rupture of his chivalric and idealised conception of the female, the result of his encounter with the vampiric Lucy, whose gestures may be perceived as the expression of a hitherto unacknowledged—by Arthur at least—libido.[30] The text, however, provides Holmwood with an almost-immediate release of the tension which, if repressed, would lead to the further development of his complaint. Mina continues:

> We women have something of the mother in us that makes us rise above smaller matters when the mother spirit is invoked; I felt this big, sorrowing man's head resting on me, as though it were that of the baby that some day may lie on my bosom, and I stroked his hair as though he were my own child. I never thought at the time how strange it all was. (*D*, p.230.)

Mina's spontaneous, 'unthinking' action, allows Holmwood to access both the recently-experienced sexual component of his trauma, and the idealised vision which it has disrupted. The scenario is reassuringly non-sexual. Mina, scripted here as nurturant mother, is the antithesis of Lucy, the sexual temptress who feeds upon children. Despite Mina's belief to the contrary, their behaviour is not really that 'strange' at all (*D*, p.211). Mina's love is selfless, innocent. But, most significantly, it is instinctive. She does not resist the biologistic call of her 'mother-spirit'. With this reassurance of the persistence of a treasured credo, life for Holmwood may go on. He has no further compulsion to repress the 'exciting cause' of his hysterical paroxysm.

The fictionalisation of male hysteria in *Dracula* represents a departure from the conventional approach to the complaint in British and Irish medicine, even while it retains the model of symptomatology associated with Carter's research. Where the popular English-language medical manuals of the *fin de siècle* regarded hysteria as a disorder suffered by women and effeminate or 'very impressionable men', *Dracula* concurs with the thought of continental physicians such as Charcot, who observed a potential for hysteria 'just like a woman' in males who are 'well developed, not enervated by an indolent or too studious mode of life[...] [and] never before emotional, at least in appearance [...]'[31]

Mental illness in *Dracula*, however, arguably may still be said to underwrite gender. It is significant that Lucy is afflicted by the hysteroid occult pathology, whilst Holmwood falls victim to its conventional counterpart. The hysteroid pathology is an *affliction* rather than a congenital defect—however closely it may mimic the specific disorders of its individual victim, Lucy. In this sense, the occult exorcism of her sexualised disorder functions equally in the text as a medical operation. Seward, in the guise of surgical assistant to Van Helsing, makes this clear:

> Van Helsing, in his methodical manner, began taking the various contents from his bag and placing them ready for use. First he took out a soldering iron and some plumbing solder, and then a small oil lamp, which gave out, when lit in a corner of the tomb, gas which burned at a fierce heat with a blue flame; then his operating knives, which he placed to hand; and last a round wooden stake [...] With this stake came a heavy hammer, such as in households is used in the coal cellar for breaking the lumps. To me, a doctor's preparations for work of any kind are stimulating and bracing, but the effect of these things on both Arthur and Quincey was to cause them a sort of consternation. (*D*, p.214.)

The surgeons are acting within a frame of reference incompletely understood by the laymen Quincey Morris and Arthur Holmwood. Seward and Van Helsing understand that the occult pathology is structured like a conventional illness. It is, quite simply, an illness whose treatment requires specialised and (in clinical terms) unfamiliar equipment. Once obtained, such equipment becomes subject to the medical discourse and may be laid out and manipulated in exactly the same manner as the conventional 'operating knives' which Van Helsing has thoughtfully provided in order to remove the patient's head at the conclusion of the operation.

Quite simply, the disease within Lucy is cut out by the operation in order that she may return to the semblance of both physical and moral health, even in death. Hysteria—that is, hysterical symptoms and their cultural associations functioning simultaneously as the stigmata of an occult disorder—thus becomes a device for asserting the innateness of female purity rather than the congenital nature of female salaciousness. Once the complaint is neutralised, the men present may gaze upon 'Lucy as we had seen her in life, with her face of unequalled sweetness and purity' (*D*, pp.216-17). Holmwood, similarly, may gaze upon a renewed and again-idealised conception of the female following his encounter with the unfeigned purity of Mina. Cured of hysteria, his resource of masculine strength becomes again available for the defence of Mina, a woman threatened with the sexualised violence associated with vampirism.[32]

Dracula, in conclusion, must be viewed as an intensely medical work—if not the most clinically-informed of *fin de siècle* fictions. The detailed symptomatology of the novel, grounded as it is in British and Continental medical and psychiatric practice, provides considerably more than an authoritative background to the misdiagnosis of an epidemic of vampirism, however. The construction in the novel of two pathologies effectively sharing the same symptoms facilitates a sense of medical confusion. Conventional medicine, empirical and unimaginative, cannot satisfactorily reconcile symptom and consequence. The occult pathology, again, is perversely contained by surgical and diagnostic techniques which, though unprecedented in detail, broadly resemble those used in conventional therapeutics. Biologistic differences of gender are challenged by the apparent (though superficial) susceptibility of both sexes to hysteroid seizures. Yet it is in relationship to gender that the co-existence of the two pathologies is perhaps most problematic. The medical script in effect draws attention not merely to itself but also to its implications in cultural terms—the moralistic and deterministic associations which are applied in the acts of diagnosis and prognosis.

NOTES

1. For an account of the development of criticism of Stoker's works from the 1960s see William Hughes and Andrew Smith, 'Introduction: Bram Stoker, the Gothic and the Development of Cultural Studies' in William Hughes and Andrew Smith, eds., *Bram Stoker: History, Psychoanalysis and the Gothic* (Basingstoke: Macmillan 1998), pp.1-11.
2. Ken Gelder, *Reading the Vampire* (London: Routledge 1994), p.66.
3. idem.
4. Nina Auerbach, 'Magi and Maidens: The Romance of the Victorian Freud', in *Writing and Sexual Difference*, ed., Elizabeth Abel (Brighton: Harvester 1982), pp.111-32, p.120; Rebecca Stott, *The Fabrication of the Late-Victorian Femme Fatale: The Kiss of Death* [1992] (Basingstoke: Macmillan 1996), p.71. Auerbach notes that Freud's 'Preliminary Communication' was 'reported enthusiastically' to the Society for Psychical Research in London, but does not assert that Stoker was present at the meeting.
5. Breuer and Freud's 'Preliminary Communication' was published in German in 1893, prefaced the German language edition of 1895, and was translated for the 1909 English language edition.
6. Harry Ludlam, *A Biography of Dracula: The Life Story of Bram Stoker* (London: Foulsham 1962), p.71.
7. Sigmund Freud, 'The Clinical Picture' [1901, 1905], *Case Histories I: 'Dora' and 'Little Hans'*, The Pelican Freud Library, Vol. 8, (Harmondsworth: Penguin 1985) p.57, n.2.
8. Elaine Showalter, *Hystories: Hysterical Epidemics and Modern Culture* (London: Picador 1997), p.82. Cf. Elaine Showalter, *Sexual Anarchy* (London: Bloomsbury 1991), pp.180-82.
9. Stoker is likely to have gained access to medical material through his brothers George, Dick and William, all of whom trained as doctors. The eldest of the brothers, William Thornley, was appointed Physician in Ireland to Queen Victoria, and was elected President of the Royal Academy of Medicine in Ireland. See Peter Haining and Peter Tremayne, *The Un-Dead: The Legend of Bram Stoker and Dracula* (London: Constable 1997), p.54, pp.62-63.
10. Bram Stoker, *Dracula* [1897] (OUP 1996), p.111; henceforth *D*.
11. Laurence Humphry, *A Manual of Nursing: Medical and Surgical* [21st edn.] (London: Charles Griffin & Co. 1900), p.160.
12. When absent from the asylum at Purfleet, Seward entrusts his medical practice to Dr Patrick Hennessey, a Licentiate of the King's and Queen's College of Physicians, Ireland (*D*, p.155). Following his single report on the behaviour of the lunatic Renfield, Hennessey makes no further contribution to the novel.
13. John M. Ross, ed., *The Illustrated Globe Encyclopædia of Universal Information*, 12 vols. (London: Thomas C. Jack 1882), Vol. 4, p.464
14. Robert Brudenell Carter, *On the Pathology and Treatment of Hysteria* (London: John Churchill 1853), pp.32-33

15 'A Medical Man', *Cassell's Family Doctor* (London: Cassell and Company 1897), p.534. In contrast to *Cassell's Family Doctor*, Seward uses the term 'functional' in the novel to refer to the functions of the bodily organs (p.110).
16 *Cassell's Family Doctor* (1897), p.536.
17 Carter, op. cit. (1853), p.21, pp.31-32, p.34; cf. W. H. B. Stoddart, *Mind and Its Disorders: A Text-Book for Students and Practitioners* (London: H. K. Lewis 1908), pp.369-70, p.374.
18 Compare here Jonathan Harker's relapse on encountering the vampire in London (*D*, p.172).
19 Carter, op. cit. (1853), p.42.
20 For example, Clive Leatherdale, *Dracula. The Novel and the Legend* (Wellingborough: Aquarian Press 1985), p.146.
21 ibid., p.147.
22 Phyllis Roth, 'Suddenly Sexual Women in Bram Stoker's *Dracula*', *Literature and Psychology* 27 (1997), p.113-21, p.114.
23 See Charles Lloyd Tuckey, 'The Applications of Hypnotism', *Contemporary Review* 60 (1891), pp.672-86, p.672.
24 Tuckey, amongst others, exercised 'a healthy scepticism about stories of hypnotism at a distance'. See ibid., p.678.
25 Jean-Martin Charcot, 'Hypnotism and Crime', *Forum* 9 (1890), pp.159-68, p.160.
26 ibid., pp.160, 162.
27 ibid., p.162.
28 Cf. Toni Reed, *Demon Lovers and Their Victims in British Fiction* (Lexington: Kentucky UP 1988), p.17, pp.64-5.
29 Tuckey, p.683.
30 Van Helsing's behaviour after leaving Lucy's funeral is *not* clinically hysterical, despite Seward's diagnosis at the time (p.174). The simultaneous laughing and crying of Van Helsing is, admittedly, hysteroid, although it arises from the grim irony of Holmwood's equation of blood transfusion with marriage. As the Dutch physician is already certain that Lucy is a vampire he experiences no functional 'shock' either at her deathbed voluptuousness or on encountering her subsequently in the churchyard. His reluctance to clarify his behaviour to Seward represents an act of discretion rather than repression (p.176).
31 *Cassell's Family Doctor* (1897), pp.535, 537; Jean-Martin Charcot, 'Hysteria in the Male Subject' [1873], reprinted in *A History of Psychology*, ed., L. T. Benjamin (New York: McGraw Hill 1988), pp.129-35, p.130.
32 Such a reaction is a common scenario in Stoker's fiction. Compare the behaviour of Don Bernardino de Escoban in *The Mystery of the Sea* [1902] (Stroud: Alan Sutton 1997), p.213.

BRAM STOKER'S *DRACULA*: POSSESSED BY THE SPIRIT OF THE NATION?

Bruce Stewart

> The days of Donnybrook Fair and all it meant, the days of the stage Irishman and the stagey Irish play, of Fenianism and landlordism are rapidly passing away [to be replaced by] a strenuous, industrious spirit, spreading its revivifying influence to rapidly over the old country (Stoker, 'The Great White Fair in Dublin', 1907.)[1]

A feature of the text of *Dracula* not commonly remarked is its curious reliance on the phrase 'plan of campaign' to describe the offensive conducted by Van Helsing and his companions against the Transylvanian vampire.[2] Though a military term of some currency in the late-Victorian period, this was more specifically deployed in an Irish context as the name given to the rent-strike policy devised by Timothy Charles Harrington and adopted by the Land League leadership in 1886 with the grudging assent of Charles Stewart Parnell.[3] That *Dracula* is grounded in the social and political conditions of its time goes without saying, especially in view of a recent spate of feminist and postmodernist readings.[4] That it is grounded in the conditions of the Irish Land War (still raging at the date to which its 'events' are sometimes ascribed)[5] has recently been suggested by several Irish critics, more or less strenuously insisting on an allegorical interpretation according to which Count Dracula is aligned with the Anglo-Irish landlords in that conflict.[6] Now, this reading of Stoker's famous novel serves the rhetorical purposes of Irish nationalism well enough—and perhaps conveys the truth of Irish history also—but does scant justice to the social and political outlook of its author and the symbolic complexity of the novel. For, however closely connected with such dramatic circumstances *Dracula* may be, it is by no means certain that it reflects the events of the Land War *as viewed from the standpoint of the victors*—that is, the agrarian class which emerged from that struggle as the dominant political formation in late nineteenth-century Ireland. Not alone is Count Dracula unlikely to have been intended by his creator as a portrait of the bloodsucking colonist of popular Irish historical memory, it is more probable that Stoker meant his vampiric tendencies to represent the kind of atavistic violence commonly attributed to Land League activists and—by implication—to Charles Stewart Parnell whom many regarded as their puppet-master.[7] At any rate, it can more easily be shown that Stoker was strongly predisposed to see the local usurer as the real blood-sucker in rural Ireland—a fact that William Gladstone noted with satisfaction on finding the 'gombeen man' blamed for Irish disorders in his presentation copy of *The Snake's Pass* (1890), Stoker's only novel set in Ireland.[8] For some, this will seem the obvious symptom of another attempt by the Anglo-Irish to exculpate themselves in the classic manner devised by Maria Edgeworth, whose character Nicholas Garraghty in *The Absentee* (1812) was the first nefarious middle-man of Irish fiction. Nevertheless it remains improbable that Stoker—consciously or unconsciously—intended to impale the Protestant landowners of Ireland on the stake prepared for them by Irish nationalist historians.

As to the wider question of national allegiances, there are strong indications that Stoker was less concerned with loyalty either to Ireland or to England considered as sovereign nations than with 'modernity'—a place or state which he looked upon as transcending such geopolitical distinctions. Perhaps this may seem a factitious idea as being the construct of the liberal-progressive world-outlook associated with imperialism and neo-imperialism. Nonetheless it was just this conception that governed his thinking in regard to the Dublin Exhibition of 1907, which he saw as a harbinger of modernisation in Ireland and which therefore caused him to express the hope that 'a strenuous, industrious spirit, spreading its revivifying influence to rapidly over the old country' would put paid to 'Fenianism and landlordism' along with the traditional associations of 'Donnybrook Fair' and 'stage-Irishism' that had so often besmirched the reputation of the country.[9] In this early outburst of Celtic-tigerism, the point to be noted is that *Fenianism* and *landlordism* are tarred with the same brush—for Stoker seems to have disliked the evicting landlords and the Land League agitators quite impartially as mutually-related manifestations of an anti-modern ethos. Acknowledgement of this fact inexorably leads us to postulate a postcolonialist reading of the novel that goes far beyond the simplistic identification of the vampire with the Anglo-Irish landlords, as well as the as-yet untried identification of Dracula with the perpetrators of Land League 'outrages', focusing attention instead upon the author's underlying concern with the conflict between modernity and atavism in contemporary society—though in this we have been anticipated by several nationalist critics in ways that we will soon consider.

I

In a remarkable discussion of Stoker's famous novel in *Strange Country* (1997), Seamus Deane has written of the central character:

> Attached to the soil by day, 'racy of the soil' in a perverse rendering of the epigraph of the Nation newspaper, he moves, like an O'Grady version of the Celtic hero, between dusk and dawn.[10]

Here the critic touches on the privileged place of 'soil' in Irish literary tradition—a note developed elsewhere in that book where he defines the lexical system in question as an 'ontological hierarchy': 'The nation is the soil; the state is the land [...]. Soil is prior to land.'[11] Further—

> The romantic-nationalist conception of the soil, its identity with the nation, its ownership by the people, its priority over all the administrative and commercial systems that transform it into land, is the more powerful because it is formulated as a reality that is beyond the embrace of any concept.[12]

In other words, Irish 'soil' is a symbolic construct residing at the very core of a definite conception of national identity and one essential to the empowerment of the nationalist project as a revolutionary ethos—a critical observation of great acuity which inevitably raises the question whether it is so for the writers under discussion only, or for the critic also.

The Spirit of the Nation: title of a famous ballad-anthology edited by Charles Gavan Duffy in 1843, drawing on the political poetry contributed by readers to *The Nation*—the newspaper that bore as its banner the epithet that Deane quotes in passing.[13] For Duffy the value of those verses was less a question of their literary merit than their authenticity, insofar as he regarded them as 'the production of educated men, with English tongues but Irish hearts' whose feelings were essentially Irish in 'character and *spirit*', and who therefore instilled their writing with 'the ancient and hereditary *spirit* of the country'—as he wrote in his Introduction.[14] Here, then, was a cultural slogan appropriate to the version of Irish nationhood sponsored by the Young

Irelanders. What that might amount to in more acutely political terms was indicated in the celebrated letter addressed to Duffy by James Fintan Lalor and printed in the *Nation* under the heading 'A New Nation' on 24 April, 1847.

In it he proposed—moderately enough—an 'Agricultural Association' between the landowners and their tenants, accompanied by a minatory observation for the former: 'If you persevere in enforcing a clearance of your lands you will force men to weigh your existence, as landowners, against the existence of the Irish people.'[15] A little later, writing for *The Irish Felon* (which he conducted on behalf of John Martin, then in prison), he penned the radical phrases that came to hold a place of prime importance in the political thinking of Eamon de Valera, who quoted it *verbatim* at Bodenstown on 25 June, 1925:[16]

> Ireland her own—Ireland her own, and all therein, from the sod to the sky. The soil of Ireland for the people of Ireland, to have and hold from God alone who gave it—to have and hold to them and their heirs forever, without suit or service, faith or fealty, rent or render, to any power under heaven.[17]

In summarising the philosophy behind the Tenant League of 1845 soon after, Lalor sketched a broad historical narrative:

> [T]he English conquest consisted of two parts [...] conquest of our liberties, the conquest of our lands. I saw clearly the re-conquest of our liberties would be incomplete and worthless without the re-conquest of our lands.[18]

Here, then, was the Land League doctrine in its germinal form. As an emotive strand of Irish political thinking, it crucially involved the branding of the Anglo-Irish landlords as aliens and beneficiaries of the legalised theft of ancestral Irish land. Interestingly enough, Lalor went on to express all this in terms that might be adapted with little alteration to describe a *clique* of aristocratic vampires:

> Strangers they are in this land they call theirs—strangers here and strangers everywhere, owning no country and owned by none; rejecting Ireland, and rejected by England; tyrants to this land and slaves to another; here they stand hating and hated - their hand forever against us, as ours against them, an outcast and ruffianly horde, a class by themselves. [...] Tyrants and traitors they have ever been to us and ours since first they set foot on our soil.[19]

This was the stereotypical view that came to dominate nationalist thought in the second part of the nineteenth-century; and it is in just such a spirit that several critics have recently been making the case that it is precisely the historical bad conscience of the descendants of the Cromwellian settlers and others of the Anglo-Irish ascendancy that gave rise to the Victorian horror stories of Maturin, Le Fanu and Bram Stoker. As Terry Eagleton puts it,

> Protestant Gothic [...] is the political unconscious of Irish [sic] society, the place where its fears and fantasies must luridly emerge. [...] For Gothic is the nightmare of the besieged and reviled, most notably of women, but in this case of an ethnic minority marooned with a largely hostile people.[20]

Applied to *Dracula*, this argues that the novel offers a portrait of the Anglo-Irish landlord of a kind that he would rather keep in the attic while continuing to parade his suaver self in the drawing-room below. The only obstacle to such a view is represented by the intentionality of the author, for it is hard to suppose that Stoker intended such a portrait. Eagleton has elsewhere suggested that a postcolonialist interpretation of *The Portrait of Dorian Gray*—presumably along these lines—should now be undertaken.[21] If Oscar Wilde did so, this must be because he was decidedly more nationalist, as several commentaries have recently suggested.[22] No such thesis can easily be adduced to fit the case of Bram Stoker and, failing that, it is by resort to the Unconscious Mind that this difficulty is best overcome. A sensational novelist, drawing energetically upon the passions of Irish history (as Anglo-Irish writers often did for patriotic no less than mercenary reasons) is thus transformed into the neurotic perpetrator of a 'Freudian slip' of mythical proportions—a tell-tale who reveals the dirty secrets of his colonist *confrères* whose comfort and security consisted in the urbane denial of their brutal origins as thieves of Irish soil.

II

Michael Valdez Moses has recently elaborated a great many points of similitude between Charles Stewart Parnell and the central character in the novel, treating the Home Rule leader as an 'overdetermined figure onto whom are cathected many of the most formidable political and social issues of nineteenth-century Ireland'.[23] In advancing his candidate, Moses embeds Parnell in a matrix of post-colonialist themes strongly militating towards a view of Stoker's novel as an expression of the author's pathological fear of Irish freedom. Viewed in this light, *Dracula* represents the Anglo-Irishman's alarm at the 'prospect that he [Parnell] might bring into existence a whole new people, a nation of free Irish citizens under his leadership', thus anticipating the collapse of the British Empire in the new century, as anti-colonial movements 'metastasised' across the globe—in an increasingly familiar conception of the tutelary role of Ireland amid twentieth-century independence movements.[24] Reading Stoker's novel as a palimpsest of colonial anxieties which inadvertently reveals the errors of colonialism, Moses identifies the 'flyman' Renfield as a 'surrogate' Land Leaguer answering the unseen commandments of his leader, Dracula/Parnell: 'More than any other figure in *Dracula* the character of Renfield serves as a stand-in for the Irish adherents of Parnell and the nationalist cause.'[25] Building on this striking identification, he next constructs a critique of the illegal procedures adopted by Dr Seward and Dr Patrick Hennessey—respectively Scottish and Irish servants of the British Union—in the course of managing Renfield's incarceration in the lunatic asylum. That these procedures culminate in a judicial cover-up of the brutal circumstances of Renfield's death leads Moses to reflect on their resemblance to the circumstances in which the ANC leader Steven Biko died somewhat nearer our own time.[26] And this directly leads the critic onwards towards an ideologically gratifying conclusion:

> In political terms, the most insidious threat that the infectious spread of vampirism poses is that even Liberal England, with its commitment to freedom, justice, peace, and the rule of law, will, like the subjugated island across the Irish Sea, become a land of darkness and misrule.[27]

This is doubtless well said, especially as underscoring the fact (also noted by Moses) that the vampire-hunters of the novel evince a marked indifference to legality in pursuit of their quarry—house-breaking being the recurrent instance—thereby breaching the very codes which they are supposed to be defending. While this is true of *Dracula* and many other quite conventional Victorian detective novels, it is not however the case the Renfield dies at the hands of his gaolers, being a victim of Dracula's appetitive conception of subservience instead. It may therefore be seen that the comparison with Steve Biko is primarily an expression of the critic's political wisdom and perhaps the political virtue of our age—as with much else that is adventitious in the postcolonialist approach to Irish literature.

The strategy of treating *Dracula* as blotting-paper for its author's post-imperial anxieties seems to have resulted here in an over-interpretation of the textual signifiers on a fairly exorbitant scale. So far from lending support to the idea that the Land Leaguers were victims of remorseless state violence, Stoker musters a critique of the violent ways of Irish agrarian agitators and implies—as Moses acknowledges—that they were subject to the remote control of a sinister aristocratic leader. This is of course an alarming idea; yet the trope of political anxiety was not necessarily intended by Stoker as an allegory of Irish politics to be interpreted as a practical position offered in support of coercion bills and so on. On the contrary: to function as it does in a sensational novel of this sort, it need be no truer to the social and political reality than the popular supposition that Jack the Ripper was a member of the English royal family. As it happens Pigott's suicide in 1890—following his fatal cross-examination by Sir Charles Russell (the Irish Catholic from Newry who was Gladstone's Attorney General)[28]—established incontestably that the documents upon which 'Parnellism and Crime' was purportedly founded had indeed been forgeries. Notwithstanding, 'Parnellism' long continued and still continues to be a term in use among historians to describe constitutional dalliance with physical force extremism. According to George Boyce, for instance, Parnellism carried Parnell to power and near-success; after 1886 Parnell disentangled himself from Parnellism with relief, and committed all to the Liberal alliance'.[29] Yet in 1888—within the period of the events of *Dracula* by some computations—Parnell was to say to an American journalist, 'a true revolutionary movement in Ireland should, in my opinion, partake of both a constitutional and an illegal character.'[30] No wonder Stoker was confused about the Irish leader's political intentions—as it falls to us in Ireland to be occasionally confused about such matters also.

III

That the novel *Dracula* shares in the common Victorian anxiety about racial degeneracy—especially associated with inward migration to Britain—is well-known. In relation to the question of agrarian crime in contemporary Ireland this theme takes on a keen significance.[31] The symptoms of criminal degeneracy form the central subject of Van Helsing's extended disquisition on Dracula's mental type, in the course of which he summons some authorities:

> 'The Count is a criminal and of criminal type. Nordau and Lombroso would so classify him, and *qua* criminal he is of imperfectly formed mind.' (*D*, p.406.)

It is this disorder that eventually leads to the vampire's downfall since it compels him to repeat the same old patterns of behaviour, making his homeward trek perfectly predictable. Van Helsing's final victory thus relies on the neurological superiority on the part of the vampire-hunters—a superiority which translates readily into an ethical rather than purely mechanical difference in the capacity of their brains:

> 'Ah! there I have hope that our man-brains that have been of man so long and that have not lost the grace of God, will come, higher than his child-brain that lie in his tomb for centuries, that grow not yet to our stature, and that do only work selfish and therefore small.' (*D*, p.404.)

Nor, of course, do the menfolk in *Dracula* single-handedly overcome the vampire. In a feminist gesture that may be taken for a chivalrous concession rather than a token of true egalitarianism, Mina Harker is permitted a crucial, mediating role:

> '[W]e want all her hope all her courage; when most we want all her great brain which is trained like man's brain, but is of sweet woman and have a special power which the Count give her, and which he may not take away altogether—though he think not so. (*D*, p.404.)

In all of this the clinical idea—though conveyed in Van Helsing's broken English (a lingo oddly reminiscent of blundering malapropisms known as 'Irish bulls')[32]—is that the plight of the vampire involves a moribund condition of the brain resulting from the damage suffered at his 'death', manifesting as a lesser stage of development in that organ than in the body it controls. In this sense Dracula is like the victim of a stroke; yet his debility is not mechanical and therefore answers better to the name of autism—since, for all his 'so great knowledge' of the English way of life acquired from books patiently scrutinised at home in Transylvania, his characteristic processes of mind and spirit remain infantile, egocentric, and ultimately alien to the ordinary community of men and women. His Achilles heel (and perhaps his essential failing) is a learning difficulty: he can acquire extraneous information yet he is not susceptible to spiritual growth or psychic modification: he is immune to the humanising influence of knowledge and experience.

Van Helsing espouses the language of contemporary criminology to describe this monstrous condition:

> 'There is this peculiarity in criminals. It is so constant, in all countries and at all times, that even police, who know not much from philosophy, come to know it empirically, that *it is*. That is to be empiric. The criminal always work at one crime—that is the true criminal who seems predestinate to crime, and who will of none other. This criminal has not

full man-brain. He is clever and cunning and resourceful; but he be not of man-stature as to brain. He be of child-brain in much.' (*D*, p.405.)

Now, criminology is a tendentious science, and never more so than in the hands of Cesare Lombroso (1836-1909), Professor of psychiatry in Pavia and later at Turin, and one of the personages explicitly cited as an authority on criminal psycho-pathology in Stoker's novel.[33] Of his career the *Encyclopaedia Britannica* (1949 edn.) has this to say:

> To Auguste Comte[,] Lombroso owed an exaggerated tendency to refer all mental facts to biological causes, but he surpassed all his predecessors by the wide scope and systematic character of his researches. He held that the criminal population exhibits a higher percentage of physical, nervous and mental anomalies than non-criminals; and that these anomalies are due partly to degeneration, partly to *atavism*. [Italics mine.][34]

In conclusion, 'The criminal is a special type, midway between the lunatic and the savage.'[35] Under "Criminology", we meet with more of the same:

> Lombroso's theory of the criminal as sub-human anthropological freak, marked by anatomical and other stigmata and doomed by his nature to a criminal career, was at once accepted by a majority of students in Italy, and [...] in other European countries. Though subjected to weighty criticism, and though never received in any English-speaking community, it became, and for a generation remained, the dominant doctrine of European students of the problem of crime.[36]

Indeed, it was left to Dr Charles Goring of H. M. Prison Service to demonstrate by statistical analysis in *The English Convict* (1913) that 'there is no such thing as a physical criminal type' and 'no such thing as a mental criminal type' either.[37]

Dr Lombroso's ideas are groundless and repugnant to democratic good sense; and what is more, they were repudiated by the British medical establishment of Stoker's day. Nevertheless they were clearly of interest to him, either as an ingredient in his melodrama or as an exponent of his racist notions about the Irish peasantry turned Land Leaguers. It may be that Van Helsing's worst fear—that the world will be taken over by a 'new order of beings, whose road must lead through Death' (*D*, p.360)—corresponded to Stoker's own alarm at the zombie-like outrages being perpetrated in contemporary Ireland; but since the metaphor is that of pandemic disease, the supposition is that what he feared was the generalisation of such behaviour to all classes. For that threat and that fear, he could only find a model of degeneracy which had proved unacceptable to the liberal community of contemporary Britain. In this regard, the author of *Dracula* shows much less enlightened than the medical establishment (if we accept the idea as his own, and not a melodramatic furnishing), or perhaps simply more frightened. In part, of course, it was the very foreignness of Lombroso's notion that makes it amenable to treatment in a sensational novel: it is, in fact, as alien as Count Dracula. In part also, the diagnosis of criminal atavism rhymes explicitly with the terminology of the Irish Land War, where agrarian 'crimes' were seen as a hateful tactic of the Land League but also as the character-stamp of a whole class of Irishmen. In such a view, the Land-League activist is a monster-figure and a genetically-determined criminal—a judgement that applies *a forteriori* to political assassins. How else, a contemporary might ask (and we might also ask), to explain the Phoenix Park murders of 1882?

The psychologist's theory of political violence against the colonial oppressor as a 'healthy expression of anger' has been developed by several postcolonialist writers;[38] and Luke Gibbons has recently based a hermeneutics of Anglo-Irish literature on Dr George Sigerson's description of the victims of famine and eviction as sufferers from clinical shock with its attendant symptoms of hysteria.[39] Such theories hold good for the social substrate—indeed, violence in colonial contexts calls for them compellingly—but need not hold good for literary works only tenuously related to those contexts. After the relation between the substructure and the base in a Marxist model of literature has been grasped, their mutual remoteness needs to be appreciated also. *Dracula* resists being turned into a case-book of Irish colonialism in action; but what is more to the point, it carries within it a definite explanation of the social violence that we assume to be within the psychic purview of its author at the time of composition. Whether his analysis be right or wrong, it is the one imprinted on the novel. For Stoker, 'colonial violence' as instanced by Land War outrages was not the produce of hysteria and shock so much as a degenerate condition which he equated with social atavism. To Van Helsing (conceivably a fictional counterpart of Sigerson) it was a result of a blocking of the learning capacity—a capacity that even animals possess in some degree:

> 'The little bird, the little fish, the little animal learn not by principle, but empirically; and when he learn to do, then there is to him the ground to start from to do more. "*Dos pou sto,*" said Archimedes. "Give me a fulcrum, and I shall move the world!" To do once, is the

fulcrum whereby child-brain become man-brain; and until he have the purpose to do more, he continue to do the same again every time, just as he have done before!' (*D*, p.406.)

'Just as he have done before': in relation to Irish dissensions, this may be read off in terms of the climactic years 1641, 1689, and 1798, comprising recurrent chapters of atavistic violence as viewed from the traditional standpoint of the Irish Protestant—for whom these were markers for the chief traumas of political history in Ireland. On this basis, *Dracula* can be aligned with the 'siege mentality' of that large and varied grouping from generation to generation.[40] From the standpoint of the ordinary middle-class Dublin Protestant of the 1890s, however, no such catastrophic soundings were necessary to import the message that violence was an intractable component of social and political life in Ireland.

An under-rated feature of the narrative of *Dracula* is the attempt that Stoker makes to dramatise the stages by which Van Helsing reaches his diagnosis of Count Dracula in successive chapters following the violent exorcism of Lucy's corpse, which Christopher Smart has called 'penetrative correction'—remarking the grisly kind of orgasm it undergoes and the covertly homo-erotic nature of this exchange in which three males share in causing this response.[41] Such psycho-sexual high drama naturally distracts from other business in the novel, notably its connections with the Irish Land-War; and, not surprisingly, Smart finds everything after this episode 'rather tedious'.[42] Yet Van Helsing's discovery is represented as the central mechanism of Stoker's novel and it is clear that a degree of suspense is supposed to attach to it—as with the triumphs of detection attained by Sherlock Holmes or other heroes of the cerebrating kind in Victorian fiction. Viewed from this standpoint, the essential narrative of *Dracula* may be regarded as the uncovering of a medical logic behind Irish social violence, importing a corresponding lesson about Irish social development at large. This is, incidentally, a thoroughly Protestant lesson as retaled by Dr Seward, who conveys Van Helsing's aetiology of vampirism in the following somewhat Pauline terms:

'In some faculties of mind he has been, and is, only a child; but he is growing, and some things that were childish at the first are now of man's stature. He is experimenting, and doing it well; and if it had not been that we have crossed his path he would be yet—he may be yet if we fail—the father or furtherer of a new order of beings, whose road must lead through Death, not Life.' (*D*, p.360.)

That might be taken as an exhortation to 'put away childish things' in keeping with the process of spiritual growth adumbrated by St. Paul.[43] The price of failing to do so is also clearly limned in likewise Pauline terms when Dracula's 'way' is typified as a 'road must lead through Death' (*D*, p.360).[44]

The whole truth about Count Dracula's mental state dawns on Van Helsing in Chapter XXV. Commenting there on Dracula's frankness in telling Harker of his ancient retreat from Turkey the vampire-hunter remarks, 'The Count's child-thought see nothing; therefore he speak so free.' (*D*, p.405). Dracula speaks 'free' because he is oblivious to the significance of his own words, his own actions. For the rest of us, the experience of mind is quite different, involving moments of mental synthesis and enlightenment denied to his kind:

> 'Just as there are elements which rest, yet when in nature's course they move on their way and they touch—then pouf! and there comes a flash of light, heaven wide, that blind and kill and destroy some: but that show up all earth below for leagues and leagues.' (*D*, p.405.)

This is a highly melodramatic conception of the process of intuition, though perhaps not remote from the actualities in a late-Victorian world of steam and high explosives, nor unconnected with the Hegelian phenomenology of mind. At any rate it is Mina Harker who next experiences the moment of epiphany: 'Oh, my dear', continues Van Helsing, 'I see your eyes are opened, and that you have the lightning flash show all the leagues' (*D*, p.406). Mina has just realised—and Van Helsing grasps it simultaneously—that just as Dracula had 'fled back over the Danube from Turkey land' (*D*, p.406) after his ancient defeat, he will now flee back to his Transylvanian eyrie after his brush with our heroes in London. In this somewhat wooden way, Stoker dramatises the essential difference in creative power between morally developed adults and monstrous creatures such as vampires and Land-League activists—a difference that consists essentially in a capacity for development and adaptation to changing times.

IV

Viewed in this light, the plot of *Dracula* seems to turns upon the helpless atavism that transforms Irish tenant farmers—or 'peasants farmers', as George Moore called them[45]—into 'lunatics and savages' (in Lombroso's coinage) in the eyes of the metropolitan community—eyes opened by Emily Lawless's *Hurrish* (1886) and novels of that sort. It hardly matters from the literary standpoint that this conception of the Land-Leaguers is patently unjust; what matters is that it informs the psychological portrayal of Count Dracula in Stoker's novel. This being so, Dracula is not simply reducible to the simulacra of an Anglo-Irish landlord; he is, moreover, very clearly affined with another figure in the Irish agrarian landscape—the 'gombeen man' whom William Gladstone loved to hate. As to how that ignoble personage featured in Stoker's political vocabulary, we need look no further than the definition of the term furnished by an incidental character in *The Snake's Pass* (1890):

> "A gombeen man, is it? Well, I'll tell ye", said an old, shrewd-looking man at the other side of the hearth. "He's a man that linds you a few shilling's or a few pounds whin ye want it bad, and thin niver laves ye till he has tuk all he've got—yer land an' yer shanty an' yer holding an' yer money an' yer craps; an' *he would take the blood out of yer body if he could sell it or use it anyhow!*" [Italics mine.][46]

In short, a gombeen man is the very model of a vampire, if we are truly seeking one. So far from being a landlord in his own person (though perhaps a surrogate of sorts), he is one of the peasant class who has made such a success of usury that he could easily prey upon that economically-troubled grouping also—

> 'if he chose an' settle in Galway [...] or in Dublin [...] and lind money to big min—landlords an' the like—instead iv playin' wid poor min here an swallyin' them up, wan by wan.'[47]

Politically-minded critics may be justified in urging that both gombeen-man and landlord were agrarian capitalists of the period and therefore equally guilty of 'grind[ing] the faces iv the poor'[48]—and that Stoker's Victorian brand of false consciousness succeeds in occluding this. For the novelist, at any rate, the bad eminence of the Irish gombeen-man elicits a Miltonic measure of demonisation when he makes the same speaker assert of Black Murdock that 'it's him that'd do little for God's sake if the devil was dead!'[49] If there were no Satan, the Irish gombeenman would perfectly fulfil his office.

Looking for an Irish substrate in *Dracula* corresponding to a single historical moment of the Land War and its social contexts is bound to be a speculative business, and perhaps a fundamentally inapposite one since the power of the novel consists in its indefiniteness of suggestion—as Franco Moretti has eloquently argued.[50] In addition to this general reservation, there are some indications that Stoker duplicated the pattern of allusion so as to foil a unilateral interpretation of precisely this kind. If so, it is a reasonable inference that he was aware of allegorical possibilities of his narrative and consciously implanted them, just as he consciously limited each to its place in the whole design. In all of this there is as much a sense of the jigsaw and the cross-word as of the psychoanalytical effusion, though *Dracula* is riddled with coded allusions of a kind readily susceptible to psychoanalysis for those who prefer that game. Take, for instance, the name 'Harker'—*one who listens*, perhaps? Barbara Belford would have us believe that its original bearer was the scene-painter at the Lyceum, who recorded in his memoirs that Stoker informed him of the debt, though not the reason why he took his name for Jonathan and Mina.[51] Peter Haining, by contrast, prints a contemporary newspaper cutting—still extant among Stoker's working papers—regarding a serious biting-attack upon a woman by her low-life partner witnessed by a Constable Harker.[52] Is this coincidence merely, or *dédoublement de signification*? On the interpretation of the diary-dates that provide the chronological framework of the novel, the commentators disagree just as widely. Belford confidently ascribes its events to the year 1893 on the strength of the desk-diary in which Stoker jotted down the main episodes.[53] Approached the matter otherwise, Haining has isolated the sole point in the text where a week-day is connected with a date—from which conjunction the year may be inferred. The signal conjunction falls in Chapter XXIII where Mina makes reference to the first encounter with Dracula in London as having occurred on 'Thursday last' (*D*, p.221), which event is notarised in her journal entry for 22 September (*D*, p.207). 22 September in the year of *Dracula* was thus a Thursday.

Now, Thursday fell on September 22nd in the common years 1870, 1881, 1887, and 1898, as well as the leap year 1892, suggesting that Haining's conjectured year of 1887—from which Constable Harker's crime report is drawn—is plausible enough.[54] As to Belford, the diary page reproduced as a plate in her book is printed with the calendar year in the top left-hand corner thus: 189– , allowing the user to fill the last digit as required.[55] Although Stoker added the dates of the days on which the events of the novel's opening chapters occurred (e.g., 'Monday May 15: Women Kissing'), he has not added the final digit to the year. Application to a 'Ready-Reference Calendar' quickly establishes that of the years within the range of time known to be associated with the planning and composition of the novel—that is, Summer 1890 to Summer 1897—Monday fell on 15 May uniquely in

1890—incidentally throwing Belford's computation out by several years.[56] If then, Stoker is assumed to have intended consistency in all the dates and days throughout, it seems to follow that he made an mistake in ascribing dates and days variously in different parts of the novel (or at least the working papers). There is only one alternative interpretation: that he consciously doubled the chronological signs so that the real events of two different years were embraced by the diary pointers of the novel.

Which of the two co-ordinates should we accept as a guide to the 'year' of *Dracula*? Dare we extrapolate from Haining's date and propose that the signal historical event which underlies the novel is the Land League demonstration at Mitchelstown with its episode of 'state violence' in October 1887? It was there that a crowd was fired on by the Royal Irish Constabulary, with the result that three Leaguers were fatally wounded. In the sequel, John Mandeville, one of the leaders, was put in prison where he occupied a cell in utter nakedness since he refused to wear prison clothes. He died in the year following his release—at which point his resemblance to the character called Renfield in *Dracula* becomes extraordinarily compelling.[57] Ought we to put aside such methods of chronological matching and set out to demonstrate that Stoker was inspired by the macabre events in Phoenix Park on May 6th, 1882? Or by the ethos of the Parnell Commission set up to investigate the libellous charges of 'Parnellism and Crime'? Or should we ascribe the events of *Dracula* to the period of Parnell's political fall and extinction in 1889-1891? (Court-revelations about his use of a ladder to scale the hotel wall while intent on visiting Kitty O'Shea might make an interesting starting-point.)[58] Reflection on such quandaries—even without broaching any non-Irish strands of commentary—reminds us that indeterminacy of signifiers is an essential component in the power of Stoker's best-known story.

Among these historical parallels the elements of a post-colonialist interpretation of *Dracula* still beckon temptingly. Yet there are precise reasons for being cautious in endorsing a merely nationalist interpretation of the novel, seen as an allegorical disclosure of the historical crimes of the Protestant ascendancy in Ireland. For one thing, such readings are apt to reveal the desires of the critics more clearly than the intentions of the author: —desires that seem (like the 'quantum of wantum' that Beckett attributes to the horse-leach's daughter) always to be constant. As such they are signs of a closed system. This is not to detract from the rhetorical analysis of Irish literary usage in regard to 'land', 'earth' and 'soil' conducted by Seamus Deane, or to question the vindication of Irish 'atavism' and supposed 'hysteria' evinced in Luke Gibbons' exploration of 'the conflicting claims of modernisation and memory on an economy in crisis' (for which read, Irish separatism vs. The Anglo-American world order).[59] What it does suggest is that nationalist—as opposed to postcolonialist—approaches are by their very nature partial as carrying within them a compulsion to represent the spirit of the nation as the source of all phenomena really or notionally connected with Irish soil. The images of Bram Stoker and his most famous creation recently offered in this spirit are all too much like Count Dracula's reflection in Jonathan Harker's shaving mirror: the original is strangely absent.

NOTES
1   'The Great White Fair in Dublin: How there has arisen on the site of the old Donnybrook Fair a great exhibition as typical of the new Ireland as the former festival was of the Ireland of the past', in *The World's Work: An Illustrated Magazine of Efficiency and Progress*, Vol. 9 (1907), pp.570-1; cited in Christopher Morash, '"Ever Under Some Unnatural Condition": Bram Stoker and the Colonial Fantastic', in Brian Cosgrove, ed., *Literature and the Supernatural* [Maynooth Bicentenary Symposium] (Dublin: Columba Press 1995), pp.95-118, p.109; see also William Hughes, '"For Ireland's Good", The Reconstruction of Rural Ireland in Bram Stoker's *The Snake's Pass*', *Irish Studies Review* (Autumn 1995), pp.17-21, p.21.
2   Viz., 'We went at once into our Plan of Campaign.' (p.385); cf. also, 'We must proceed to lay out our campaign' (p.288); 'Plan of attack' (p.363). See *Dracula* [Penguin Popular Classics] (London: Penguin 1994). Henceforth cited as *D*.
3   The Plan of Campaign consisted in offering a 'fair rent' to the landlord agreed by the League, to be contributing to a League fund should he refuse to accept it as quittance. See R. V. Comerford, 'The Parnell Era, 1883-91' [Chap. III], in W. E. Vaughan, ed., *A New History of Ireland*, V: Ireland Under the Union, II: 1870-1921 (Oxford: Clarendon Press 1996), pp.53-80; Laurence M. Geary, *The Plan of Campaign, 1886-1891* (Cork UP 1986), p.145.
4   The *Norton Critical Edition of Dracula* (NY: Norton 1997) contains representative essays in this vein by Phyllis Roth, Franco Moretti, Christopher Craft, Bram Dijkstra, Stephen Arata, and Talia Schaffer—all of which previously appeared elsewhere—together with Stoker's working papers and other source materials.
5   For the dating of those 'events', see Sect. IV infra.
6   See Seamus Deane, 'Land and Soil: A Territorial Rhetoric', in *History Ireland*, 2, 1 (Spring 1994), pp.31-34; reprinted as 'Landlord and Soil: *Dracula*', in 'National Character and the Character of Nations' [Chap. 2], *Strange Country* (Oxford: Clarendon Press 1997), pp.89-94; and Terry Eagleton, 'Form and Ideology in the Anglo-Irish Novel', in *Bullán: An Irish Studies Journal*, Vol. 1, No. 1 (Spring 1994), pp.17-26, reprinted in

Mary Massoud, ed., *Literary Relations: Ireland, Egypt and the Far East* (Gerrards Cross: Colin Smythe 1996), pp.135-46, and incorporated under the same title though a variant form as a Chapter V in *Heathcliff and the Great Hunger* (London: Verso 1995), pp.145-225.

7   The identification of Dracula with Parnell has been piloted in unrelated essays by Chris Morash and Michael Valdez Moses. See Morash, '"Ever Under Some Unnatural Condition": Bram Stoker and the Colonial Fantastic', in Brian Cosgrove, ed., *Literature and the Supernatural* (Dublin: Columba Press 1995), pp.95-118; Moses, 'Dracula, Parnell, and the Troubled Dreams of Nationhood', in *Journal X: A Journal in Culture and Criticism*, Vol. 2, No. 1 (Autumn 1997), pp.66-11.

8   See Barbara Belford, Bram Stoker: *A Biography of the Author of Dracula* (NY: Knopf 1996), p.230.

9   'The Great White Fair in Dublin [... &c.]' (1907); see William Hughes, '"For Ireland's Good": The Reconstruction of Rural Ireland in Bram Stoker's *The Snake's Pass*', in *Irish Studies Review* (Autumn 1995), pp.17-21; p.21; Morash, '"Ever Under Some Unnatural Condition": Bram Stoker and the Colonial Fantastic' (1995), p.109.

10 *Strange Country* (Oxford: Clarendon Press 1997), p.90.

11 ibid., p.76. The reference is to Standish James O'Grady.

12 ibid. p.77.

13 [Charles Gavan Duffy, ed.,] *The Spirit of the Nation: Ballads and Songs by the writers of the Nation with Original and Ancient Music* (Dublin: James Duffy 1843). Ironically, the epithet 'racy of the soil' was attributed on the title page to Arthur Woulfe, Lord Kilwarden, the principal government victim of Emmet's Rebellion of 1803. For a full commentary on the history of this epithet, see my paper '"Racy of the Soil": The History of an Irish Literary Epithet', in the Transactions of the IASIL Conference at Hofstra, New York, in 1996, ed., Maureen Murphy [forthcoming].

14 Cited in Seamus Deane, gen. ed., 'Introduction', *Field Day Anthology of Irish Writing* (Derry: Field Day Company 1991), Vol. 1, p.5.

15 'A New Nation, Proposal for an Agricultural Association between the Landowners and Occupiers', a letter addressed to Gavan Duffy, dated 17 April 1847; reprinted in Seamus Deane, gen. ed., *Field Day Anthology of Irish Writing* (1991), Vol. 2, pp.165-72; p.171. See also Deane, *Strange Country* (1997), pp.75-78.

16 Reprinted in *Field Day Anthology* (1991), Vol. 2, pp.746-47.

17 *The Irish Felon* (24 June, 1848); *Field Day Anthology of Irish Writing* (1991), p.172; see also Deane, *Strange Country* (1997), p.76f.

18 'The Faith of a Felon' (*Irish Felon*, 8 July 1848), quoted in Justin McCarthy, ed., *Irish Literature* (Washington: Catholic University of America 1904) [under 'Lalor'].

19 *Field Day Anthology of Irish Writing* (1991), p.174.

20 'Form and Ideology in the Anglo-Irish Novel', in Mary Massoud, ed., *Literary Relations: Ireland, Egypt and the Far East* (1996), p.140. Cf. Siobhán Kilfeather's version of the same idea, 'Ireland provided a gothic closet or priest-hole for many colonial skeletons of the English imagination.' ('Origins of Female Gothic', in *Bullán: An Irish Studies Journal*, 1, 2, Autumn 1994, pp.35-45; p.42.)

21 See *Heathcliff and the Great Hunger* (1995): 'Ireland figured as Britain's unconscious [... &c.]' (p.9).

22 See for instance Declan Kiberd, 'Oscar Wilde: The Artist as Irishman', in *Inventing Ireland* (London: Jonathan Cape 1995), pp.33-50; Davis

Coakley, *Oscar Wilde: The Importance of Being Irish* (Dublin: Town House 1993), Pine, *The Thief of Reason: Oscar Wilde and Modern Ireland* (Dublin: Gill & Macmillan 1995), and Jerusha McCormack, ed., *Wilde the Irishman* (Yale UP 1998).
23 'Dracula, Parnell, and the Troubled Dreams of Nationhood', in *Journal X: A Journal in Culture and Criticism*, Vol., 2, No. 1 (Autumn 1997), p.69.
24 ibid. pp.83, 103.
25 ibid., p.84.
26 ibid., p.99.
27 ibid., p.100.
28 1832-1900; created Lord Killowen in 1894.
29 See D. George Boyce, *Nationalism in Ireland* [rev. edn.] (London: Routledge 1991), p.223.
30 ibid., pp.332-33. Note further: 'When this alliance broke his leadership of the party in 1890, he sought to save his position by playing upon the sentiments that had helped him to power in the first place, and directing them against the Liberal alliance. But the party and the country would not follow him; they shared his emotions, but disapproved of his tactics. It was perhaps tragic, but appropriate, that in 1886 Parnell destroyed Parnellism, and in 1891 Parnellism destroyed Parnell.' (idem.)
31 See for instance Daniel Pick, '"Terrors of the Night": *Dracula* and "Degeneration" in the Late Nineteenth Century', in *Critical Quarterly*, 30, 4 (Winter 1988), pp.72-87, and Ludmilla Kostova, '(En)gendering a European Periphery: Images of the Balkans in Nineteenth-Century British Fiction', in *The European English Messenger* (Autumn 1997), pp.52-58
32 The classic text is Maria Edgeworth [with Richard Lovell Edgeworth], *Essay on Irish Bulls* [1802] (NY: Garland Publ. 1979).
33 *Dracula* (London: Penguin 1994), p.406.
34 *Encyclopaedia Britannica* (Chicago UP 1949), Vol. 14., p.345. Among Lombroso's best-known works, *L'uomo di genio* (1888) and *La donna delinquente* (1893) were translated into English respectively in 1891 and 1895.
35 idem.
36 *Encyclopaedia Britannica* (Chicago UP 1949), p.720.
37 idem.
38 See for instance Geraldine Moane, 'A Psychological analysis of colonialism in an Irish Context', in A. Halliday and K. Coyle, eds., *The Irish Journal of Psychology*, 'The Irish Psyche' [Special Issue], Vol. 15, Nos. 2 & 3 (Psychology Society of Ireland 1994), pp.251-65; p.261.
39 See '"Some Hysterical Hatred": History, Hysteria and the Literary Revival', in *Irish University Review*, 27, 1 (Spring/Summer 1997), pp.7-23; espec. pp.18-20.
40 See Terence Brown's Field Day pamphlet, *The Whole Protestant Community: The Making of a Historical Myth* (Derry: Field Day Company 1985), stressing the resistance of Protestantism in Ireland to uniform definition.
41 Christopher Smart, '"Kiss Me with Those Red Lips", Gender and Inversion in Bram Stoker's Dracula', in Elaine Showalter, ed., *Speaking of Gender* (London & NY: Routledge 1989), pp.216-42; pp.216, 232.
42 ibid., p.231.
43 See 1 Cor. 13:11.
44 Cf., 'For the wages of sin is death.' (Romans 6:23.)
45 See *Parnell and His Island* (1887), pp.48-49.

46 *The Snake's Pass* [1890] (Dingle: Brandon Press 1990), p.26.
47 ibid., p.27.
48 idem.
49 idem. See *Paradise Lost*, Bk. II, l.1-6.
50 See Franco Moretti, 'Dialectics of Fear', in *Signs Taken For Wonders: Essays in Sociology of Literary Forms* [trans. David Forgacs] (London: Verso 1983), pp.82-108.
51 Viz., Joseph Harker. See Belford, op. cit. (1996), pp.203-04.
52 See Peter Haining, *The Dracula Scrapbook* (London: Chancellor Press 1987), pp.29-30. Haining is not perhaps taken very seriously, but his book contains a photocopy of the newspaper article.
53 Belford, op. cit. (1996), p.263. Mina is of course née Murray.
54 I am grateful to Colin Smythe for supplying a copy of the *Ready Reference Calendar*.
55 idem.
56 The reason for this is hard to determine since the only rule she is concerned to observe is that the events should be contemporaneous with the composition of the novel.
57 Mandeville was released within the year but died in July 1888. A namesake issued *Zoologica Medicinalis Hibernica* in 1744.
58 See *Dracula* (Penguin Edn. 1994), p.90. Parnell did not in fact employ this method of access, but those who followed the O'Shea divorce trial would be forgiven for supposing that he did.
59 '"Some Hysterical Hatred": History, Hysteria and the Literary Revival', in *Irish University Review*, 27, 1 (Spring/Summer 1997), pp.11-12. A longer version of this paper responds more fully to Gibbons's article.

FABULATION, ONEIRISM AND IRONIC DISTANCE IN LORD DUNSANY'S SHORT FICTION

Gilles Menegaldo

Even though there is currently a renewed interest in fantasy and the fantastic, the work of the Anglo-Irish Baronet Lord Dunsany is widely overlooked, except for a few academic works.[1] Yet he is one of the great figures of twentieth-century fantasy and his contribution to the field is essential, both on account of his own voluminous production (novels, plays, short stories, essays), and through his influence on other writers such as Fritz Leiber, Ursula K. Le Guin, and Howard Phillips Lovecraft.

Indeed, Dunsany's reputation seems to have been primarily sustained by the tribute paid to him by Lovecraft who considered Dunsany as one of his masters in the field of weird fantasy. The American writer admits his debt in a letter to Clark Ashton Smith in 1923:

> Truly Dunsany has influenced me more than anyone else except Poe—his rich language, his cosmic point of view, his remote dream world and his exquisite sense of the fantastic, all appeal to me more than anything else in the modern literature.[2]

Lovecraft points here to some of the key aspects of Dunsany's fiction from which he would borrow extensively, both in terms of style and content between 1920 and 1926 in such stories as "The White Ship", "Celephaïs" or "The Quest of Iranon". Lovecraft also wrote an essay on Dunsany that might serve as an introduction to his poetic art.[3] According to Lovecraft, Dunsany's finest achievements are his early fantasy novels and short stories, especially the stories gathered in such collections as *The Book of Wonder* (1912) and *A Dreamer's Tales* (1910). For him what some critics have contemptuously dismissed as 'a literature of escape' is the result of a deep scrutiny of reality on

Dunsany's part and, as such, it is an appropriate material for literary creation:

> Some of Dunsany's tales deal with the objective world and of strange wonders therein; but the best of them are about lands conceivable only in purple dream. These are fashioned in that purely decorative spirit which means the highest art, having no visible moral or dramatic element save such quaint allegory as many inhere in the type of legendary lore to which they belong. Dunsany's only didactic idea is an artist's hatred of the ugly, the stupid and the common place.[4]

Lovecraft lays stress upon the dominance in Dunsany's outlook of a gift of fabulation that consisted in the ability to conjure up entire magical landscapes in his fiction. Lovecraft also emphasises the importance of dream to Dunsany as a privileged medium reaching beyond the limits of the familiar 'beyond the fields we know' in the unreal. In this way, the empirical, objective world is reduced to the status of a back-cloth acting as a foil to the wonders that make up the central interest of the tale. Dunsany's art thus involves a fundamental contradiction. The apparently naïve—even reactionary—celebration of outmoded social values which characterises them in many places is simply the consequence of his social formation and quite remote from the real 'wonder' of his writing. For this is the key term in his artistic vocabulary, conveying as it does a sense of the marvellous in its connection with the essential condition of ignorance from whence all real belief inevitably springs.

Yet the writer himself must never be taken in by his fantasies. His aim is to conjure up an emotion involved in the depiction of a certain inscape, but also to imply a certain critical and ironic distance. The artist plays with illusions extracted from legends and myths without losing sight of the fact that these outmoded materials are discounted by modern science as guides of any sort to the reality of experience. Faced with confusion, Dunsany manages to achieve a synthesis between the critical approach of modern times and a form of mythical perception based on older cultural traditions, thus engendering his own imaginative universe and his own literary myths.

The Gods of Pegana, published in 1905, provides a good illustration of Dunsany's approach. This book purports to be a transcription of forgotten mythical lore. Indeed, if we detect various influences—notably Greek and Eastern mythology—there is certainly no definite model. *The Gods of Pegana* projects the reader into the world of origins, of absolute beginnings. Unlike the fairy tale, which presupposing the existence of a normal reality—Dunsany's mythical world is not yet regulated, nor ordered by any specific set of values. The text is represented as the history of creation not only of a world, but of possible worlds generated by a central god-figure Mana-Yood-Sushaï around which other, less powerful gods gravitate—in particular the trinity Mung-Sish-Kib, so reminiscent of the Hindu trinity Civa, Vishnu and Kali. In general, the narration takes the form of a rather complex cosmogony featuring the various avatars of an imaginary universe as they are involved in conflicts with each other on a cosmic scale. These conflicts are sometimes presented in a serious, and sometimes a playful—or even trivial—light, akin to the depiction of the petty conflicts in which Greek gods are involved.

A notable feature of the text, apart from the highly poetic quality of its incantatory prose, consists in its relativistic, even indifferentist, outlook on the world. In this it is remote from the moralistic approach that underlies much of fantasy writing, as in fairy-tales. Indeed, even if *The Gods of Pegana* (the last word is etymologically close to Pagan) touches on such quasi-metaphysical themes as creation, knowledge, destiny, death, origins, and secrecy, none of these are specifically foregrounded. Creation is discussed not as a grand design or even a serious business, but as a game or a routine, as something trivial. Thus Mung the God of Death is assigned the task of visiting both palaces and humbler abodes to make his sign. The gods themselves who are at the origin of all the conflicts are presented as vulnerable, ephemeral, subjected to the power of time.

The effect is to underscore the radical puniness and insignificance of human beings, who are often manipulated like pawns on a huge chessboard in the course of these cosmic and even comic games. Our Earth itself is only one world among many. Indeed the origin of our world lies in the dream activity of the central God-figure, who alone knows the truth about the source of creation. Reality thus appears as the product of an eternal, but also immaterial and evanescent process, itself threatened with extinction. In this way Dunsany anticipates the Borgesian paradox expressed in the short story "The Circular Ruins", which concerns a reality that is nothing more than the dream of an avatar. This ironic vision obviously diminishes the importance of the human since, in Dunsany's developing mythology, even the lesser gods depend upon the dream activity of Mana Yood Sushaï, the central God: should he awake, they will vanish since they are no more than parts of his dream. If it is thus for Gods, how is it with men?

Dunsany's next collection *Time and the Gods* (1906) also concerns creation stories and elemental conflicts such as that between the oceanic forces and telluric forces embodied by Tintaggon, the iron mountain which supports these deities. At the same time, the novel marks a shift in emphasis from cosmogony to war between men. Dunsany underlines the role of prophets and poets as intermediaries between gods and common humanity; he also introduces kings who exercise powers that are often revealed to be illusory. In Pegana, the earth is a world among many others, devoid of privileged status. The storyteller mostly devotes his art to describing the mechanisms of creation and destruction. If the motif of the secret already appears, for instance in "Eye in the Waste", it is not really foregrounded. Indeed, every fragment of the discourse men hold concerning gods is seen as unreliable and inappropriate. Even the prophets only know one thing: that men should be kept in ignorance. As to false prophets such as Yug or Kabok, their lies are as fragile and ephemeral as their own existence.

In contrast to this, a principle of duality is manifested in *Time and the Gods* involving a system of exchanges between two worlds, two realities, and two equally legitimate sets of values. The title story provides a good example of this interaction. Here the dreams of the gods are materialised as a city of marble, Sardathrion, where the gods, disguised as men, come to rest and wander among the symbolic figures of the world. However, some men elected by the gods are allowed to dwell in this city and later, when the gods have deserted it, they carve statues representing them and celebrating their original act of creation. This exchange of signs breaks down the univocal character of previous narratives; yet the ephemeral character of creation is still emphasised. Even the most ideally beautiful city dreamt by the gods is subject to time and destruction—and this represents a major, almost obsessional motif in Dunsany's fiction.

Duality and exchange are also illustrated in another story whose title "The Vengeance of Men" adumbrates the theme. Here gods continue to manipulate men, ruling their destiny according to their own whims, condemning them and their cities to ruin; yet they cannot prevent a human prophet from heralding their own downfall, and here the human word acquires a special value and is seen as potentially challenging the divine Word itself, while also serving as the medium in which is inscribed the very fate of the gods.

In "The Cave of Kaï", the omnipotence of gods is questioned. No magician seems to be able to satisfy the desire of King Khanzar to recover past time, but a harp player manages to interpose himself between the memory of the King's glorious actions and the guardian of the cavern where the hours are being swallowed. The law of the irreversibility of time established by the gods is challenged and checked by one kind of human activity in particular—that is, artistic creation in the form of music, which perpetuates memory and thus flows against the course of time.

In another tale, "The Men of Yarnith", it is the very existence of the gods which is challenged. The tale starts with a description of a cosmogony (different from that of Pegana) in which Yarni-Zaï, the earth god, holds sway over the universe. When however the inhabitants of Yarnith, threatened with starvation, decide to send a messenger to the god and ask for help, the god is hidden by mist. When the veil of mist is lifted, the messenger discovers carving instruments close to the towering statue of Yarnith-Zaï—a sign that the god is a creation of man. Thus, made aware that nothing is any greater than themselves, men take up the struggle on their own account and actually manage to overcome the famine. However, some kind of ambiguity remains at the end of the story since the inhabitants still worship Yarnith-Zaï even though he may not exist, but apparently because he can still serve as a medium through which they can reach the true gods whose identity no one knows.

In this way the subversion of divine power and even of God's existence becomes a dominant motif in Dunsany's fiction. In "The Sorrow of Search", King Khanazar, who seeks to find out who the true gods are, is told the story of a prophet, who meets on his quest a multitude of temples and priests, each worshipping a different god, though each believes there is only one god. The prophet ultimately reaches an abyss at the bottom of which lies hidden in the dark a tiny god who can only expostulate: 'I don't know.' In the same story, Shaun (another prophet), meets in turn during a life quest for the genuine gods, four ancient divinities, then three apparently more important ones, then two gods who poke fun at the previous ones, and lastly the allegedly unique deity. While he is carving the image of the latter, he sees in the distance four tall figures. After a difficult trip through a marshy land, he realises these are only the gods whom he has previously encountered. Thus the quest for truth proves vain since the prophet finds himself coming back to the point from which he has departed. Ominously, the ending stresses the relation between the power of the king and the power of gods. When the king asks: 'Who are the true gods?', the prophet can only answer, 'Let the King command.'

Thus, whereas *The Gods of Pegana* relied upon a self-sufficient and univocal system, *Time and the Gods* implies a critical vision, where mirror effects, illusions and delusions trigger a sense of uncertainty closer to the fantastic than to the tale of wonder. A similar duality is expressed in subsequent collections (*The Book of Wonder*, *The Dreamer's Tales*, *The Tales of Wonder*, *New Tales of Wonder*)—that of the conflict between dream and reality. Here mythological creation is relegated in the background, the narrative mostly representing the power of imagination and dream as a strategy of compensation for an alienating, deceiving reality. The dreamer now comes centre stage, represented by the Lovecraftian arch-dreamer Randolph Carter, the hero of the well-known Kadath cycle of stories. This dreamer-hero is often an ordinary man such as the clerk Mr Shap, who leads a highly regulated existence but suffers from increasing frustration leading to imaginative flights whose main vehicle is the dream. Seized with a demiurgic intoxication, he generates, like the gods themselves, his own universe.

This universe is not, however, a 'never-never land' or a cosmic 'elsewhere' in which creative euphoria knows no limits since its creation is paid for at the cost of the character's mental balance and created at the expense of his own existence. This duality involves an interaction between two realms of the imagination, between two codes and two languages which contaminate each other. Thus *The Coronation of Mr Thomas Shap* celebrates the power of dream, its ability to construct autonomous universes as a compensation for the monotony and poverty of the real, empirical world; yet it also stresses the problem of dual identity which induces a schizophrenic condition in the protagonist and alienates him from his real surroundings.

Even still the capacity to create imaginative worlds through dreaming is not given from the outset. It can only be acquired through a gradual and methodical form of labour which is, ironically enough, to some extent reminiscent of the dreamer's real job. At first a source of frustration and dissatisfaction, the oneiric quest is never actually easy. It is often interrupted. The dreamer must overcome many obstacles and also needs to secure the help of a reliable guide. The creation itself is fragile, constantly threatened by awakening and the return to day to day reality. In the end, Thomas Shap is crowned king over all the lands of Wonder, but he also loses touch with reality and ends up in an asylum:

> The doctors downstairs were sitting over their supper, the warders softly slipped from room to room, and when in that cosy dormitory of Hanwell they saw the king still standing erect and royal, his face resolute, they came up to him and addressed him: 'Go to bed', they said—'pretty bed'. So he lay down and soon was fast asleep: the great day was over.[5]

This also conveys the notion that the dreaming faculty, however exhilarating and creative it may be, leads also the protagonist to utter psychological collapse from which there appears to be no return.

The dream world also involves an ambivalent relation to time. If the creation of Mr Shap seems to be unaffected by time, in another story, "The Shop in Go By Street", Dunsany suggests that things age more quickly in the world of dreams than in the real world. When the narrator finds the boat in which he had sailed along the river Yann in dream two years before, he only finds some scattered fragments of it. If the dream world acquires eventually as much reality and vividness as the real world, Dunsany ultimately reintroduces in the dream world the limitations inherent to the real world. This can be felt also in terms of space. There is a certain hierarchy of places in the lands generated by dreams. Some are more 'real' or probable than others. Space is characterised by its uncertainty like this staircase in Shap's dreamworld which leads 'we know not wither'. So in a way Lord Dunsany subverts the categories of the real and the unreal. We may wonder which of the two is the most tangible.

Another trait of some of these stories is that of the reversal of view point. Indeed in "The Coronation of Mr Shap", London appears as if it were embodying all the evils of urban modernity. However in "A Tale of London", through the magic of poetic evocation, it becomes the most marvellous city in the world—a wonder almost beyond the power of words to describe. Only the sultan's hasheesh-eater can find, with difficulty, an adequate language, while he also expresses fear and awe at having gone beyond the limits to probe into a forbidden territory:

> Indeed of many cities have I dreamt but of none fairer, through many marble metropolitan gates hasheesh has led me, but London is its secret, the last gate of all; the ivory bowl has nothing more to show. And indeed even now the imps that crawl behind me and that will not let me be are plucking me by the elbow and bidding my spirit return, for well they know that I have seen too much. 'No, not London,' they say.[6]

This relativistic approach—which is quite in keeping with a modernist and scientific approach (even though Dunsany satirises many aspects of modernity)—is also interesting to consider in relation with the concept of the fantastic which depends upon the relation between an object and a perceiving subject. The very conditions of perception are seen to alter the nature of the object. In the same way, Dunsany also experiments with perspective, taking for his protagonists giants or dwarves, men or insects, in order to provide alternative angles on reality.

In "Blagdaross" the protagonists are discarded objects, a cork, an unburnt match, a broken kettle, a rope used by a suicide, all recalling their memories. Blagdaross is a forsaken rocking horse who remembers nostalgically how he could, through the imagination of his young owner, impersonate such famed creatures as Bucephalus, Roland's horse or even Rossinante. However the tale ends on a positive note as a young boy rides the toy horse again. Another story, "Where the Tides Ebb and Flow", provides an original angle since the narrator—who has apparently committed some unmentionable crime—tells his story from beyond the grave. His executed body is constantly desecrated, taken out of its grave, plunged in the muddy waters of the river, gnawed by rats, buried or exposed according to the workings of the tide. Meanwhile his spirit or soul witnesses historical evolution: the gradual transformation of the city and its ultimate downfall. Eventually man disappears replaced by millions of birds while nature is restored, symbolised by a wild rose standing over the ruins of wharves and warehouses. This powerful evocation which stresses once more the ephemeral fate of man provides another example of an alternative point of view.[7]

Dunsany was explicitly concerned with the issue of perspective and shared that interest with Lovecraft, who brought it to focus in such stories as "The Shadow out of Time", dealing with the notion of mind transference. Dunsany wrote in a letter:

> Probably if we were suddenly made to live amongst insects, it would come out that we knew nothing about the smell of grass or even its exact colour, and the insects would wonder how any creature living in the world could be ignorant of a thing so common as grass.[8]

In Dunsany's tales, however, speech is foregrounded even more than the look and, indeed, the creative power of language is constantly asserted. In a way, poetic discourse provides an adequate substitute for reality, without the dangers for sanity that the dream activity entails. In "A Tale of the Equator" (in *The Last Book of Wonder*), the Sultan wants to build a palace upon the boundary that divides the North from the South, so that summer should reign in the Northern courts while winter would prevail in the South. He summons the poets to describe such a palace; some manage to attract his attention and 'make him smile', but only one is able to give a full account of it according to his notion. Indeed, the evocation is so vivid and so meticulous in detail that once the poet finishes speaking the Sultan gives up his project of actually building the palace: 'It will be unnecessary for my builders to build this palace, Erlathdronion, Earth's Wonder, for in hearing thee we have drunk already its pleasures.'[9]

Dunsany asserts the power of language in many ways, either by celebrating the creative gift of poets, or by emphasising the deadly power of prophecy and malediction. In "The Loot of Loma", the four tall Indian men who return home after having ransacked the city of Loma do not realise that a priest of the doomed city has written a curse (in an unknown language) on a parchment that has been slipped in with the loot by a dying nomad. In time the curse proves effectual and retribution shall come upon the robbers, even though the reader is left in ignorance as to the cause of death:

> [...] but the curse in the mystical writing that they had unknown in their bag worked there on that lonely pass six leagues from the ruins of Loma, and nobody can tell us what it was.[10]

Language can be a means to conjure up the realm of wonders; it can even replace reality itself since words have a performative function. They can make things happen, command or at least orientate the fate of the characters. The symbolism of writing and reading is ever-present through objects, engraved stones, and books of course. Indeed the motif of reading, of page-turning, is recurrent in Dunsany's fiction. Everything that exists is written down; knowledge is consigned within the pages of the ultimate register to which very few have access—a theme that might easily be compared with the Borgesian concept of the Central Library to which the records of all events, past, present and future are consigned. To this conception Dunsany comes closest in his adumbration of the "Book of Secret Things" in "The Men of Yarnith", a tale that associates writing with the theme of transgression.

Writing no less than telling is endowed with a supernatural power in Dunsany's stories, and is indeed presented as a necessary ritual on occasion. Thus the narrator of "The Secret of the Sea" fails to consign to paper the strange and frightening sailors' tales told by a reticent gnome and confesses that, when he tries to write them down *verbatim*, the ancient words make him shiver until he is compelled to destroy what he has written. This is why he must tell the story in his own words even though something of the authenticity and vividness of the original may be missing from his account since it no longer smacks 'of rum and blood and the sea'.[12]

This points to the self-reflexive quality of Dunsany's work, as is best illustrated in the story entitled "Probable Adventures of the Three Literary Men". An apparently simple narrative tells how some nomads, hankering after new songs to sing around their camp fire at night, ask Slith, a famous thief, to steal for them a Golden Box which is supposed to contain poems of fabulous value. However, as Donald Burleson has shown,[13] this text develops an extended metaphor concerning the transmission and the transcription of texts but also concerning writing and the reading process. At the outset, poetry is a treasure, jealously guarded by its owner who keeps for himself the best pieces, reading them 'selfishly and alone'. The exploits of Slith who manages to steal the precious Box, may be taught after his spectacular fall into the black abyss. We shall never know if he escapes death or not, but the theft itself becomes a fable, a material for fiction to be transmitted to a new generation of readers. Burleson sees the thieves as a slightly ironic or even sarcastic image of the reader (or the critic), seeking in texts nuggets of interpretation and succeeding or failing to find them according to their reading competence.

Dunsany's fiction is also characterised by its subversion or reversal of some common conventions of the fairy tale, one recurrent device being the absence of closure. A number of stories have no real, satisfying ending. The reader is left with a sense of frustration as the narrator is either deliberately withholding information for intellectual or moral reasons, or pretending that there is a limit to his knowledge, as in "The Loot of Loma". As for "Bethmoora", another tale of a doomed city threatened by an allegorised desert, the reader shall never learn what dread message is delivered. Many hypotheses are suggested but none is confirmed. In "The Hasheesh Man", however, the narrator of "Bethmoora" (Dunsany himself?) learns who it was that brought the curse: thus, Dunsany manipulates the information, disclosing only part of the mystery, leaving the reader in a state of delicious frustration. The motif of partial or forbidden knowledge is involved in a wider symbolic pattern since most stories are structured in terms of quest or initiation; but it seems to apply beyond the limits of the diegetic universe to the writer himself as if he had some hidden, transgressive and potentially dangerous connection with an unknown world.

Another device is the ironic deflation of the questing hero. In "The Hoard of the Gibbelins", the main protagonist, the knight Alderic is indeed bent on a quest, but this quest is not aimed at ridding the world of the monstrous, cannibal gibbelins but rather at getting hold of their hoard. Ultimately, the knight, having spoken a fiery dragon into submission, manages to overcome the many obstacles that are set on his path. Dunsany plays here with the various conventions of the epic quest such as the impassable forest over which the protagonist sails thanks to the dragon. Alderic ultimately reaches the evil tower (joined to *terra cognita* by a bridge) where the Gibbelins dwell, breaks into the emerald cellar only to find, like many other thieves in Dunsany's fiction, retribution and untimely death: [14]

> By a faint ray of the moon, he saw the water was green with them and, easily filling a satchel, he rose again to the surface. And there were the Gibbelins waist-deep in the water, with torches in their hand! And, without saying a word, *or even smiling*, they neatly hanged him on the outer wall—and the tale is one of those that have not a happy ending.[15]

Subversion is here explicit, as the last sentence testifies provocatively.

I shall end by evoking another motif subverted in Dunsany's fiction, that of marriage, so much a stable of conventional fairy-tale endings. In "Poltarnees, Beholder of Ocean", the three little kingdoms of Toldees, Mondath and Arizim named the Inner Lands are separated from the ocean by Poltarnees, a huge, sublime mountain. Through the centuries, all the young men, drawn by the call of the ocean which lies beyond, have been eager to leave. They steal away from the country by climbing over Poltarnees, alas never to return, even though they have sworn to do so. So no one in the Inner Lands knows what the ocean looks like, or why all young men have fallen under its spell. However, Hilnaric, the beautiful daughter of the King of Arizim seems to be a match for the attractions of the ocean. Her extraordinary beauty is subjected to a test in which she is variously compared to the moonrise, or to the rising sun at morn.

Among those who praise her, a bold young hunter called Athelvok goes so far as to say she is more beautiful than the ocean—a comparison that seems blasphemous to all those present. For his part, the king offers him his daughter Hilnaric as a bride if, on climbing over Poltarnees, he returns to the kingdom to report what lies beyond, and what the ocean looks like. The young man make his journey but does not return, as might be expected, to the Inner Lands—he too having yielded to the spell of the sea. The bride waits in vain and her dowry is set aside in order 'to build a temple wherein men curse the ocean'. In this way, Dunsany challenges a major convention of the fairy tale and offers something of a satire on marriage while at the same time paying tribute to the sublimity of the sea. In this connection, he employs rhythmical, incantatory prose, freighted with poetic images and biblical tones:

> And the whole plain of water glittering with late sunlight, and the surges and the currents and the white sails of ships were all together like the face of a strange new god that has looked a man for the first time in the eyes at the moment of his death; and Athelvok, looking at the wonderful Sea knew why it was that the dead never return [...].[16]

Dunsany thus creates, 'at the edge of the world', a most unusual fictional universe, with his invented gods, his imaginary kingdoms, his marvellous but elusive cities. Beyond that poetic vision, however, the writer seeks also to contrast modern life, presented as drab and alienating, with the more appealing world of fantasy. Most of his human protagonists seek some kind of escape, and dream becomes the ideal vehicle for conjuring vivid images that build up a new personal reality at the expense of the old one. This oneiric journey often assumes the form of a quest for identity and self-knowledge, hence the prominent motif of transgression and retribution. Indeed, through the depiction of outlandish characters, Dunsany exposes also the shortcomings of men, whether they be kings or knights, fools or prophets. By shifting perspectives, he offers a distantiated, humorous, even cruel, approach to mankind. His fiction heavily emphasises the power of words, oral or written. Poetic language is seen as a kind of struggle against the tyranny of time, to perpetuate through generations a sense of the past and capture the essence of things. Lastly, Dunsany seeks to subvert the conventions of the fairy tale by introducing some uncanny, at times macabre touches, and to establish with a reader a new contract, involving various kinds of manipulation but also a certain complicity through a common celebration of fantasy.

NOTES
1 See for instance, Mark Amory, *A Biography of Lord Dunsany* (London: Collins 1972); S. T. Joshi, *Lord Dunsany: Master of the Anglo-Irish Imagination* (NJ: Greenwood Publ. 1995), and Joshi, *The Weird Tale* (Texas UP 1990), containing a chapter on the writer. See also Max Duperray's articles in issues of *Études Irlandaises* during 1975 and 1984 and his unpublished thesis on Dunsany (University of Toulouse Le Mirail).

2   H. P. Lovecraft, *Selected Letters* (Sauk City: Arkham House 1944), Vol. 1, p.243.
3   'Lord Dunsany and his Work", in *Marginalia* (Sauk City: Arkham House 1922), pp.148-60.
4   ibid., p.151.
5   "The Coronation of Mr Thomas Shap", in *The Book of Wonder* (NY: Books for Libraries Press 1972), p.68.
6   "A Tale of London", in *The Last Book of Wonder* ([1910] rep. NY: Books for Libraries Press 1969), p.3.
7   The end is however anti-climactic as the narrator awakes in his London bedroom. For once, Dunsany sticks to the convention, explaining away the deep uncanniness of the tale.
8   Quoted by Linda Pashka in her excellent article '"Hunting for Allegories" in the Prose Fantasy of Lord Dunsany', in *Studies in Weird Fiction*, No.12.
9   "Tale of the Equator", in op. cit. (1969), p.158.
10 "The Loot of Loma", in op. cit. (1969), p.79.
11 Juan Luis Borges, "The Library of Babel", in *Labyrinths* (1953).
12 ibid, p.83
13 See his article: 'On Dunsany's "Probable Adventure of the Three Literary Men"', *Studies in Weird Fiction*, No. 10.
14 Some of them escape however such as Nuth in the story entitled: "How Nuth Would Have Practised His Art upon the Gnoles" which ends with the following words: 'Nobody ever catches Nuth.'
15 "The Hoard of the Gibbelins", in *The Book of Wonder*, op. cit. p.49.
16 "Poltarnees, Beholder of Ocean", in *A Dreamer's Tales* (Philadelphia: Olswick Press 1979), p.15.

'GREEN FIRE INTO THE FROZEN BRANCH'- VIOLENCE AND THE RECOVERY OF IDENTITY IN VINCENT WOODS'S *AT THE BLACK PIG'S DYKE* & SEAMUS HEANEY'S *THE CURE AT TROY*

Bernard McKenna

In "Solstice", Gerald Dawe writes of the birth of his son, who arrived in 'that bad winter/when I was like a man/walking in a circle no one else was near' (ll.1-3).[1] Further, nature and the crisis of violent history accentuate the speaker's personal feelings of isolation. 'The lakes had frozen, [...] and the news was all discontent/of *Sell-Out* and blame for the dead/country-boy faces that already were/fading from church wall and gate' (ll.4, 6-9). However, with his child's birth, the poet

> [...] saw the ice outside fall
> and imagined the fires burning
> on the Hill of Tara ring
> across the concealed earth
> towards a silent hospital
> and our standing still
> all around you, Olwen,
> transfixed by your birth
> in such a bitter season. (ll.16-24)

The speaker comes to terms with the violence and sites of traumatic rupture that surround him, as a consequence of the birth of his son, converting his introspective and solipsistic circling into an image of rebirth and renewal. Moreover, he transforms his private circle into a communal one paying homage with friends and family to his child. In addition, his new circle finds a resonance in ancient Irish myth and legend, consciously referencing the solstice rites on Tara. Furthermore, the poet's careful use of assonance in the lines that detail his renewal reinforces the natural thaw and consequent personal, spiritual rejuvenation felt at the birth of his son. The speaker 'saw' the ice 'fall' and imagined the rites of 'Tara' leaning 'towards' the hospital where he and his friends are 'standing'. The vowel sounds create a subtle unity between the speaker's personal images of renewal, the rebirth of the natural world, and ancient spiritual rites of resurrection. The speaker reconstitutes his identity, through the birth of his child, developing a personal alternative to the violent forces of the Troubles.

The process for developing alternative, reconstituted identities, within the framework of Vincent Woods's *At the Black Pig's Dyke* and Seamus Heaney's *The Cure at Troy*, involves components akin to Gerald Dawe's reflections and to clinical stratagems for recovery. Specifically, in terms of the 're-establishment of secure social and cultural contacts',[2] the two plays establish rituals, based in part on received images and traditions but also based on personal variation and revisions to those traditions, designed to recognise the factors that rupture identity and perpetuate that rupture. In addition, Woods's and Heaney's theatre provides an alternative identity that incorporates traumatic structures into a fully reconstituted sense of self. Furthermore, in a process similar to the clinical matrix of recovery that stresses the 'accumulation of restorative experiences',[3] the plays explore a process through which individuals regain control and mastery of their environment by recalling and incorporating into their consciousness the ruptured memories that cause trauma. Within both plays characters come to terms with violence and transform the ruptured components of identity into a newly fashioned identity by combining received mythic images and a personal spirituality.

Many of the characters in the plays make a distinction between the emotional repercussions of violence and the objective factors that ultimately inform identity. As a consequence, they reconstitute a personal spirituality which enables them to re-establish meaningful interpersonal, historical, and mythic contacts. As Carl Jung put it,

> if we can succeed in discriminating between objective knowledge and emotional value-judgements, then the gulf that separates our age from antiquity is bridged over. [...] The importance of this realisation should not be underestimated, for it teaches us that there is an identity of fundamental human conflicts which is independent of time and place [, ...] an indissoluble link binds us to the men of antiquity [which represents] the way of inner sympathy on the one hand and of intellectual comprehension on the other. By penetrating into the blocked subterranean passages of our own psyches we grasp the living meaning of classical civilisation, and at the same time we establish a firm foothold outside our own culture from which alone it is possible to gain an objective understanding of its foundations.[4]

Green Fire into the Frozen Branch 99

Applying Jung's program for 'transformation' to Northern Irish drama, it becomes clear that the characters come to understand the foundations of their personal and community history by severing the link that trauma has created between themselves and the violent factors that inform their understanding of their society. Moreover, once the link is severed, individuals, like the speaker of Gerald Dawe's "Solstice", can then achieve a sense of the 'living meaning' of their own classical civilisation. Specifically, they come to terms with Irish historical, mythological, and geographical images and places that help them recover from traumatic experiences by refashioning their identities to include socially and historically engaging imaginative constructions.

Restoration of Social Support

In response to the ruptures to identity created by traumatic events, Vincent Woods's *At the Black Pig's Dyke* and Seamus Heaney's *The Cure at Troy* ritualise a method for re-establishing social and cultural support. Through allegory, the playwrights detail a process for integrating the traumatic event into a character's consciousness in order to come to terms with trauma and to refashion a fully-integrated identity. In clinical terms,

> [e]motional attachment is probably the primary protection against being traumatised. People seek close emotional relationships with others in order to help them anticipate, meet, and integrate difficult life experiences. [...] In recognition of this need for affiliation as protection against trauma, it has become widely accepted that the central issue in acute crisis intervention is the provision and restoration of social support.[5]

In plays that detail the restoration of social support, the process for overcoming traumatic disruption involves several parts. Initially, individuals must come to terms with the extent of the traumatic disruption and the extent of their emotional isolation. In terms of the North of Ireland, this part of the process involves recognising the full impact of sectarian and colonial rupture. Subsequently, individuals exposed to trauma must put behind them flawed dynamics of protection, including masks of historical or cultural resonance that seem to disrupt traumatic threat. Within the context of Northern Ireland, the process includes structures that enabled the individual to find status or protection from violence: roles of martyr, Republican volunteer, and Orange loyalist are just a few examples. Next, individuals must articulate a framework for overcoming violence that contains within it elements with a non-sectarian cultural resonance. Finally, individuals must provide their own variation on the cultural framework, adapting it to their individual needs and to their particular traumatic reaction.

Ultimately, both playwrights produce an allegorical resolution to the particular interpretations of recovery. The individual interpretation of the cultural framework, the articulation of difference, proves essential in the development of a type of hybrid identity that integrates not only traumatic elements into an individual's consciousness but also serves as a model for a fully integrated society. As Homi Bhabha has said,

> the representation of difference must not be hastily read as the reflection of *pre-given* ethnic or cultural traits set in the fixed tablet of tradition. The social articulation of difference, from the minority perspective, is a complex, ongoing negotiation that seeks to authorise cultural hybridities that emerge in moments of historical transformation. The 'right' to signify from the periphery of authorised power and privilege does not depend on the persistence of tradition; it is resourced by the power of tradition to be reinscribed through the conditions and contradictoriness that attend upon the lives of those who are 'in the minority.' The recognition that tradition bestows is a partial form of identification. In restaging the past it introduces other, incommensurable cultural temporalities into the invention of tradition.[6]

Thus individual interpretation of cultural tradition insures that the tradition will not overwhelm an individual's identity or become a mask of identification with no internal, substantive resonance. The individual must improvise, using the cultural forms as a starting point, in order to re-establish ruptured cultural and social dynamics and identifiers.

In specific terms, the final image of *The Black Pig's Dyke* suggests a type of ritual healing of communal bonds. Elizabeth, whose character creates a narrative of the Strange Knight at the beginning of each act and just before the final curtain, details a three-part process by which the land can be renewed after violence. The process involves a series of movements from harmony to strife. The first part includes the recognition that the land exists in a state of chaos as a consequence of violent disruption:

> The Strange Knight remained in his castle. He watched from the ramparts and no one came. The land around him grew rancid from the decay of bodies in the ground.[7]

The Knight realises that his kingdom is 'rancid' and that he is alone. His acts of violence that created the decaying bodies distance himself of communal involvement. Significantly, he initially seeks others from his 'ramparts', from the defences of his castle. He comes to terms with the world inside his protective cocoon of violent conquest. Subsequently, in the second part of the process, the Knight attempts to bring harmony back to the land.

> He ordered a banquet but there was no food; a ball but there were no musicians; a duel but there was no one to fight. He posted orders that a beautiful woman be brought to him to sire an heir; all night he lay alone, naked, in his bed. And the Strange Knight grew lonely and came to be filled with sorrow.[8]

The Knight requests four forms of ritual healing. Each begins with a ceremonial attempt to restore harmony to the land but ends with a further recognition of chaos. The first form, a banquet, includes components not only of a communal gathering but a type of spiritual communion as well, a ceremony in which food is digested to restore an equilibrium and vitality to the land. However, at this point within the Knight's tale, there is no sacred communion. The second type of healing involves a courtship ceremony. Through dance and ritualised movement, a type of mating ritual occurs on a large scale. However, in the Knight's tale, the music, a necessary component of the ritual, is unattainable. Next, the Knight orders a duel, a ceremonial form of sacrifice. However, once again, the Knight's desires are thwarted because there is no one to sacrifice. Ultimately, the Knight seeks to restore vitality to the land through a ritualised sexual encounter. An heir would serve as a metaphor for the vitality of the kingdom. However, once again, circumstance frustrates the Knight's plans. No one comes to consummate his ceremonial act of replenishment. Despite the Knight's recognition of the emptiness of his landscape and his efforts to restore vitality through a series of rituals, each attempt to replenish his kingdom finds frustration, representing an attempt to bring harmony to chaos but culminating in simply a recognition of further chaos.

Ultimately, in a process reminiscent of ancient sacred rituals, the Knight emerges from his castle.

> He walked back along the road he had travelled till he came to the place where he'd met the woman with the riddle. He fell to the ground and begged to be forgiven. His tears fell like rain on the soil and the water soaked down, down into the heart of the dead woman, and out of her heart grew a flower—a blood-red poppy. And the Strange Knight plucked it and when he did it fell asunder. (*Elizabeth lets the poppy petals in her hand drift to the ground.*) Petal after petal drifted to the

> ground and out of each sprang a dozen women with hooks and seeds and implements to sow and harvest. They yoked the Strange Knight to the ground and so began the endless task of restoring the land to life and the beginning of happiness. *(Elizabeth scatters the final petals of the poppy and stands still as the lights fade, very slowly, into darkness.)*[9]

In ancient ceremonies the ritual elements include 'the centre of the campsite, which will become the hearth, the ceremonial meeting place, the threshing floor, and finally the agora, [...] the dancing ground'.[10] On the land where he committed his first crime, the Knight's tears and blood create the ritual components. On this land, a ceremonial dance occurs through which a harvest of sacrificial death emerges. His recognition of his isolation creates an empty centre onto which his tears can flow. Likewise, in ancient rites, the dancers 'leave the centre empty, like the evening sky, and into this potent emptiness' the 'dancing is directed, unself-conscious, mirrorless, questioning. The circle is charmed because it encloses emptiness. The emptiness is charged not only because' it was 'constructed by joining hands and gazing inward, but also because it is what our dancing bodies address' (Young 98). Within the Knight's story, the 'women with hooks' engage in a dance addressing the Knight's empty space to restore potency to the ravaged land. The Knight's ritualised empty centre becomes a threshing floor which produces seeds to replenish the land and sacred food, the Knight's body. Moreover, as the ritual components come together in the Knight's final acts, they express, on an individual level, the formulaic ceremonial cures he attempted earlier. The ceremonial dance finds expression in the women's movements. The Knight becomes the sacred communion, the ceremonial sacrifice. Initially, his tears and later his blood inseminate the earth producing a harvest that will renew the land. Ultimately, the Knight's individual interpretation enables the healing ritual to proceed. Indeed, in ancient ceremonies of healing, the participants in the rite 'find that the secret of song and dance composition is the emergence of solo work from the ensemble'.[11] Again, in the ancient rituals, individuals must offer their own creative interpretation, their own variation of received ceremony and ritual in order for the rite to prove successful. Indeed, the Knight becomes not simply the organiser or a participant in the rite of healing. Rather, he becomes a component in the ritual. Consequently, within the Knight's tale, ancient ceremonies, music and ritualised dance become not simply masks behind which the rupture of traumatic experience can lie but components through which the land can be restored. Woods's play provides the ceremonial elements of confrontation of violence, the recognition of traumatic disruption and emptiness, and the allegorical healing of the land. His character of the Knight, then, finds not a sense of futility in death and destruction but a sense of purpose within ritual.

Earlier components of the Knight's story detail recognition of rupture and nuances of sectarian history particular to the North of Ireland, offering a vision of sectarian conflict which recognises the animosity and violent rivalry between the two sides but also recognises the role the English play in accentuating the rivalry. From the outset of Woods's play, it is apparent that the Knight stands for the British:

> The Strange Knight went on till he arrived at a fair where two men were havin' a dispute over a piece of land. He said he could settle it and offered a fine price to whichever of them would sell it to them. One man said he'd sell it that minute, the other said he wouldn't sell it for love or money. So the Strange Knight said to the second man: you're the owner, it's your land. [...] Then he shot the two of them and had the land for himself.[12]

Exploiting the tensions between the two parties, the Knight imposes a settlement on them, using his vision of justice to arbitrate the dispute. Ultimately, however, the Knight exploits the weakened condition of both sides to take the land for himself. Like the British in the North, whose troops imposed on both Protestant and Catholic communities decisions from a remote parliament, the Knight's arbitrary use of power uses the rivalries between two factions to benefit himself. At this point in the Knight's story, there is no offer of reconciliation between factions. However, that the sectarian history of the North would find allegorical representation in the image of two parties exploited by an interloper suggests a common history for warring factions. Furthermore, it is in this imagining of a common past, that reconciliation may come to fruition. Indeed, as Kiberd argues:

> '*Imagine* is the operational word for the liberationist who, far more than the nationalist, needs the sanction of previous authority if history is to be blown open. That sanction comes from history not as a chronological narrative but as symbolic pattern, in which certain utopian moments are extracted from its flow.'[13]

Liberation from sectarian divisions finds expression in the 'imagined' symbols of pluralism. In the Knight's tale, the created story of a common enemy simultaneous with the recognition of sectarian conflict creates a utopian moment which can be extracted from the violent past in order to offer the possibility for reconciliation or at least the imaginings of a common heritage. The Knight's tale offers—to borrow a phrase from Seamus Deane—a counter to a Romanticised, sectarian history and 'seeks to escape from it into a pluralism of the present'.[14] The plural dream, as articulated by the Knight's tale, does not dismiss the sources and heritage of violence but rather explores the violence in which third parties have exploited the divisions in the North to the disadvantage of both Protestant and Catholic communities. Within the common history of exploitation, the possibility for negotiations towards a pluralistic and non-sectarian identity can begin.

In a further allegorical representation of sectarian history, the Knight's tale details elements of common struggle against a king, recalling the co-operation between Protestants and Catholics in rebellions such as the 1798 rising.

> The Strange Knight walked on again till he came to a castle. There was a rook perched on the rampart with blood on its beak. The Knight asked whose blood was it and the rook said: 'It's the king's blood. The people have killed the King and his body is in pieces in the courtyard inside.' So the Knight thanked the rook and went inside to the people. He told them they had done a wonderful thing and he wanted to be their leader. So they elected him their leader and that night held a great banquet where he set one half of them against the other; and they fought till there was no one left alive but the Strange Knight. [...] And he was happy then: to have evaded answering the riddle, to have the piece of land for himself and to have the castle without King or people to bother him.[15]

Once again, the allegory of the Knight details how a third-party exploits the divisions within a community. However, within this portion of the tale, the Knight does more to create sectarian conflict than in his earlier sectarian allegory. Here, he literally disunifies the rebellious populace so he might better control them. English colonial history in Ireland is full of such reports of British interference in Irish affairs with the intention of disrupting inter-community relations in order to more easily govern the island. Once again, in the recognition of a common history of exploitation, the allegory offers the possibility of a unified, pluralistic society in the North, Indeed, the plural vision 'need not always take the high road: where there are borders to be crossed, unapproved roads might prove more beneficial in the long run than those patrolled by global powers' (Gibbons 180). As Luke Gibbons argues, the 'unapproved' roads of allegory and narrative, of symbolic imagination, without the interference of outside powers might prove beneficial in short-circuiting the colonial divide. Within the

Green Fire into the Frozen Branch 105

recognition of the British role, in creating and accentuating colonial divisions, lies the seeds of a potential pluralistic vision for the North, uniting Protestant and Catholic parties in opposition to outside forces. The Knight's tale also recognises the created colonial divisions between the Republic and the North. It begins with the confrontation between the riddle woman and the Knight.

> At that time there was a Strange Knight on the road. He met a woman with a riddle. How many people were in the world before the world was made? How many graves did it take to bury them? What way were they laid?—Facin' north, south, east or west? And did they rest or not from then till now? He said he'd answer any riddle in three parts but not in four. As she rose her hook to kill him—but if she did he shot her first—through the heart with a golden bullet.[16]

Within the four parts of the riddle lie the symbols of the four provinces of Ireland. The geographic divisions stand for the Northern province of Ulster, the Southern province of Munster, the Eastern province of Leinster, and the Western province of Connaught. Further, within the riddle woman's questions, reference is made to ancient traditions in Ireland, that recognise not only previous civilisations but alternative traditions to contemporary English customs. The allusion to the direction of the bodies recalls the ancient manner of burying the dead standing up and ready for battle. However, the Knight refuses to answer her questions because they are in four parts and he will only answer a riddle in three, recalling the partition of the four provinces. Essentially, the Knight creates a division in the riddle woman's questions where no division existed. The allegorical tale of the riddle woman's death functions in two ways. As Richard Kearney has written, '[b]y creatively reinterpreting the past, narrative can serve to release new and hitherto concealed possibilities of understanding one's history; and by critically scrutinising the past it can wrest tradition away from the conformism that is always threatening to overpower it'.[17] By creatively recognising that there are four parts to one riddle, the allegorical tale recognises that there are four parts to one Ireland. In addition, the tale releases the understanding that the Knight, an outsider, divides the riddle into separate parts not just separate components and destroys the unifying principle behind the parts, the riddle woman. The Knight's tale then, in Kearney's words, wrests tradition from the conformism of a divided history. The tale recognises the ruptures created by sectarian and colonial history and attempts to reconcile them within its allegorical components.

A similar allegorical process occurs in Seamus Heaney's *The Cure at Troy* where a poetic expression recognises and metaphorically heals components of cultural and social identity ruptured by violence. However, Heaney's play emphasises not so much the factors that directly contribute to the destruction of identity but rather the masks of identity that certain characters adopt in order to come to terms with violence. The chorus in Heaney's play acknowledges the transitory and limited nature of masks of identity and posits an alternative that directly confronts all the implications of violence, attempting to incorporate them into a new identity capable of re-integrating traumatic elements into individual identity. Heaney's chorus creates a type of hermeneutic identity in a sense consonant with Paul Ricoeur's account of it.

> Hermeneutics is concerned with the permanent spirit of language [...] not as some decorative excess or effusion of subjectivity, but as the creative capacity of language to open up new worlds. Poetic and mythic symbols (for example) do not just express nostalgia for some forgotten world. They constitute a disclosure of unprecedented worlds, an opening onto other possible meanings which transcend the established limits of our actual world.[18]

In *The Cure at Troy*, Heaney's choric poetry discloses new possibilities for the re-establishment of secure social contacts outside the masks of ideological representation. The actual world of the North then is transformed from one in which the archetypes of history dominate individual consciousness, because of their seemingly invulnerable facades, to a world of possible reconciliation within the allegorical representation of unprecedented worlds of common memory and heritage within not just common exploitation but also common suffering.

Just as the process of the Knight's tale's rejuvenation of the land begins in the recognition of the damage to the landscape, Heaney's chorus begins the process of coming to terms with masks of violent identity by recognising the nature of masks. The chorus observes

> Gods and human beings
> All throwing shapes, every one of them
> Convinced he's in the right, all of them glad
> To repeat themselves and their every last mistake,
> No matter what.[19]

For the gods and men who 'throw shapes' their 'whole life [is] spent admiring themselves/For their own long-suffering'.[20] Essentially, 'they're fixated,/Shining with self-regard like polished stones'.[21] For the gods and men, the adoption of masks of identity, of 'shapes' of identity, enables them to create an image of themselves that is like a 'polished stone', an image that removes all stain of blame from their consciousness and makes their vulnerable identities impenetrable behind the stone mask. Essentially, rather than come to terms with suffering, each comes to terms with an image of a long-suffering character, created in response to traumatic threat but unable to adequately shield the individual from violence because the polished mask prevents the individual from coming to terms with anyone beyond himself.

However, just as in the Knight's tale, a curative is offered in allegorical representation. The chorus recognises that it was '[p]oetry' that '[a]llowed the gods to speak. It was the voice/Of reality and justice'.[22] Poetry offers a 'real' alternative to the imagined identities rooted in 'long-suffering' and solipsism. Poetry offers the possibility for communication, for communal interaction; it '[a]llowed the gods to speak.' Just as the Knight recognises the necessary elements for rejuvenation but is at first incapable of realising their individual potential, the chorus in *The Cure at Troy* recognises ritual elements and procedures, advising the spectators to

> hope for a great sea-change
> On the far side of revenge.

And to:
> Believe that a further shore
> Is reachable from here.[23]

Within the chorus's speech, just as in the Knight's survey of the landscape, there exists a recognition of the devastation of the land. However, in Heaney's play, the chorus goes beyond a simple recognition of chaos and penetrates into the causes for chaotic violence. The chorus challenges the individual to reach beyond 'revenge' for 'self-healing' that is the product of a 'self-revealing' acknowledgement of emotions. Therefore, within the traditional symbols of 'healing wells' and 'fire on the mountain', the chorus indicates there is communication—'someone is hearing'. Within the revelation that self exists independent of the masks of identity, a curative of social discourse offers itself, a discourse that proves regenerative, a discourse of 'new life' that recalls Gerald Dawe's "Solstice".

The product of this recognition supplies a poetic counterpart to the Knight's individual interpretation of the ceremonial elements. The chorus explicitly refers to the masks of violence and martyrdom in the

North and penetrates into the common bond between communities' mutual suffering. Essentially, the masks of violent identity fall away to reveal genuine human emotion rather than avoidance and a sense of community rather than solipsism. The chorus observes that 'Human beings suffer,/They torture one another,/[...] get hurt and get hard.' He talks about the sufferings of the hunger striker's father and the policeman's widow, and then comes to the justly celebrated lines:

> History says, *Don't hope*
> *On this side of the grave.*
> But then, once in a lifetime
> The longed-for tidal wave
> Of justice can rise up,
> And hope and history rhyme.[24]

The chorus recognises the masks consequent of traumatic disruption. Individuals 'get hurt and get hard'. They fail to recognise their individual identity behind their hard masks of 'polished stone'. Moreover, nothing, not even poetry can 'fully' compensate for suffering and violence. However, within the 'rhyme' of 'hope and history', within the poetic expression of historical suffering and the possibilities for reconciliation, the chorus can 'leave/Half-ready to believe/That a crippled trust might walk/And the half-true rhyme is love'.[25] The promise for the 'crippled trust' lies in the mutual suffering behind the masks of traumatic disruption. Both the family of the hunger striker and the dead policemen, martyrs from both communities, suffer. Their suffering, and its recognition and expression of commonality with violence through poetry equips the society, so the chorus suggests, to form a communal bond beyond pain and in 'love'. The 'half-true rhyme' then is that both communities are united, despite the masks of violence that separate them, by a common history. If the violent and disruptive particulars can be acknowledged but then set aside, the remaining half truth of common suffering can supplant the divisive masks of identity that prevent communal interaction. Essentially, commonality through suffering is only half of the truth. The whole truth is a history of division. Just as the Knight's tale allegorically recognises the rivalries of sectarian history and the divisions of colonial intervention, the chorus acknowledges the masks and histories of both communities. Similarly, just as the Knight's tale forms a bond in mutual victimisation, the chorus forms a bond between the sides through a mutual recognition for the consequences of history in the suffering of both communities, uniting them into one community and metaphorically healing the cultural and social divisions consequent of traumatic disruption and skewed adaptation to violence.

Accumulation of Restorative Experiences

At the Black Pig's Dyke and *The Cure at Troy* also detail a process by which individuals regain control and mastery of their environment by recalling and incorporating into their consciousness the ruptured memories that cause trauma. The characters confront traumatic experiences and convert them from factors that destroy identity into conditions that inform a reconstituted identity. Within this process, mythic and personal memories combine to counteract the traumatic rupture. In clinical terms,

> because the reliving and warding off of traumatic memories are the central psychological preoccupation of traumatised people, there is little room for new, gratifying experiences that might allow for reparation of past injuries to the self. Patients need to expose themselves actively to experiences that provide them with feelings of mastery and pleasure.[26]

The reconstituted identities of Woods's and Heaney's plays base themselves in a framework similar to the clinical matrix. Essentially, characters achieve a sense of mastery and pleasure when they abandon the traumatic structures in favour of a personally reconstituted identity that incorporates the violence into their consciousness within a matrix that gives individuals a sense of control over the violence. Carl Jung defined such a process as

> the *objectification of impersonal images*. It is an essential part of the process of individualisation. Its goal is to detach consciousness from the object so that the individual no longer places the guarantee of his happiness, or of his life even, in factors outside himself, whether they be persons, ideas, or circumstances, but comes to realise that everything depends on whether he holds the treasure or not. If the possession of that gold is realised, then the centre of gravity is *in* the individual and no longer in an object on which he depends.[27]

The subjects of Jung's analysis and the characters in *At the Black Pig's Dyke* and *The Cure at Troy*, must wrest control from 'circumstances of life', such as traumatic violence in order to achieve a sense of contentment. Essentially those characters are faced with the necessity of finding an individual method

> by which the impersonal images are given shape. For they have to take on form, they have to live their characteristic life, otherwise the

> individual is severed from the basic function of the psyche, and then he is neurotic, he is disoriented and in conflict with himself. But if he is able to objectify the impersonal images and relate to them, he is in touch with that vital psychological function which from the dawn of consciousness has been taken care of by religion.[28]

In order to repair the 'individual psyche' that has been 'severed' by traumatic rupture, the characters must 'find an individual method' through which they can incorporate traumatic structures into their consciousness and gain control over them.

One such method occurs in *At the Black Pig's Dyke*'s mummers musical and dance sequences, in which they come to terms with sectarian violence and, as a consequence, accumulate restorative emotional experiences that confront trauma, integrate it into their personalities through music and dance, but do not avoid it or attempt to fashion an escape from it. Initially, however, Captain Mummer appeals to music as a diversion from violence, saying that '[p]igs squeal in Ulster, echoed all 'round/Strike up the music to block out the sound'.[29] Indeed, the most immediate musical sequence could be read as an escape. However, shortly thereafter, the mummers' performance imaginatively re-creates Sarah and Lizzie's death.

> Captain Mummer picks up the lantern and holds it aloft with one hand; with the other hand he raps his stick on the ground, moving/swaying as if he were trying to shoulder open a door. The circle of mummers moves/sways to the same rhythm and on the fifth rap the straw wall bursts open and falls, the mummers scatter and the bodies of Lizzie Boles and Sarah fall to the ground with a scattering of red confetti.[30]

Within the play, the mummers create a space through which Lizzie and Sarah will eventually tell the story of their own lives and the factors surrounding their deaths. Rituals recreating the moment of the women's deaths, through the repetition of movement and sound, allows for a sense of control over the violent event and simultaneously allows for an emotional coming to terms with the act. Symbolically, the Captain illuminates the scene; he sheds light on the deaths of the women by 'pick[ing] up the lantern and hold[ing] it aloft'. He confronts the stark reality of violence in his effort to 'shoulder open a door'. At the same time, he initiates a ritualistic recreation of the violence with his other hand. As he moves and sways, the 'circle of mummers moves/sways to the same rhythm'. Subsequently, the red confetti recreates the moment of death and casts the mummers as the cause of the women's death; the mummers let loose the blood. By taking the role of the assassins, Captain Mummer and his troupe take the sin of murder upon themselves, coming face to face not only with a horrific moment of sectarian violence but also ritually beginning a process through which they can purge themselves and their society of the most serious repercussions of the traumatic event by integrating it into their personalities. Subsequently, through music, the mummers ritualistically resurrect Lizzie and Sarah. Captain Mummer tells his men to '[p]lay the tune-play the tune that was her favourite. And make a good job of it for the last time'.[31] The troupe responds by playing the first verse of the Enniskillen Dragoons. While they are playing the second verse they are

> interrupted by the return of Tom Fool (minus mask) who rushes in stage left beating a badhran. [...] The musician plays another verse of the Enniskillen Dragoons. Tom Fool then begins a slow single-note beat on the badhran. The mummers pick up the straw wall, Lizzie Boles and Sarah rise up and stand still for a few beats, looking out at the audience. They exit through the small door as the mummers move upstage, hang the straw wall in two sections on the side-walls and stand facing the audience, backs to the walls. Tom Fool and Miss Funny stand stage left and when all the others are in place they march downstage-centre to the badhran beat.[32]

The drum beat, with its ceremonial repetition and the 'favourite' song repeated one 'last time' conjure Sarah and Lizzie from the dead. When they rise, they stare directly into the audience, summoning the audience into the ritual as witnesses to the circumstances and hatred surrounding the murders. The ceremonial elements of the ritual, even though they recall the traumatic event in clear and unambiguous terms, provide the basis for emotional recuperation. Indeed, the

> paradox of the restoration of behaviour resides in the phenomenon of repetition itself: no action or sequence of actions may be performed exactly the same way twice; they must be reinvented or recreated at each appearance. In this improvisatory behavioural space, memory reveals itself as imagination.[33]

Like the Knight's tale and the choric elements of Heaney's play, it is not simply in the recognition of the traumatic event but in the imaginative coming to terms with the event that recuperation occurs. Moreover, by pulling the audience into the play, Woods makes the spectators participate in the ritual. He imaginatively engages with them so that they become not simply observers but a part of the performance. By breaking down the 'fourth wall', he refuses to allow them to be passive but demands imaginative engagement and involvement. In this sense, the mummers and the audience become part of the ritual restoration and coming to terms with traumatic violence. The house has a stake in the production.

Throughout the play, Vincent Woods stages moments of restorative rites. However, not all of them engage the audience in terms of tragedy and suffering. In one scene, Woods uses humour to recognise and then resolve sectarian divisions.

> CAPTAIN MUMMER: The straw wren—it's a long time since I saw one of them. Do you know the story of the wren? *(Sarah shakes her head.)* Well, the way I heard it, it was the wren betrayed Saint Stephen and him hidin' on the Roman soldiers in a field of corn. The bird flew up and gave away his hiding place and ever after he was hunted and killed for a traitor. *(Some of the mummers have been nodding their heads in agreement; others shaking their heads in obvious disagreement. Of the latter Tom Fool and Miss Funny are the most vehement.)* That's my version of it—though I know some of ye heard different.
> TOM FOOL AND MISS FUNNY: No, no, no, The way we heard it was [...]
> TOM FOOL: it was the wren that betrayed a regiment of Billy's men at the Battle of the Boyne [...]
> MISS FUNNY: They were creepin' up on a gantry of others that was asleep [...]
> TOM FOOL: And didn't the wren fly up and waken them [...]
> MISS FUNNY: They routed Billy's men and killed every last one of them [...]
> TOM FOOL: That's why the Orange men kill the wren the same as everybody else. [...]
> CAPTAIN MUMMER: Isn't that a good one? The same wee bird in a field of corn in the East and in a battlefield in this whelp of a country.[34]

The wren, a symbol of ritual sacrifice, becomes a tool for comic resolution. Captain Mummer identifies himself as a Catholic by recalling the tradition of St. Stephen and the wren. His story loosely conceals an allegory of colonial relations. Within the tale, Rome and Britain and the Irish and early Christians parallel one another. The wren stands as the informer. By ritualistically purging the wren from their society, those sympathetic to this version of the story symbolically purge themselves of not only colonial dominance but cultural impurities; the allegory takes on further significance later in the play as Hugh is killed for being an informer. The alternative version of the tale also isolates traitorous or impure components of a society and singles them out in the body of the wren for sacrifice—'the Orange men kill the wren the same as everybody else'. However, rather than resolve the conflict between the two stories through sectarian confrontation, the captain humorously points to the similarities between the stories. Moreover, he takes on the role of the fool, assuming the guise of someone who believes both versions of the stories. The subsequent laughter, from the audience, symbolically kills the captain and resolves the sectarian differences. Essentially, the captain offers himself up as the object of ridicule in order to resolve the tension surrounding both versions of the stories, the alternative stories standing for the alternative traditions of both communities. Within his humorous representation of the verity of both traditions, the captain undermines the earnestness and claims of exclusiveness of both sides, offering a space for reconciliation. Subsequently, the laughter focuses the tension and subtle aggression on the figure of the captain, whom the audience marks as a fool by their inevitable reaction. Once again, Woods engages the audience in the rituals of the play, makes the spectators participants in the ceremonial restoration. The captain's act of insurgent humour finds a resonance with more serious restorative rituals. To quote Bhabha,

> the borderline work of culture demands an encounter with 'newness' that is not part of the continuum of past and present. It creates a sense of the new as an insurgent act of cultural translation. Such art does not merely recall the past as social cause or aesthetic precedent; it renews the past, refiguring it as a contingent 'in-between' space, that innovates and interrupts the performance of the present. The 'past-present' becomes part of the necessity, not the nostalgia, of living.[35]

Thus the captain straddles the borderline between the two traditions, comically legitimising yet subtlety undermining both. His act does not simply recall the past but rather renews the past with laughter focused on him as the figure of the fool who undermines both traditions but also brings them together and brings audience and actors together in the simultaneous act of laughter.

Conversely, in Sarah's and Lizzie's story, the motif of sacrifice and informer takes on more horrific proportions in order to come to terms with a post-traumatic, reconstituted identity. Their narrative does not resolve confrontation through humour. Indeed, their stories do more to recognise the horror of traumatic rupture. Specifically, Lizzie, through her thoughts about her lover Hugh, comes to terms with the violent history of her family and focuses on the masks of violence and how they distort individual identity.

SARAH: (singing)
The Wren, The Wren, The King of all Birds

On Saint Stephen's night was caught in the furze.
LIZZIE: You remember that?
Sarah: I remember it. Daddy singin' it to me. I remember his eyes. (*louder/direct*) Hugh's eyes have changed since Sean was killed. I don't know him any more.[36]

In their exchange, mother and daughter introduce the wren as a symbol of sacrifice and associate that sacrifice with a father who was murdered and a lover whom violence has changed. After the death of Sean, Hugh adopts a mask of the violent Republican volunteer to achieve revenge, to combat a sense of helplessness in the face of death, and to protect himself from emotional vulnerability. The mask distorts Hugh's identity so much that his lover no longer recognises in him the image of her father. Indeed, Sarah, later in the play, explicitly associates Hugh with memories of her father.

I always imagined his eyes were the same as Daddy's. I had it in me head since I was a child that father's eyes were brown. I remember sittin' on his knee and starin' at him—tryin' to make him blink. And Hugh's eyes—though they were different—they were like his. When I told him—it was a Sunday and we'd driven over to Leitrim, up to The Dawn of Hope. He got annoyed first and then he laughed a bit and he told me how his grandfather had one blue eye and one brown. [...] Brolly and Clements. Brown eye and blue. Oh, he told me it all. How his grandfather with the two different coloured eyes was the child of May Brolly and Clements—the man who drowned her brother. Can you imagine what it was like for that woman? Dragged up to the Big House and left pregnant and then promised the lot—that he'd follow her on and marry her if she'd go to America, then nothing and nothing again till she got word he was drowned on the lake and John, her own flesh and blood, drowned with him.[37]

Significantly, Sarah's recollections and further association between Hugh and her dead father, recalls even earlier sectarian violence and death. Sarah goes even further, linking Hugh not only to historical and personal instances of death and sacrifice but also to mythic images of ritualistic violence.

Remember after we met Hugh—and we went on that drive across over The Black Pig's Dyke. We looked out over the lake where your ancestor was drowned by Clements and sat by the old nunnery where we could see out to the Holy Island. Remember the place we went to—with the view out over all the counties—The Dawn of Hope.[38]

In her recollections and associations, Sarah summons subtle and deliberate motifs of sectarian violence and sacrifice. The theme of the wren merges with images of Hugh, whose later death will eerily parallel the wren's. Both merge with an image of her father, slaughtered on his farm, his innocent blood pouring onto the fields, recalling the guilty Strange Knight's death. Those images subsequently find resonance with class and religious distinctions and the violence those differences can bring. Ultimately, the image of Hugh, Sarah's father, and the sectarian strife in Ireland merges with geographical locations. The Black Pig's Dyke, both the ancient boundary of Ulster and the mythic location of the battle marking the end of the world, becomes the ultimate symbol for sectarian violence. However, the images culminate in a more optimistic location—The Dawn of Hope. Sarah comes through her myriad associations, marking violence and sacrificial death, to a symbol of resurrection. Mysteriously, in her acknowledgement of death and the horror of violence, she converts both the negative memory of slaughtered ancestors and the transformation of her lover image from that of father to that of a gunman into the possibility of renewal. Within her reconstituted spiritual recollection of the past, of her lover, and of the mythic geography of her home, Sarah comes to terms with the possibilities for renewal and an end to violence. She, like the audience whose laughter creates an image of a sacrificial fool, converts the deaths and violence of her community and familial history into sacrificial acts that can renew her identity. Essentially, by acknowledging the complete extent of traumatic rupture, Sarah creates a personal mythology, with a resonance of local and familial history and local myth, which can reconstitute her self-conception despite and even as a consequence of violence. In her act, Sarah converts the traumatic event from one of rupture alone into one which can be used to renew identity. As one Mbembe and Roitman have written:

> According to this formulation, we are not interested primarily in the problematics of resistance, emancipation, or autonomy. We distance ourselves from these questions in order to better apprehend, in today's context, the series of operations in and through which people weave their existence in incoherence, uncertainty, instability, and discontinuity; then, in experiencing the reversal of the material conditions of their societies, they recapture the possibility for self-constitution, thus instituting other 'words of truth.' [39]

In just these terms, Sarah comes to terms with the 'incoherence, uncertainty, instability, and discontinuity' of sectarian violence and then reverses the 'material conditions' of traumatic rupture, using myth and personal memory to 'recapture the possibility for self-constitution'. Vincent Woods' multi-layered dramatisation of renewal and reconstitution finds a resonance with Seamus Heaney's translation of *The Cure at Troy* in an Irish context. Heaney's characters too, through a communion with a mythological past, come to terms with the personal traumatic ruptures of their lives, converting a scene of violent rupture into one that offers the possibility for renewal. Within the play, Neoptomemus escapes the mask of traitor and deceiver and is won over to his true self through an emotional bond with Philoctetes and through communion with Hercules. Initially, Neoptomemus was sent to trick Philoctetes into handing over the bow. Neoptomemus says that 'The bow/Is like a god itself. I feel this urge/To touch it./For its virtue/Venerate it'.[40] Heaney uses short lines to signify Neoptomemus' internal struggle. Previously, his certainty was mirrored in the steadiness of his speech, characterised by a pentameter or hexameter, mostly iambic rhythm. However, the rhythm of these lines, although it begins in iambic hexameter quickly changes. Initially, Neoptomemus remains certain of his deception. As he sees the bow, and all that it implies, so freely offered, he becomes uncertain about his mask. His speech deteriorates into a series of excited spondees only to culminate in a more relaxed rhythm with the word 'virtue' and then the word 'venerate'. The abrupt change in metre signifies a change in personality. Neoptomemus drops his mask and offers himself in devotional reverence leaving behind his lust for glory and coming to terms with his true character. Significantly, the bow is a symbol of death and skill. Like the straw wren, it serves as a marker for both sacrifice and renewal. Neoptomemus claims the divine object by accepting the renewal of his personality in his reverence for the instrument of death. He accepts that the instrument itself stands for much more than a useful weapon of war. He realises that its meaning implies a communion with the gods, beyond the transience of human conflict. In his acceptance of the bow, Neoptomemus praises not its destructive potential but rather a whole 'economy of kindness/Possible in the world; befriend a friend/And the chance of it's increased and multiplied'.[41] Essentially, Neoptomemus sacrifices his old self, within his mask of deception, in favour of an emotional bond, through the bow, with his former enemy. The sight of the bow essentially kills his masked self and gives birth to his true self.

Neoptomemus abandons the ruptured personality, adopted in order to gain recognition in war and adopts a more integrated personality. Likewise, Hugh Brolly, from *At the Black Pig's Dyke* drops his mask of revenge and war in favour of a more integrated personality; he allows emotion and pity to purge him of his mask. He begins with the intention to do violence.

> What I've been doin' tonight I've been doin'—since they killed Sean. Delivery work. [...] Tonight was to be a pick-up in the yard like I always did. They promised me it'd be the last run. There was no sign of anyone when I drove in, so I went up to knock on the back door. I could hear them inside talkin'. (Pause) What I was bringin' over tonight—the stuff I was collectin'—it was to be used on Stuart's weddin' on Tuesday. They're bound to have known half the country would be there. [...] I didn't let on a thing, but collected the lot. I drove the back road like they said, but I stopped, south of the Dyke and I dumped the lot in the lough there—into the deepest spot at the Long Point. I stopped again, over this side—at the loneliest phone box I could find—and I rang the police. If anyone lifts a finger at that weddin' they're behind bars or dead.[42]

Like Neoptomemus, Hugh rejects his mask of violence and embraces emotional engagement with his former enemy. He abandons the instruments of war in the mythic symbol of the battle of the end of the world. He rejects the symbols of violence in favour of life. In doing so, he realises that he marks himself for death. However, within his sacrifice, he embraces emotional interaction with a larger community, offering the possibility for at least a limited halt to sectarian violence. Both Hugh and Neoptomemus, within their masks of warriors were 'confined within too narrow a spiritual horizon'—as Jung put it, before going on to say of people in such a predicament: 'Their life has not sufficient content, sufficient meaning. If they are enabled to develop into more spacious personalities, the neurosis generally disappears.'[43] Accordingly each adopts a more spacious personality that embraces emotional involvement and rejects their masks.

Vincent Woods's *At the Black Pig's Dyke* and Seamus Heaney's *The Cure at Troy* function as forums to expose the masks of those powers that have control of the lives of their characters. Specifically, through the accumulation of restorative experiences and through the establishment of secure social contacts, characters wrest control of their lives from the forces and powers of the Troubles that disrupt identity and personal, historical, and spiritual ties. Like the speaker in Gerald Dawe's "Solstice", many of the characters in Heaney's and Woods's plays draw from a mythological heritage to express a personal hope for communal renewal. Moreover, like the speaker of Robert Greacen's poem, "A Wish for St. Patrick's Day", who calls on 'Holy Patrick [...] [to] Exorcise the demons of intransigence,/[and to] Send your green fire into the frozen branch',[44] the characters from the plays summon the gods of their classical heritage to transform an environment and individuals ruptured by violence and the threatened trauma.

NOTES
1. Gerald Dawe, in *The Lundys Letters* (Loughcrew, Oldcastle: Gallery Press 1985). "Solstice", ll.1-3. Ensuing line-numbers refer to this poem.
2. See Van der Kolk, Alexander McFarlane, and Onno Van der Hart, 'A General Approach to the treatment of Post-traumatic Stress Disorder', in Bessel Van der Kolk, et. al., eds., *Traumatic Stress: The Effects of Overwhelming Experience on Mind, Body, and Society* (London: Guilford Press 1996), pp.417-40; p.432.
3. ibid., p.432.
4. *Symbols of Transformation*, trans. by R. F. C. Hull (Princeton UP 1990), pp.4-5.
5. Van der Kolk, op. cit. (1996), pp.432-33.
6. *The Location of Culture* (NY: Routledge 1994), p.2.
7. Vincent Woods, *At the Black Pig's Dyke* [unpublished typescript], p.80.
8. idem.
9. idem.
10. Dudley Young, *Origins of the Sacred* (NY: St. Martin's Press 1991), p.97.
11. idem.
12. Woods, op. cit., p.2.
13. *Inventing Ireland* (London: Jonathan Cape 1996), p.293.
14. 'Heroic Styles: The Tradition of an Idea.' *Ireland's Field Day*, ed., Roger McHugh. (Derry: Field Day Theatre Co. 1985): pp.45-59; p.45.
15. *At the Black Pig's Dyke* [typescript], p.44.
16. ibid., p.2.
17. Richard Kearney, *Poetics of Modernity* (Atlantic Highlands: Humanities Press 1995), p.40.
18. Paul Ricoeur, 'The Symbol as Bearer of Possible Worlds', in Mark Hederman (OSB), et al., eds., *The Crane Bag of Irish Studies* (1982), p.17.
19. *The Cure at Troy* (London: Faber & Faber 1990), p.1.
20. ibid.
21. ibid.
22. ibid.
23. ibid., p.77.
24. ibid., p.78.
25. ibid., p.81.
26. Van der Kolk, op. cit., p.433.
27. Carl Jung, *Analytical Psychology Analytical Psychology* (NY: Vintage Books 1968), p.186.
28. ibid., p.187.
29. *At the Black Pig's Dyke* [typescript], p.10.
30. ibid., p.15.
31. ibid., p.17.
32. idem.
33. Homi Bhabha, 'Culture and Performance in the Circum-Atlantic World', in *Performitivity and Performance*, ed. by Andrew Parker and Eve Kosofsky Sedgewick. (NY: Routledge 1995), p.46.
34. Woods, op. cit., pp.58-59.
35. Bhabha, op. cit. (1995), p.7.
36. *At the Black Pig's Dyke* [typescript], p.51.

37 ibid., pp.66-67.
38 ibid., p.75.
39 Achille Mbembe and Janet Roitman, 'Figures of the Subject in Times of Crisis', in *The Geography of Identity*, ed. Patricia Yaeger (Michigan UP 1996.), pp.153-86, p.153
40 Heaney, op. cit., p.36.
41 ibid., pp.36-37.
42 *At the Black Pig's Dyke* [typescript], pp.73-74.
43 Jung, *Memories, Dreams, Reflections* (NY: Vintage Books 1972), p.140.
44 "A Wish for St. Patrick's Day", *Collected Poems of Robert Greacen, 1944-1994* (Belfast: Lagan Press 1995); ll.1, 3-4.

'THAT OTHER WORLD': THE MYTHIC AND THE FANTASTIC IN CONTEMPORARY IRISH DRAMA

Csilla Bertha

It is not the fantastic that needs the theatre but the theatre that needs the fantastic—to paraphrase T. S. Eliot's statement about Christianity and drama. Contemporary theatre, especially the postmodern theatre seems to rediscover the fantastic and its ability to reflect deeper truths than mimesis and realistic presentation can. The fantastic which 'seems now to be an aesthetic mode extremely compatible to postmodernism's various interpretations of the "real"' features in the theatre 'not in opposition to reality [but as its] new *mise-en-scène*'.[1]

In this respect, postmodern theatre appears poised to catch up with Irish drama: the postmodern mind consciously forms attitudes and views that are immanent in Irish thinking. What has been a *re*discovery of long lost views or a nostalgic *re*viving of the world of folk and fairy tales in the fantastic literature of the Western world since about the 1960s, is an organic continuation of tradition in Irish literature. What occurred as a result of questioning realism's power, a mistrust of its validity, a reaction to its dominance in other Western cultures, is for the Irish a preservation of their all-embracing vision of reality which naturally incorporates both the visible and the invisible world.

'That other world'—'The undiscovered country from whose bourn/No traveller returns'—is not so sharply separated from 'this' empirical world in the Irish imagination as in other Western European cultures. Moreover, 'travellers' keep returning from there, ghosts reliving moments of their earthly existence or participating in the lives of the living. Nor are these ghosts fearful, frightening, or 'unnatural' as, for example, those in Dickens's *A Christmas Carol*, neither do the characters show much astonishment when encountering them. As Mary in Stewart Parker's *Northern Star* remarks: 'we're well used to the walking dead, we have more spooks than living bodies round these parts.'² The poet Nuala Ní Dhomhnaill observes that even today the Other World is 'no big deal' for the Irish, whereas 'James Hillman and these post-Jungian psychologists [...] talk about the "other world" as if they had just discovered it [...] like Columbus felt when he discovered America. But that doesn't mean that America wasn't there before, and there weren't aboriginal Americans living here—quite happily'.³ Her point can be confirmed by the sobering reply of a West-of-Ireland Irish woman to the inquiry of an American anthropologist if she believed in the fairies: 'I do not, sir—but they're there, anyway.'⁴

Today's advocates of the fantastic in world literature still find it necessary to argue with the 'popular understanding' in which '"fantasy" is always opposed to "reality" [...], fantasy is the *negative* of reality',⁵ and have to assert that fantasy is *not* a 'parasite' on reality.⁶ The Irish, on the other hand, have always naturally incorporated the fantastic in their literature probably just because it has *not* been felt as fantastic but a part of their reality. Eighteenth-century enlightenment, the exclusive dominance of reason and rational thinking did not influence Irish thinking as extensively and as deeply as it did other Western European cultures. Instead, in that century Ireland saw George Berkeley's subjectivist immaterialist philosophy, Swift's fantasy of *Gulliver's Travels* and what is often regarded as the first 'postmodern' novel, Laurence Sterne's *Tristram Shandy*.⁷ As opposed to the 'either/or' exclusive binaries that in other Western cultures postmodernism tries to discard as 'poor reflections of the complex world',⁸ the Irish mind always preferred a more inclusive and tolerant 'both/and' attitude to the world.⁹ Weldon Thornton can rightly assert that as late as the beginning of the twentieth century Irish writers such as Yeats, "A.E.", Lady Gregory, or O'Casey were aware of the Descartesian split between matter and spirit, but they were less severely affected by it than modern writers generally, partly because of the presence in their cultural *milieu* of certain pre-scientific or archaic attitudes.¹⁰

The fantastic mode of representation—indeed a mode, an 'aesthetic category' rather than a genre,¹¹ 'a perceptual orientation rather than a structural one; a way of getting at significant cultural and psychological issues [...] unamenable to realistic methods of writing and representation',¹² has received much less critical attention in drama than in other genres. And yet it has always been present in drama from its beginnings, and it can effectively help to bring to the stage, in a visible and tangible manner, very real but invisible, hidden or inarticulate feelings, events, dramatic tensions; present 'inner landscape[s], one might almost say [...] spiritual landscape[s], which may well have psychological and mythological depths',[13] the working imagination, dreams, unconscious and subconscious processes or spiritual dilemmas; it can also subvert well-accepted meanings, or can be 'an appropriate form of expressing social estrangement'.[14] That is why, after the dominance of the mimetic mode in the nineteenth century, European modern and *avant-garde* playwrights began to experiment with non-realistic, non-mimetic modes of dramatic presentation, aiming at the expression of deeper, inner realities, cosmic rules, or the eternal validity of psychological archetypes. 'The various experimental forms used in the theatre since the 1890s, symbolism, expressionism, surrealism, and so on, may all be regarded as various attempts to bring fantasy into an active relationship with realism.'[15] Looking at realism from the angle of the fantastic, 'the relation of realism and the realistic to reality itself' will be questioned. In Patrick Murphy's analysis,

> [a]ll realist constructs must necessarily be reductionist, closing down alternatives and possibilities in order to present a certain arrangement of events in a 'plausible' series of relationships. As a result, an ontological argument might contend that fantastic texts concern themselves with the inadequacy of the referential dimension of language and with the failure of mimesis to capture the depth of reality rather than merely mirroring its surface appearances.[16]

Epistemologically, the fantastic is usually regarded as a mode that enables the writer to perceive and present 'the impossible'.[17] This approach always raises the question of what is impossible, and hence, what is possible, where, when and in whose view. It is common knowledge that our perception of what is real and what is unreal, what is possible and what is impossible, changes with the times as well as with the cultures. '[F]antasy and our conception of what is fantastic depend upon our view of reality: what we find improbable and unexpected follows from what we find probable and likely, and the fantastic will therefore necessarily vary with the individual and the age.'[18] As noted earlier, Irish culture has preserved a more inclusive view of reality than other Western Europeans—in Berkeley's words: 'We Irish think otherwise'[19]. The giants, descendants of gods and goddesses or ghosts, who are *both* impossible—to the modern consciousness—*and* possible since familiar from tales and living story-telling, dwelling in the imagination still, can find their way more

The Mythic and the Fantastic in Contemporary Irish Drama 123

naturally into contemporary literature and drama, perhaps transformed or domesticated, than in other cultures. They, in fact, *extend* reality only if we confine reality to the visible world, but if we agree that reality includes all the dreams and memories, and phenomena we cannot explain, then they bring to the surface layers of reality otherwise hidden. Hence the Irish fantastic, with a few exceptions, would not fall into the category of pure fantasy but rather into a mode of heightened realism, including what in other cultures would belong to the realms of the impossible.

The Irish fantastic, consequently, remains closer to the ancient mythic view than modern fantasy, the creation of the individual mind. It is true in general that 'The space left empty by the withdrawal of myth [...] has been filled with stories, and the stories which have so far been closest to myths are fantastic stories'.[20] But for the Irish, the mythic did not withdraw as early and as finally as with other peoples and, what is more, it did not leave a gap. Rather, it transformed itself into folktales, stories of folk imagination, which—as is the nature of folklore—lend themselves to be altered, modified, continued by individual imagination into imaginative stories. The borderline between the mythic and the fantastic thus is often blurred.

Myths themselves are not fantastic inasmuch as they symbolically and/or metaphorically reflect reality. The all-inclusive mythic view holds the four-dimensional universe, the empirical and the transcendental worlds, together in a unity, in a natural interrelation with each other. In fantasy, on the other hand, 'the supernatural will remain perforce on a different plane, with both the reader's belief and disbelief sustained at the same time'.[21] Mythic figures and events were believed to be real because they arose out of the collective experience of a community hence myth, while being universal, is also closely related to the life of a community where it has the function of uniting its members. Fantastic beings, on the other hand, are mostly products of an individual imagination. Mythic time is timeless, cyclical instead of linear or circular (as often in fantasy), annihilates natural time, and, similarly to what Mircea Eliade calls 'sacred' or 'holy' time, dissolves past and future in a continuous, eternal present, which can be experienced again and again through rites.[22] The synthesising power of myth thus unites not only the natural and the supernatural, but also past, present, and future.

While both myth and fantasy present the quest for wholeness and completion, in myth the quest is based on a commonly shared belief in certitudes about human beings and the universe, in fantasy it is an individual endeavour to realise dreams and desires or to escape from the existing, frustratingly incomplete world.[23] These and other differences are both manifestations and consequences of the contrasting overall attitudes behind myth and fantasy: the certainty and security of an order, of clear proportions, relationships, and values behind myth as opposed to the elusiveness and unknowability of truth in the modern world behind fantasy.

It is not surprising, therefore, that today no purely mythic works can emerge. Contemporary Irish drama does not directly deploy mythic or legendary figures and events, as Yeats did at the beginning of the century, nor form characters living entirely in their fantasy world as do George Fitzmaurice's fantasists. Contemporary plays tend to draw on myths and the mythic view in much less obvious ways, while introducing fantastic elements into realistic created worlds. The proportion of and the relationship between the mythic and the fantastic varies from play to play as does fantasy's relationship to realism. Today the mythic seems to be evoked either through the archetypal quality of some—otherwise realistically drawn—characters, or through the presence of ritual or ritualistic scenes whereas the fantastic through some unexpected, miraculous event within the mostly naturalistic plot, through the appearance of ghosts and the communication between the living and the dead or through characters that turn out to be the doubles of each other. This also means that in the majority of contemporary Irish drama the fantastic intrudes into the realistic—which itself is already a heightened realism owing to the mythic, archetypal references—and the atmosphere created in this way allows an oscillation on the brink of the possible and the impossible.

The variety of manners in which the mythic and the fantastic appears in contemporary Irish drama, might be classified into the following, often overlapping groups:

> 1) more or less pure fantasy plays where the fantastic dominates in the arrangement of the events, in the drawing of character, and/or the treatment of place and time; where the mythic, symbolical, half-realistic half-fantastic characters and events appear either in themselves or in their combination within one space and time as 'impossible' as in, for example, Thomas Kilroy's *Tea and Sex and Shakespeare* (1976), Frank McGuinness's wild fantasy, *Mary and Lizzie* (1989) and, to a great extent, his *Mutabilitie* (1997), Tom Murphy's *The Morning After Optimism* (1993)

2) plays in which realism and the fantastic are more mixed: plays dramatising split characters through doubles and ghost plays with ghosts appearing in their corporeality, interacting with the living, often forming the 'double' or doppelgänger of a living counterpart, and modern, secular 'miracle' plays in which some sudden, unexpected event breaks out of the established naturalism of the play as in most of Tom Murphy's plays;

and

3) seemingly naturalistic plays clothing a character (or a group of characters) in some archetypal attributes of ancient gods—more frequently goddesses—or inviting the mythic through ritual as in Brian Friel's *Wonderful Tennessee* (1993) or Pat Kinevane's *The Nun's Wood* (1998).

Most often some ambiguity is created as to whether the appearances are only the memories, dreams and visions of the characters or existing entities. Not included here as fantastic are plays that use fantastic elements merely as stage technique to help to project the psychological, emotional, or intellectual processes of the character as in, for instance, Brian Friel's *Philadelphia, Here I Come!* (1964) where Private Gar is the stage embodiment of the invisible inner half of Public Gar. Also not included are plays where the fantastic only offers a means of making visible dreams, visions, memories as in Tom Murphy's *A Crucial Week in the Life of the Grocer's Assistant* (1978).

Of the first group perhaps the most remarkable contemporary play is McGuinness's *Mary and Lizzie* (1989). The historical figures (such as Marx, Engels, Mary and Lizzie Burns) move in an entirely imaginative space and time. The protagonists, on their spiritual journey cross not only geographical boundaries (for example going instantly from Ireland to England) but also travel across time and space, walk both *on* and *in* the earth, across boundaries of life and death. The fantastic makes it possible to bring different times and places, events and characters into the same theatrical space, and to present, confront and subvert ideas, notions, views of history. With the help of the fantastic 'many details are telescoped into one moment, as events are compressed, intensified, fractured and multiple, as the pressures within the psyche can materialise ghosts or energies which either haunt or restrain'.[24] The very form and structure of *Mary and Lizzie*, with its fluidity, discontinuity, lack of comfortable linearity of narrative, as Eamon Jordan repeatedly suggests, undermines 'both the concepts of the real and of the historical', 'challenge[s] the repressive and prejudicial received historical narratives' and 'the stereotypes of being woman and of being Irish', while reinforcing defiance, rebellion, 'choice and opportunity'.[25]

This wild surrealist fantasy is set in nineteenth-century, pre-famine Ireland (although with the famine predicted), at the peak of Victorian colonisation and oppression. In powerful, many-layered images, McGuinness evokes the suffering and misery of the Irish, especially of Irish women but also of Irish emigrant men in England, thus linking gender and colonial exploitation and humiliation. The first scene, 'The City of Women', depicting women left alone and pregnant by English soldiers, living in trees, dramatises those banished from society, and at the same time also evokes the mad king Sweeney, turned into a bird after losing his kingdom, thus connecting the present with the past, and the real with the legendary. Since McGuinness's attention in this play is focused on Irish women's fate, the old king's place in the trees is taken by women.

The 'Old Woman' figure, an allegorical Mother Ireland, after centuries of embodying the independent, vital forces of Ireland, has by now become compulsive, demanding, and basically destructive. Instead of giving consolation or support to the wandering Mary and Lizzie, she guides them down into the earth. Mother Ireland being at home in the earth rather than on it, evokes associations with Mother-Earth and her attribute of fertility. But the play dramatises the opposite of fertility as emphasised in many images from the women in the trees exiled because of their unwanted babies to the Pregnant Girl killing whatever she gives birth to. So Mother Ireland combined with Mother-Earth acquires the reverse attribute: not life but death. Yet another reversal has Mary and Lizzie meeting their dead mother, together with several other women who died in childbirth, inside the earth. The real mother, a life-in-death figure, a counterpart of the death-in-life Old Woman, actually emerges after the Old Woman fades away. Unlike the Old Woman, the mother has no desire to dominate, but is more personal, more emotionally related and more concrete and practical minded. She thus proves more helpful even in death than the allegorical Mother Ireland in life.

The transmutation of the old image of Mother Ireland into the resurrected, personal loving mother promises a transformation of old-fashioned sectarianism, exclusivity and male-centeredness. While the Old Woman-Mother Ireland was fighting for her exclusive Catholicism, and loved only her *son*, the personal mother becomes a partner of God in her non-dogmatic faith and thus recreates life: 'God did not make the earth. We sung it. He heard us and joined in. We did it together, creation.'[26]

If the mother-image was split into two (with a third, colonial 'mother-figure' Queen Victoria, appearing in a comico-grotesque scene), the next generation divides even more antagonistically, theatricised through Mother Ireland's son, the 'Magical Priest' and the two girls. This underworld magical priest represents the dualism of Catholicism and Protestantism: having united them in himself in a destructive way, he inverts both to their opposites, teaching hatred instead of love: 'a killing combination of two defunct faiths that can only survive by feeding off each other' (*M&L*, p.11). The two girls, on the other hand, are independent and irreverent, defy the priest's intention of devouring them by threatening to devour him—LIZZIE queries: 'Shall we eat him?' (*M&L*, p.11)—evoking in the process matriarchal images of the all-powerful goddesses before patriarchy subdued them.

Instead of hatred, the girls are seeking love and fulfilment, and together embody the depth of the feminine psyche,[27] so little explored in Irish drama up to the past few years. They are *both* spirit, since they easily travel across the boundaries of life and death, *and* very definitely, sometimes quite vulgarly flesh, stressing the right of the repressed physical side of human experience. Their indivisible natural unity between soul and body sharply contrasts with the social division and the 'repression of the body on a grand scale [...] on both individual and collective levels',[28] especially of the female body so conspicuous in Irish literature and arts. The play dramatises this division in several situations, including the confrontation of Mother Ireland's son, who so far has been provided with women only to 'sin' with, with Mary and Lizzie's independence and strong mindedness which shocks and frightens him.

In encountering Marx and Engels, the materialist, rational thinkers, the girls experience the conventional gender view combined with colonial stereotypes. Engels identifies them with the darkness he fears (itself a powerful irony); with the dark powers of instinct and flesh as well as with the uncivilised Irish, living 'little above the savage [...] on the lowest plane possible in a civilised country'.[29] Probably the most subversive use of the fantastic occurs in these richly comic, grotesque scenes between the girls and Marx and Engels. These encounters bring to the surface 'how unfree Engels and Marx were of the cultural stereotypes in circulation within their own society', how they 'are implicated in the production of stereotypes of both woman and of Irishness', how Marx failed to recognise that his theory that '"it is not the consciousness of men that determines their being but on the contrary, their social being that determines their consciousness" [would] apply just as easily to himself', and how much, incidentally, he hated the poor, 'of whom the Irish in Britain constituted a significant portion'.[30]

Representing daring femininity, freedom of speech, liberation of instincts, the rebellious spirit which will not put up with conventional social roles or with colonial prejudices, the two sisters, having experienced much frustration, betrayal, and loss, emerge the wiser from the journey. The two heroines *together* are able to preserve integrity, in situations and roles very different from what society would accept. They are cast out of society, a pair of those socially marginalised people whom McGuinness in his plays moves into the centre: the gay, 'the outsider, the wanderer, the rebel',[31] to emphasise their right to their otherness, to being different. Against the background of conventional role-expectations and prejudices, these fantastic inversions and subversions throw into sharp relief Mary and Lizzie's 'fierce and joyous sense of self' and 'new, utterly Irish, indominatibility',[32] their independent womanhood, acknowledgement of the rights of the body, and new, direct contact with God through love and beauty.

The fantastic gives McGuinness the opportunity to form symmetrically arranged scenes. For instance, those utilising trios of characters where the qualities juxtaposed are counterbalanced or overpowered by one another. One such subversive scene is the encounter of the two women with the magical priest in which they counterbalance overgrown male spirituality turned inhuman. Another is their threesome with Engels where they make the repressive dominance of reason and rationality ridiculous. But the play ends with an affirmative use of the trio-image: that of a trinity of women who, after much suffering and frustration, find a note of peace and love. In the concluding scene, Mary and Lizzie with their (dead) mother in between them, pace up and down the stage, singing about love which 'is lord of all' (*M&L*, p.49). The three woman, similarly to the three women in Tom Murphy's *Bailegangaire* and the 'unholy trinity' in *The Sanctuary Lamp*, form a symmetric threesome, an image of wholeness, completion, equilibrium, a promise of healing. It is tempting to see the prevailing threesomeness in such plays bringing about reconciliation, completion or at least a temporary balance, as an echo of the three-faced ancient Celtic goddesses such as Brigit. The 'concept of three or the trinity seems [...] nowhere [...] more prominent than in Celtic culture. [...] In both Irish and Welsh myth the gods came in threes, triune gods and goddesses. Three and three times three permeates Celtic philosophy and art.'[33]

In the second group of contemporary Irish plays deploying the fantastic, the realistic is mixed in with the fantastic. This group is the largest and probably the most varied in its use of the fantastic. Within this group, the proliferation and variety of doubles and split characters is a striking feature and can be accounted for by all the historical dualities and divisions in Irish personal and national existence. Also, since the literary doubles embody the problem of identity, this form is congenial for the dramatisation of this major concern of the colonial and post-colonial psyche. Brian Friel's *Philadelphia, Here I Come!* (1969) projects the division between the internal and external self, Thomas Kilroy's *Double Cross* (1986) more directly that of the colonial psyche, Tom Murphy's The *Sanctuary Lamp* (1975) and *The Gigli Concert* (1985) the complicated relationships between matter and spirit, body and soul. The splits, including the living and the dead, add to their dividedness the well-known Irish dimension of the co-existence of past and present, the haunting of history.[33] Hugh Leonard's *Da* (1973), Stewart Parker's *Northern Star* (1984) and *Pentecost* (1989) dramatise such coexistence of past and present, with the first and the last pointing towards a possible meaningful integration of the past rather than its dominance over the present, while Frank McGuinness's *Mary and Lizzie* calls attention to the great variety of the mixture within these groups.

While most postmodern split characters reflect fragmentation and postmodern instability, the relativity of the self,[35] and the lack of value in unity, their Irish counterparts—at least those created through 'doubling by division',[36] that is, the complementary doubles—in most cases strive for union, integration, and reconciliation. Rosemary Jackson, working with Freud and Lacan's theories, finds the chief motive in literary works of doubles in general to be 'a desire for that state *preceding* the fall into alienation [...] for the non-relationship of zero, where identity is meaningless'.[37] But the Irish doubles move in exactly the opposite direction. After waking up from false idealism and 'optimism' (dramatised, for instance, in Tom Murphy's *The Morning After Optimism*), for instance, some doubles go through the hard and painful stages of loss and disintegration to arrive at a new level of consciousness and identity. Others take a different direction, such as in the most recent haunting ghost plays, such as Marina Carr's *Portia Coughlan* (1995), which focuses on the relationship between indivisible twins who are, however, divided by death. Like Jackson's examples, Carr's heroine *does* want to go back to the state 'preceding the fall into alienation'. She does so consciously not to achieve the 'non-relationship of zero where identity is meaningless' but rather to achieve the perfect relationship of total union with her other half, that is, completion, wholeness without complications. Death becomes the only place or state where she can find her identity. She cannot find it on earth after having lost her twin brother, the other half of her self. That this identity and wholeness can be found only in death becomes a new, psychological exploration of the Yeatsean philosophy according to which Unity of Being can be achieved only at the cost of physical life.

The ghost of Gabriel, the fifteen-year-dead twin-brother haunts *Portia Coughlan*. Not only does Portia see him hovering over the river and hears him singing but several other members of the small community do as well. He thus gains more of an independent existence than if he were only an embodiment of Portia's thoughts and feelings. He is a living presence in Portia's life, more real than the living members of her family, more important than her husband and children. The loss of her twin brother inflicts suffering through all the rest of her life as she makes her family suffer in a hell from which there is no redemption, where every attempt at reconciliation or the rekindling of relationships only deepens the inferno. The archetypal twins, belonging together, sharing one soul, feeling each other's pain, living in each other, is one of the most direct possible embodiments of the double. Jung described the ideal harmony and happiness of marriage which holds true for the twins in Carr's play (except, of course, for the fatal difference that Carr's characters are sister and brother). Jung maintained that

> the return to that original condition of unconscious oneness is like return to childhood. [...] Even more it is a return to the mother's womb, into the teeming depths of an as yet unconscious creativity. It is, in truth, a genuine and incontestable experience of the Divine, whose transcendent force obliterates and consumes everything individual; a real communion with life and the impersonal power of fate.[38]

Exactly this kind of relationship is clearly spelled out in the play, especially in Portia's keen awareness of her belonging to her twin brother Gabriel and her longing to return to their togetherness in the womb. The chief archetypal symbol of the play, the river Belmont, where Gabriel drowned and where Portia sees and hears him all the time and where she is ready to follow him again—is obviously a reference to that prenatal state. The deep, mythical union between the twins—one that obliterates every other relationship no matter how many years pass after the death of one of them—is reinforced by Portia's mythical relationship to the river to which 'she is wedded [...] just as fatally as a legendary mermaid to the sea'.[39] The Irish Midland twin-lovers' irrepressible passion for each other echoes the unfathomable depth of love between Heathcliff and Catherine, their indivisible oneness that ordinary human beings can never understand nor influence, but which, if circumstances hinder its fulfilment, turns into destructive and self-destructive power. But whereas incest was only hinted at as a possibility in the nineteenth-century *Wuthering Heights,* it is openly discussed as psychological torment in *Portia Coughlan.*

Portia, a woman misplaced, unfitted to her narrow environment, has experienced something deeper than ordinary life can offer: the depth of the unmeditated, inescapable, absolute which is for her natural, since offered by nature in the natural process of her growing together with her twin-brother in the womb—yet is forbidden. This predetermined love and passion appears stronger than human will, ethics, or social acceptability. On one level, the play contributes to the list of Irish dramas in which the past still defines the present (apart from being conceived as twins, the family's inbreeding, hatreds, and other ills form part of their legacy), and provides little room for awakening from history's nightmare. Set in a small, choking rural community and dramatising the heroine's suffering and struggle with deep psychological realism, *Portia Coughlan* at the same time lends to this struggle a mythic depth. Portia becomes the embodiment of the suffering human soul itself, torn in twine, in search of completion.

The third group of plays rarely at first glance reveals the presence of the fantastic and/or the mythical. Dominantly naturalistic plays or memory-plays full of projected figures and events, they come close to the mythic in borrowing some archetypal features or through enlarging a character and placing him/her within a wider context than the immediate theatrical world. Perhaps the most frequently occurring reminders of the ancient Irish mythic world may be found in the modern woman characters clad in some archetypal attributes of goddesses.

One of the longest-lasting Celtic mythic concepts is embodied in the Sovereignty figure. The descendent of the goddess of the land, whose marrying the king was necessary to sanctify his reign, later turned into the Shan Van Vocht, the Poor Old Woman, or into Cathleen Ní Houlihan—both personifications of Ireland. The Mother Ireland figure has dominated the Irish imagination for centuries. Included among her features are both healing and destroying, both youth and old age at the same time—another example of the Irish capability for holding together seemingly exclusive qualities without contradiction— oxymorons, in one view, which are manifest features of the modern fantastic.

Contemporary Irish drama is teeming with heroines enlarged by archetypal qualities, sometimes with mythical echoes. Portia Coughlan, Marina Carr's The Mai in the play of that name, Mommo in *Bailegangaire*, are only a few prominent examples. In Sebastian Barry's *Our Lady of Sligo* (1997), the main character, Mai O'Hara, even in her destroyed, reduced, dying condition, dominates the scene and the lives of her closest family members. Behind this almost larger-than-life figure lurks the mythical old and young woman, goddess, queen:

> The Shan van Vocht personifies defiance and resistance. [...] The image of the poor old woman merges with that of the hag and war goddess of the early literature, and this image is united with that of the 'beautiful maiden' in the figure of Cathleen Ní Houlihan. Cathleen resembles the Hag of Beare, also an Irish sovereignty figure, in her combined youth and age. Both are poor, miserable, and lonely in their old age, and both remember their youth and beauty when they had many lovers.[40]

Mai miserable, ill, and fearfully alone in her dying, has only the ghosts of her lost loved ones, especially her father for company. And yet her family members and sometimes her own memories of her earlier self evoke her queenliness, when she was the 'beauty-queen of Sligo', 'impervious, imperial'. Her daughter's bitter memory of the nights when she had to go 'beyond where the hag of Beare sat in the sucking shadows' up into her mother's bed, make more explicit references to Mai's descending from the goddess-queens. The daughter had to guard her like 'the warrior asleep in his stone hut on Knocknarea at the foot of Maeve's gigantic cairn, guarding his queen eternally'.[41] And as in the Irish imagination where pagan notions and objects of worship become mixed with Christianity, so here the daughter associates her mother with "Our Lady of Sorrows". She concludes that her mother is 'Our Lady of Sligo except you had lost your little boy and instead had the sliver of your tattered girl, a coin of fear and sleeplessness in the palm of your hand'.[42]

Also, like those mythical figures, Mai embodies both old age and youth. On stage her fragility is paramount. She needs every support in her sickbed, and yet she—her soul in her memories, dreams, imagination—gets out of bed and moves about as young and beautiful. These archetypal features lend Mai in Barry's play a larger-than-life quality and place her in Ireland beyond all the references to places, history, or contemporary events. Barry's play underlines the bitterness and the irony by its echoes of one-time goddesses and queens. Mai is a warrior but instead of heroic confrontations, she fights a losing battle with herself, with alcohol, with Jack, her husband; and she is left without any healing power: she cannot save the land, not even herself, but rather destroys herself and all the others around her. Rather than embodying the land, the country, she no longer fits the country, as she herself recognises in a scene set in Omard where she desperately runs to her country aunt and uncle in hope of rescue, but finds none.

All Mai's life lies in the past, as her response to her visitors makes clear. She rarely even acknowledges her husband's and daughter's presence or their relationship to her and many times she blatantly denies them—'I was never married'—whereas she happily communicates with her ghostly visitors, especially her long-dead father and aunt. The appearance of the dead may be seen in part as simply the projection of her thoughts, memories, morphine-dreams but, like so many other Irish stage-ghosts, they do appear in their corporeality and go beyond a convenient stage-technique of dramatising psychological processes. This is especially true of the father's presence, because he is not only a memory but has his own existence. His presence as a fantastic phenomenon, as more than the embodiment of Mai's dreams, becomes the most noticeable when, in the concluding scene, his voice approving Mai is heard after her 'eyes stay open'.[43] 'Good girl, Mai-Mai, good girl'.[44] While clearly naturalistic, Barry's *Our Lady of Sligo* is also equally fantastic in its mythic overtones, its archetypal figure of the woman larger than life, and the corporeality of the dead.

While not deploying figures directly from myth and legend or creating characters who live wholly within a fantasy world, as earlier dramatists did, contemporary Irish playwrights draw on mythic and legendary elements as well as the fantastic which they then introduce into what may otherwise appear as a realistic realm. All the examples cited confirm that Irish imagination and writing anticipates post-modern's preference for the fantastic to the purely naturalistic. Speaking about the tendency in Irish drama to extensively use palimpsest, Christopher Murray arrives at a similar conclusion: 'Irish drama was in some measure post-modernist before ever the term was coined.'[45]

NOTES
1. See Christopher Murray, 'Irish Drama and the Fantastic', in Donald E. Morse and Csilla Bertha, eds., *More Real Than Reality: The Fantastic in Irish Literature and the Arts* (Westport: Greenwood Press 1991), pp.85-96.
2. *Northern Star*, in *Three Plays for Ireland* (Birmingham: Oberon Books 1989), p.52.
3. Interview, *An Nasc.* 3, 1 (1990), p.25.
4. Quoted in Declan Kiberd, *Inventing Ireland: The Literature of a Modern Nation* (London: Jonathan Cape 1995), p.2.
5. Burgin et al., quoted. In Veronica Hollinger, 'Playing at the End of the World: Postmodern Theater', in Patrick D. Murphy, ed., *Staging the Impossible* (Westport: Greenwood Press 1992), p.185.
6. Nicholas Ruddick, 'Introduction: Learning to Resist the Wolf', *State of the Fantastic* (Westport: Greenwood Press 1992), pp.xiv-xv.
7. See for instance Lance Olsen, *Ellipse of Uncertainty. An Introduction to Postmodern Fantasy* (Westport: Greenwood Press 1987), p.10.
8. ibid. pp.9-10.
9. See Richard Kearney, ed., *The Irish Mind* (Dublin: Wolfhound Press 1985), p.9.
10. Weldon Thornton, *J M Synge and the Western Mind* (Gerrards Cross. Colin Smythe 1979), p.51.
11. Nancy H. Traill, Possible Worlds of the Fantastic: The Rise of the Paranormal in Fiction (Toronto UP 1996), p.7.
12. Patrick D. Murphy, *Staging the Impossible* (Westport: Greenwood Press 1992), p.3.
13. David Pringle, 'Introduction', *Modern Fantasy: The Hundred Best Novels* (London: Grafton Books 1988), p.10.
14. Rosemary Jackson, *Fantasy: The Literature of Subversion* (London: Methuen 1981), p.159.
15. Murray, op. cit. (1991), p.87.
16. Patrick Murphy, op. cit. (1992), p.4.
17. See, for instance, Gary K. Wolfe, 'The Encounter with Fantasy', in *The Aesthetics of Fantasy Literature and Art*, ed., Roger C. Schlobin (Indiana: Notre Dame 1982), pp.2-3; Colin N. Manlove, *Modern Fantasy: Five Studies* (Cambridge UP 1975), p.3, and Olsen, op. cit. (1987), p.17.
18. George P. Landow, '"And the World Became Strange": Realms of Literary Fantasy', in Schlobin, op. cit. (1982), p.197.
19. Quoted in Richard Kearney, *Postnationalist Ireland: Politics, Literature, Philosophy* (London: Routledge 1996), p.146
20. András Sándor, 'Myths and the Fantastic', in *New Literary History*, 22 (Spring 1991), p.339.
21. Manlove, 'On the Nature of Fantasy', in Schlobin, op. cit. (1982), p.18.

22 *A szent és a profán*, trans. Gábor Berényi (Budapest: Európa 1987), p.62.
23 For a fuller exploration of the differences between myth and the fantastic, see Csilla Bertha, 'Myth and the Fantastic: The Example of W. B. Yeats', in Morse and Bertha, op. cit. (1991), pp.17-27.
24 Eamon Jordan, *The Feast of Famine: The Plays of Frank McGuinness* (Bern: Peter Lang 1997), p.126.
25 ibid., pp.127, 194, 128, and 127.
26 *Mary and Lizzie* (London: Faber & Faber 1989), p.48; henceforth *M&L*.
27 Richard Cave, review of *Mary and Lizzie*, in *Theatre Ireland*, 21 (Dec. 1989), p.58.
28 Cheryl Herr, 'The Erotics of Irishness', in *Critical Inquiry*, 17, 1 (Autumn 1990), p.6.
29 McGuinness, op. cit. (1989), p.40.
30 Jordan, op. cit. (1997), p.134.
31 Richard Pine, 'Frank McGuinness: A Profile', in *Irish Literary Supplement*. 10, 1 (Spring 1991), p.29.
32 Cave, op. cit. (1989), p.59.
33 Peter Berresford Ellis, *A Dictionary of Irish Mythology* (London: Constable 1987), p.223.
34 For a more detailed analysis see Anthony Roche, "Ghosts in Irish Drama" in Morse and Bertha, op. cit. (1991), pp.41-66.
35 Cris Hassold, 'The Double and Doubling in Modern and Postmodern Art', in *Journal of the Fantastic in the Arts*, 6, 2-3 (1994), pp.253-54.
36 Robert Rogers, A Psychoanalytical Study of The Doubles in Literature (Wayne State UP 1970), p.5.
37 op. cit. (1981), pp.46-47.
38 'The Relations Between the Ego and the Unconscious', in *The Portable Jung*, ed. Joseph Campbell (Harmondsworth: Penguin 1976), p.167.
39 Christopher Murray, *Twentieth-Century Irish Drama: Mirror up to Nation* (Manchester UP 1997), p.238.
40 Rosalind Clark, *The Great Queens. Irish Goddesses from the Morrígan to Cathleen Ní Houlihan* (Gerrards Cross: Colin Smythe 1991), p.169.
41 Olsen, op. cit. (1987), pp.43-44
42 Olsen, op. cit. (1987), p.44
43 Olsen, op. cit. (1987), p.44
44 Olsen, op. cit. (1987), p.64. The printed text makes clear that the father is present on the stage and speaks on stage. In the London premier production the voice was amplified as if from afar.
45 Christopher Murray, 'The State of Play: Irish Theatre in the 'Nineties', in Eberhard Bort, ed., *The State of Play: Irish Theatre in the 'Nineties* (Trier: Wissenshaftlicher Verlag Trier 1996), p.22.

DANIEL CORKERY AND THE GROTESQUE

Alexander G. Gonzalez

When Daniel Corkery is remembered at all, it is only for his conservative ideas on Irish cultural nationalism or his role as mentor to Sean O'Faolain and Frank O'Connor. His own fiction goes virtually ignored, despite strong thematic and symbolic connections to such contemporaries of his as George Moore and James Joyce. For instance, his extensive use of the paralysis motif has already been documented,[1] and reveals a writer who—in spite of his narrow and idealised views regarding Irish literary culture—in his fiction almost always saw Ireland very realistically, enough to point out the same spiritual paralysis seen by Moore and Joyce. When Corkery did wax romantic, it usually was restricted to his largely propagandistic collection *The Hounds of Banba* (1920).[2] Part of Corkery's generally unrecognised realistic view of his nation's emergence from what was, in essence, a feudal state is his willingness to—indeed, need to—write about Ireland in such a way as to reveal not only its people's widespread paralysis but also the concomitant grotesqueness that accompanied it and helped symbolise it. That is, Ireland's rapid emergence brought with it a spiritual and social anomie that left many Irish men and women directionless, paralysed, and exhibiting forms of grotesqueness symbolic of this debilitating spiritual state. Some of this ugliness is evident in Yeats's poetry, where the middle-class Irishman is reduced to fumbling in a greasy till, but it is even stronger, of course, in Joyce's *Dubliners* (1914), where we see the likes of the truly grotesque Father Flynn in "The Sisters", the old sexual pervert in "An Encounter", or even the witch-like Maria in "Clay".

Corkery, like Yeats, sees a grotesqueness in Ireland's new materialism. In "Understanding" (*Earth Out of Earth*, 1939),[3] the protagonist, Peter Farrell, long ago went into exile to America, where, in his fifty-fifth year, he met and married a young Irish emigrant, whose ignorance, uncouthness, and indulgence in materialistic values eventually estranged him from her. Upon her sudden death after five years of marriage, the disillusioned Peter returns to Ireland in an attempt to revive his spirit after long bouts of depression. Seeking the simple, idyllic values he remembers from his boyhood, he finds instead a changed land whose values are as grubby and materialistic as those that his wife appeared to have adopted and that he had assumed were blameable on America. Ireland does, however, help him to recover from his depression, but he also realises that he is no longer of that country—even though so much of it appears exactly as he remembers it. He does come to understand why modern Irish values are as depraved as they are and, concomitantly, why his young wife was as *gauche* as she was; he also feels a release from the guilt that has been causing his depression—guilt that his snobby rejection of her had somehow hastened her death. After his recovery, he finds that Ireland ultimately bores him and that he must go back 'home', as he calls America—where life is faster-paced and people are willing to take risks. The grasping, clutching materialism of the new Ireland seems unbearably grotesque to him now, so with his new-found understanding he re-exiles himself, leaving behind his paralysis and assuming a new sense of activity and enterprise.

The story is important for several reasons. First, it is one of many stories to feature paralysis as an integral part of its thematic development; the recurring phrase, 'he was dead in himself', along with Peter's frequent physical sluggishness, cannot be missed. Second, the story is one of the strongest indictments of the new values in all of Corkery's work. Peter's memory of horses bred and raised in Ireland is of the animals themselves—their fiery nature, their beauty, his boyhood ability to 'talk' to them; but now all he finds is haggling over the prices they will bring, which repulses him. A third reason for the story's relative prominence is that Corkery for once allows his protagonist to go into exile, a fact that further underscores his revulsion at these new values; significantly, these extreme circumstances are roughly analogous to those under which the similarly conservative Seumas O'Kelly permits a character to exile herself in "The Derelict". Throughout, Peter's detachment from any sense of community also is emphasised, as we see him scouring the countryside, alone, searching for anything that will feed his hunger for the simple, wholesome memories of his youth. The family and friends with whom he lives sympathetically attempt to offer him support, but his strange words and actions, such as his disappearing daily with little explanation, alienate him from them until all interaction is reduced to the most superficial of levels. His inability to become integrated into the community quickens his mania for exile; it has become a society of which he no longer wants any part. Some readers will be reminded of George Moore's story, "Home Sickness", whose protagonist feels a comparable sense of estrangement in Ireland and re-exiles himself in America.

Because Corkery's realism was, in light of his conservative ideas on Irish cultural nationalism, necessarily also pessimistic, he often created an atmosphere of severe gloom in many of his stories. His first collection, *A Munster Twilight* (1916),[4] is by far the darkest of all in its general mood, with the word 'gloom' itself occurring frequently. The effects of such gloomy conditions, however, are not always entirely negative, as in "The Breath of Life", a story where 'the dreary hills that surround Clonmoyle on every side and overlay it [...] with a sort of perpetual gloom' (*MT*, p.44) are what in fact provide artistic inspiration to Ignatius O'Byrne, who is prevented from joining an orchestra because of his extreme poverty. We thus see the escarpments of his region informing the story with a well-conceived irony: not only do they inspire him and protect him from the external 'contamination' that would pollute his natural genius, but they also keep him so poor—lacking in gainful opportunities—that the visiting orchestra, full of jealous and snobby musicians, can point to his inability to 'pay his way' as an excuse for not permitting him to join them.

The 'architectural gloom' (*MT*, p.49) of Ireland's cities does not necessarily prevent their inhabitants from maintaining a certain dignity, as in "The Child Saint", where, despite a 'squalid environment' (*MT*, p.101), an old paralytic's life—in a small room that sits atop 'crazy, box-like stairs'—is so selflessly devoted to helping his community that he exhausts himself until he dies. Such conclusions, sentimentalised as they may sometimes be, indicate well the depth of Corkery's pessimism, as even these few efforts to combat Ireland's spiritual gloom seem ultimately wasted, or at least severely limited.

The protagonist of "The Child Saint" has his 'crazy, box-like stairs'; Ignatius has his enclosing hills in "The Breath of Life"; Phil has his labyrinthine passages in "A Looter of the Hills"; an old man lives in a small part of his 'hive' of a tenement house in "Refuge"; and in "The Priest" Corkery has the protagonist's withdrawal from complacency occur degree by degree as Reen rides his horse deeper into the night. Indeed, many cases exist where Corkery demonstrates the isolation of his characters by underscoring their disconnection in physical terms. Starting with a large overview, he quickly and methodically narrows that view until it becomes oppressive in the extreme. Sometimes, as in "The Priest", the disconnection develops over a number of pages, but most often, as in "Vanity", very quickly, establishing an instant atmosphere of gloom and alienation:

> From that great mountain-wall which divides Cork from Kerry great spurs of broken and terraced rock run out on the Cork side like vast buttresses; and in the flanks of these great buttresses are round-ended glens, or cooms, as they are called in Irish. Those on the northern flanks of such spurs are gloomy beyond belief. (*MT*, p.83)

The rapid subdivision of open space, so that we eventually focus on just one of these gloomy northern flanks, gives a perfect external correlative for the spiritually starved condition of that area's unfortunate inhabitants. This kind of rapid focus yields the same effect in quite a number of stories, whether they be urban or rural in setting.

With so much social and political turmoil occurring within a relatively short period of years, Corkery realised that any truly realistic depiction of his country and its people would have to include some treatment of the psychological, as well as physical and moral, scars that seared rural Irishmen. It is therefore appropriate that Corkery's fiction offers us so many cases of grotesque characters, often fools, and otherwise psychologically unbalanced people. As Sean Lucy has observed, Corkery studies their 'strangeness, without flinching from some of its more gross and grotesque manifestations'.[5]

Corkery's fascination with the grotesque is a trait he shares with fellow conservative Seumas O'Kelly, albeit for different purposes: where O'Kelly utilises grotesque characters as a means of puncturing the unrealistically inflated dreams of romantic characters, Corkery's grotesques play an important symbolic role in the mood of his stories, contributing an additional layer of almost gothic gloom to his evocation of the rural landscape. Such is the case in "The Stones" (*The Stormy Hills*, 1929),[6] where we find old John Redney, a physically repulsive denizen of a mountain coom who is in some ways very much like Diarmuid MacCoitir, the protagonist in "Vanity". The sense of gloom in such an isolated place is symbolically enhanced by Redney's physical description: he seems as grey and colourless as the stones that dot the hillside, his face as worn, uneven, and angular as their surfaces. 'Looking out from under his shaggy brows, his head down, his left hand clenched across the small of his back, his right hand tight and heavy upon the knob of his stick' (*TSH*, p.132), Redney is the harsher, utterly humourless counterpart of O'Kelly's wizened old men in *The Weaver's Grave*.

Other noteworthy cases are the Larty family in "The Lartys" (in *The Stormy Hills*), who keep to themselves in the savage land near the ocean cliffs of western Ireland; and the 'Master' in "The Ruining of Dromacurrig" (in *TSH*). Also worth mentioning is "The Death of the Runner" (in *Earth Out of Earth*), a story about a weird old man who suffers fits of insanity that can be traced back to his youth. These fits stem from a rash action taken many years ago, when he drowned his father's favourite colt because the father had disapproved of his son's marriage choice. Instead of asserting himself and marrying the woman, The Runner bows to parental pressure and then takes his revenge. The result is his fits of insanity, which manifest themselves in his long runs from place to place—miles of running, which signify his attempts to relieve the guilt he has always carried with him since his clash with his father. As the story's title suggests, The Runner's exhausting fits can result only in his death, which occurs as he tries to outdistance himself from an old horse, which, he feels convinced, bears the spirit of the young colt he drowned so long ago.

Other characters in Corkery's fiction are also probably better termed 'psychologically disturbed' than purely grotesque, such as the reclusive Maurice in "Refuge", the neurasthenic cutler in "Strange Honeydew", and the infirm Sylvie Moriarty in "There's Your Sea!" (all in *Earth Out of Earth*). The last of these is worth further consideration here. Sylvie, who has been raised inland and has since moved to the western coast, suffers from severe fits of mental agitation and is preoccupied with the 'thousand different voices that could come from the sea's throat' (*EOE*, p.263). He is described as a 'wild-eyed' man, one who has 'gone away into his own world' and whose 'spirit was dead within him'; he is 'in a stupor, [with] a rigid stillness of body' (*EOE*, pp.267-70). Sylvie is jarred from his obvious paralysis one day when he finds a drowned baby on the seashore after a powerful storm has passed over. The incident initiates in him the resolve necessary for him to abandon the cabin he has shared with his wife—a property that came to him as part of his wife's dowry—and to move inland with his family. He seeks thus to relieve his spiritual agony, for he has discovered that he is too sensitive a man to live on the coast, where one must be psychologically calloused in order to endure. The townspeople in the story are exactly that: accustomed to sudden random deaths and mutilating accidents. We are perforce reminded of the naturalistic cruelty of the events in Synge's *Riders to the Sea* (1904), where Maurya is at the play's end in the position that Sylvie now foresees for himself. The figure of the fool plays an important role in Corkery's concept of the grotesque. Dull-witted idiot boys are for various reasons made the focus of several pieces: in *The Threshold of Quiet* (1917),[7] which Derry Jeffares[8] has praised for its 'sound psychological insight' (*TTQ*, p.271), Ned Connell's mental incompetence is stressed, perhaps as an 'excuse' for his eventual exile; and Phil, in "A Looter of the Hills" (*TSH*), is strangely retarded, but his capacity for love transcends his mental drawbacks as he struggles to help his mother survive in Cork's labyrinths. And Nick Motherway, in "A Bye-Product" *(Hounds of Banba*, 1920), is by all outward appearances a grotesque:

> No one had ever seen those flat, unshapely features, those wandering eyes, take on the keenness of intelligence: at best one caught in that empty face only a vague expectancy, a gleam that began to die away before it had half ripened. The mouth was now active, and the strength of the jaws was plainly seen, but no sooner would the feeding be done with than the lips would droop open again and the whole chin and lower face sag down helplessly. (*HB*, p.170.)

This idiot son is the only one remaining, for all the 'trusty sons' have 'gone to America' (*HB*, p.178). Thus, at least for the moment, the idea that Moore and Joyce so strongly propounded, that the able emigrate while the inept remain, seems to be holding true, but, as we shall see, Corkery will give the truism a twist in an attempt to prove it false. When the English threaten to enforce conscription of Irishmen to fight in Europe, Mr Motherway gives his son over to a recently formed gang of local guerrillas.

After a long night spent in drills and manoeuvres, Nick bursts into the house 'with unaccustomed noise and vigour' (*HB*, p.174). Moreover, Nick's whole misshapen body seems to be responding to his new-found responsibilities as a patriot: 'his height was huge, huger than before, for that ungainly droop with which he used to carry his shoulders was falling away from him' (*HB*, p.177). Nick tosses his head now 'with a new pride, a new alertness'.

When soldiers come to search the house one night, we see young Nick described as one 'in whom life had come suddenly to the blossoming' (*HB*, p.191). He has previously unexpectedly assaulted a policeman in order to obtain a rifle that actually works, but the soldiers' search for that rifle is now unsuccessful. Later the same night, the guerrilla leader, who has earlier warned the Motherways of the impending search, returns to find the father asleep with his son keeping watch—rifle firmly in hand.

The sight constitutes an epiphany for the guerrilla, 'one of those moments when we see into the life of things'. This vision he keeps in his head thereafter:

> the meagre, death-like figure laid flat upon the bed, the wild creature watching by it, the gun across the huge knees, the fierce grip. And in the light of that vision the task of freeing his native land that he and others like him had taken upon their shoulders seemed suddenly to have become immensely heavier, infinitely more involved, more surely fraught through and through with living pain. (*HB*, p.193)

Corkery thus attempts to prove that it is not necessarily intelligence and initiative that are needed to free Ireland, but courage and devotion, for it is possible that one simpleton can do more for his country than his four able brothers who have escaped abroad. Inspired by his vision, the guerrilla leader makes progress 'not unlike Nicholas Motherway's, only on a higher plane' (*HB*, p.193). The inspiration to fight Ireland's lethargy is to be found on the most basic of levels. Corkery's rudimentary use of epiphany is fairly successful and provides the story with a strong conclusion—strong not only in its attempt to influence the Irish men and women of his day, but also in its artistic effect, which needs to be affirmed, as *The Hounds of Banba* is often justly criticised for being mostly mere revolutionary propaganda. In stories such as this, Corkery the artist supersedes Corkery the propagandistic patriot; that is, Corkery reaches beyond his initial intentions in spite of himself.

Corkery's grotesque fools are each imbued with a tremendous will, which enables them to fix their minds on a certain purpose and, actually aided by their mental simplicity, to persevere in attaining their goals. Thus where intellectually superior characters may stray from their responsibilities, Corkery's fools usually serve as models for the total commitment Corkery romantically wished to see widespread in the Irishmen of his day. Corkery's theory obviously is that if a fool can give himself over unshakeably to a cause, then Ireland's more able citizens should be able to do the same, especially when the stakes—the future of Ireland—are so great.

Other salient figures worth brief mention are Liam, in "The Ploughing of the Leaca" (in *Munster Twilight*), who is manipulated by the squire into ploughing holy ground after being subjected to extreme psychological pressure; the 'pathetic' labourer with the 'joyless, dull eyes' that have 'but little comprehension in them' in "The Bonny Labouring Boy" (in *Munster Twilight*); and the distracted lunatic who wanders about in "The Old Stevedore" (in *Earth Out of Earth*). Ireland may be producing grotesque figures as the nation emerged from its virtually feudal state, but Corkery found ways to promote his nationalist views by ironically using many of them as models from which the average Irishman could, he hoped, draw some active inspiration.

NOTES
1 See Alexander G. Gonzalez, 'A Re-Evaluation of Daniel Corkery's Fiction', in *Irish University Review*, 14, 2 (Autumn 1984); pp.191-201.
2 Daniel Corkery, *The Hounds of Banba* (Dublin: Talbot 1920), henceforth *HB*.
3 Corkery, *Earth Out of Earth* (Dublin: Talbot 1939), henceforth *EOE*.
4 Corkery, *A Munster Twilight* (NY: Stokes 1917), henceforth *MT*.
5 Sean Lucy, 'Place and People in the Short Stories of Daniel Corkery', in *The Irish Short Story*, eds., Patrick Rafroidi and Terence Brown (NJ: Atlantic Highlands: Humanities 1979).
6 Corkery, *The Stormy Hills* (London: Jonathan Cape 1929), henceforth *TSH*.
7 Corkery, *The Threshold of Quiet* (Dublin: Talbot 1917), henceforth *TTQ*.
8 A. N. Jeffares, *Anglo-Irish Literature* (NY: Schocken 1982).

TREATING THE WORLD AS A TRAMPOLINE: THE ALTERNATIVE REALISM OF MATTHEW SWEENEY

Michael Faherty

> The poet who is not a realist is dead, and the poet who is only a realist is also dead. The poet who is only irrational will only be understood by himself and his beloved and this is very sad. The poet who is all reason will even be understood by jackasses, and this also is terribly sad.
>
> Pablo Neruda

Matthew Sweeney would probably be the first to admit that his reality may not be ours. He is as aware as anyone that his poetry may well seem to the average reader to be populated with an excessive proportion of carcasses and corpses, of deaths and drownings, of suicides and severed penises. These somewhat fantastic elements, however, are not there simply to give an effect of the gothic but to give a real sense, more or less, of the world in which he lives. Sweeney is famous for his fear of falling prey to a fatal disease, whether the rarest of pathogenic parasites or the commonest strain of flu, and as one of his friends, the American poet and undertaker Thomas Lynch, recently reported, that world is fraught with a whole host of both actual and anticipated physical and psychological dangers:

> There are accounts of his inflation of the common cold to pneumonia or tuberculosis. His headaches are all brain tumours, his fevers meningitis, his hangovers all peptic ulcers or diverticulitis. Any deviations from the schedule of his toilet are bowel obstructions or colon cancer. He has been tested for every known irregularity except pregnancy, though he takes, on a seasonal basis, medication for PMS from which, no one doubts, he suffers. He is a consumer of medical opinion and keeps a list of specialists and their beeper numbers on his person. A cardiologist, an acupuncturist, an immunologist, an oral surgeon, an oncologist, a proctologist, and a behavioural psychologist join several psychic and holistic healers from regional and para-religious persuasions to make up Matthew's medical retinue. The same numbers are programmed to speed-dial from his home phone. And where most of his co-religionists

wear a medallion that reads *In Case of Emergency Call a Priest,* Sweeney's reads *Call an Ambulance. Call a Doctor. Please Observe Universal Precautions.*[1]

While Lynch may be having a little fun here at his friend's expense, there is little doubt that Sweeney's concerns about the outside world and what it holds in store for him are nothing but sincere and it would be somewhat of a surprise if they did not affect the poems he writes. As he himself has confessed: 'I'm a hypochondriac and any serious hypochondriac is not just play-acting. Whenever you get something, you think it's the end, so a sore toe is motor neurone disease. And how would you not write about it if that's a preoccupation?'[2]

This does not mean, however, that Sweeney only gives us his version of reality, repeatedly seen from the perspective of some hapless neurotic lurching from one life threatening disorder to the next. It has always been terribly important to him that poetry, above all else, not lose contact with a more general sense of reality in the late twentieth century and that the poet does not simply secrete himself away in some garret, secluded from the papers and politics of the streets outside. Sweeney sometimes cites a fellow Irishman, Louis MacNeice, who felt much the same way: 'I would have a poet able-bodied, fond of talking, a reader of the newspapers, capable of pity and laughter, informed in economics, appreciative of women, involved in personal relationships, actively interested in politics, susceptible to physical impressions.'[3] He often repeats this advice when teaching workshops, warning young writers of the dead end that lyrical solipsism can so often turn out to be and encouraging them instead to bring more of the outside world into their writing:

> During one of my residencies, I told a woman whose poems I'd been looking at that they showed no evidence whatsoever that the 20th century had happened, not to mention that we were at the tail end of it, or that she was in it. 'So?' she said. I said: 'We're living through the century of zeppelins, jazz bands, mushroom clouds, concentration camps, sputniks, computers and mobile phones. I can't get any sense from your poems that you've noticed.'[4]

While Sweeney is convinced of the need for contemporary poetry to reflect a reality beyond itself, this should not suggest that he is an old-fashioned follower of the theories of mimesis. He knows better than most writers these days that realism no longer works and that the borderline between fantasy and reality has never been more elastic, allowing the poet to play with this boundary pretty much as he sees fit.

Even though his early work shows that he was well aware of this elasticity long before he began to gather poems together for the anthology of contemporary poetry that he recently edited with Jo Shapcott for Faber and Faber, it was while reading through volume after volume of verse from around the world for *Emergency Kit* that Sweeney began to appreciate just how prevalent this tendency to move from the mimetic impulse to the fantastic, and back again, had become. Both editors began to believe that this could not be mere coincidence but must reflect a serious effort on the part of writers almost everywhere in the second half of this century to translate their experiences of the world around them into text:

> We live in an age when scientists can see inside every cell in the body and are learning more and more, through space exploration and the advances of astrophysics (Voyager, the Hubble telescope, for example), about the outer reaches of the universe and the distant history of life itself. It occurs to us that, just as Donne and Marvell were compelled by the discoveries of their time, so the poets in this book are responding to or reflecting the surprises of ours.
>
> TV, tabloids, movies, virtual reality, the Internet—all these have encouraged us to take the extraordinary for granted. We have watched men walk on the moon, we talk to each other across space and time, we conduct our business and our courtships on the 'net'. Isn't it inevitable, then, that these days poetry should be written which makes free with the boundaries of realism, crossing this way and that, at will?[5]

Although both Sweeney and Shapcott applaud such crossings and hope their anthology will only encourage more poets writing in English to make the same journey, neither editor recommends sheer flights into fantasy, into texts that do not have at least one foot still planted somewhere on the ground. As they say in their introduction about the poems they have selected for this anthology: 'But however far and freely they travel, they always come back to the world we wake up to, illuminating, from whatever angle, our day-to-day concerns.'[6]

While Sweeney acknowledges that a healthy suspicion of that foreign import known as realism has always been there in Irish literature—including the hyperbole of much medieval verse and the exaggerated stories of Swift—it has largely been Eastern European writers like Miroslav Holub and Vasko Popa and South American writers like Jorge-Luis Borges and Pablo Neruda who have served as mentors for many contemporary poets. For Sweeney himself, another Eastern European, Franz Kafka, played an early and decisive role in his development as a writer, opting as a student at the Polytechnic of North

London and, later, the University of Freiburg to study German in order to read his works in the original. What Kafka taught Sweeney, among other things, is the importance of accurate detail to all good writing, regardless of whether its subject matter is the wholly familiar or the wildly fabulous. This is the only way, Sweeney argues, for the writer to take the reader with him, to convince him to suspend his disbelief:

> Think of his story "Metamorphosis", with its preposterous opening sentence: Gregor Samsa awoke one morning from uneasy dreams to find himself transformed into a gigantic beetle. How can you be expected to believe such a statement? Kafka gradually persuades you by the accumulation of detail. When Samsa, the beetle, falls off the bed and onto his back, he can't turn over again, just as beetles we've observed can't turn over. And when he does get rightway-up again, he bangs his soft underbelly on the bed corner, gouging a deep wound, then when he reaches the wall, insect instinct takes over and he scurries happily across the ceiling, forgetting for the time being his predicament. After a few pages of this, his situation seems no more unnatural than waking up with a bad hangover.[7]

In those early days as a student of German literature, Sweeney says he used to consider Kafka's work to be pure fantasy but, once he realised that Kafka's approach to writing was essentially the approach of realism with its strict adherence to everyday detail, he decided that it was neither fantasy nor realism but a kind of 'alternative realism'. This is not to be confused with surrealism, according to Sweeney, since it is a style of writing 'where the realism is distorted or exaggerated somewhat but still comes back to the world and its concerns, and where the distortion paradoxically permits things to be more clearly seen'.[8] Moreover, he insists that this distortion or exaggeration remain consistent within the text and that whatever laws the writer invents for this alternative world remain, likewise, as consistent as the laws of the natural world that realism does its best to obey. If pigs fly in the first stanza, cautions Sweeney, they had better be still flapping those porcine wings in the last.[9] In order to make this point in workshops, he sometimes hands out postcards of various paintings and sculptures, explaining that these are pictures of other worlds, and asks the students to imagine some laws that would function within those worlds. He then asks each of them to write a dramatic monologue speaking as someone from that world, adhering to its laws without actually saying what those laws are.[10] As Sweeney knows, Kafka convinces because he follows the rules of the worlds that he himself has created but, unwilling to let our world completely alone, he just as surely draws our attention to the often unspoken rules that govern it, bringing the reader's notice back to the mundane, in the end, instead of the marvellous.

It is a similar talent for slipping quietly from the mundane, to the marvellous that many fellow poets, including Carol Ann Duffy and Peter Porter, have praised in their reading of Sweeney's poetry, suggesting that it almost seems to come second nature to him, as if he were raised on this stuff as a child in Donegal, having been taught at an early age that the one often goes hand in hand with the other. Some of those lessons no doubt took place at his great uncle's house, where he would stop as a boy to listen to the story-telling sessions held there, the tail end of an oral tradition that, unfortunately, no longer exists:

> He had this friend called Dan, and they were both probably in their seventies then, and Dan would come round and take some whiskey and stretch himself on the sofa, and I would sit in the corner with the dog, listening to them tell these stories from the turn of the century. And you got to know if you heard them a few times that the stories would change. I realised then that there was a lot of fictionalising going on. And the stories were all larger than life. You've often heard that when Gabriel Garcia Márquez is accused of magic realism and fantasy, he says, 'Well, that's what it's like in Colombia'. Well, where I come from, all the local stories have a little bit of magic realism thrown in. It's a natural thing. There were characters with weird names and maybe one arm.[11]

Sometimes everyday life in Donegal was, however, a little bit like that, with no need for fantasy to improve upon reality, including one day when a fisherman who had drowned out to sea was carried on a door to the Sweeney family home. It is this image of the drowned man that appears indirectly in poems such as "Where Fishermen Can't Swim", "The Bells" and "Reconfirming Light" and quite directly indeed in "The Sea at Pollan", "The House" and "Never in Life":

> Never in life had he drawn a crowd
> like the one spread out
> along the clifftop, to witness
> a door being dropped on ropes
> then raised again with him tied on,
> before being carried by six men
> at the head of a procession,
> a mile uphill to an ex-dancehall
> which was ours.[12]

Sweeney returns to this image over and over again—as well as the other central image of his poetry, the close friend who hung herself in the 1980s, a memory he revisits in poems such as "The Long-Legged

The Alternative Realism of Matthew Sweeney

Chair", "Goodbye to the Sky" and "Elm"—not simply to try and make sense of them, though that may be there too, but to try and get them right this time, just as the old men in Donegal would tell their stories over and over again in an attempt to get them right. According to Sweeney, this has as much as anything to do with what makes one writer unlike another:

> Dennis Potter said in an interview ten years ago that every writer has only a handful of themes and images which mean something to him, and you keep coming back to them because this time you hope to do it right. But you will never do it right. So I think that what you have to do is keep going deeper, and hope you're building a distinctive world, little by little, till it becomes recognisable, so no-one can read something you've written, even without your name on it, without knowing it's by you.[13]

Sweeney would be pleased that another Eastern European poet he greatly admires, Charles Simic, feels very much the same way, arguing that 'all great poetry is the contemplation of a few essential images—essential to the poet first, that is'.[14] While for Sweeney these essential images are the drowned fisherman and the old friend who hung herself, for Simic, who spent his childhood in a Serbia occupied by the Nazis, those essential images are the neighbours with their throats cut that he saw in a ditch as he walked to the market as a boy and the lice he picked up from wearing a German helmet he had found.[15] Whether these images are rooted in Serbia or Donegal, they still seem to suggest a much larger world where, as Tzvetan Todorov said of a whole movement within literature since Kafka, 'the fantastic becomes the rule, not the exception'.[16]

In order to convey a satisfactory sense of that world in his poetry, Sweeney has been asking his own questions about the literary conventions that have come to dominate its depiction in the West for at least the last two hundred years, wondering whether Kafka was on to something worth pursuing when he decided to describe the fantastic as if it were the real and to write in the third person as if he were writing in the first. It is Kafka, of course, who has often been the stickler in the debate amongst theorists of the fantastic, with even Todorov famously admitting that nothing he had learned about this genre in his study of the literature up to Kafka could help him account for the puzzling effect of his "Metamorphosis", that the lack of surprise at Samsa's shift into the form of an insect is, after all, the story's greatest surprise, with everyone concerned accepting it with a mere shrug of the shoulders, as if to say it is no more significant than a broken ankle.[17] Another such theorist, Rosemary Jackson, agrees, arguing that when it comes to Samsa's transformation, questions as to how or why simply become irrelevant: 'Strangeness is taken as a given, before the narrative begins: it is the inevitable condition of being, apprehended as an external disorder which the text tries to reproduce and comprehend.'[18] Those very same questions seem equally irrelevant to the transformation that takes place prior to a poem from Sweeney's most recent collection, called "Russian", in which a man awakes, much like Samsa himself, only to find that he is no longer the same man he once was:

> He woke up speaking Russian.
> He lay there, amazed,
> as sentence after sentence emerged and sailed to the window —
> it was verse, it had to be
> to flow that rhythmically,
> but he hadn't written it,
> nor had he been to Russia.[19]

As with Kafka, this change is clearly not some dream that can be undone by simply going back to sleep and, as with Kafka, it is absolutely crucial that the narrative position itself this side of consciousness, making it as clear to the reader as possible that we are not being given—as Jackson put it in her own discussion of the travelling salesman turned beetle—the perspective of our protagonist's 'fevered mind', thus not offering the reader the easy option of dismissing any of the text's obvious peculiarities on those grounds alone: 'The dizzying effect of a tale such as Kafka's "Metamorphosis" derives from this inability to push away the hero's experience as delusory: it is not the dream of an "I", but the reality of a "he" in terms of its presentation. Gregor's "unreal" transformation is "real": he *is* another being than himself, with his reason intact.'[20] The reason that remains intact in Sweeney's poem, of course, is not only that of our Russian-speaking hero but, much more importantly, that of the narrative itself, sticking as close to the rules of realism as the fantastic incident itself will allow, particularly to a tone that provides all the reassurance of nothing other than realistic objectivity. In order to corroborate its story, the narrative calls the protagonist's wife to the bedroom, asking her, with all her evident common sense, to verify its version of the event, begging her to back it up with her very own eyes and ears as well as her previous knowledge of just who this man was only the night before:

The Alternative Realism of Matthew Sweeney

> His wife came in from church
> to find pages of Cyrillic
> on the bed, and her man
> on the telephone, in Russian.
> He was arguing, she knew that,
> though about what?
> When had he been to night class?
> Was it him here at all?
>
> She remembered the tapes
> and his never-right French,
> or that time in Prague
> at the tram terminus
> grasping for a phrase of Czech.
> He had to be seriously sick
> or possessed. In the pauses
> she heard the answering Russian
> faintly, a world away.

Todorov would say, of course, that the wife here has just entered the realm of the fantastic, stuck somewhere between a natural and a supernatural solution to this transformation—making the situation 'uncanny' should she choose sickness and 'marvellous' should she plump for possessions[21]—but it could not be clearer that the text itself is having none of this. The husband may at first be 'amazed' by what has happened to him and his wife may feel that he is suddenly 'a world away' but, by keeping the narrative focused on the consequences rather than the possible causes of this transformation and by describing it with all the deliberateness of George Eliot in her witness-box, Sweeney has made sure that the reader is not and does not.

For just this reason, Sweeney takes some pains to make certain that the world in which these strange things happen cannot be confused with any world other than our own, a world where people wake up in the same bed in which they went to sleep, where they go out to church on a Sunday morning and where they fail to learn proper French from cassette tapes. These people live on streets like ours, where the sun rises in the morning and sets in the evening, even though, once again, that world sometimes finds itself suddenly in collision with another where other laws operate. While Samsa took a moment or two to adjust to his additional legs and the Russian-speaking husband woke slowly to the fact that those sentences were coming from his own mouth, the protagonist in Sweeney's poem "Hanging" barely seems to notice when he nips from one world to the next:

> Hanging from the lamppost
> he could see far —

> cars parked to the street's end,
> the few late-night walkers
> most of whom ignored him
> hanging there. He could hear
> screams and running feet,
> also quick shuffles away
> and, eventually, the wah-wahs
> that came with blue lights
> that led in the dawn.
> Then the lights in all the houses
> went on, and dressing-gown
> wearers gathered, killing yawns.[22]

When the wife walked into the bedroom to find her husband speaking Russian, the laws that governed her world found themselves in sudden opposition to the laws governing her husband's tongue but, in both of these poems, there is a more significant opposition at the level of the narrative itself, telling us things that such an objective perspective ought not. In "Russian", the narrative does not even think to hesitate where the wife herself certainly does and, in this poem, it observes one set of rules on the outside and another on the inside, allowing the consciousness upon which the limited narrative itself depends to continue while the corpse follows its expected course of decomposition:

> And flashbulbs exploded,
> though he couldn't hold
> his head up, and his face
> was blue. A megaphone
> asked the crowd to go home
> as a ladder leant on the lamppost
> for someone to ascend.
> He looked into this man's eye
> as the knife cut him down.

Even though both poems are written in such a way as to allow the reader to hold both worlds and their opposing laws in mind simultaneously, making the familiar suddenly strange and the strange suddenly familiar, the texts can only maintain this double-vision for so long, with the wife finally feeling 'a world apart' from her husband as she hears the faint sound of Russian coming from the telephone and the dead man staring into the living man's eyes, receiving no sign of recognition in return. In another poem employing the same central image, simply called "Postcard of a Hanging", two worlds collide once again, although the rules that may be violated this time are not necessarily those of the natural world as they are those governing darkrooms and the etiquette of the breakfast table and the worlds themselves are, likewise, the more recognisable cultures of the East and the West. Using the device of a postcard to bring these two worlds into contact, Sweeney manages to move the reader of the card—and, with him, the reader of the poem—back and forth between feelings of comfort and discomfort, between moments when we seem to be confronted with something true and other moments when we suspect something might be false. The poem begins in an appropriately unsettling manner:

> I sent you a postcard of a hanging,
> the first one I attended, not thinking
> I'd like it, or even stand it, as you
> must have loathed my postcard too
> till you realised it must be a trick,
> a decadent, oriental gimmick
> to put liberals off their breakfast
> of an egg, toast, jam and the rest.[23]

In this Chinese-box of a poem where the speaker addresses the second person about an earlier address to the same second person, Sweeney shows how readers attempt to accommodate the uncomfortable, how they can make it less of a threat merely by deciding that it is not real after all, even if the evidence appears to be photographic. Thus somewhat comforted, the reader then flips the postcard over and begins to read the story on the other side, telling the friend in the one world how well the friend in the other is getting on, with the reader temporarily suspending the disbelief expressed just moments before: 'And you believed it, you knew / that all my varied antics were true'. Disbelief creeps back in, however, as soon as the unwise reader flips back to that offensive photograph on the front of the postcard:

> And you turned to the picture again,
> a colour print—a gallows, two men,
> one hooded, one holding a noose
> of whitest rope, for the moment loose,
> and low in the foreground, a crowd
> of men mainly, silently loud,
> all eastern, except for two or three —
> one of whom, if you look closely, is me.

Although the reader could believe that a friend so familiar to him could thrive in a world so equally foreign to him, he still cannot make his eyes see both worlds at the same time, finding it all but impossible to hold both images in his mind at once and, therefore, impossible to decide whether the photograph is a trick or not. From his past experience of postcards, the reader has learned that a world we do not know appears on one side of the card while a world we do know appears on the other. When they violate this convention and collide on a single side, the combination, as Jackson said earlier of the Kafka story, tends to make us dizzy. It is almost as if the reader needs to hold a hand over one eye here, like the wife in "Russian" who can either see the husband who fumbled at French and Czech or the husband who is suddenly fluent in a foreign language, but not both.

And yet it is precisely this sense of uncertainty that Sweeney is trying to convey in his poetry, the giddiness that seems to be such an integral part of the way in which we experience, contemporary reality, what Bakhtinians would no doubt feel a need to call our 'dialogical' debate with the outside world. For Sweeney, however, it is still terribly important that poetry not get too caught up in its own reeling motion, that it not entirely lose its sense of balance, completely forgetting what side is up and what down. While he wholeheartedly joins Seamus Heaney in his recent admiration for writers who work with fantasy and 'treat the world as a trampoline' and while he would probably also subscribe to Simone Weil's law which states that 'the greatest sin' a writer can commit is 'obedience to the force of gravity', Sweeney would no doubt add Heaney's own words of caution here, urging poets to create a 'counterreality' but warning them, all the same, that their alternative world only 'has weight because it is imagined within the gravitational pull of the actual'.[24] In order to defy gravity without losing all sense of its ineluctable tug, Sweeney simply turns common poetic conventions against themselves, whether making the fantastic seem familiar, as in the poems discussed above—borrowing the methodology of mimesis to transmit the bizarre and inverting the first and third person perspectives—or making the familiar seem fantastic, as he often does in poems such as "Whatever", where the third-person speaker is denied the authority that usually comes with that perspective, refusing his narrator access to the thoughts and feelings of those under poetic observation and offering his reader far more questions than answers:

>What does he think, this man
>in the hospital bed, knowing
>he's dying because he heard
>she was sleeping with a neighbour—
>perhaps she taunted him
>until he grabbed the bottle

> of weedkiller, and swallowed,
> and now his kidneys are dead,
> dead as he'll be soon?
>
> And what does she think, knowing
> she called in the other man
> who, showing it was harmless,
> swallowed weedkiller too —
> and he's in another hospital,
> fighting to live, and the whole
> town is talking about her
> and her two kids, and all
> because of sex, love or whatever?[25]

In this poem and many others like it, the world of the everyday becomes as inexplicable as the world of the fantastic, their third-person speakers clearly not capable of making sense of these things any better than anyone else. Perhaps it should not be a surprise, then, that when he turns his attention to things closer to home, what initially proclaims itself an outright lyrical poem—taking the terribly straightforward title of "Sweeney"—becomes instead a strange sort of dramatic monologue, playing upon the tragic figure of the mad Celtic king by the same name, turned reluctant bird and, subsequently, poet. Once again, the reader is asked to hold the two images in mind simultaneously, that of the fretful worrier who now lives in Bloomsbury and writes poems for a living and that of the fearful warrior who once lived just east of Donegal and later spoke poems for the sake of his sanity:

> Even when I said my head was shrinking
> he didn't believe me. Change doctors, I thought,
> but why bother? We're all hypochondriacs,
> and those feathers pushing through my pores
> were psychomatic. My wife was the same
> till I pecked her, trying to kiss her, one morning,
> scratching her feet with my claws, cawing
> *good morning* till she left the bed with a scream.
>
> I moved out then, onto a branch of the oak
> behind the house. That way I could see her
> as she opened the car, on her way to work.
> Being a crow didn't stop me fancying her,
> especially when she wore that short black number
> I'd bought her in Berlin. I don't know if she
> noticed me. I never saw her look up.
> I did see boxes of my books going out.
>
> The nest was a problem. My wife had cursed me
> for being useless at DIY, and it was no better now.
> I wasn't a natural flier, either, so I sat
> in that tree, soaking, shivering, all day.
> Every time I saw someone carrying a bottle of wine

> I cawed. A takeaway curry was worse.
> And the day I saw my wife come home
> with a man, I flew finally into our wall.[26]

What happens in this poem is that Sweeney becomes Sweeney as much as Sweeney becomes Sweeney, that while Kafka convinces his readers of Samsa's transformation into a beetle by closely observing a beetle's behaviour, Sweeney convinces his readers of his transformation into Sweeney by closely observing his own behaviour, relying, of course, to some extent on their knowledge of his well known hypochondria and his inability to resist a decent curry. While the medieval Sweeney acquires an entirely new personality along with his plumage, the postmodern Sweeney experiences no more than a physical alteration, his enthusiasms and tastes and concerns still very much earthed in the side streets of Holborn, perhaps pushing feathers through his pores but still smacking his shrunken skull into that wall like Dr Johnson putting the boot in.

NOTES

1 Thomas Lynch, *The Undertaking: Life Studies from the Dismal Trade* (London: Jonathan Cape 1997), p.146.
2 Martin Sonenberg, 'The Lyricism of Menace' [interview], *Magma*, 7 (1996), pp.17-27 (p.22).
3 Quoted in Matthew Sweeney and John Hartley Williams, *Writing Poetry and Getting Published* (London: Hodder & Stoughton 1997), p.1.
4 ibid., p.75.
5 Jo Shapcott and Matthew Sweeney, 'Introduction', in *Emergency Kit: Poems for Strange Times*, ed. by Shapcott and Sweeney (London: Faber and Faber 1996), p.xvii.
6 ibid., p.xviii.
7 Sweeney and Williams, op. cit. (1997), p.12.
8 'Matthew Sweeney on *The Bridal Suite*', in *Poetry Book Society Bulletin* (Winter 1997).
9 Sweeney and Williams, op. cit. (1997), p.77.
10 ibid., pp.92-95.
11 Sonenberg, op. cit. (1996), p.21.
12 Sweeney, *The Bridal Suite* (London: Jonathan Cape 1997), p.4.
13 Sonenberg, op. cit. (1996), p.25.
14 Charles Simic, *Wonderful Words, Silent Truth: Essays on Poetry and a Memoir* (Ann Arbor: Michigan UP 1990), p.115.
15 ibid., p.67.
16 Todorov, *The Fantastic: A Structural Approach to a Literary Genre*, trans. by Richard Howard (Ithaca: Cornell UP 1975), p.173.
17 ibid., pp.169-70.
18 Jackson, *Fantasy: The Literature of Subversion* (London: Methuen 1981), pp.159-60.
19 *The Bridal Suite* (1997), p.38.
20 Jackson, op. cit. (1981), p.30.

21 Todorov, op. cit. (1975), p.41.
22 Sweeney, *Cacti* (London: Secker & Warburg 1992), p.21.
23 Sweeney, *Blue Shoes* (London: Secker & Warburg 1989), p.25.
24 Heaney, *The Redress of Poetry* (London: Faber and Faber 1995), p.3.
25 Sweeney, *Cacti* (1992), p.16.
26 I would like to thank Matthew Sweeney for permission to publish this uncollected poem, which has previously appeared in *Poetry London Newsletter* and *Princeton Library Journal*.

IRISH FANTASY, ENGLISH FANTASY: BECKETT AND LEWIS CARROLL

Antony Easthope

With outrageous exaggeration Jacques Lacan asserts that 'the slightest alteration in the relation between man and the signifier [...] changes the whole course of history'.[1] On the basis of a little less exaggeration we might agree that all of us live our lives in an inescapable relation to the various discourses we each inhabit; and further that many of these discourses come to us from our national culture. Of course we do not live only in relation to culture, nor is national culture the only form of culture there is. I mean to offer a definition of the fantastic in Irish culture and seek justification for this by offering a brief speculative contrast between the national cultures of England and Ireland. Fantastic discourse is distinguished by transgression and excess but it refers, I propose, to the dominant national culture because that sets the norms fantasy exceeds.

English Culture

The real is real and discourse is discourse. If we ask ourselves about the relation between discourse and reality that question falls under the heading of epistemology—how do I have knowledge of the external world? Many (probably most) epistemologies are rationalist—they assume that reality is rational, we are rational, so we should be able to work out the logic of a correspondence between discourse and reality. The English intellectual inheritance, however, is not rationalist but predominantly and overwhelmingly *empiricist*, a tradition established in writers such as Bacon, Hobbes and Locke.

Not to be confused with 'the factual' or 'the empirical' empiricism is the epistemological belief that the real can be experienced and understood more or less directly by the unprejudiced observer—you don't have to work to achieve knowledge, it is self-evident. Empiricism functions in a scenario with three terms:

1) Reality is supposedly pregiven. All you have to do is observe the real 'objectively', that is, without prejudgment or self-deception, and it will yield knowledge of itself. In a well-known incident, Boswell and Johnson came out of church and stood talking about Bishop Berkeley's idealism until Johnson, 'striking his foot with mighty force against a large stone', exclaimed, 'I refute it *thus*'.[2] Johnson's boot has the full weight of Englishness behind it (and Bishop Berkeley was an Irishman brought up in Kilkenny).

2) The means of representation by which reality is represented to the subject is presumed not to interfere significantly with the subject's access to objects. In principle, language is transparent so that the only problem for knowledge is to go and look and see what things are *there*.

3) In an epistemology subject and object always imply each other—thus the English subject and the English real correspond. If for the English reality is simply a given, then the English subject is envisaged as always already *there*, knowing and experiencing things.

Irish Culture

I am not going to trust my own opinion for an account of the tradition of Irish national culture but shall call on a recent and compelling observer who, moreover, has the advantage for my purposes of being a hostile witness. Terry Eagleton in his book *Heathcliff and the Great Hunger* (1995) aims to write a narrative of Irish cultural history insofar as it may be explained by a theory of political economy, in fact an unashamedly Marxist one.[3] I have no quarrel with that here but it does mean that in principle Eagleton's history must deny there is a national discursive tradition which maintained a degree of its own autonomy beyond any determinations of political economy, autonomy in what I would want to call the inheritance of the signifier.

Yet, in Eagleton's account, traces of the great Irish oral tradition—bardic, heroic and romantic—constantly return like the repressed. A main argument of his, and not a surprising one, is that Irish writing generally eschews realism, and he acknowledges that one factor at work is that such textuality recycles 'the riddling wordplay and extravagant world of the ancient sagas'.[4] Part of an Irish willingness to elevate culture over politics, Eagleton says, derives from 'the Gaelic political order', brought low in the seventeenth century, but 'in the form of bards and ballads, music and memories' living on as 'one of the few remaining repositories of a "national" consciousness'.[5] And that structure of feeling, he concedes, still bears an 'anti-mimetic aesthetic' down as far as Wilde and Yeats.[6]

In fact, with his customary brilliance, Eagleton does include a most suggestive description of the structuring of Irish national culture. Discussing Maria Edgeworth he notes how the line between fiction and reality becomes dangerously undecidable and affirms that:

> [...] one name for this blurring of the real and the rhetorical is Ireland. For there are several truths in Ireland depending on whom one is talking to; and if truth is in this sense elusive it is because it is in the service of power.[7]

Eagleton is immediately anxious to pull this possibility back into the secure corral of a political explanation; such 'verbal stratagems', he reassures us, 'are at once an effect of colonialism and a form of resistance to it'.[8] Perhaps, but this does not prevent him noting acutely:

> Language in Ireland is a field of struggle and dissimulation, performative rather than constative [...]. Language is weapon, dissemblance, seduction, apologia—anything in fact, but *representational*.[9]

I find this intuitively persuasive but we should not forget that it involves a covert denigration, for Irish discourse is being defined here by implicit reference to Englishness. It is of course English empiricist discourse which likes to imagine itself as constative (asserting truth) rather than performative (transforming meaning), English discourse which obsessively seeks to be representational and *only* representational: the truth and nothing but the truth. (Having had a dig at Terry for judging Ireland by English standards I should offer you a warning—if you need it—against my own pretences to objectivity and neutrality).

To regain an appropriate balance—to set the English norm at a distance—let me invoke someone who is definitely not Irish, Jacques Lacan. 'A signifier', he states more than once, 'is that which represents the subject for another signifier.'[10] One might think, if one believed language was in principle transparent to meaning, that a signifier represented a subject for another *subject*, that I communicate with you, you communicate with me, and we get on fine. But no, for Lacan it is ontologically and necessarily the case that to perform as a speaking subject I must enter an order in which signifiers relate in the first place to each other so it is only secondarily, on this basis, that an effect of communication can be brought about.

Lacan's proposal brings us closer, does it not, to Eagleton's affirmation that in Irish national discourse (my term, not his)

'Language is weapon, dissemblance, seduction, apologia—anything in fact, but *representational*.' I feel therefore encouraged to advance a hypothetical and conjectural definition of the structuring of Irish national discourse to set against that I put forward with rather more confidence for Englishness.

Mainstream inherited discourse in Ireland is characterised by acceptance of the priority of the signifier over the signified and of the completed sign over any truth, experience or knowledge that sign would refer to. So:

1) Language, speech, writing is acknowledged as a process in which the signifier is determined in relation to other signifiers. Discourse is accepted as a materiality constituted by sounds, figures, tropes, repetitions, in sum the work/play of the signifier. And Irishness, one might hazard, is constituted in its search for the magic word and the magic of the word, in its desire for the signifier which, impossibly and apocalyptically, might bring all discourse to an end by saying everything completely and at once.

2) But priority of the signifier means that the subject cannot be regarded as autonomous, separated, self-sufficient. If a signifier represents the subject for another signifier, and if language consists of the endless movement of the signifying chain, then the subject cannot be specified apart from that operation. Naturally language is seen as weapon, dissemblance, seduction, apologia and many other things, because the subject is caught up in what Emile Benveniste calls 'the unceasing present of enunciation'.[11] Always deictic and demonstrative, all utterance has to be acknowledged as inseparable from a situated act of uttering, all statement ineluctably entramelled in enunciation. Is it for this reason that Irish culture prefers speech to writing, and if writing (one thinks of Swift, Wilde, Joyce) a writing conscious of its own textuality?

3) On this basis, then, there is no possibility that discourse can be assumed, in naive empiricist fashion, as essentially a vehicle for transmitting a self-standing truth, one independent of who is writing about what for whom. Truth we cannot escape but the Irish tradition concedes that truth is inescapably an effect of discourse. Obviously 'truths in Ireland depend on whom one is talking to' and obviously language is envisaged as 'performative rather than constative'.

The preceding invites a tempting digression. English and Irish national discourses are mirror opposites, contradicting each other point by point, swerving past each other alarmingly when the same words are taken up in diametrically opposed interpretations, each the other of the other. Almost any invading culture—French, Chinese—would have made a better shot of understanding the particularities of Irish culture than the poor benighted, empiricist, stone-kicking, truth-obsessed Brits.

If even the gist of this preliminary analysis is granted, it indicates a salient difference between the place of fantasy and the fantastic in Irish and English discourse respectively. Irish discourse will not want to demarcate fantasy from other forms with a hard and fast border since the fact/ fiction opposition though available will not emerge in as stark a contrast. English discourse, however, certain it can found itself in fact, will be confident it can delimit the fantastic behind a strictly policed boundary. For Ireland fantasy will be present to a degree in most discursive forms and to an extent will typify discourse in general: in England fantasy will be a specially licensed discursive enclave.

Two Texts

Enough generalisation. I want to go some way towards substantiating these theoretical arguments from two examples even though no two examples are ever precisely comparable. One is from an English text published in 1865 and has received the attentions of (among others) Gilles Deleuze; the other from an Irish text published in 1951 in French. They are firmly distinct, then, in that one is from a Victorian comic novel, the other from a piece of Modernist writing. They are, however, somewhat uncannily comparable in their out-of-the-way subject matter—someone's reflections about their identity as inhabitants of their own body, this focused on the subject's relation to their extremities and specifically the feet. Both texts express fear of the idea of the body-in-pieces.

After falling down the rabbit-hole at the beginning of her adventures Alice finds a small cake labelled 'EAT ME'; when she eats it, she finds herself getting bigger and bigger:

> 'Curiouser and curiouser!' cried Alice (she was so much surprised, that for the moment she quite forgot how to speak good English); 'now I'm opening out like the largest telescope that ever was! Goodbye, feet!' (for when she looked down at her feet, they seemed to be almost out of sight they were getting so far off). 'Oh, my poor little feet, I wonder who will put on your shoes and stockings for you now, dears? I'm sure I shan't be able! I shall be a great deal too far off to trouble myself about you: you must manage the best way you can—but I must be kind to them,' thought Alice, 'or perhaps they won't walk the way I want to go! Let me see: I'll give them a new pair of boots every Christmas.'
>
> And she want on planning to herself how she would manage it. 'They must go by the carrier,' she thought; 'and how funny it'll seem, sending presents to one's own feet! And how odd the directions will look!
>
> Alice's Right Foot, Esq.
> Hearthrug,

near the Fender,
(with Alice's love).
Oh dear, what nonsense I'm talking![12]

Lewis Carroll exemplifies the English tradition of the fantastic that runs from (say) *Midsummer Night's Dream* through *Comus* and Pope's sylphs down to *Peter Pan*, *Wind in the Willows*, Tolkien and even, I would guess, 'Monty Python'. A commonsense empirical fact (the body is the body) becomes distorted into fantastic shape. That bodies do not open out like telescopes is explicitly remarked; Alice describes the process as 'Curiouser and curiouser', and concludes, 'Oh dear, what nonsense I'm talking!' The real is invoked by the way this passage is marked off as a comic departure from it.

Yet it is significant that when it comes to the process of the body empiricist discourse always risks losing control—Locke speculates how much of the body you could cut off (an arm, a leg, another arm) without the individual losing their identity. If our bodies really did go on growing we would be in very serious trouble. So Alice's responses to her experience are comically inappropriate, as she starts to talk about her disappearing feet as though they were children leaving home and needing a loving mother who at Christmas will send them presents (boots fittingly enough). The tone and attitude is therefore one of pleasurable transgression, of fantasy *known* to be fantasy, like that at the end of *The Life of Brian* when the people being crucified join in a chorus of *Always Look on the Bright Side of Life*. It is consistent with the general effect—the fantastic measured against the real and enjoyed precisely as a departure from it—that the language is assumed to be more or less transparent to meaning, with description sustained in a clear and ordered syntax. Alice's deviations from conventional usage are noted precisely as deviations, and when she says 'curiouser and curiouser', the text remarks her failure 'to speak good English'.

A very different kettle of fish is represented by Molloy in Samuel Beckett's novel of that name though Molloy also worries about his relation to his feet:

> And when I see my hands, on the sheet, which they love to floccillate already, they are not mine, less then ever mine, I have no arms, they are a couple, they play with the sheet, love-play perhaps, trying to get up perhaps, one on top of the other. But it doesn't last, I bring them back, little by little, towards me, it's resting time. And with my feet it's the same, sometimes, when I see them at the foot of the bed, one with toes, the other without. And that is more deserving of mention. For my legs,

corresponding here to my arms of a moment ago, are both stiff now and very sore, and I shouldn't be able to forget them as I can my arms, which are more or less sound and well. And yet I do forget them and I watch the couple as they watch each other, a great way off. But my feet are not like my hands I do not bring them back to me, when they become my feet again, for I cannot, but they stay there, far from me, but not so far as before. End of the recall.[13]

Here it is much harder to impose a decisive line between a sense of the real and a sense of the fantastic. Is this a description of the not unusual effect that lying awake in bed produces, when inactivity weakens my sense of living the body and so that it becomes like an object for me? Granted that Molloy is watching the movements of his own hands, how do we respond to the unnervingly plausible suggestion that they are trying to have sexual intercourse with each other? Is this fact, fantasy or a joke aided by the pun on 'pair'? And if it is a joke, it seems about to be repeated at another extreme with the pair of feet, a 'couple' who 'watch each other'?

While Alice's tone of voice was cuddly, domestic and reassuring, Molloy's tone is uneven, unreliable—shifting uncertainly between comedy and horror (why, for example, is there no good answer to the question why Molloy's other foot has no toes?). What blurs the line between fact and fantasy and what makes the tone undecidable is that, far from being a means of stating a truth beyond itself, the language of this text is conscious of itself as *producing* the very possibility of meaning. Symptomatically, the reference to 'my arms of a moment ago' refers to the arms not as they are but as they were *spoken* of a moment ago. The self-consciously abstruse word 'floccillate' (the more familiar term is 'flocculate') confirms this effect, as does, throughout, the 'spokenness' of the short, staccato phrasing. This is writing which impersonates the movements of speech, but not speech as the ideal effect of presence (against which Derrida preaches so instructively) but rather speech as event, event both within discourse known as discourse and event for the subject positioned in relation to discourse. Alice ends with a self-reflective gesture restoring her to commonsense, 'what nonsense I'm talking', while Molloy finishes with a reflection on his own text, 'End of the recall'.

I would like to close by opening a fresh topic, for there is a distinct contrast between the place of rationality in the two passages and I would like to know how far this particular insight might hold for a wider contrast between two opposed national cultures. In Lewis Carroll the departure from empirical fact leads into questions of logic and rationality. If Alice is so much larger, will her head lose contact with her feet? If she is so distant from her feet will she have to treat them as an other? And this fancy in turn leads into her exploring the need (reasonable given the circumstances) to send them new boots 'by the carrier' and so on into the details of how the label on the package would have to be (affectionately) addressed. All this reasoning is based on a logical fallacy, for if she is 'opening out' like a telescope, then presumably her arms will be in proportion, and the problem of their reaching her feet would not arise (as Carroll's drawing of Alice, despite its Magritte-like phallic head and neck, makes clear).

This fantasy deriving from logical extension based on the premiss of the ever-spreading body is part of the pleasurable transgression, and is dismissed in the words 'she went on planning to herself'. It seems the hegemony of empiricism *fears* logic and assigns it a place along with fantasy as a form of deliberate self-indulgence. Not so for Molloy, carrying out a detached and self-critical inspection of his bodily parts, striving for precise distinctions (having said his hands 'are not mine', he hurries to qualify this as 'less than ever mine'), and from the point of view of his own consciousness scrupulously differentiating his arms from his feet on the grounds of

1) pain versus absence of pain

2) which is more easy to forget and

3) possibility of retrieval (he notes that he can bring his arms back but can't bring his feet).

In this discourse rational induction serves instead of empirical knowledge. For Molloy rationality seems to be the only possible source of meaning and coherence yet it is one that constantly fails.

NOTES
1   Jacques Lacan, *Ecrits: A Selection* (London: Tavistock 1977), p.174.
2   James Boswell, *Life of Dr Johnson* (New York: Scribners 1945), p.130.
3   Terry Eagleton, *Heathcliff and the Great Hunger* (London: Verso 1995)
4   ibid., p.149.
5   ibid., p.234.
6   ibid., p.333.
7   ibid., p.170.
8   idem.
9   ibid., pp.170-71.
10 Lacan, op. cit. (1977), p.316.
11 Emile Benveniste, *Problèmes de linguistique générale*, Vol. 2 (Paris: Gallimard 1974), p.84.

12 Lewis Carroll, *Alice's Adventures in Wonderland* (London: Dent 1952), pp.9-10.
13 Samuel Beckett, *Molloy* (NY: Grove Press 1955), p.89.

YEATS AND BECKETT:
FANTASTIC DISCOURSES ON THE STAGE

Irene Eynat-Confino

The perception of the fantastic denotes the ability to distinguish among the many elements that go into the texture of human experience those which escape the rule of reason and consensus reality. As such, the fantastic includes the supernatural as well as the uncanny (or Freud's *umheimlich*).[1]

For is expression, the fantastic requires the structure of a deliberate discourse, artistic or philosophical, a discourse using an accepted code and intending to give an account of an unaccountable phenomenon. The paradox lies in the very act of translating the untranslatable, for the use of an accepted code requires the application of its rules to a phenomenon that escapes them. In other words, the world of the fantastic can be translated only by using the elements and rationale of the world of consensus reality.

The theatre is yet another world, a work of art. As such, it embraces visions of the fantastic as well as visions of consensus reality. Both Yeats and Beckett wrote plays. I propose to dwell here not on the signs and symbols they used as keys to the fantastic, but on the substantiation of the fantastic and its function in their works for the theatre. Each of the two offers a different aesthetic approach to the integration of the supernatural into consensus reality by the mediation of the theatre.

In 1901, in his essay 'Magic', Yeats asserted his belief

> in the practice and philosophy of what we have agreed to call magic, in what I must call the evocation of spirits, though I do not know what they are, in the power of creating magical illusions, in the visions of truth in the depths of the mind when the eyes are closed.[...][2]

He believed, as he carefully explained,

'in three doctrines, which have [...] been handed down from early times, and been the foundations of nearly all magical practices. These doctrines are:

(1) That the borders of our mind are ever shifting, and that many minds can flow into one another, as it were, and create or reveal a single mind, a single energy.

(2) That the borders of our memories are as shifting, and that our memories are a part of one great memory, the memory of Nature herself.

(3) That this great mind and great memory can be evoked by symbols.'

Yeats never disowned his belief in the supernatural as a symbol and key to a parallel system of thought, the product of archetypal imagination.

A brief look at the manifestations of the fantastic in Yeats's plays will first reveal the many supernatural beings who people these plays. In *The Countess Cathleen* (1892), written not long after he compiled the book of *Fairy and Folk Tales of the Irish Peasantry*, the audience hears during the first scene about the bizarre events in the famished countryside. There 'graves are walking'; a man is seen 'with ears spread out [that] moved up and down like a bat's wing'; another 'had no mouth / Nor eyes, nor ears; his face a wall of flesh', while two birds are spotted 'with a human face'.[3] These phenomena take place offstage; onstage, however, two demons disguised as simple merchants take a lively part in the action. In another play, *In The Land of Heart's Desire* (1894), a fairy child, messenger of the Sidhe—the Irish mythological Otherworld or land of the fairies—takes possession of the newly-married bride and claims not only her soul but also her life. In *The Shadowy Waters* (1900) there is magic also. In *The Hour Glass* (1903), an angel, the creature of a dream, materialises onstage; in *On Baile's Strand* (1904)—a changeling turns out to be the reincarnation of Bricriu, an Irish god and one of the chief characters in the play. Bricriu appears again in *The Green Helmet* (1910), as does a unicorn in *The Unicorn from the Stars* (1908) and in *The Player Queen* (1922). A supernatural hawk is placed centre-stage *in At the Hawk's Well* (1917), near the miraculous source of the title. The Sidhe are at work in *The Only Jealousy of Emer* (1919), as are spirits of the past in *The Dreaming of the Bones* (1919). Nor are Yeats's late plays lacking in fantastic characters: for instance, Morrigu, the legendary Irish goddess of war, appears in *The Death of Cuchulain*, the last play he wrote before he died.

The fantastic materialises in Yeats's theatre as dramatic characters, both onstage and offstage, but not only that: it is also communicated by linguistic signs—that is, verbal images which may be construed as symbols and as metaphors, but also by kinetic signs such as the woman's dance in *At the Hawk's Well*, and finally as three-dimensional objects serving as visual signs such as the magic well in the same play. As several commentators have shown, the supernatural characters in Yeats's plays were generally taken from old Irish tales and legends, just as the metaphors and symbols were taken from occult and esoteric philosophy, and the dramatic techniques from French Symbolist theatre and the Noh drama.[4] Yet, while the fantastic has been variously explored as a trope in Yeats's work, it is the power of its physical presence in his theatre that sets it apart. On Yeats's stage, the fantastic is primarily present as an expressive *audial* sign: the sound of the chosen word voiced by the actor or singer. This sound is enhanced by the rhythm of the spoken line, the use of multiple voices (like the chorus in *On Baile's Strand*), and by chant, song and music.

The audial sign is the dominant component of the synchronic orchestration of theatrical devices and the main agent of the affective and cognitive import in Yeats's theatre. A second source of the potency of the fantastic on Yeats's stage is the use of the non-realistic visual signs: masks and non-realistic costumes (as in *At the Hawk's Well* or *The Only Jealousy of Emer*); non-realistic settings (like the 'diapered or gold background' in *The Countess Cathleen*); the empty stage which can function as a non-restrictive metaphor; and kinetic signs like dance and stylised or restricted movement. To this last category belong the dramatic units or 'actions' unaccounted for by 'real', consensus logic. So, for example, in *On Baile's Strand*, the Fool has put 'a curse upon the wind' and was therefore punished by blindness. In *Deirdre*, the supernatural character of a woman is inferred because of an action: 'She never could have played [chess] so, being a woman.' In *The Only Jealousy of Emer*, Bricriu animates Cuchulain's dead body; in another scene Cuchulain returns from the dead, and in *Resurrection* (1931), the resurrected Jesus appears on the stage.

While these devices operate synchronically or diachronically, their rigorous orchestration creates not only a distinct, mythical world but also a special mood, aiming to induce a trance-like state in the spectator—a distinct state of receptivity by means of which he is subtly led to comprehend the world offered to his senses and be engulfed by it. This approach to audience control was prevalent in the Noh and the

Symbolist theatre.[5] The spectator's transition from consensus reality to this fictitious, though sensorally-perceptible world is accomplished so masterfully and smoothly that the auditor comes to share the author's faith, taking the poet's symbolic network into his mind as if it were native to it.[6] In these ways Yeats adapts theatrical medium to his own ends. The theatrical mask thereby ceases to be a masking device and becomes an instrument revealing the hidden but real and potent world of the supernatural. Yeats's purpose is to demonstrate the parallel existence of a supernatural order by means of the lived-experience of the theatre.[7] That experience gives rise to a collective acknowledgement and a living proof of the interpenetration of the real and the supernatural. It is therefore a ritual—sensuous, emotional, and ultimately persuasive.

Yeats was not alone to use the medium of the theatre to introduce, conjure, animate and impart the sense and significance of the fantastic, nor was to use the fantastic in theatre as 'strange' as James Flannery would seem to think.[8] In fact, Yeats shared this theatrical strategy with symbolist playwrights such as his contemporaries Maeterlinck, Jarry and Claudel, while the same strategy was occasionally used by Wilde, Ibsen and Strindberg, as also by Cocteau, Beckett, Ionesco, Arrabal, Ghelderode, Albee, or Tennessee Williams.

Yeats attempts to communicate his belief in the supernatural to those who had not been endowed with visionary powers like his own, be they readers or spectators, though of course the reader's experience must always be different from the spectator's. The reader is often alerted to occurrence of the fantastic *before* it happens by means of the *didascalia*, whereas the spectator apprehends it only at the moment of its actual occurrence on the stage. Because of the linearity of written discourse, the reader often feels himself to be possessed with partial (and often plausible) explanation of the fantastic event, and therefore experiences a diminished sense of mystery and ambiguity while it is unfolding on his 'stage' of his imagination. As for the spectator, the information that he acquires (both diachronically and synchronically) reaches him in the course of a continuous process of intellectual response, arising from the sensory and affective elements of the theatrical experience. Furthermore, group dynamics and the captive situation of the theatre audience work together to intensify the bonding and bounding state of receptivity created by the sights and sounds of a stage such as Yeats's, producing a form of compliance audience.

To accept what seems a self-contradictory attitude may be puzzling to a scientifically-trained mind; yet Yeats firmly believed in the existence of a spiritual world quite distinct from consensus reality and consciously employed elements of this separate world as dramatic figures in his art. For Yeats this contradiction was non-existent. His belief in a parallel system of thought, the product of archetypal imagination, gave sense and purpose to his life both as an artist and as a human being. His system of spiritual beliefs enlarged the scope of his daily experience occurrences and conferred on them a spiritually sustaining aura of significance. In this way Yeats used the theatre as a vehicle for his all-encompassing system of belief, and thus fulfilled the shamanistic role that he associated with the office of the modern bard.

Samuel Beckett, too, uses the fantastic for epistemological purposes. The blossoming of the old, withered tree within one day in his play *Waiting for Godot* (1949) is not a natural phenomenon. This resort to the fantastic has been variously construed by Beckett scholars, but the Irish soil out of which the mound is raised has been strangely overlooked. If Beckett's use of symbols has been examined intently, not so his use of the fantastic.

The mound in *Waiting for Godot* is a supernatural property borrowed from ancient Irish culture and mythology, as is many another fantastic element in Beckett's plays. On such Celtic sites, trees were venerated in ancient times, as the classical writers tell us. By virtue of that mound, it may be said that the world of Beckett's play borders on Otherworld. The French text specifies only '*route à la campagne avec arbre*' (or, 'country road with tree'); but lest the metaphorical significance be lost on an English-speaking audience, Beckett has added other fantastic elements such as the telescoping most overtly displayed by the device of making the withered tree blossom in one day.[9] As in the Irish Otherworld, life seems here an endless period of waiting. Like the Otherworld also, it has two aspects: sometimes it is a Land of Youth and sometimes a dark realm full of monstrous creatures. The monstrous dimension of Beckett's otherworld is represented by Lucky, whose mental and physical degeneration is a testimony to the fate that awaits us all and the reward for human *hubris*. Something of a bard, Lucky has his counterpart in the Gaelic *fili* or learned poets— those seers, teachers, and royal counsellors whose satirical poems could cause deaths.

In another of Beckett's plays, *Happy Days* (1960), an Irish mythological mound is again the centre of the action. Act I opens on an 'expanse of scorched grass rising centre to low mound'. Winnie is 'embedded up to above her waist in exact centre of mound'.[10] The connotations of the Otherworld and the mound as burial place are clearer now. The image of Winnie halfburied in her mound readily connotes the literary effects of the fantastic, while the uncanny is conjured by the juxtaposition of her commonplace activities with her unaccountable immersion in the earth. The ringing of the bell that punctuates her daily rituals reinforces a sense of the uncanny. In this gloomy version of the Otherworld, the descent into the earth is apparently an unending process—a gradual transition from one state to another. In the course of the play Winnie advances from the human condition, shared with the audience, to the condition of a half-human half-elemental being, effectively taking us with her.

The cauldron, or the Beckettian urn or bin, is a comparable visual sign of the fantastic. The huge cauldrons of Irish mythology had magic powers of restoration: in *Endgame* (1956) Beckett plays upon these mythological connotations in placing Nagg and Nell in bins, a fate not which—though intelligible in terms of family history—is not explained in any part of the play. One thing is clear: the magic cauldron's powers of restoration are put in question, as are real-life familial relationships throughout the play. In *Play* (1963), the placing of three big urns on stage, each with a head protruding from it, reinforces the mythological dimension of drama: the restoring power of the Irish mythological cauldron has remained intact. Here the supposedly dead are not only thriving in the Other World, they are condemned to re-enact a horrendous vaudevillian parody of the network of adultery in which they were involved in this one (a Dantesque touch recurring in the adventures of Belacqua). In the ancient Irish tale, the head of the slain Sualtam, Cuchulain's father, did not cease shouting out its message until it had succeeded in dispelling the curse cast on the men of Ulster by Macha. Likewise, Beckett's sarcastic message derides human emotion and destroys whatever illusions the reader/spectator may be harbouring.

Triads, a recurrent motif in Irish mythology, is used by Beckett in *Come and Go* (1965), where the three interchangeable female characters, Flo, Vi, and Ru evoke the three identical figures of Irish mythology, Fodla, Eriu and Banbha, the eponymous goddesses of Ireland recorded in the *Lebor Gabala* (*Book of Invasions*). Beckett's three characters are likewise reminiscent of the three deities who wreaked havoc in Irish mythology by their presence alone: that is, the

Morriga, variously known as the Morrigan, Nemhain and Macha. Beckett's three characters hold hands 'in the old way', arms intertwined like circles in old Irish works of art.[11] A pervasive sense of the supernatural is further sustained in the play by the audial signs (i.e., repetitious and enigmatic speech); telescoping of time (i.e., the brevity of the ritualistic performance); as much as by the visual effect of the three such outlandish characters.

The devastating scream, a recurrent motif in Irish mythology, furnishes Beckett's drama with a further audial token of the fantastic. Such was Deirdre's scream while she was still in her mother's womb, or Macha's screams that cast the spell on the men of Ulster for nine generations. Beckett's play *Breath* is built around a single 'faint brief cry', an apocalyptic sound amidst the horrifying spectacle created by the visible decay on the stage.[12]

The theatre allows Beckett not only to make visible and audible a mental condition, but also to reach, stimulate, and control his audience emotionally. In his drama, the visual element is the dominant sign by which the fantastic is expressed. The radio provides him another medium where invisibility enhances the threatening effect of the horrific fantastic elements. The audience cannot see now, it can only hear. In Beckett's radio plays, the impossibility of seeing is in fact an essential component in the blurring of the boundaries between fantasy as a subjective state of mind, the fantastic as a parallel world, and consensus reality. In *Embers* (1959), Henry—and the audience—hears the voice of his dead wife Ada. This voice is clearly not that of a ghost—another fantastic element—but the audible manifestation of a disembodied consciousness. However, in *Cascando* (1962), another radio play, a pervasive ambiguity about the nature of the double (itself a sufficiently fantastic element) persists throughout the play, and ambiguity is by definition one of the main foundations of the fantastic. If doubt is eliminated and an explanation offered, the fantastic vanishes into consensus reality.[13] In this radio play, the presence of the double is made audially perceptible by the dissociation between the voice of the character referred to in the text as 'Opener' and his presumedly separated identity as the 'Voice'.

From the outset this dissociation invests the play with a feeling of the uncanny, as when the Opener says: 'It is the month of May [...] for me.'[14] By his appropriation of time, the Opener places the unfolding occurrence in a different realm. However, Beckett soon dissipates the illusion of a newly created, fantastic, coherent world by another defamiliarising device, the disrupted speech of the Voice, the Opener's double. The feeling of the uncanny introduced by this disrupted speech—where the word ceases to function as a vehicle for meaning and becomes instead an audible sign initiating an exegetical process in the audience—is so overwhelming that it debunks the coherence of the newly invented parallel world. Our doubts about the independent existence of the Voice persist even after the Opener's own voice merges with it and with what seems now to have been still another 'double', the sound of the Music. The same audial technique of dissociation is used in *That Time* (1975), where the self is embodied, to threatening effect, by three voices.

The dissociation of self by physical multiplication is a technique often used by Beckett in his later plays. Doubles are used in *Ohio Impromptu* (1980), and quadruples in *What Where* (performed in 1983). In *Nacht und Traume*, a television play from 1982, the double is visualised as the dreamt self, and thus pertains to 'consensus imagination' rather than the fantastic. On the other hand, another fantastic theme appears in this play, dismemberment: parts of the body move of their own—a visual effect made possible by the television medium.

Although Beckett commentators have, as a rule, highlighted other aspects of his work, the fantastic as a narrative element is essential in creating the apocalyptic mood that permeates his plays.[15] Unlike Yeats, however, Beckett integrates the fantastic into a realistic discourse where it takes on a catalytic, subversive role, thereby initiating an exegetical process. As a result, not only is the fictive realistic discourse on-stage questioned, but so is consensus reality itself. Beckett's apocalyptic fantastic triggers various significant effects, philosophical and psychological, and creates a mood of gloom and negation that permeates the spectator's mind long after he has left the theatre.

Theatre is structured on binaries, a play between visibility and invisibility, between the presentation of consensus reality and that of consensus imagination. The use of the fantastic as a dialectical tool that debunks the myth of consensus reality is common to Yeats and Beckett. For Yeats, the fantastic was the initiatory key to the understanding of an existing parallel world obscured by consensus reality. His theatrical achievement, decried by some and praised by others, stood out as a poetic experiment among a plethora of realistic productions, from the beginning of the twentieth century until our own time; but more recently the non-realistic postmodern theatre has legitimised new aesthetic norms. Yeats's minimalist stage, with its mesmerising rhythmic sounds, unobtrusive settings, stylised gestures, costumes and masks, offers a captivating solution to the representation of the fantastic onstage. To a postmodern aesthetics based on shock tactics and nihilism, horror and pity, Yeats's theatre offers an aesthetics of wonder and belief, fear and compassion. Yeats offers the vision of a different realm that combines the lessons of a symbolic, mythical past with the hope of a better future. His is not a phantasmagorical theatre, as Flannery maintains, but the substantiation of a coherent vision, the vision of a realm that is not separate from everyday experience but part of it.

For Beckett, the fantastic was an epistemological tool adroitly used to reveal not a parallel world of hope and redemption, like Yeats's, but one of unredeemable, endless suffering. For both writers, the fantastic was a key to a better understanding of human experience. Unfortunately, for today's audience the fantastic is too often an enigmatic key. The multiple meanings of the various culturally-embedded signs are seldom apprehended by an audience brought up on *ET*, *Superman*, or *Star Wars*. The key to the apprehension of old Irish mythological symbols belongs now to a small, cultured elite, while the larger theatre audiences are better acquainted with the newer myths disseminated by mass media. This is why in Beckett's *Waiting for Godot*, the mound, site of the fairies, is literally overshadowed by the eye-catching withered tree. Reality is not what it used to be. But neither is the fantastic.

NOTES
1   See Kathryn Hume, *Fantasy and Mimesis: Responses to Reality in Western Literature* (London: Methuen 1984), p.xii.
2   W. B. Yeats, *Essays and Introductions* (London: Macmillan 1969), p.28.
3   W. B. Yeats, *Collected Plays* (London: Macmillan 1969), pp.3-4.
4   See, for example, Richard Taylor, *The Drama of W. B. Yeats: Irish Myth and the Japanese No* (Yale UP 1976); George Mills Harper, ed., *Yeats and the Occult* (London: Macmillan 1975); Reg Skene, *The Cuchulain Plays of W. B. Yeats: A Study* (London: Macmillan 1974); Denis Donoghue, *William Butler Yeats* (NY: The Echo Press 1971, rep. 1988); W. Y. Tindall, 'The Symbolism of W. B. Yeats', in *Yeats: A Collection of Critical Essays*, ed., John Unterecker (Englewood Cliffs, N.J.: Prentice Hall 1963), pp.43-53.
5   Donoghue, op. cit. (1988), pp.107-12; R. Taylor, op. cit. (1976).
6   Skene, op. cit. (1974)
7   For the specific dramatic techniques involved in this, see Yeats's essay 'Emotion of Multitude' (1903).

8   J. W. Flannery, 'Staging the Phantasmagorical: The Theatrical Challenges and Rewards of William Butler Yeats', in *Visions of the Fantastic*, ed. A. R. Becker (Westport, Conn.: Greenwood Publishing 1996), pp.149-65.
9   Samuel Beckett, *En Attendant Godot* (Paris: Editions de Minuit 1952), p.11; *Waiting for Godot* (London: Faber & Faber 1965), p.9.
10 Beckett, *Happy Days* (London: Faber & Faber 1966), p.1.
11 Beckett, *Collected Shorter Plays* (London: Faber and Faber 1984), p.195.
12 Beckett, *Breath and Other Shorts* (London: Faber and Faber 1971), p.11.
13 Tzvetan Todorov, *Introduction à la littérature fantastique* (Paris: Seuil 1970); N. Cornwell, *The Literary Fantastic: From Gothic to Postmodernism* (Hemel Hempstead: Harvester Wheatsheaf 1990); Brian Attebery, *Strategies of Fantasy* (Bloomington: Indiana UP 1992).
14 Beckett, *Collected Shorter Plays*, p.137.
15 K. H. Burkman, *The Arrival of Godot: Ritual Patterns in Modern Drama* (London and Toronto: Associated UP 1986); Lance Olsen, 'Beckett and the Horrific', in *Staging the Impossible: The Fantastic Mode in Modern Drama*, ed. Patrick D. Murphy (Westport, Conn.: Greenwood Publishing 1992), pp.116-26.

TERMINAL FANTASIES: BECKETT AND KAFKA

Mark Harman

In the unending days and nights
Of unending melancholy

Beckett, *Malone Dies*

A first sign of nascent knowledge is the desire for death.

Kafka aphorism

Samuel Beckett's fantasies are written on the edge of silence and of death. So, too, are Franz Kafka's:

> [...] the best things I have written have their basis in this capacity of mine to meet death with contentment. All these fine and very convincing passages always deal with the fact that someone is dying, that it is hard for him to do, that it seems unjust to him, or at least harsh, and the reader is moved by this, or at least he should be.[1]

In Beckett as in Kafka, this preoccupation with death is often displaced into febrile reasoning about inconsequential activities. Both writers profited from Pascal and Schopenhauer, and their characters' obsessive cogitations are merely a distraction—in the Pascalian sense—from the death that awaits them. Out of this preoccupation with melancholia and death each evolves a comparable aesthetics and creates what one might call self-erasing fantasies.

Kafka had an early epiphany in which he glimpsed the self-annihilating form that would underlie his fiction:

> Many years ago I sat one day, in a sad enough mood, on the slopes of the Laurenziberg. I went over the wishes that I wanted to realise in life. I found that the most important was to attain a view of life in which life [...] would be recognised [...] as a nothing [...] a dream, a dim hovering [...] somewhat as if one were to hammer together a table with painful and methodical technical efficiency, and simultaneously do nothing at all, and not in such a way that people could say: 'Hammering a table together is nothing to him' but rather: 'Hammering a table together is really hammering a table together to him, but at the

same time it is nothing', whereby certainly the hammering would have become still bolder, still surer, still more real, and if you will, still more senseless.[1]

Beckett and Kafka both endeavour to create analogues for that table which is both something and nothing. In this they are not unique. There is a long tradition of self-conscious—and self-cancelling—fantasy from Don Quixote all the way through to Borges and Flann O'Brien. Kafka and Beckett push this self-questioning form of fantasy toward an extreme, and mine it for its philosophical implications while rarely resorting to the conceptual language of philosophy.

Kafka's vision of art as something and at the same time nothing— 'a nothing, a dream, a dim hovering'—is remarkably close to Beckett's aesthetics of failure. In a 1937 letter to Axel Kaun (written in Beckett's self-taught but remarkably proficient German), Beckett speaks of wanting 'to bore one hole after another into it (language), until what lurks behind—be it something or nothing—begins to seep through'. His goal in ripping apart the veil of language is 'to feel a whisper of that final music or that silence that underlies all'.[2]

Later, in the much-quoted *Dialogues with Georges Duthuit* (1949), Beckett calls for an art that would prefer 'the expression that there is nothing to express, nothing with which to express, nothing from which to express, no power to express, no desire to express, together with the obligation to express'. In June 1921—three years before his premature death of tuberculosis—Kafka connects his comparable recognition of the futility of writing with the difficulties Jews encounter writing in German:

> They [i.e., Jewish writers of German] existed among three impossibilities, which I just happen to call linguistic impossibilities [...] These are: the impossibility of not writing, the impossibility of writing German, the impossibility of writing differently. One might also add a fourth impossibility, the impossibility of writing [...].[3]

Like so many of Beckett's stories and plays, Kafka's late stories threaten to lapse into silence. In "Josefine the Singer, or the Mouse Folk", for instance, the narrator stresses that he and the mouse folk value Josephine more for her silences than for the undistinguished piping sounds on which she prides herself. And when it comes to wasting away, Kafka's "Hunger Artist" surely outdoes all of Beckett's figures, since he quite literally consumes himself to death. Like some of Beckett's *œuvre*, Kafka's late works represent 'a peculiar sophistication of expressionist theory, for the art is still a self-dramatisation, but a dramatisation of the self's wasting'.[4]

In post-war Paris, just when Beckett was struggling to step out of Joyce's shadow, Kafka was all the rage. Even in Dublin, as Beckett himself sadly informed Joyce the intellectuals were not interested in *Ulysses*, because they were too busy reading Kafka.[5] In this context it is not surprising that Beckett should have gone on the offensive to prevent his being perceived as a Kafka epigone. However, it is clear now, especially thanks to James Knowlson's recent biography, that Beckett's knowledge of German literature and art is deeper than we used to suspect.[6] If Beckett's comments about Kafka betray a certain anxiety of influence, they also show how closely he read his Prague rival:

> 'I've only read Kafka in German—serious reading—[...] only *The Castle* in German. I must say it was difficult to get to the end. The Kafka hero has a coherence of purpose. He's lost but he's not spiritually precarious, he's not falling to bits. My people seem to be falling to bits. Another difference. You notice how Kafka's form is classic. It goes on like a steamroller—almost serene. It *seems* to be threatened the whole time—but the consternation is in the form. In my work there is consternation behind the form, not in the form.'[7]

Beckett's remark that he found it difficult to get to the end of *The Castle*—a phenomenon not entirely unknown among readers of Beckett's own prose—doesn't quite square with his acute perception that Kafka's form goes on 'like a steamroller'. Beckett thus seizes on a key feature of Kafka's prose—its relentlessness—a stylistic trait that had passed unremarked in the voluminous discussions of *The Castle* by German-language writers and critics. Sometimes it takes an outsider with the linguistic discernment of a Beckett to spot essential characteristics of foreign masterworks.

Beckett's astuteness about *The Castle* is all the more remarkable given that he was reading the original in the edition of Kafka's friend and first editor Max Brod. Brod normalised Kafka's punctuation and made other significant changes—roughly two per page.[8] Malcolm Pasley's edition restores the loosely punctuated sentences and the breathless effect of his seemingly never-ending paragraphs, which do not separate out the dialogue from the narrative and thus create a rush of language.

There has been some dispute about the wisdom of adhering to Kafka's punctuation. Like Beckett, who avows his dislike of semicolons in *Watt* and abandons them thereafter, Kafka restricts his punctuation to commas and the occasional full-stop. Some German critics have argued that Kafka would have inserted orthodox punctuation had he prepared the manuscript of *The Castle* for publication. But Kafka, like Beckett, was fully aware of the expressive function of commas and full stops. In a diary entry dated 26 March, 1911 he writes:

> Omission of the full stop. In general the spoken sentence starts off in a large capital letter with the speaker, bends out in its course as far as it can towards the listener and with the full stop returns to the speaker. But if the full-stop is omitted, then the sentence is no longer constrained and blows its entire breath at the listener.

When Beckett says that in his own writing the 'consternation is behind the form, not in the form', he is putting his finger on a significant difference between Kafka's *Castle* and his own work: Kafka's narrative is linear; his is disjunctive. On another level, however, Kafka's deepest preoccupations do indeed lie behind the form. In *The Castle,* as in most of his other works, Kafka is playing a cat and mouse game with his character and with the reader. Unlike his hero, Kafka himself has no faith in the relentless quest to penetrate through to the Castle.[9]

On first reading Beckett's comment on the steamroller-like quality of Kafka's prose I couldn't quite see what Beckett meant. Only while preparing a new translation of *The Castle*—based on Pasley's critical edition—did it suddenly become clear to me that Beckett is right. There is an odd discrepancy in Kafka's third and final novel between the lack of action—the hero K. goes round and round in circles and never penetrates through to the mysterious Castle—and the relentless momentum of the language itself which presses on and on in a manner that anticipates Beckett's own steamroller effect. While Beckett's prose is more colloquial than Kafka's, it too has an urgent forward drive.

The Castle is Kafka's most Beckettian novel. For one thing Kafka began writing the novel in the first person—a mode more characteristic of Beckett than of Kafka. In the beginning there was no K., only an I. In the course of penning the third chapter Kafka went back and replaced all the "I's" with "K.'s". The traces left by these first-person origins accentuate the sensation that we are stuck inside K.'s head, eavesdropping on his obsessive thoughts.

Kafka may well have given up on the first person narrative out of unease at the thought of writing in the first person lovemaking scenes such as the following:

> Hours passed there, hours breathing together with a single heartbeat, hours in which K. constantly felt he was lost or had wandered farther into foreign lands than any human being before him, so foreign that even the air hadn't a single component of the air in his homeland and where one would inevitably suffocate from the foreignness but where the meaningless enticements were such that one had no alternative but to go on and get even more lost. (*C*, p.41.)

Malone's lovemaking is equally desolate:

> 'Let us think of the hours when, spent, we lie twined together in the dark, our hearts labouring as one, and listen to the wind saying what it is to be abroad, at night, in winter, and what it is to have been what we have been, and sink together, in an unhappiness that has no name.'[10]

In Beckett, sex is often no more than a gateway to nameless unhappiness. In Kafka, it provides new air which, however, suffocates rather than replenishes. Malone claims to find in his literary creations a new source of air. His invention of the dull-witted child Sapo— endowed with Beckett's 'palest blue' eyes (*MD*, p.191)—yields 'the air I needed, a lively tenuous air, far from the nourishing murk that is killing me' (*MD*, p.193).

The most Beckettian passage in *The Castle* occurs when a barmaid called Pepi invites K. to come live with her and two other girls in a cellar room. The ensuing exchange suggests a climactic as well as temporal stasis that points forward, beyond Kafka's nameless village and Castle, to Beckett's even more abstract landscapes:

> 'So will you come? How much longer is it till spring?' asked K. 'Till spring?' repeated Pepi, 'the winter here is long, a very long winter, and monotonous. But we don't complain about that down here, we're safe from the winter. Of course at some point spring does come and summer too, and they certainly have their day, but in one's memory spring and summer seem short, as if they didn't last much longer than two days, and sometimes even on those days, throughout the most beautiful day, snow falls.' (*C*, p.312.)

There is no doubt that Beckett's reading of *The Castle* left discernible traces in *Watt*, as Ruby Cohn and Edith Kern have shown.[11] Kafka's depiction of the elusive Castle official Klamm clearly inspired Beckett's remarkably comparable rendering of Mr Knott, who is of course the forefather of Youdi in *Molloy* and of Godot in *Waiting for Godot*. By a piquant coincidence, one of Kafka's original chapter headings, not included by Max Brod in his editions but restored by Malcolm Pasley in the 1982 German critical edition, was "*Das Warten auf Klamm*", or "Waiting for Klamm".

Kafka, who anticipated ending *The Castle* with the death of K., concedes in his diaries that such death scenes deliberately exploit the discrepancy between the reader's fear of death and his own longing for it: '[...] for me, who believe that I shall be able to lie contentedly on my deathbed, such scenes are secretly a game; indeed, in the death enacted I rejoice in my own death, hence calculatingly exploit the attention that the reader concentrates on death, have a much clearer understanding of it than he, of whom I suppose that he will loudly lament on his deathbed.' (*D*, p.321)

As Christopher Ricks suggests in his witty book *Beckett's Dying Words*, Beckett is a writer who reveals to us in stark form the fact that most of us at some point, at some level long for death.[12] Yet Beckett does not entirely banish his characters' fear of death. A comparison of *Malone Dies* and Kafka's late stories shows that the fear goes underground in Beckett, as it does—quite literally—in Kafka.

Beckett's characters are so intent on welcoming death that they seldom acknowledge their fear of it. Malone is disgruntled he cannot rid his mind of Democritus's bleak aphorism, a favourite of Beckett's—*Nothing is more real than nothing*. He fears the melancholia into which such phrases plunge him, for they 'rise up out of the pit and know no rest until they drag you down into its dark' (*MD*, p.192). Only rarely does he admit his reluctance to die: 'Yes, there is no good pretending, it is hard to leave everything' (*MD*, p.107).

In Kafka's story "The Burrow"—though "The Construction" would be a more precise equivalent for Kafka's neutral title "*Der Bau*"—the anonymous animal hero describes in great detail an underground maze it has constructed, partly by smashing its own forehead against the earth. He—I am assuming the animal is male—never explicitly owns up to the fact that his obsessive reasoning is driven by a fear of death. As in "Josephine the Singer, or the Mouse Folk" and in "Hunger Artist", the hero is about to disappear. The animal's disappearance will come about when his adversary—around whom his thoughts continuously circle—and he come face to face. Then they will lock together in a fight to the death. This other creature may well be a fictional representation of the tuberculosis that is galloping through the body of Kafka, who has only months to live when he writes "The Burrow". That vision of mortal combat represents the closest depiction of death that we get in the story, which then breaks off.

Although Kafka evidently finished the story, the ending was lost. We can only speculate as to whether that missing ending came close to the perfect lament that Kafka envisages in his diaries: 'my lament is as perfect as can be, nor does it suddenly break off, as is likely to be the case with a real lament, but dies beautifully and purely away' (*D*, p.321). Still, the non-ending we are left with is not an inappropriate conclusion for this terminal tale. Like Kafka's *Castle* in the restored text of the critical edition,[13] Beckett's *Malone Dies* tapers off, with the following fragmentary phrases:

> never there he will never
> never anything
> there
> any more

While Beckett's characters claim to be much in love with easeful death, the fantasies that they spin are actually designed to distract them from the death that they ostensibly welcome. This tension is already apparent in the opening lines of *Malone Dies*. In the first sentence Malone announces his imminent departure—'I shall soon be quite dead at last'—only to add 'I would not put it past me to pant on' (*MD*, p.179). And on and on, I would add. However much Beckett's characters may look forward to their demise, their's is a protracted farewell.

Ostensibly, Malone is attempting to observe himself dying by penetrating through to an Ur-self behind the self. Nevertheless, he announces in the opening lines: 'I shall not watch myself die, that would spoil everything' (*MD*, p.179). Spoil everything because he wants to die—at least on the surface. In the course of his jottings he invents alternate selves such as Saposcat and Macmann only to extinguish them. As he dryly notes, 'my notes have a curious tendency [...] to annihilate all they purport to record' (*MD*, p.259).

In "The Burrow" the level of violence is unusually strong for Kafka. The animal imagines what he may do to his antagonist: 'I might in my blind rage leap on him, maul him, tear the flesh from his bones, destroy him, drink his blood and fling his corpse among the rest of my spoil.'[14] That violence testifies to the extremity of the predicament in which Kafka's mole-like creature is trapped. Kafka was fascinated with moles, who occasionally surface in his letters. Beckett, too, felt a kinship with moles, once observing of himself: 'I am like a mole in a tunnel.'[15]

Malone alludes to characters such as Watt whom he—or rather Beckett—has conjured up in the past. Likewise, Kafka reflects about his own literary *œuvre* through his alter ego's musings about his underground lair. The various passages in the labyrinth that the animal is attempting to construct correspond to individual works. For instance, in describing the earliest part of the construction, the animal may be alluding to Kafka's literary breakthrough "The Judgement": 'a labyrinthine burrow which at the time seemed to me the crown of all burrows, but which I judge today, perhaps with more justice [...] to be [...] a flimsy piece of jugglery that would hardly withstand a serious attack [...]' (*TB*, p.97).

In his final moments Malone wants to observe the death of the other self he has created: 'To show myself now, on the point of vanishing, at the same time as the stranger, and by the same grace, that would be no ordinary last straw. Then live, long enough to see, behind my closed eyes, other eyes close. What an end.' (*MD*, p.195.) The animal in the "Burrow" has a comparable obsession: he wants to be simultaneously inside and outside the burrow. As with Malone, this quest to split himself in two is futile.

Like so many of Beckett's characters, Kafka's animal is a recluse who has attempted to seal himself off from the world. In this he has been only partly successful. He cannot avoid all contact with an outside world perceived as a constant threat. He creates inventories of his possessions—his prize items being not hats and sticks, as in Beckett, but food stores. He worries constantly about the security of his food—a leitmotif in Kafka's fiction and the crux around which "A Hunger Artist" is constructed: 'The place is so spacious that food for half a year scarcely fills it. Consequently I can divide up my stores, walk about among them, play with them, enjoy their plenty and their various smells, and reckon up exactly how much they represent. That done, I can always [...] make my calculations [...] for the future.' (*TB*, p.94.) Malone also prepares for his demise—or, as he puts it, his 'great day'—by counting his possessions: 'I want, when the great day comes, to be in a position to enounce clearly [...] all that its interminable prelude [...] had brought me and left me in the way of chattels personal.' And then he adds: 'I presume it is an obsession.'

Kafka's characters fret as much as Beckett's do. However, unlike their counterparts, they eschew psychological terms such as obsession. Kafka was wary of Freud and kept his distance from psychoanalysis whereas Beckett underwent therapy at the Tavistock Clinic in London and drew on depth psychology in his writings.[16]

The digging of Kafka's animal involves laborious calculations and the sheer pleasure of the mind in its own keenness is often the sole reason why he persists. Beckett's characters fill the interminable wait with equally futile activities. Malone, for instance, questions whether he should go on compiling an inventory of his possessions: 'So I wonder if I should go on [...] and if I should not rather cut it short and devote myself to some other form of distraction, of less consequence, or simply wait, doing nothing, or counting perhaps, one, two three and so on [...]' (*MD*, p.251). The characters derive a sort of grim joy from their futile endeavours. Kafka's animal has his 'joy in labour'. Beckett's Malone speaks in Schopenhauerian terms of 'the black joy of the solitary way, in helplessness and will-lessness' (*MD*, p.278).

Malone is more playful than the heroes of Kafka's late stories. At the outset he declares: 'From now on it will be different. I shall never do anything any more from now on but play' (*MD*, p.180). It is of course a rather morbid form of play. But this, too, does not escape Malone, whose self-awareness is one of his saving graces: 'What tedium. And I call that playing.' (*MD*, p.186.) He speaks of having overcome 'the wild beast of earnestness' in the course of which he 'padded up and down, roaring, ravening, rending'. Whereas Kafka's heroes in stories such as the "Burrow" and "Hunger Artist" are still 'ravening, rending', Malone strives to introduce 'a little variety' into his 'decomposition' (*MD*, p.254).

He can even crack jokes about his own morbidity: 'I pause to record that I feel in extraordinary form. Delirium perhaps.' (*MD*, p.257.) Kafka, too, has a bleak sense of humour, but it is not particularly evident in the "Burrow". Of course, unlike Beckett, who wrote *Malone Dies* in Paris in the late forties, Kafka knew while writing "The Burrow" in late 1923 or early 1924 that he had not much longer to live.

In Beckett's *Watt* a character called Arsene defines the 'mirthless [...] dianoetic laugh' as 'the laugh that laughs [...] at that which is unhappy'.[17] Readers of both writers are well acquainted with that kind of laughter. It is as difficult to suppress a quiet chuckle on reading the dismal first fine of Beckett's *Murphy*—'The sun shone, having no alternative, on the nothing new'—as it is on hearing the following exchange between Kafka and Brod:

> Kafka: I believe we are not such a radical relapse of God's, only one of his bad moods. He had a bad day.
> Brod: Is there hope for us?
> Kafka: Plenty of hope—for God—no end of hope, only not for us.

In 1983 Beckett complains of feeling 'inertia and void as never before' and recalls an entry in Kafka's diary: 'Gardening. No hope for the future.' Savouring an opportunity to trump Kafka's pessimism, Beckett adds wryly: 'At least he could garden.'[18] However, by 1922 gardening was no longer an option for Kafka.

Kafka is never more Beckettian than when he is envisioning his own death. In a letter to Max Brod dated 5 July, 1922, he characterises writers like himself: 'Such a writer is continually staging a scene: He dies (or rather he does not live) and continually mourns himself. From this springs a terrible fear of death [...].' There are two reasons why such a writer so fears death: 'First he has a terrible fear of dying because he has not yet lived.' Second, says Kafka, switching to the first person: 'I have not bought myself off by my writing. I died my whole life long and now I will really die.' Kafka then envisages the twin deaths of his writer's self and of his biographical persona: 'Of course the writer in me will die right away, since such a figure has no base, no substance, is less than dust [...]. But I myself cannot go on living because I have not lived, I have remained clay, I have not blown the spark into fire, but only used it to light up my corpse.' To readers of Beckett's novels and plays, Kafka's subsequent vision of his final days may sound uncannily familiar:

' [...] from now on I may not go out of Bohemia, next I will be confined to Prague, then to my room, then to my bed, then to a certain position in bed, then to nothing more.'

NOTES
1 Kafka, *The Diaries 1910-1923*, ed., Max Brod, trans., Joseph Kresh, et al. (NY: Schocken Books 1976), p.321; henceforth *D*.
2 Samuel Beckett, *Disjecta* (London: John Calder 1983), pp.171-73. Trans. Martin Esslin. In the letter to Axel Kaun, Beckett explicitly disavows Joyce as a model: 'With such a program, in my opinion, the latest work of Joyce has nothing whatsoever to do.' That disclaimer ought to give pause to those who persist in linking Beckett's modernism to his assertion that *Finnegans Wake* is *not* about something but is that something itself. It is surely high time to acknowledge that Kafka's negative aesthetics, with its inherent scepticism about language, is closer to Beckett's artistic program than Joyce's ever was.
3 Kafka, *Letters to Friends, Family and Editors*, trans., Richard and Clara Winston (NY: Schocken Books 1977), p.289; henceforth *L*.
4 Daniel Albright, *Representation and the Imagination: Beckett, Kafka, Nabokov, and Schoenberg* (Chicago UP 1981), p.143.
5 Richard Ellmann, *James Joyce* [new & rev. edn.] (OUP 1982), p.702.
6 See James Knowlson, *Damned to Fame: The Life of Samuel Beckett* (NY: Simon & Schuster 1996).
7 Interview, *New York Times*, May 6, 1956.

8   For further discussion of the Beckett-like features of Kafka's style in the critical edition of *The Castle,* see Mark Harman, 'Digging the Pit of Babel: Retranslating Franz Kafka's *Castle*', in *New Literary History,* 27 (1996), pp.291-311.
9   Tzvetan Todorov—whose name has been frequently invoked throughout this conference—has great difficulty incorporating Kafka into his definition of the fantastic. I would suggest that the difficulty may have something to do with Todorov's failure to acknowledge that Kafka's deepest preoccupations are often hidden under, or behind, the form of his texts. Todorov writes that 'the Kafkaesque narrative abandons what we had said was the second condition of the fantastic [...]: the hesitation represented within the text'. (Todorov, *The Fantastic: A Structural Approach to a Literary Genre,* Cornell UP 1975, p.173.) Yet Kafka's own aphorisms indicate quite clearly that he believed that such hesitation was the only appropriate response to the supernatural. In *The Castle,* K. is impatient and wants to barge into the Castle. For Kafka the aphorist, impatience is the cardinal sin: 'Because of impatience we were driven out of Paradise, because of impatience we cannot return.' ('Reflections on Sin, Pain, Hope, and the True Way', p.3.) In *The Castle* K. ought to hesitate but he does not. Unlike Kafka, he ignores the paradoxes implicit in the very notion of the way: 'The true way goes over a rope which is not stretched at any great height but just above the ground. It seems more designed to make people stumble than to be walked upon.' ('Reflections', p.1). *The Castle* is a modernist fantasy that must be read against the grain.
10 *Malone Dies,* in *Molloy, Malone Dies, The Unnamable* (NY: Grove Weidenfeld 1965), p.262; henceforth *MD.*
11 Ruby Cohn, '*Watt* in the Light of *The Castle*', in *Comparative Literature,* 13 (1961), pp.154-66; Edith Kern, 'Reflections on the Castle and Mr Knott's House: Kafka and Beckett', in *Franz Kafka: His Place in World Literature* [Proceedings of the Comparative Literature Symposium] (Tech. University 1971), pp.97-112
12 Christopher Ricks, *Beckett's Dying Words: The Clarendon Lectures 1990* (OUP 1993)
13 In the new edition of *The Castle* the novel ends in mid-sentence. In the final fragmentary sentence, which follows, the pronoun 'she' refers to the mother of a coachman called Gerstacker: 'She held out her trembling hand to K. and had him sit down beside her; she spoke with great difficulty, it was difficult to understand her, but what she said.' *The Castle,* trans. Mark Harman (1998), p.316.
14 *The Basic Kafka,* trans., Edwin and Willa Muir, et al, intro, Erich Heller (NY: Washington Square Press 1979), p.103.
15 Charles Juliet, 'Meeting Beckett' [trans., Suzanne Chamier], in *Triquarterly,* 77 (1989-90), p.13.
16 A comparative study of Beckett and Kafka from the perspective of depth psychology—along the lines of J. D. O'Hara's stimulating recent study, *Samuel Beckett's Hidden Drives: Structural Uses of Depth Psychology* (1997)—might yield worthwhile insights.
17 *Watt* (NY: Grove Weidenfeld 1953), p.48.
18 James Knowlson, op. cit. (1996), p.601.

FLANN O'BRIEN'S OTHER WORLD OF FANTASY

Joseph M. Hassett

Serious readers of Flann O'Brien's novels are quick to find them fantastic. When Graham Greene encountered Flann O'Brien's first novel, *At Swim Two Birds,* as a reader for Longman's Green, he found its 'books inside books' structure 'a wild, fantastic, magnificently comic notion'.[1] His successor, the Longman's reader for O'Brien's second novel, *The Third Policeman,* said this: 'We realise the author's ability but think that he should become less fantastic and in this novel he is more so.'[2]

What does it mean to say that a novel is fantastic? Bakhtin said that fantasy presents 'extraordinary situations' in order 'to provoke and test a philosophical idea'.[3] Todorov had this notion in mind when he defined the fantastic as 'a narrative marked by an event that defies the laws of nature, thereby evoking in the reader a hesitation as to whether the event or phenomenon belongs to reality or to imagination, that is [...] whether or not it is real'.[4] If the event is a product of the imagination, then the laws of the world remain what they are; if 'the event has indeed taken place, it is an integral part of reality—but then this reality is controlled by laws unknown to us'. (*TF*, p.25).

Todorov's elaboration reflects Bakhtin's insistence that the hallmark of the fantastic is not 'the positive *embodiment* of truth, but [...] the search after the truth, its provocation and, most importantly, its testing'. To this end, the heroes of fantasy 'ascend into heaven, descend into the netherworld, wander through unknown fantasy lands, and are placed in other extraordinary situations'.[5]

This notion of the fantastic aptly describes O'Brien's enterprise in *The Third Policeman.* For one thing, as the reader learns only in the final pages of the novel, its hero has descended into the netherworld. Unbeknownst to either reader or hero, all of the novel's action takes place after the hero's death in, as O'Brien said in a letter to William Saroyan, 'the world of the dead—and the damned—where none of the rules and laws, not even the law of gravity holds good [...]'.⁶ More importantly, the fantastic adventures of the nameless hero are best understood as efforts to test troubling ideas about the nature of reality that were forced on O'Brien's generation by Einstein's revolution in physics. Those ideas—particularly the radical idea that neither space nor time exists independently of the other—were bound to trouble students of the Aristotelian-Thomistic metaphysics taught at University College Dublin in the era of both O'Brien (Class of 1932) and his predecessor, James Joyce (Class of 1902).

Einstein's physics required that the world of absolute space and time, in which events occurred in a particular place in a chronological sequence, give way to a unified concept of space-time, in which the time sequence of events may be different for observers who are in motion relative to each other. The shock effect of this profound transformation of reality is reflected in the observation of O'Brien's madly inventive scientist, De Selby, that, Einstein 'befuddled man' by showing that 'space and time had no real existence separately but were to be apprehended only in unison'.⁷ O'Brien said the same thing himself in his "Cruiskeen Lawn" column, observing that 'Einstein's discoveries entail the radical revision of conventional concepts of time, space and matter, and a person who undertakes to discourse on such subjects while ignorant of Einstein, must necessarily rely on premises shown to be inadmissible [...]'.⁸ For Joyce and O'Brien, who not only sought to apprehend reality, but to describe it in words, there was a further befuddlement stemming from the inadequacy of existing language to the task of depicting reality so that its multiple space-time dimensions could be apprehended in unison. George W. Gray's comment on the mathematical core of relativity theory highlights the nature of the writer's problem:

> Inasmuch as the theory of relativity is presented by its author in mathematical language, and in strictness of speaking cannot be expressed in any other, there is a certain presumption in any attempt to translate it into the vernacular. One might as well interpret Beethoven's Fifth Symphony on a saxophone.⁹

Writers of the post-Einstein world needed to find words to depict four dimensions at once. Mary McCarthy has remarked that Picasso sought to 'compress time and space into a single Einsteinian dimension'.¹⁰ Both Joyce and O'Brien grappled with the question how a writer could perform a similar feat of compression.

Joyce, for example, sought to invent a new language, writing of the post-Einstein world as a 'collideorscope' that a hypothetical human being would see if he had 'plenxty of time' and 'vacants of space' to be apprehended in that multi-tiered, non-instant of time, 'this auctual futule preteriting unstant'.[11] O'Brien rejected the Joycean path of tinkering with language. When Joyce appears as a character in O'Brien's *The Dalkey Archive,* he confides that he is having difficulty with his new book because

> I'm rather at sea as to *language.* I have a firm grip as to my thoughts, my argument ... but communicating my ideas clearly in English is my difficulty. (*DA*, p.147.) [Original emphasis and ellipsis.]

In a "Cruiskeen Lawn" column of 7 July, 1958, O'Brien himself held Joyce responsible for the 'attempted disintegration, dissipation and demolition of language'.[12] O'Brien would struggle to portray—and to test—the new physics, but, above all, he would be clear.

Confronted with a theory that reduced familiar objects to a mass of swirling sub-atomic particles, O'Brien constructed a fantasy to test the idea, but did so in language of crystalline clarity. '[T]he Atomic Theory is at work in this parish', according to *The Third Policeman*'s Sergeant Pluck, and thus

> [e]verything is composed of small particles of itself and they are flying around in concentric circles and arcs and segments and innumerable other geometrical figures too numerous to mention collectively, never standing still or resting but spinning away and darting hither and thither and back again, all the time on the go. These diminutive gentlemen are called atoms.[13]

And they 'are lively as twenty leprechauns doing a jig on top of a tombstone'. As a result, Michael Gilhaney—like most members of the parish, an ardent bicycle rider—has exchanged so many of his own spinning sub-atomic particles with those of his bicycle that he has become 'nearly half a bicycle' (*TP*, p.98) and 'spends a lot of his time leaning with one elbow on walls or standing propped by one foot at kerbstones'. (*TP*, p.102)

When the policemen discover 'omnium', the 'inherent interior essence which is hidden inside the root of the kernel of everything' (*TP*, p.129), the narrator struggles to find a language adequate to a shifting reality that can only be described in a mathematical formula:

> I can only say that these objects, not one of which resembled the other, were of no known dimensions. They were not square or rectangular or

circular or simply irregularly shaped nor could it be said that their endless variety was due to dimensional dissimilarities. Simply their appearance, if even that word is not inadmissible, was not understood by the eye and was in any event indescribable. That is enough to say. (*TP*, p.161)

The instability at the heart of the new reality was more troubling to O'Brien than its defiance of description. One of the fundamental comforts of traditional metaphysics was the thought that time stretched back in a straight line from the moment of birth to the beginning of creation. This notion underlies Joyce's reverie on linked umbilical cords stretching back to the beginning of time, like so many monks bound together by their girdles:

> The cords of all link back, strandentwining cable of all flesh. That is why mystic monks. Will you be as gods? Gaze in your omphalos. Hello. Kinch here. Put me on to Edenville. Aleph, alpha: nought, nought, one.[14]

The Einsteinean notion of a unified space-time, with the same event happening at different times for different observers, left the universe with no fixed beginning point, and threatened an endless stretch to nowhere. The nameless narrator of *The Third Policeman* poses the problem in terms of the concern of his conscience, Joe, that he might have a body:

> Why was Joe so disturbed at the suggestion that he had a body? What if he *had* a body? A body with another body inside it in turn, thousands of such bodies within each other like the skins of an onion, receding to some unimaginable ultimum? Was I in turn merely a link in a vast sequence of imponderable beings, the world I knew merely the interior of the being whose inner voice I myself was? Who or what was the core and what monster in what world was the final uncontained colossus? God? Nothing? (*TP*, pp.141-42)

O'Brien's disturbed questions illustrate Borges' observation that infinity is the conception that 'corrupts and upsets all others'.[15] The notion of infinite regress had a powerful hold on O'Brien's mind. He studied it in J. W. Dunne's books on serial theory,[16] and returned to it often, never more felicitously than in the amazing woodworking of Sergeant MacCruiskeen, who crafted an endless series of tiny boxes within increasingly tinier boxes, one of them so small it took him three years to make and another year to believe he had made it. (*TP*, p.85)

O'Brien tested—and had fun with—the fantastic and comic possibilities inherent in a marriage of the theory of infinite regression with the notion of the new physics that 'if it were possible to conceive of a human being attaining speed greater than the velocity of light [...] he could overtake his past and his birth would occur in the future'.[17] No doubt aware of this theory, the ingenious De Selby constructed an arrangement of parallel mirrors through which he observed his face in an infinity of reflections by means of 'a powerful glass' (*TP*, p.76). O'Brien tells what De Selby saw:

> He claims to have noticed a growing youthfulness in the reflections of his face according as they receded, the most distant of them—too tiny to be visible to the naked eye—being the face of a beardless boy of twelve, and, to use his own words, 'a countenance of singular beauty and nobility'. He did not succeed in pursuing the matter back to the cradle 'owing to the curvature of the earth and the limitations of the telescope'. (*TP*, p.76.)

Todorov thought that psychoanalysis had 'replaced (and thereby made useless) the literature of the fantastic' (*TF*, p.160) and that the themes of fantastic literature had become the themes of psychological investigations (*TF*, p.161). O'Brien's novels, however, show that, while psychoanalysis may have taken over what Todorov called 'themes of the other'—concerns of 'the relation of man with his desire—and thereby with his unconscious' (*TF*, p.139)—there is still a rich world of fantasy to be explored in terms of what Todorov called 'themes of the self'—those that 'concern the structuring of the relation between man and the world' (*TF*, p.120).

Moreover, the genre of the fantastic remains perfectly suited to testing and exploring one of the fundamental paradoxes explored by twentieth-century mathematics and logic, a paradox that lies at the heart of fiction itself. The underlying idea is intriguingly described in Douglas Hofstadter's *Godel, Escher, Bach*. Hofstadter's book deals with what he calls 'strange loops', a phenomenon that occurs 'whenever, by moving upwards (or downwards) through the levels of some hierarchical system, we unexpectedly find ourselves right back where we started'.[18] Bach's 'endlessly rising canon', *Musical Offering,* is a strange loop, as is Escher's *Ascending and Descending,* a lithograph in which monks walk up (or down) steps only to find themselves at the beginning again, fated, as Hofstadter says, to 'trudge forever in loops'.[19]

Godel's Theorem arose out of efforts to come to grips with the strange loop in the Epimenides' paradox, a wrinkle in the foundation of logic illustrated by the statement, 'This statement is false.' If you think the statement true, it loops back on itself by being false. If you are thus moved to conclude that the statement is false, it backfires again, by being true.

Samuel Beckett planted the Epimenides' paradox smack in the middle of his Trilogy. In *Malone Dies,* the narrator confesses that 'I shall say nothing that is not false',[20] thereby forcing the reader along the strange loop where Beckett's narrator is telling the truth only if he is lying.

O'Brien has a delicious way of testing this strange loop, and illustrating how it lies at the heart of the very idea of fiction. The narrator of *The Third Policeman* reports, excitedly and in detail, on the various readings taken by the two policemen on the mysterious machine that seems to be controlling all reality. The readings are recorded carefully in Sergeant MacCruiskeen's notebook and frequently consulted for purposes of preventing a looming catastrophe adumbrated by changes in the all-important 'readings'. The narrator reproduces a page of the Sergeant's notebook with the introductory observation that: 'For obvious reasons the figures themselves are fictitious' (*TP,* p.122).

Why fictitious? And for what obvious reasons? Obviously, *The Third Policeman* is a fiction and thus every word of it is fictitious. The introduction to MacCruiskeen's notebook, like Epimenides' paradox, loops back on itself by professing its own status as a fiction. O'Brien's use of the fantastic to test and explore the notion of fiction shows that Todorov was wrong to think that the fantastic died with psychoanalysis. Indeed, as Brian McHale has pointed out, 'the fantastic has been co-opted as one in a number of strategies of an ontological poetics that pluralises the "real" and problematises representation [...] a sort of jiu-jitsu that uses representation itself to overcome representation'.[21] O'Brien found a happy vehicle to explore this theme in *At Swim Two Birds,* which turns the reader toward a series of circles within circles revolving around the facts that the narrator of O'Brien's novel is himself writing a novel about a novelist writing a novel, one of whose characters—but I anticipate too far into the circles.

To begin closer to the beginning, the narrator, *à la* Stephen Dedalus, sets forth his theory of the novel, thus 'affording an insight into its aesthetic, its daemon, its argument, its sorrow and its joy, its darkness, its sun-twinkle clearness'.[22] Anticipating Borges' conviction that all literature is plagiaristic, and that—as Harold Bloom puts it, 'Homer and Shakespeare [are] everyone and anyone'[23]—the narrator holds that 'characters should be interchangeable as between one book and another' and that 'the entire corpus of existing literature should be regarded as a limbo from which discerning authors could draw their characters as required, creating only when they failed to find a suitable existing puppet' (*ASTB*, p.33).

True to this aesthetic, the novelist in the narrator's novel, Dermot Trellis, dips liberally into the limbo of existing character, creating only when necessary. When necessity calls, Trellis uses his new scientific-literary invention 'aesthoautogamy', a method by which characters are created fully grown and without conception or fertilisation.

Contrary to the narrator's belief in 'self determination' for all characters, Trellis controls the action of his characters when he is awake, although they go their own way when he sleeps. Trellis's sexual assault on one of his own creations, the beautiful Sheila Lamont, leads to the birth of young Orlick Trellis who, for better or ill, inherits his father's literary gifts. These gifts prove useful when he joins a group of his father's disgruntled characters who object to the course charted for them by the elder Trellis. As that unhappy father sleeps, young Trellis writes a novel in which the renegade characters inflict a brutal beating on Trellis senior.

As it becomes possible to wonder what is happening to the renegade characters in the pages of the father's novel while they are pursuing him in his son's opus, O'Brien has developed a fantasy to explore the strange loop at the heart of fiction. The loop doubles back on life as well. As Borges says, such inversions remind the reader that he too may be fictitious.[24] O'Brien illustrates the reader's precarious position in this whole process with the Good Fairy's observation, in connection with the possibility of mating between material and spiritual bodies, that 'angelic or spiritual carnality is not easy and in any event the offspring would be severely handicapped by being half flesh and half spirit, a very baffling and neutralising assortment of fractions since the two elements are forever at variance' (*ASTB*, p.149). Man, as one of the narrator's cronies observes, is 'tortured by his body and the illusion of existence' (*ASTB*, p.137).

O'Brien's novel is a fantasy adequate to the plight of humanity. If, as Anna Maria Barrenechea asserts, Borges was 'an admirable writer pledged to destroy reality and convert man into a shadow';[25] O'Brien is an admirable writer who, finding reality disintegrated into shifting borders of space and time, championed the power of language to construct fantasies capable of exploring its mysteries.

NOTES

1. Anthony Cronin, *No Laughing Matter* (London: Grafton Books 1989), p.89.
2. ibid., p.101.
3. Mikhail Bakhtin, *Problems of Dostoevsky's Poetics*, trans. R. W. Rotsel (Ann Arbor: Ardis 1973), p.94.
4. Tzvetan Todorov, *The Fantastic*, trans. Richard Howard (Cornell UP 1975), pp.25; henceforth *TF*.
5. Bakhtin, op. cit. (1973), p.94.
6. Flann O'Brien, letter to William Saroyan (7 September 1940), cited in Anne Clissman and David Powell, eds., "A Sheaf of Letters," *Journal of Irish Literature*, 3, 1 (January 1974), p.73.
7. Flann O'Brien, *The Dalkey Archive* (NY: Macmillan 1965), p.14; henceforth *DA*.
8. *The Irish Times*, 3 August 1942, cited in Anne Clissman, *Flann O'Brien: A Critical Introduction to his Writings* (Dublin: Gill & Macmillan 1975), pp.153-54.
9. Cited in Robert B. Downs, *Books That Changed The World* (NY: Mentor 1965), p.186.
10. Mary McCarthy, *The Stones of Florence and Venice Observed* (Harmondsworth: Penguin 1972), p.83.
11. James Joyce, *Finnegans Wake* (NY: Viking 1939), p.143 [143.05-08].
12. Clissman, op. cit. (1975), p.221.
13. Flann O'Brien, *The Third Policeman* (NY: Lancer 1967), p.97; henceforth *TP*.
14. James Joyce, *Ulysses* (NY: Random House 1934), p.38.
15. Jorge Luis Borges, *Labyrinths*, ed. and trans., Donald A. Yates and James E. Irby (NY: New Directions 1964), p.202.
16. Cited in Mary A. O'Toole, 'The Theory of Serialism in "The Third Policeman"', *Irish University Review*, 18 (1988), p.215
17. Downs, op. cit. (1965), p.188.
18. Douglas R. Hofstadter, *Godel, Escher, Bach* (NY: Basic Books 1979), p.10.
19. ibid., p.13.
20. Beckett, *Malone Dies* in Three Novels by Samuel Beckett (NY: Grove Press 1955), p.207.
21. Brian McHale, *Post-Modernist Fiction* (NY: Routledge 1991), p.224.
22. Flann O'Brien, *At Swim Two Birds* (1939, rep. NY: New American Library 1976), p.32.
23. Harold Bloom, *The Western Canon* (NY: Harcourt Brace 1994), p.473.
24. Borges, op. cit. (1964), p.196.
25. Bloom, op. cit. (1994), pp.470-71.

THE THIRD POLICEMAN: A GRAVE YARN

Monique Gallagher

When Brian O'Nolan died in 1966 he had, as Flann O'Brien, achieved world-wide celebrity due to his extraordinary novel *At Swim-Two-Birds*, and had, as Myles na Gopaleen, become a popular figure in Ireland on account of his 'Cruiskeen Lawn' column in *The Irish Times*, where for twenty five years he had cultivated the role of a clownish jester. When illness overcame him he departed with what could seem to many to be a last jest—the date on the calendar was April Fools' Day. The joke seemed to be pushed even further with the publication, one year after his death, of a new book, *The Third Policeman*—though written as early as 1940—for there is an additional irony in the fact that this posthumous novel purports to have been written from the grave.

One can recognise in *The Third Policeman* O'Brien's whimsical playfulness and taste for innovation and delirious extravaganza. The unexpected narrative standpoint, a grave, gives him opportunities to express his imaginative inventiveness and create comic effects. Yet, despite hilarious passages, there is a perturbing overall atmosphere and a certain *malaise* subsists even after all the tricks of the fantastic genre have been recognised. How O'Brien has transformed a potentially playful fantasy into a disturbing oeuvre is what we intend to explore.

The Third Policeman begins as an autobiography. The narrator mentions how his devotion to the work of an eccentric philosopher-cum-scientist, de Selby, led him, with the complicity of a friend, Divney, to murder old Mathers, a rich neighbour. It is when, several weeks after the crime, he goes to Mathers's house intending to retrieve the box supposed to hold the old man's fortune that he starts encountering eerie phenomena: first, Mathers appears to him, and talks to him; the narrator also reports a change in his own self, which becomes double; and a series of strange adventures follows, involving two eccentric policemen in weird barracks, where the narrator's brain and senses are tormented by many divergences from the norms of human existence. After three days of mental tension, he is enlightened by a third policeman as to the logic behind the disruption of the familiar universe: this third policeman, Policeman Fox, has been playing with reality, making 'ribbons' of it, as he puts it, using the powers of a substance he calls omnium, contained in fact in Mathers's black box, now located in the narrator's home, where the narrator immediately goes, and finds his friend Divney again, looking strangely aged. On seeing him Divney has a heart attack, shocked by the apparition of what he believes is a ghost, for he reveals just before collapsing that sixteen years before he had caused the death of the narrator, putting a bomb at the place where the box was supposed to be. The text proceeds with the account, in the selfsame words, of the exact same eerie adventures, but now shared by Divney. The narrator does not seem to be endowed with memory or to understand that he and Divney are both trapped in the eternal circle of hell.

A certain amount of estrangement is to be expected in a story allegedly written from the world of the dead. It was precisely because of its eeriness that the manuscript of *The Third Policeman* had been rejected in 1940 by Longman who explicitly referred to the 'fantastic' element as having induced their refusal to publish the novel: 'We realise the author's ability but think that he should become less fantastic and in this new novel he is more so.'[1] They still had *At Swim-Two-Birds* in mind, published the year before. However, if *The Third Policeman* can be described as 'fantastic', it is not on the same grounds as *At Swim*. The initial postulates are different: *At Swim* deals with the imagined world of fiction, *The Third Policeman* with the imagined world of after life. O'Brien, who enjoyed working with outlandish situations, from which he could work out networks of implications and complications, drawing them to their most extreme consequences, boasted that with *The Third Policeman* he had entered territory never yet treated in literature—'I think the idea of a man being dead all the time is pretty new'[2] and rejoiced in the infinite number of odd situations he could invent: 'When you are writing about the world of the dead—and the damned—where none of the rules and laws (not even the law of gravity) hold good, there is any amount of back-chat and funny cracks.'[3]

Back-chat and funny cracks: O'Brien introduces 'eccentric, queerly-spoken' characters. The characters' use of language, their activities, follow the same whimsical logic as those of Myles na Gopaleen in his dissection of *clichés* and surrealistic dramatisations of his word-play. *The Third Policeman* resembles O'Brien's other productions insofar as it is a vehicle for the creation of another reality, an 'unreality', with new connections between people and objects, new spaces, new elements: man is presented as capable of calculating the time of his death by a mere examination of the thickness of a robe bestowed upon him at birth; a bicycle can be hanged for murder; a cigarette can burn endlessly without being consumed. We find grotesque situations, in which policemen become thieves, in which molecules dance and whirl their way from object to object in a reality that is permeable, mutable, where sounds become colours which in their turn can produce electricity and heat. One reaches eternity by taking a lift, in company of policemen exchanging views on Turkish Delights and jelly-sweets. A world where liquorice-chewing policemen carve diminutive chests with the help of invisible tools and microscopes, while embarked on a crusade to save mankind from the threat of turning into bicycles is a fantasy-world, or wonderland. *The Third Policeman* indeed seems to be a 'yarn' from the grave, the grave providing the context for play with ideas, with language, with objects, with institutions, foils for O'Brien's fertile imagination. Everything is possible, even the role of autobiographer assumed by a dead narrator.

We cannot say however that this world corresponds to a paradise or a fairyland. Apart from one episode in which the narrator recounts his progress through a 'supernally good-looking countryside',[4] the environment encountered is far from idyllic. Although the hero once meets a male counterpart of a fairy-tale godmother just in time to save him from the scaffold, his nerves and his brain are frequently submitted to intolerable pressures and disturbances. To 'wonderland' motifs have been added disquieting features which make this world a hell rather than a paradise. In the realm of the dead, the hero unsurprisingly meets ghosts and spectres. The ghost of the man he has killed is there, suitably appalling: 'the hand was yellow, the wrinkled skin draped loosely upon the bones [...]' (*TP*, p.24). The hollowness of the pit of hell is also suggested by peculiar resounding echoes and the supernal quality of voices: 'my own words were also soft and light as if they had no breath to liven them [...], I heard his voice coming back to me softly called across a fathomless valley [...]. Here I heard myself give a hollow laugh [...].' (*TP*, p.158.) The hellish horror of the place is underlined—'I felt I was standing within three yards of something unspeakably inhuman and diabolical which was using its trick of light

The Third Policeman: A Grave Yarn 199

to lure me on to something still more horrible' (*TP*, p.178). However the hell of *The Third Policeman* is not a world of hideous monsters, frightening ghosts of criminals or other damned creatures. If O'Brien has been tempted by the baroque presentation of abominable repulsive beings—'Millions of diseased and decayed monsters clawing the inside latches of ovens to open them and escape, rats with horns walking upside down along the ceiling pipes, trailing their leprous tails on the policemen's heads' (*TP*, p.190)—they are described as part of tortures contemplated but not exercised, remaining half-way between the parody of the Celtic extravaganzas and that of the tale of horror, a pure exercise in style: O'Brien has skilfully introduced within the pattern of his extraterrestrial story reminders of the fantastic genre; the tale of horror is indeed reflected in it, albeit discretely.

In spite of the violence his imagination is able to envisage, and the frenzy demonstrated in his killing of Mathers, the main character, the narrator, is not presented as a dangerous, awesome criminal, nor is the hell to which he is doomed like the hell of a horror tale. Although his individual self becomes dislocated into two distinct voices, and his soul addresses him in a separate audible way, the narrator is not so much a 'fantastic' character as a witness and victim of fantastic experiences. As is often the case in a fantastic story, his adventure is a solitary one; he leaves his village for a countryside that seems to be the end of the world, full of malefic mystery: Mathers's house resembles the castles of gothic tales; the police barracks lacks 'one of the customary dimensions', depth, and keeps changing appearance; time has a spatial location—'the middle of the day is situated five miles away' (*TP*, p.157); the sun rises and sets at the same spot. The hero has entered a world where the laws of common experience are disrupted, where bicycles can think (*TP*, p.171) and behave as humans, where the humans he meets are not altogether human: Mathers's voice sounds like 'the hoarse toll of a rusty bell' (*TP*, p.26), and his eyes are 'not genuine eyes at all but mechanical dummies animated by electricity or the like, with a tiny pinhole in the centre of the pupil through which the real eye gazed out secretively with great coldness' (*TP*, p.24); Policeman Pluck sounds hollow and tinny when he taps his forehead, and Policeman McCruiskeen looks like 'a walking emporium [...] on wires'. The occupations of these characters are supernatural: Mathers is familiar with magic and sorcery since he can perceive the colour of winds and is intimate with a policeman who can foretell a man's death by watching his birthwind. Equally extraordinary are the constructions of de Selby, the mad '*philosophe-savant*', and the bewildering statements expressed by the policemen, supported on apparently plausible scientific grounds. The pseudo-scientists are presented at work, manipulating microscopes, mirrors, through which the hero is able to perceive phenomena his everyday experience had so far never acquainted him with. He receives new sensations, observes objects for which no name has ever been devised because no-one has ever perceived them before; he can feel the prick of a spear so sharp that its extremity has a half foot of invisibility. If a novel is fantastic when it dramatises the puzzlement of a consciousness confronted with an environment which has lost the stability of its once rigorous, immutable laws, then *The Third Policeman* is a fantastic novel.

Roger Callois speaks of the fantastic experience in terms of 'scandal' for the mind and senses.[5] In *The Third Policeman* the 'scandal' proceeds from the fact the hero keeps after death the system of perception and reflection that was his before, and assesses his new environment according to the standards of his past experience as a living person. Only when he tries to discard the memory of such norms can he soothe his mind. 'The best thing to do was to believe what my eyes were looking at rather than to place my trust in a memory' (*TP*, p.26). O'Brien has transposed to the situation of bewilderment of a consciousness passing from life to death the traditional experience of shock associated with the fantastic genre. The agony of the mind in its attempt at adjustment is specified in terms belonging to the fantastic tradition. The lexicon is quite eloquent: 'agonising disturbance', 'distress', 'sick utter horror', 'chilling', 'momentous and frightening'; the senses are racked, the brain is similarly tormented. O'Brien introduces the physiology of fear, 'a heart pausing for a time and working on again with slow heavy hammer-blows' (*TP*, p.26); the hero describes himself 'dry-throated and timorous', or in another circumstance with 'a weakness in [his] spine'; 'the blood ran away at once from my startled face [...]'; 'sweat was gathering on my brow, my heart was thumping loudly [...]' (*TP*, p.177). His body becomes so powerfully stirred that he can even perceive his heart valves (*TP*, p.96), as if his physical self had become a conglomeration of individually assaulted dislocated parts: 'Every part of me that was behind me—neck, ears, back and head—shrank and quailed painfully before the presence confronting them, each expecting an onslaught of indescribable ferocity' (*TP*, p.180).

But is it sufficient to evoke the anguish of a character and the anatomy of his fear, for the reader to sympathise with his emotion and share his fantastic experience? For a novel to be considered fantastic, it must not just be 'about' the fantastic, or borrow its style. *The Third Policeman* offers a whole inventory of fantastic themes and motifs, as if O'Brien had deliberately scanned the *répertoire* of the *genre*. The impression that he may be merely playing with the devices is corroborated by the comic exploitation he makes of the strange situation of his hero. If we laugh, can we still speak of fantastic literature?

When we laugh reading *The Third Policeman* it is not particularly when the hero experiences his fantastic fear. When we laugh at the burlesque situations derived from the impracticable theories of an '*idiot-savant*', which the hero himself finds absurd, we never think that they could leave the domain of words to threaten the hero's security; as to the unscientific aberrations drawn from an immature interpretation of molecular physics on the part of eccentric policemen, they amuse us at a stage when the hero's security does not seem to be endangered. Such episodes are distinct from what the narrator considers fantastically disturbing. Just as it is not the mere presence of fantastic motifs or emotions that makes a tale fantastic, it is not because one episodically finds matter for comedy that the whole effect is necessarily comic. One of the complexities of *The Third Policeman* is that it provides matter for both laughter and fear. What the 1940 publishers rejected was probably not this ambiguity inherent in the novel; they had kept to the level of the fantasy of the situation, the first impression a reader may have. And yet, if O'Brien's friend Niall Sheridan recalls his first reaction as 'one of great amusement', he also expresses his opinion that *The Third Policeman* represents 'a world of nameless fears, sinister undertones, strange obsessions'.[6] Anthony Burgess also referred to the duality of his response: 'To say that it is mad Irishry is not enough: it is mad Irishry used for a profound and terrible end.'[7]

And did not O'Brien himself confess his own hesitation as to the tone of his book? 'It's supposed to be funny but I don't know about that.' How then has O'Brien maintained the effects of the fantastic *genre* in his amusing novel? One of the *sine qua nons* of the fantastic is the reader's participation in the hero's adventures, the sympathy he must feel for him. In *The Third Policeman* the reader's laugh is never in discordance with the hero's mood. O'Brien takes steps to make his hero an average man, with whom it is easier to assimilate oneself. The fact that the hero of the fantastic adventures is a narrator rather than a mere character makes his story more trustworthy. The tone of confession, from the opening sentence—'Not everybody knows how I killed old Phillip Mathers'—conditions the reader into believing an account that starts so honestly. Moreover, the realism of the description of the murder sets the tone for the rest of the narration, which describes a familiar environment, with pubs, schools, roads, books, money, drink. When the text deals with the world of death, the choice of the autobiographical mode and of a narrator who—though dead keeps the warm sensation of being alive—allows the author to maintain the illusion that it is our world that is perceived and described. The experiences related suggest life, and not death. The hero goes to sleep, wakes up, goes back to sleep, dreams; as if he were not already dead he dreams of death, is sentenced to death, narrowly escapes death. His moments of unconsciousness enhance the impression he gives of being the rest of the time fully conscious, as well as physically and mentally alert, analysing his experiences with the logic of a scientific mind. Besides, hell has enough normal characteristics for the intrusion of the strange elements to disturb the reader: the countryside traversed by the hero on his way from Mathers's house to the police-barracks has familiar Irish characteristics. On the other hand, from the very beginning of the novel and in the 'safe' framework of the narration are introduced elements of uncertainty, imprecision. The hero's relationship with time is mysterious ('I was born a long time ago'); Mathers's murder is followed by cosmic manifestations, the murdered victim continues staring at the murderer in an eerie way: we are thus prepared for the future apparition of Mathers's spectre, and mystery will impose itself the more easily in the incoherence that follows. In the care given to the texture of his novel, O'Brien has achieved more than a mere *pastiche* of the fantastic *genre*.

Towards the end of the book the narrator thinks his adventure is no longer 'fantastic': when the 'third policeman' provides explanations about the existence and nature of omnium, the substance which allowed him to play with the fundamental laws of space and time, the narrator thinks he now holds a rational 'key' to get out of his fantastic situation. But in fact he has received a mere illusion of rational explanation; his situation has not changed; however the situation of the reader has. It is now clear, as O'Brien remarked in a letter to his friend William Saroyan, 'that all the queer ghastly things which have been happening to the [narrator] are happening in a sort of hell which he earned for the killing'.

There shouldn't be any fantastic effect for the reader who reads *The Third Policeman* for a second or third time.[8] The auto'necro'graphical nature of the narrative establishes the text as fiction, and what was judged 'fantastic' should then be redefined in terms of 'fantasy'. However the novel remains disturbing on a second reading. Waiting until the last pages to reveal that this dislocated frame is the representation of hell, O'Brien increases the effect of disorientation, for instead of relieving the reader the end confirms that the real world can also be a hell. We recognise in the extraterrestrial world too many echoes of the world in which we live not to feel a certain malaise. One cannot really speak of a distinction between two worlds; that in which the reader lives and that which the author has imagined as a hellish environment for his hero.

O'Brien goes beyond the usual premise of the fantastic according to which the real is natural and normal and assaulted by the fantastic: for O'Brien the real world itself is nightmarish. The meticulous policemen doing scrupulously their duty, or zealously inventing meaningless activities, stealing bicycles better to retrieve them, express the absurd fussiness of our bureaucracy, with its means without ends and its ends without means. The whimsical policemen who handle the hero as a tool or plaything, making him a pretext for a display of wit and cunning, the very style of *The Third Policeman*, the non-sequiturs, the false rhetoric, the lack of cohesion between the different episodes, the discontinuity of the text, reflect the distortions of an infernal universe. The structure of *The Third Policeman* gives an impression of aimlessness: much time is spent on mere 'embroidery'—the endless footnotes, slowing down the reading and contributing to the inertia of the book, the circular structure, are the expression of a hellish feeling of 'claustrophobia'. The narrator progresses without moving forward, in the closed universe of his hell; he walks but his destination keeps receding; the circle of the hero's journey, his futile escape on a bicycle that takes him back where he started, may be an echo of a Sisyphian reading of life. This hell in which the narrator is trapped is part of an atmosphere which we can feel in the whole of O'Brien's 'Man moves on in the coil of his dark destiny' ("Cruiskeen Lawn" 05-01-1944). *The Third Policeman* appears then as the projection of what O'Brien found mysterious, strange, disturbing, not just the unknown of after life, but the mystery of existence itself.

De Selby discourses at length on the subject of a mirror reflecting a mirror reflecting another mirror. This endless '*ricorso*' of mirrors is but one among many illustrations of a serialist view of reality, like Mathers's eyes '[giving rise in his mind] to interminable speculations as to the colour and quality of the real eye and as to whether, indeed, it was real at all or merely another dummy with its pinhole on the same plane as the first one so that the real eye, possibly behind thousands of these absurd disguises, gazed out through a barrel of serried peepholes' (pp.24-25). Chinese box universes create the fantastic of the absurd. This impression of depth, of abysmal vertigo resulting from the accumulation of serial effects, subsists on a second reading, supported by the metaphysical, existential erring of the narrator: he has a dream of death; he dreams of being in his coffin, is happy to wake up and find himself alive, but in fact we know that what he thought was a dream of death was a real state of death, and that it is an illusion of life he wakes up to! The erring of the narrator suggests the metaphysical vertigo Genette evokes: '*ce que nous prenons pour réalité n'est peut-être qu'illusion, mais qui sait si ce que nous prenons pour illusion n'est pas aussi réalité?.*'[9] O'Brien produces a similar effect of mystery when he dissects and measures the unfathomable notion of silence: 'the silence of the room was so unusually quiet that the beginning of it seemed rather loud when the utter stillness of the end of it had been encountered' (*TP*, p.105). This feeling of dizziness before the mysterious layers of reality is comparable to that of modern man, for whom the world is no longer homogeneous or unique but part of a complex universe where a multiplicity of worlds are embedded within each other, where reality doesn't exist in and of itself but only as a passage to another possible reality, which in its turn leads to another. The endless series and concentric circles in *The Third Policeman* express more than a feeling of claustrophobia in an infernal circle, they express the mental *malaise* of modernity, the restlessness of a century deprived of all certainty, having witnessed the collapse of man's trust in the rationality of the universe.

Because the modern world is no longer immutable, the reader is prepared to accept a non-Euclidian interpretation of reality. De Selby's, the policemen's revelations are tinged with the disconcerting mathematics of relativity or atomic physics. When O'Brien conceived *The Third Policeman* he had probably in mind two books by J. W. Dunne, which he was to evoke when writing *The Dalkey Archive*, a novel largely based on *The Third Policeman*: 'You may remember

Dunne's two books, *An Experiment with Time* and *The Serial Universe*, also the views of Einstein and others, the idea is that time is a great flat motionless sea. Time does not pass; it is we who pass.'[10] According to Dunne, what consciousness grasps of time is not absolute time but an image, transformed by our mental habits. The barriers erected by consciousness are destroyed by dream, ecstasy, death, and the mind then communicates with the true nature of time. Dunne asserts that after death the mind continues to exist on another scale of time, which he calls 'time 2'. When the mind penetrates inside this time, which in fact is absolute time, immutable and permanent, it wanders, unable to take its bearings, for it needs to learn how to adjust its understanding; if it fails to do so, its new environment appears nightmarish. It is the impression we have in *The Third Policeman*: the hero at the beginning of the novel and until he dies, lives with Divney in a time (time 1) appreciated according to human criteria, made of a succession of days and months. At the moment of the explosion he enters a new level, time 2, which has nothing to do with time 1 but, as the hero is undergoing a punishment, a hell, he is not allowed to achieve the adjustment of his mind, and still uses in the new time his system of references of before his death, continuing to measure time 2 as if it were still time 1, hence his impression of a duration of three days, distinct from the 16 years of Divney's time 1 experience.

As Charles Kemnitz demonstrated, there are also close connections between the narrator's experience and Einstein's discoveries. The return of the narrator after sixteen years of absence is an echo of the return of the 'prodigal son' proposed in Einsteinian thought ('If one twin were to take a trip at a velocity approaching the speed of light, time for the travelling twin would slow down so that only days pass in his life while years pass for the twin remaining in the middle zone on earth').[11] The sun rising and setting at the same place represents the absence of direction of particles in the four-dimensional time-space continuum. As to the idea of the series of mirrors which might allow one to see a younger version of oneself, it was formulated by Einstein who expressed the idea of a mirror big enough to allow light to reach the confines of the universe and come back again—one could then see one's hair growing. It is difficult to determine where logic stops and the absurd begins in this reclaiming of the past with a system of mirrors. Plank and Einstein's theories proceed from the field of mathematical physics, which is superimposed on experimental physics, and allows logicians' demonstrations that make the universe appear as a succession of discontinuous fragments. It is very close to the nonsensical world of Carroll. To replace empirical methods by the abstraction of reasoning leads to logical labyrinths.

In *The Third Policeman*, O'Brien takes literally the conclusions of modern thought on space and time, showing the abyss between the ordinary perception man has of the universe and the universe as scientists present it. De Selby defends in the pure abstraction of his logical discourse reasonings leading to shocking negations of experience: 'His theory seems to discount the testimony of human experience and is at variance with everything I have learnt myself' (*TP*, p.50). The infernal torture of the hero is that of modern man trying to establish a coherent link between the concrete testimony of his senses and the logical discourse which science communicates to his brain. His hell is the absurdity of a universe which reasoning and intuition perceive differently.

The grave message of *The Third Policeman* is that an excess of reasoning may lead to folly. It exposes the horror of a life entirely based on reasoning, where a multitude of systems attempt to grasp an elusive universe. O'Brien borrows from several systems without explaining any completely, making the overall impression more bewildering, suggesting the confusion and danger for the psyche of imperfectly understood scientific or philosophic systems. He has selected in philosophical and scientific theories what could create an atmosphere of estrangement suggesting the leap into the other world. Because this estrangement corresponds to that of a Euclidian brain steeped in a relativistic system, it also represents the puzzlement of modern man who, having lost the solid foundations of the Newtonian system, has the impression that his world has become another world. Thus the trickster, the jester, while playing with a fantastic genre, has written a complex, puzzling, disquieting, genuinely fantastic novel. If the novel is fantastic, it is not by the presence of separate motifs, which, extracted from their context, appear frail examples of fantasy or imaginative play; what makes *The Third Policeman* so fascinating is that O'Brien's playfulness with 'that other world' has been cleverly integrated into a disturbing commentary on 'this our world'. Having started with the intention of writing a fantasy, O'Brien has organised his work according to a thematic coherence, original and harmonious, providing a unique experience, both entertaining and disturbing.

NOTES

1. Letter from A. M. Heath to Brian O'Nolan, 11 March, 1940.
2. Letter from Brian O'Nolan to William Saroyan, 14 February, 1940.
3. ibid.
4. Flann O'Brien, *The Third Policeman* (London: MacGibbon & Kee 1967), p.39; henceforth *TP*.
5. Viz., '[U]n scandale, une déchirure, une irruption insolite, presque insupportable, dans un monde réel'. (Roger Callois, *Anthologie du Fantastique*, Paris: Gallimard, 1966, p.8).
6. Niall Sheridan, 'Brian, Flann and Myles', in Timothy O'Keeffe, ed., *Myles, Portraits of Brian O'Nolan* (London: Martin Brian & O'Keeffe 1973), p.51.
7. Anthony Burgess, 'Surprise from the Grave', *The Observer*, 1 September, 1967, Sect. 1, p.22.
8. As Tzvetan Todorov observes, the reader's hesitation is the first condition of the fantastic: '*l'hésitation éprouvé par un être qui ne connaît que les lois naturelles, face à un événement en apparence surnaturel'; and further: 'En fait à la deuxième lecture, l'identification n'est plus possible, la lecture devient inévitablement méta-lecture: on relève les procédés du fantastique au lieu d'en subir les charmes.*' (*Initiation à la Littérature Fantastique*, Paris: Editions du Seuil 1970).
9. Gérard Genette, *Figures I* (Paris: Editions du Seuil), p.18.
10. Letter from Brian O'Nolan to Timothy O'Keeffe, 21 September 1962.
11. Charles Kemnitz, 'Beyond the Zone of Middle Dimensions: Relativistic Reading of TP', *The Irish University Review*, XV, 1985, p.61.

Keynote Lecture 3

MAGIC AND REVOLUTION: YEATS'S "EASTER 1916"

Terence Brown

Yeats's early poetry invokes a world of wavering indeterminacy in which 'meditative, organic rhythms' induce a prolonged 'moment of contemplation, the moment when we are both asleep and awake' when, hushed by an 'alluring monotony' and held 'waking by variety', we are kept in 'that state of perhaps real trance, in which the mind liberated from the pressure of the will is unfolded in symbols'.[1] So mesmeric therefore are many of the early poems that readers often fail to note one of their most intriguing characteristics. They are poems, as Helen Vendler has astutely observed, in which 'at the other extreme from hovering sensitivity, undecidibility, lack, and ambiguity stand full power and command'.[2] She rightly attributes those moments in the early poetry which hint at such 'full, even coercive, rhetorical strength' with 'language used with magical intent and confident will'.[3] For the symbol-filled *reveries* of his early work do in fact accommodate a bold assertiveness; they suggest a mind about to reveal portentous truths: 'He made the world to be a grassy road/Before her wandering feet' ("The Rose of the World"); 'All the heavens bow down to Heaven,/Flame to flame and wing to wing' ("A Dream of A Blessed Spirit", subsequently "The Countess Cathleen in Paradise"). Indeed the *grandeur* of some of these deceptively authoritarian poems can make them seem works whose oracular persuasions are intended to raise them from mere textuality to communal existence, as a sacred book is the basis in its rubrics and *verbiage* of liturgical celebration.

Vendler has further alerted us to the fact that the repetitive structures of the syntax and the verse patterns of Yeats's early poetry suggest indeed that they were executed with manifest will and control:

> The incantatory power of reduplicative language (learned in part from Swinburne but not abused) served Yeats as an index of magical writing all his life [...]. Repetition by spell-casting, is the guarantee of

revolution; and so transformative or revolutionary spells must be repetitive first, and then [...] revolutionary.[4]

"The Sorrow of Love" supplies, in its original version, an apt example:

> And then you came with those red mournful lips,
> And with you came the whole of the world's tears,
> And all the sorrows of her labouring ships,
> And all the burden of her myriad years.
>
> And now the sparrows warring in the eaves,
> The curd-pale moon, the white stars in the sky,
> And the loud chaunting of the unquiet leaves,
> Are shaken with the earth's old and weary cry.

This is incantatory, ritualistic, syntactically repetitive, rhetorically commanding. It also employs words in the curious agglutinative fashion which was Yeats's habit as a young writer. In this strange way with words, closely examined by Vendler in the article cited above, rhyme develops by addition so that words contain prior words ('eaves' becomes 'leaves'). And the keyword in this poem in its revised form (the version in the *Collected Poems*) is 'arose' which makes the figure of Helen in the poem—the female presence of these stanzas—even more fully a symbol of the demonic, spiritual power of womanhood: a rose in a sequence entitled "The Rose". Furthermore the rhyme on 'lips' and 'ships' links girl and her beauty which launched a thousand ships more 'magically' than Marlowe's famous lines, where merely face and ships are in apposition.

What I am arguing therefore is that Yeats's early poems are more complex artefacts than is usually acknowledged by criticism. For in their powerful liturgical patterns of syntax and verse structure, their ingenious deployment of words as if language was constituted by a complex system of inter-relating, essentially significant signs, which could be shaped by diligent craft into magical mandalas, mantra-like symbols, they are artefacts designed to transform consciousness. Which gives a special meaning to the line 'Words alone are certain good', in the poem "The Song of the Happy Shepherd" (in *Crossways*), the poem Yeats chose to stand at the head of his *Collected Poems*. For, in Vendler's words: 'magical, non-rational, non-etymological connections between words are as important to Yeats as logical, semantic, or etymological relations'.

In 1916 in Dublin it seemed to Yeats, who had waited in vain for the trembling of the veil at the century's end, that the kind of transformation in consciousness that his early poetry had sought to induce, had at last taken place. The poem he composed to mark the event is accordingly one in which artefact, magic and daimonic female powers conjoin as they had done in his early poems of commanding conjuration. Like the early poetry "Easter 1916" traffics with the occult, with the ritual, magical powers of language; and at last Yeats as poet and mage had an occasion worthy of his dual calling. Full power and command could be exercised by the poet as magician to sustain for ever the transformation that had been wrought so remarkably in the dimension of lived history.

The complex female presences evoked in the poem require detailed analysis. For in them much of the occult significance of a magical event finds its source.

It is not certain when the poem was composed. It is dated 25th September in the typescript which was used for a private printing in 1917. However we know that Yeats read a version of it to Maud Gonne on a beach in Normandy during the summer of 1916. So we can assume it was much on his mind through the summer and early autumn of 1916, as the public mood in Ireland swung irresistibly behind those who had given their lives in the Rising and its bloody aftermath. The poet spent July and August with Maud Gonne and Iseult in Normandy. On 1 July he proposed to Gonne once more, offering her a life away from politics in a world of writers and artists, and was again rejected. Yet her image and imaginative experience found their way, as so often before, into the poem which preoccupied him through the summer of 1916. The repeated phrase 'terrible beauty' inscribes her in the poem.

From Yeats's earliest writings onwards the concept of ideal beauty and Gonne's earthly form had been woven together to suggest an intermingling of erotic feeling with expectation of imminent apocalypse and death. From early in Yeats's *œuvre*, feminised beauty, an abstract idea made languorously available in verses that breath erotic longing and swooning death wishes, was also associated with something more authoritative: with height and nobility, with instinctive, solitary aristocracy of presence. In "The Arrow" in *In the Seven Woods* a woman's beauty had been recalled at its inception as 'Tall and noble but with face and bosom/ Delicate in colour as apple blossom'. "No Second Troy" had added martial prowess to the complex of associations which the term 'beauty' involved for the poet. Gonne and a female ideal—erotic, death-haunted, noble in dangerous hauteur—constitute in Yeats's poetry a reiterated idea of the beautiful,

Magic and Revolution: Yeats's "Easter 1916" 211

so that the term is vested in his work with a powerfully female, sexual aura. As it is in this poem.

In the charged atmosphere of the months after the Dublin tragedy, Yeats knew any poem by him on the Rising would be a public statement and would be read in the future as his contribution to what increasingly seemed likely to prove a defining moment in his country's history. Yet for the Yeats who had written dismissively in prose and verse of the generation of Irish men who had now proved their mettle in battle, to be accepted as the poet of the Rising required some adroit rhetorical manoeuvres. The poet met this challenge by casting "Easter 1916" as a palinode, which answers his own "September 1913" in terms that imply that its harsh judgements have been overtaken by events. The opening movement of "Easter 1916" magnanimously acknowledges how wrong he had been in thinking that the martyrs and he himself had inhabited a world of drab inconsequentiality, which could not change. For now all has changed, 'changed utterly'. Such an atmosphere of concessive recantation does however allow the poet his own reservations, which are related to the poet's sense of what in fact had transpired. And that involved the female daimon, her beauty, allure and occult power.

The poem does not, should be noted, fully retract Yeats's earlier assessment of a generation and a society. Rather, the second rhetorical move of the poem is to suggest how the martyrs' characters and behaviour had enforced an estimate of them and their world in which the heroic played no part, and to accept with a touch of astonishment, as well as humbled recognition, that they have been changed. It is striking certainly that the heroes of a revolution (male apart from the desexualised Markievicz) which had brought back tragic dignity to Ireland are represented here as passive figures, altered, in some instances beyond recognition, by a historical change over which they seem to have no control. So powerful has been this transformative energy that even the disreputable MacBride has been affected by it and made fit matter for a noble elegy:

> This other man I had dreamed
> A drunken, vain-glorious lout.
> He had done most bitter wrong
> To some who are near my heart,
> Yet I number him in the song;
> He, too, has resigned his part
> In the casual comedy;
> He, too, has been changed in his turn,

> Transformed utterly:
> A terrible beauty is born.

The phrase 'in his turn' here implies that the actual agent of transformation (and we note the passive voice in which acts of rebellion are recounted) is death by execution itself, for the prisoners in Kilmainham Gaol in Dublin were dispatched in batches over a grim period of days. Yet the poet is not satisfied by that simple response to what had happened, which he could not share with Gonne who accepted that her husband, whatever their unhappy personal history, had been apotheosised by dying for Ireland. The poet wanted to understand what had made the martyrs risk and even, in some cases, court death. He wanted to comprehend how they and he himself had been changed as individuals and as figures in a national drama that had taken so tragic yet heroic a turn. He wanted too to participate in the magic of a momentous transformation.

In the brief portraits of the rebels in the poem's second stanza, feminine attributes are emphasised in two cases and suggested in another. Countess Markievicz, who as Constance Gore-Booth of Lissadell had won Yeats's admiration in her girlhood in the 1890s, is remembered 'young and beautiful' riding to harriers. Her career as a suffragist and socialist agitator, worker among the poor of Dublin, had made of her a ' shrill' voice in argument, when once no voice had been 'more sweet than hers'. 'Sweet' is a key-word here, for Yeats found true femininity to lie in the sweetness of the female voice (in a late poem he asserted 'The women that I picked spoke sweet and low', "Hound Voice"). The critic and lecturer Thomas MacDonagh, another of the 1916 martyrs, is evoked in the following ambiguous terms: He was

> [...] coming into his force;
> He might have won fame in the end,
> So sensitive his nature seemed,
> So daring and sweet his thought [...]

'Force' reminds us here that MacDonagh, the intellectual and university-educated man of letters, had fatefully cast in his lot with men of the 'physical force' tradition in Irish politics. Yet his nature is a feminised one, combining as it does, sensitivity and sweetness of thought with daring. Even the sanguinary Pearse (his poetry and oratory had made much in the years immediately before the Rising of a necessary shedding of blood) whose 'helper and friend' MacDonagh had been, is gathered, in the revised 1920 version of the poem, into this nimbus of beauty and sensitivity—of the gentler, cultivated, even womanly virtues—for '[t]his man had kept a school' as well as riding 'our wingèd horse'. (The 1916 version of the poem here reads 'wingèd mettlesome horse'.)

In her detailed analysis of the gender politics of this poem, Elizabeth Butler Cullingford boldly asserts that

> Markievicz stands in for Gonne in "Easter 1916". The Countess, condemned to death for her part in the Rising but reprieved because of her sex, offered a mirror image of Gonne's devotion to her country and what might have been her fate had she stayed in Dublin.[5]

Certainly Yeats had often expressed a fear that Gonne would lose her femininity in a political fanaticism bred of abstract patriotism (or ideological commitment) which he did not think proper for women. Such abstraction had made the beautiful girl Constance Gore-Booth had once been, a strident, ignorant woman, wasteful of time and her own beauty. By extension such fanaticism (and the image of the revolutionaries' 'vivid faces', contrasted with the measured sobriety of 'grey Eighteenth-century houses', with which the poem opens, highlights a freakish fanaticism) can destroy the feminine in a man also. So Cullingford has it that '"Easter 1916" [...] asks whether the sacrifice of change occasioned by obsessive love of country may not give political men as well as political women hearts of stone'.[6]

Cullingford is referring in this summary to the central metaphor of the poem, the implications of which are explored in its third and fourth movements—that between the flux of natural life and the stone of the fanatic heart which troubles the living stream. Stone as metaphor here, in the context of Yeatsian imagining, intensifies the sense of Maud Gonne as presiding presence in the poem, for it had played a recurrent part in Yeats's fascination with her and in his concept of woman generally. When in 1898 Gonne had told him of her former sexual relations with her lover Lucien Millevoye, they had shared a strange dream in which 'She thought herself a great stone statue through which passed flame, and I felt myself becoming flame and mounting up through and looking out of the eyes of a great stone Minerva'. Yeats had asked himself 'were the beings which stand behind human life trying to unite us, or had we brought it by our own dreams?'[7] Yeats in 1898 would have known that in popular ideas of the Celt (the writings of the Breton scholar and critic Ernest Renan for example, which he read for his own article of 1898, 'The Celtic Element in Literature') the Celtic race was reckoned 'an essentially feminine race'[8] which had made a fetish of stone:

> The stone, in truth, seems the natural symbol of the Celtic races. It is an immutable witness that has no death. The animal, the plant, above all the human figure, only express the divine life under a determinate form; the stone on the contrary, adapted to receive all forms, has been the fetish of peoples in their childhood.[9]

Yet for a woman, for a man with a sensitive nature and sweet thought, for a feminine race, to worship stone is to risk petrification of the heart. The worship of any ideal, even the ideal beauty of a nation, is to worship the immutable and to miss the living, determinate reality of animal, plant and the human figure. The consequences can be fateful. A few days before the death of Synge in 1909, Yeats had communicated to his journal his fear that such a process would take Gonne in its chill grip:

> Maud Gonne writes that she is learning Gaelic. I would sooner see her work at Gaelic propaganda than any other Irish movement I can think of, except some movement for decorative art. Women, because the main event of their lives has been a giving of themselves, give themselves to an opinion as if [it] were some terrible stone doll. We [men] take up an opinion lightly and are easily false to it, and when faithful keep the habit of many interests [...]. They grow cruel, as if [in] defence of lover and child, and all this is done for something other than human life. At last the opinion becomes so much a part of them that it is as though a part of their flesh becomes, as it were, stone, and much of their being passes out of life. It was part of her power in the past that, though she made this surrender with her mind, she kept the sweetness of her voice and good humour, yet I cannot but fear for her.[10]

Yeats had dreaded what Ireland could do to Gonne and must have been secretly relieved that her estrangement from MacBride had largely kept her out of the country in the years when the sweet voice of a beautiful Gore-Booth had been made strident in the turmoil of agitational politics. He knew too that an entire generation could be affected by the same petrification. For those who had destroyed Synge, he had sensed, had been like 'an hysterical woman who will make unmeasured accusations and believe impossible things, because of some logical deduction from a solitary thought which has turned a portion of her mind to stone'.[11] In the meditative heart of his own poem, Yeats represents the dangers of fervent, even fanatical, commitment to an ideal, as a dialectic between stone and a living stream, between the immutable and flux. The dialectic brings the terrible beauty, longed for by the obsessive and fanatical (the 'enchanted' of the poem), to birth, in an occult dynamic which the poet seeks to comprehend in his brooding verses—a dynamic which might indeed have claimed Gonne as another of its victims, even though her ideal beauty epitomises the Ireland for which the revolutionaries died.

Gonne also pervades the poem, not only because for the poet she embodied beauty itself and because he had feared her vitality might have been hardened to stone had she stayed in Ireland to become a martyr for the cause, but in the special sense that the imagery and form of the poem in part derived from her imagination. Her role in its composition helped to make "Easter 1916" a work which, like many of Yeats's early lyrics, an incantation which seeks the status of magical, consciousness-transforming artefact.

In September 1911 Gonne had written to Yeats, in sensitive awareness of the complex gender exchanges that constituted their long relationship, that 'Our children were your poems of which I was the Father sowing the unrest and storm which made them possible & you the mother who brought them forth in suffering & in the highest beauty & our children had wings [...]'.[12] "Easter 1916" is a compelling example of an even more intimate, immediate kind of literary erotics.

In September 1901, when the spiritual marriage they had contracted in 1898 was still compulsively intact, Gonne had written to Yeats of one of her vivid waking visions. In a haunted glen she was led by a god and goddess to a stream:

> I went a long way up the stream till I stood by stones marked with 7 & 9. There standing in the middle of the stream dressed in lily green was a beautiful girl. She stood still & presently sat down by a rock & and laughing baby child came also dressed in green & leant up against her. (*GYL*, p.144.)

Gonne associated this vision with the music of the fairy folk, which she told Yeats she had heard once 'quite distinctly', with 'physical ears'. In 1915 she heard it again. On 7 November she wrote to Yeats that she had been haunted for three days 'by an air with the Rhythm of a dance reel' (*GYL*, p.362). She then recalled where she had heard the air before, when it had seemed to come out of the heart of a mountain, from Slieve Gullion. It had seemed in the past to be connected with the number 16. The air from the mountain, she recollected, had shared the rhythm of an '8 hand reel', which she had heard at a Gaelic League music festival. As she thought of this rhythm, which obsessed her in the early days of November 1915, she sensed its colour was green.

The imagery and curious numerology (stream, rock green-clad fairy folk, the numbers 7 and 9) of Gonne's earlier vision had been bathed in a blissful, almost pastoral, light, as in a Samuel Palmer canvas. The haunting fairy music of 1915, which she had heard before on Slieve Gullion in association with the number 16, provokes in 1915 a prophetic, Wagnerian vision of Irish destiny in the war raging in Europe. She thought of all Europe as dancing to the rhythms of the fairy reel and of the many Irish soldiers who had already given their lives on the battlefield. They were being brought back 'to the spiritual Ireland' from which they had wandered. Some had died without hate and so they could be part of the dance, but others among them had

> died with a definite idea of a sacrifice to an ideal, they were held by the stronger & deeper Rhythms of the chants, leading in wonderful patterns to a deeper place, the peace of the Crucified, which is above the currents of nationalities & storms, but for all that they will not be separated from Ireland for as an entity she has followed the path of Sacrifice & tasted of the Grail & the strength they will bring her is greater. (*GYL*, p.363.)

In the summer of 1916, when Gonne's vision of nationally efficacious Irish sacrifice had been vindicated (the poet was reading, with Iseult's help, the writings of the French Catholic school with, in Jammes and Péguy, its intense version of sacred sacrificial patriotism), Yeats's poem on the Rising entered the territory of his hostess's strange envisioning and numerological arcana. As Helen Vendler has pointed out—with an acknowledgement to Nathan Rose (one of her students), the poem itself is a deliberately numerological artefact, based on the date when the Rising began, 24 April 1916. It is constructed as four movements: the first of 16 lines, the second 24, the third 16 and the final movement 24 once more. This gives magical force to the act of poetry itself, for it participates in the mystery of the occasion it honours. 'I write it out in a verse' avers the poet/mage, 'I number him in the song'.

One of the most moving aspects of this powerful, troubled poem— its taut trimeter disallowing any too easily earned elevation of tone—is its consciousness of two orders of time. In one, day follows day, winter follows summer, minute by minute things change, 'close of day' brings 'nightfall', time is wasted in lingering in the street, in 'nights in argument', sacrifice can be sustained 'too long'. In another order of time, the martyrs of 1916 are monuments which inhabit eschatological reality, in a permanent present tense that suffuses futurity with national meaning:

> MacDonagh and MacBride
> And Connolly and Pearse
> Now and in time to be,
> Wherever green is worn,
> Are changed, changed utterly:
> A terrible beauty is born.

The numerological structure of the poem enforces a sense that quotidian time has been mastered by a deep structure in history which occasions recurrence. For the basic pattern of the poem, based on the date of the Rising, is rendered twice (16, 24, 16, 24). Just as the declaration of the Republic which Pearse read aloud outside the Post Office in central Dublin that Easter Monday justified his actions as a culmination of a repetitive history (the Irish people have risen in rebellion six times before, at Easter they rise again for the seventh time to complete the process with a sacred number, at a sacred time), Yeats's poem embodies recurrence in the sacral dimension of an eternal present. Yet the cost to individuals caught up by the process which the poem makes palpable, is also sorrowfully, even agonisingly, acknowledged. For 'death' in "Easter 1916" is not some counter in a saga of patriotic *grandeur*, as it seems to have been for Maud Gonne. It is a cruel, ineluctable and consequently radical interruption of the minute by minute vitality of daily existence and of the uncertainties of future political possibilities: 'Was it needless death after all?/For England may keep faith/For all that is done and said'. Yet for all that, patriots and poet have dwelt together at an apocalyptic moment, in a transformed order of time and being, which recalls the younger Yeats's conviction at the end of the 1890s that Ireland would be a site of magical renewal, when occult powers would elevate her to a transcendent spirituality: 'a terrible beauty is born'.

Yeats had twenty-five copies of the poem printed in 1917 for private circulation. The date appended to this version (the first published version made some changes to stanza two) was retained in subsequent publications. The effect is uncanny, for the precision of the date (25 September 1916) highlights how time has run on in the days and months since that fateful 24 April, to which the poem is a kind of monument, composed for future reading. It collapses back into the daily order of time from a period of five months when time has been experienced on another dimension. The 25 September seems the day after 24 April, which has been brooded upon in arrested, sacral time.

NOTES
1. W. B. Yeats, 'The Symbolism of Poetry', in *Essays and Introductions* (London: Macmillan 1961), p.159. Henceforth *E&I*.
2. Helen Vendler, 'Technique in the Earlier Poems of Yeats, in *Yeats Annual*, edited by Warwick Gould, No. 8 (London: Macmillan 1991), p.16.
3. Elizabeth Butler Cullingford, idem.
4. ibid., p.19.
5. W. B. Yeats, *Gender and History in Yeats's Love Poetry* (Cambridge: UP 1993), p.121.
6. idem.
7. *Memoirs*, ed. Denis Donoghue (London: Macmillan 1972), p.134. Henceforth *Mem*.
8. Ernest Renan, *The Poetry of the Celtic Races and Other Studies* [1896], trans., William G. Hutchison (Port Washington, NY: Kennikat Press 1970), p.8.
9. ibid., p.23.
10. *Mem*, pp.191-92.
11. W. B. Yeats, *Essays and Introductions* (London: Macmillan 1961), p.314.
12. Anna MacBride White and A. N. Jeffares, eds., *The Gonne-Yeats Letters, 1893-1938*, ed., Anna MacBride and A. Norman Jeffares (London: Hutchinson 1992), p.302; Henceforth *GYL*.

THE INCURSION OF THE WILDES INTO TÍR-NA-NÓG

Maria Pilar Pulido

> But the best book since Croker is Lady Wilde's *Ancient Legends*. The humour has all given way to pathos and tenderness. We have here the innermost heart of the Celt in the moments he has grown to love through years of persecution, when, cushioning himself about with dreams, and hearing fairy songs in the twilight, he ponders on the soul and on the dead. Here is the Celt, only it is the Celt dreaming.' (W. B. Yeats, *Fairy and Folk Tales of the Irish Peasantry*, 1888.)[1]

In 1881 Lady Wilde published *Ancient Legends, Mystic Charms, and Superstitions of Ireland* followed, two years later, by *Ancient Cures, Charms, and Usages* of Ireland. The contents of both volumes were based on the copious notes which Sir William Wilde had taken from the eighteen thirties onwards, partly from the Irish peasants (often in exchange for the customary medical fees they were unable to pay in cash)[2] and, partly, as the result of his own personal archaeological research on the treasures of Celtic Ireland. He was to carry out this research right up to his protracted death in 1876.

Wilde had planned the publication of such rich material but the project had to be shelved because of his numerous and time-consuming occupations. In the nineteen-eighties, Lady Wilde decided to discharge the terms of her late husband's will by taking on the enormous task of organising and compiling his notes into book form, a task which only her deep respect and great admiration for her husband's work together with her passion for the culture of her own native land allowed her to accomplish with success.[3] Her aim in undertaking its publication, as she states in the preface to *Ancient Legends*, had been to pay tribute to the Celtic people as the imaginative and mystical bearers of a sort of *docta ignorantia* which should never perish:

> In a few years such a collection would be impossible, for the olde race is rapidly passing away to other lands, and in the vast working-world of America, with all the new influences of light and progress, the young

generation, though still loving the land of their fathers, will scarcely find leisure to dream over the fairy-haunted hills and lakes and raths of ancient Ireland.
I must disclaim, however, all desire to be considered a melancholy Laudatrix temporis acti. These studies of the Irish past are simply the expression of my love for the beautiful island that gave me my first inspiration, my quickest intellectual impulse, and the strongest and best sympathies with genius and country possible to a woman's nature.[4]

Both the Wildes, in particular Sir William, had been conscious of the harmful influence exercised by the National School system on the Irish language and culture and were also deeply concerned about the ravaging effects of the Famine which had decimated the Irish-speaking community in a few short years. Somehow, Sir William's scientific mind was to blend perfectly with Lady Wilde's idealistic temperament echoing as they did her nationalist past.[5] Lady Wilde's concern with the supernatural can be traced back to 1849 when her translation of Johann Wilhelm Meinhold's *Sidonia the Sorceress*, which tells the story of Sidonia von Bork who was tried for witchcraft and executed in 1620, was published. Lady Wilde had felt attracted by Sidonia's verbal skills which had enabled the Pomeranian noblewoman to survive among a people whom she had sworn to exterminate and who had accused her of having cast a spell on the royal race of Pomerania in order to ensure its sterility and final disintegration.[6] The pre-Raphaelites submitted at once to Sidonia's charm; Burne-Jones did a painting of her and, in 1893, William Morris undertook the re-edition of Lady Wilde's translation 'which he praised as an almost faultless reproduction of the past, its action really alive'.[7]

Tír-na-nÓg is defined by Yeats as 'The Country of the Young': 'for age and death have not found it; neither tears nor loud laughter have gone near it. The shadiest boskage covers it perpetually'.[8] By extension, it can be regarded as the world where the fairies dwell, that of the supernatural which, in Ireland, is so closely linked to the peasantry's ancient usages and superstitions, what in Irish is known as *piseog*. The supernatural had acquired a noticeable presence in the everyday lives of the Irish peasants who, downtrodden by a hostile political and social reality, had clung to those ancestral beliefs thus creating, out of their pre-history, a sort of 'parahistory' which was closer to their own reality and, paradoxically, easier to comprehend and control than the oppressor's official written History. The conclusion of the reconciliatory quality of folklore was reached by Sir William through his ethnological research. In his book entitled *Irish Popular*

Superstitions (1852), Wilde states his belief in the existence of a common cultural base entwined in the very fabric of popular superstitions: 'There are certain types of superstitions common to almost all countries in similar states of progress or civilisation, and others which abound in nearly every condition of society.'[9] A cultural concept whose ideological implications had already been put forward by the Young Irelanders in their claim to a unifying cultural past in which men of letters had a decisive role to play as leaders of the nation: 'Culturally and politically, the concern of Young Ireland is precisely to articulate the 'otherness' of Ireland around its own centre, both geographically and politically, and in relation to the myth of a unified and coherent cultural past.'[10] Yeats regarded the poetry of Thomas Davis, the spiritual leader of the Young Irelanders, as the turning point in his awakening to Ireland's cultural nationalism as had been the case with Lady Wilde forty years earlier.[11]

Sir William's research into the archaeological treasures of Celtic Ireland had its beginnings in the 1840's when he was a member of the Ordnance Survey. This commission had on its staff Gaelic scholars of renown such as Eugene O'Curry and John O'Donovan and worked under the supervision of Captain Thomas Larcom. Its aim was 'to collect all available information, antiquarian or topical, about the particular part of the Country which at the time was being surveyed'.[12] The department's activities produced quite a number of publications among which Sir William's *The Boyne and the Blackwater, the Beauties of the Boyne and its Tributary the Blackwater*, published in 1849, which resulted in its author's rise to fame within the scholastic community of the Dublin of his time. Two years after the publication of this book, Dr Wilde married Miss Jane Francesca Elgee 'Speranza' whose ambiguous brand of republicanism was to fade away on her husband's being knighted in 1863.[13] Nevertheless, Speranza's nationalistic views were to remain with her throughout her life and permeate the final version of the folk material taken down by Sir William by adding an ideological stance almost totally avoided by its compiler. A member of the Royal Irish Academy since 1839, Wilde was appointed Census Commissioner two years later. His main activity for many years was to catalogue the archaeological treasures of the Academy's museum and the diffusion of the works of artists such as the painter Gabriel Béranger who had contributed to the revitalisation of Ireland's monumental past.[14]

While on their honeymoon the Wildes decided to set off for Denmark whose Royal Society of Northern Antiquities had sent a representative to Dublin the previous year. While Dr Wilde stood in awe before the Danish archaeological remains so carefully treasured in the Museum of Antiquities of Copenhagen, and inquired about further and more prolific co-operation between the two countries, his wife set down her own literary and ethnological impressions of a journey which was to end in their visiting all the Scandinavian countries including Germany. In Sweden, Lady Wilde read with enthusiasm the ancient manuscripts of the *Codex Argentus*, the poems of Edda, the Scandinavian mythological saga and the ballads which narrate the deeds of Thor, Odin and Freya. Thus, her personal appreciations dealt not only with the archaeological treasures of those countries but also with the cultural heritage that the Scandinavian ballads and legends represent for those countries. She was to record some of those ballads and legends which she later translated and inserted in *Driftwood from Scandinavia* published in 1884. The deep interest which the Wildes took in ancient cultures and folklore becomes essential in order to understand firstly, the scholarly approach which lay at the basis of Sir William's passion for Irish culture and secondly, Lady Wilde's invaluable contribution which suited both her idealistic temperament and the folk images which, only a few years later, were to feed the Celtic Renaissance's lyrical approach to myth.[15]

Whereas Lady Wilde's two volumes on folklore were both warmly received by the Irish public nevertheless she came in for a great deal of criticism from some Dublin scholars. Among those critical of Lady Wilde's methods—or lack of—was Douglas Hyde whose conviction of the priority of a scientific approach to the sources deterred him from taking the Wildes' work too seriously. In *Beside the Fire* (1898), he regretfully admitted that,

> Lady Wilde's volumes, are, nevertheless, a wonderful and copious record of folk-lore customs, which must lay Irishmen under one more debt of gratitude to the gifted compiler. It is unfortunate, however, that these volumes are hardly as valuable as they are interesting, and for the usual reason—that we do not know what is Lady Wilde's and what is not.[16]

The literary value of folk compilations which had assured the celebrity of authors such as William Carleton, Samuel Lover and Patrick Kennedy was to take a mere second place in Hyde's methodological approach to myth, scrupulously conscious as he was of the concept of 'authenticity' and faithfulness when applied to the sources of any given folk material. On the contrary, the Wildes' approach to folklore gave priority to imagination as the essence of the people's 'intuitive science' which the printing process was determined to save at all costs. Unfortunately, the numerous spelling errors in the transcription of Irish words left the Wildes defenceless against Hyde's criticisms based on what he considered to be an essential premise, namely, that one should be perfectly bilingual in order to be a trustworthy folklore compiler. As it happens, Sir William's doubtful mastery of the Irish language was at no stage a drawback in his research. Nevertheless, while staying at Moytura House, he had made good use of the linguistic skills of native interpreters such as Dr Conor Maguire of Claremorris who became his constant and ever helpful guide when travelling around the county in search of new material.[17] For Sir William, the challenge lay in the preservation of the lyrical element which permeated the fatally wounded Gaelic oral tradition, a precious jewel he was determined to save from the mists of oblivion with the same zeal he had applied to the preservation of the Irish archaeological treasures of the Royal Irish Academy.

But Hyde and the Folklore Society could hardly regard the Wildes' 'unfaithful' contribution to folklore as truly reliable. However, as far as Sir William was concerned, the transcription of the native oral tradition in a foreign written language, from an unconscious collective memory and experience to its conscious and individual literary contextualisation, involved an irretrievable loss which he considered to be a minor evil if compared with the certainty of its total disappearance. As Sir William put it: 'Nothing contributes more to uproot superstitious rites and forms than to print them [...].'[18] According to this theory, the works of Carleton, Banim, Griffin, and the Wildes themselves would constitute the literary epitaph of a bygone oral tradition.

More appreciative of the Wildes' vision of the task of the folk compiler than Douglas Hyde, Yeats encouraged the imaginative approach as a means of reintroducing the mytho-poetic element of Irish culture into Ireland's cultural reality,

> The various collectors of Irish folk-lore have, from our point of view, one great merit, and from the point of view of others, one great fault. They have made their work literature rather than science, and told us of the Irish peasantry rather than of the primitive religion of mankind, or whatever else the folk-lorists are on the gad after. To be considered scientists they should have tabulated all their tales in forms like

grocers' bills—item the fairy king, item the queen. Instead of this they have caught the very voice of the people, the very pulse of life, each giving what was most noticed in his day.[19]

Thus, Lady Wilde's errors in transcribing Irish words in the stories, which had been one of Hyde's strongest arguments in attempting to diminish the scientific validity of her compilations, were to be regarded as a symptom of the fallibility of any attempt to uproot Celtic lore from its oral environment. In any case, at that time, the term 'authenticity' seemed to be often used and abused by all folk compilers, whether they were scientific or imaginative, as if it were a password for both the folklorist and indeed the contemporary English reader to that world of eternal youth which was fading away before their very eyes. Thus, the so-called 'fidelity to the sources' becomes devoid of sense, and is not only a *cliché* but a rhetorical or argumentative element vital to the outsider's incursion into the supernatural through a pre-established accord between the anonymity of the teller, the known compiler and the possible reader. In order to give credence to this point of view, Lady Wilde had added Sir William's 'Address to the Anthropological Section of the British Association' at the end of *Ancient Legends*, by far, the better documented and better structured of the two volumes dedicated to Irish folklore. In this speech delivered in Belfast in 1874, Sir William traces one of the causes which may account for the lack of detailed knowledge of Druidism or Paganism in ancient Ireland by blaming the Christian missionaries who had undertaken the transcription of legends with the purpose of obliterating 'every vestige of the ancient forms of faith'. Transcribing a story which belongs to the oral tradition becomes, even for the scrupulous researcher of the original manuscript of the legend, a betrayal to the sources.

Thus, the label of authenticity represented for the literary compiler a sort of rhetorical device whose degree of veracity would be scarcely questioned by the English speaking readers of the time, and Lady Wilde dutifully reproduces the well-known formula in her introduction to *Ancient Legends of Ireland*,

> These narrations were taken down by competent persons skilled in both languages, and as far as possible in the very words of the narrator; so that much of the primitive simplicity of the style has been retained, while the legends have a peculiar and special value as coming direct from the national heart.[20]

The Wildes' incursion into *Tír-na-nÓg* leaves aside the legendary Ireland in which the deeds of mythical heroes were to be revived by other authors such as Lady Gregory. The heroes of their stories are the Irish peasants themselves whose superstitions faithfully portray the ritualistically established rapport between their anodyne everyday lives and the invisible world. Somehow, rituals represent for Lady Wilde the only way both strata can be linked in order to counteract the maleficient attraction fairies feel for the human world. Throughout the numerous stories she narrates, the reader comes into contact with the world of ritualistic behaviour through a series of druidic charms which have been preserved in manner though the wording has been 'translated' into a more acceptable Christian mode. This transformation can be easily 'diagnosed', for instance, in the prescription given against a nasty toothache, 'drink water from a human skull; or take a pinch of clay from a priest's grave, and put it in your mouth. Then kneel down, say a *Pater* and an *Ave*, and you will have no more toothache as long as you live'.[21] In *Ancient Cures*, Lady Wilde analyses this pious passage from the bardic tradition to the Christian tradition, from pagan Ireland to Saint Patrick's Ireland, from what is considered *piseog* to the official religious rites,

> Meantime, the ancient Druidic charms and invocations continued to hold their power over the people, who believed in them with undoubting faith. No doubt, in pagan times, the invocations were made in the names of Baal and Ashtaroth, and by the power of the sun, the moon, and the winds; but the Christian converts, while still retaining the form of the ancient charms, substituted the names of the Trinity and the words of the Christian Rituals as still more powerful in effecting cures.[22]

Sir William's opthalmological practice led him to further inquire into the peasants' treatment of eye diseases, especially blindness which had caused an endless flow of pilgrims towards the numerous sacred wells of Ireland.[23] John Millington Synge found, among the stories and anecdotes dealing with the sacred wells taken down by Sir William, that of *ceathair aluinn* in Aranmore where he was to place the protagonists of his play *The Well of the Saints*. Inevitably, after the peasant's last disease came death and, accompanying it, the wake, a deep-rooted cultural event Dr Wilde eagerly attended in the area surrounding Moytura House where he spent his holidays. A sympathetic ethnological study of the wake follows a description of the activities of the peasant community around the deceased, in which games, dances, music, and drink are 'respectfully' fused in between prayers.

The Wildes' approach to the numerous stories they transcribed opened up a double tracked passage into Tír-na-nÓg: that of the archaeologist and that of the political idealist, both in search of the roots of a unifying cultural past. Their compilations show Irish culture as the basis of unity, a common property capable of being appreciated, rehabilitated and recreated thanks to its everlasting lyricism which Yeats so appreciated. The Wildes' main contribution to folklore was that they put forward yet another potent argument towards proving that the Celt far from being dead was alive to all those who had been given the gift of interpreting the language and dreams of a never to be forgotten legendary past.

NOTES
1 See William Butler Yeats, *Irish Fairy and Folk Tales* (New York: The Modern Library, n.d. [1925]), p.xv; first published as *Fairy and Folk Tales of the Irish Peasantry* (London: Walter Scott 1888).
2 'It was said that when he was offered presents of butter and fowl by peasants in return for medical assistance he would often ask that a piece of poetry or folklore be recited instead.' Ulick O'Connor, *Celtic Dawn: A Portrait of the Irish Literary Renaissance* (London: Black Swan Books 1985), p.100.
3 The prospect of a ameliorating her financial difficulties may be have been a factor also.
4 Lady Wilde, *Ancient Legends, Mystic Charms, and Superstitions of Ireland* (London: Ward & Downey 1881), p.xii.
5 'There was a point in her idealism and his enthusiasm where their natures met. It was established when she finished his unpublished work and included his last speech in her book of Irish customs, the harvest of his life's gleanings shared with hers.' Terence de Vere White, *The Parents of Oscar Wilde* (London: Hodder & Stoughton 1967), p.234.
6 *Sidonia the Sorceress* was one of Oscar Wilde's favourite readings as a child. In the preface to the book, the reader is presented with the heroine's dual portrait: in the first one, Sidonia is represented 'in the prime of mature beauty' painted in the style of Lucas Cranach, whereas, behind it, one can distinguish Sidonia's aged and witch-like features dressed for her ready execution, this time painted in the style of Rubens. This dual portrait, as well as the way Sidonia makes use of her exceptional beauty, should be duly added to the possible sources which inspired Oscar Wilde's masterpiece in prose, *The Picture of Dorian Gray.*
7 Richard Ellmann, *Oscar Wilde* (London: Penguin Books 1987), p.19.
8 William Butler Yeats, op. cit. (1925), p.214.
9 William Wilde, *Irish Popular Superstitions* [1852] (Shannon: IUP 1972), p.30.
10 David Lloyd, *Nationalism and Minor Literature, James Clarence Mangan and the Emergence of Irish Cultural Nationalism* (Berkeley: University of California Press 1987), p.3.
11 'Under O'Leary's influence he half intended to start up some day a new Young Ireland movement like that of Thomas Davis forty years before; it would produce nationalist literature, too, but of better quality, and would

play a less active role than Davis's group in practical politics, in which Yeats had no interest.' Richard Ellmann, *Yeats: the Man and the Masks* [1948] (London: Penguin Books 1987), p.102.
12 G. Wilson, *Victorian Doctor: Being the Life of Sir William Wilde* (Yorkshire: EP Publishing 1974), (1942), p.145.
13 On 15th September 1849, *The Nation* published an article by Miss Elgee (later Mrs Wilde) about Wilde's *Boyne* book in which, in fact, he had quoted some of "Speranza's" poetry.
14 As in the case of the folk material left behind by Wilde, his wife finished and published his notes on the Dutch painter in book form entitled *Memoirs of Gabriel Béranger* in 1880.
15 'From Sir William Wilde, however, Yeats learned the far-reaching importance of the folk imagination and its tales and beliefs. Sir William Wilde was one of the earliest to comment upon folk material as a form of poetry in and of itself'. Steve D. Putzel, *Yeats's Use of Irish Folklore and Mythology in the 1890's* (Toronto 1980), p.13. Thesis.
16 Douglas Hyde, *Beside the Fire* (Dublin: Irish Academic Press 1978), (1898), p.xix.
17 'Sir William would always take me with him as an interpreter with Irish speaking farmers when he was investigating old forts or any archaeological remains.' Cited in Terence de Vere White, *The Parents of Oscar Wilde: Sir William and Lady Wilde* (London: Hodder & Stoughton 1967), p.220.
18 Quoted in Seamus Deane, 'Fictions and Politics: The Nineteenth Century National Character', in *Gaéliana*, VI (1984), p.97.
19 William Butler Yeats, op. cit. (1925), p.xiv.
20 Lady Wilde, op. cit. (1888), p.xii.
21 Lady Wilde, *Ancient Cures, Charms, and Usages of Ireland* (London: Ward & Downey 1890), p.12.
22 ibid., p.88.
23 In *Legends of Saints & Sinners* (1915), Douglas Hyde retakes the theme of the sacred well's curative powers. He had also found a few prayers or charms against the Evil Eye which he published in the second volume of *Religious Songs of Connacht* (1906).

OSCAR WILDE, THE FAIRY TALE, AND THE CRITICS

Neil Sammells

Until quite recently such little critical attention as had been paid to Wilde's fairy tales regarded them principally as a quarry for biographical speculation. For instance, Richard Ellmann—although he has little to say about the stories in his 1987 biography—introduced Wilde's *Selected Writings* in 1961 by noting that 'the fairy tale was a natural form for him to choose to write in, and perhaps all his creative work belongs to this genre': in these fantasies he could cancel 'his nightmare of being found out with light-hearted dreams of pardon and transfiguration'.[1] Similarly, Christopher Nasaar has argued that they are Wilde's attempt 'to remain within the charmed circle of his children, innocent and safe from evil' and to assert 'the primacy of his family life and to reject the siren call of homosexuality'.[2] Such a critical approach reached its nadir in Robert K. Martin's reading of "The Happy Prince" as Wilde's covert celebration of his newly discovered homosexuality over the heterosexual life he had lived before. Martin says of the relationship between the swallow and the reed: 'A good deal of Oscar's experience with Constance undoubtedly went into this passage: she, although attractive, was hardly literary and was intellectually incapable of sharing her husband's life'.[3] However, that biography might be displaced by politics in a more stimulating analysis of the fairy tales had been noticed by George Woodcock in 1949:

> This ["The Young King"] is a parable on the capitalist system of exploitation as severe as anything in William Morris, and it can stand beside the grimmest passages of Marx as an indictment of the kind of horrors which, Wilde was fully aware, were inflicted on the toilers in this world for the benefit of the people he satirised in his plays.[4]

Apparently taking her cue from Woodcock, Jerusha McCormack insists that the fairy tales are to be read 'from the perspective of the poor, the colonised, the disreputable and dispossessed'.[5] I want to concentrate less on the tales as political commentary than on the political implications of Wilde's choice to use this particular form, a choice which—if Ellmann is right in describing it as natural—would be perhaps the only natural thing Wilde ever did.

The Happy Prince and other Tales (1888) and *The House of Pomegranates* (1891) are contemporaneous with the composition and publication of 'The Decay of Lying' and 'The Critic as Artist': essays in which Wilde expounded his anti-naturalistic aesthetic theories. It is thus reasonable to suppose that these fairy tales might bear the same self-conscious relationship to those theories as does *The Picture of Dorian Gray*, first published in 1890. Indeed Wilde talks about the fairy tales in much the same terms. In defending *Dorian Gray* against the charge of immorality, Wilde described it as 'an essay on decorative art. It reacts against the brutality of plain realism'.[6] In a letter to Leonard Smithers (July 1888) he says that "The Happy Prince" 'is a reaction against the purely imitative treatment of modern art—and now that literature has taken to blowing loud trumpets I cannot but be pleased that some ear has cared to listen to the low music of a little reed'.[7] In defending Ricketts's cover-design for *The House of Pomegranates* against the questionable taste of the reviewer of the *Speaker*, Wilde made the link with his novel explicit. The reviewer had objected to Ricketts's abstract design, claiming to discern in what Wilde called 'the delicate tracing, arabesques, and massing of many coral-red lines on a ground of white ivory' an Indian club with a house-painter's brush on top of it. Wilde was imperious in his dismissal: 'Now, I do not for a moment dispute that these are the real impressions your critic received. It is the spectator, and the mind of the spectator, as I pointed out in the preface to *The Picture of Dorian Gray* that art really mirrors.' For Wilde, Ricketts had managed to orchestrate a colour-effect culminating in 'high gilt-notes'—'what the gilt notes suggest, what imitative parallel may be found to them in the chaos that is termed Nature, is a matter of no importance' (*LOW*, p.301). Characteristically, Wilde collapses the distinction between surface and depth, form and contents, in outlining the aesthetic strategies of the stories by theorising the pleasure to be had from the designs they are bound with. That the fairy tales generally were for Wilde, at an important level, experiments in form is confirmed by his comments to Thomas Hutchinson on "The Nightingale and the Rose":

> I like to think that there may be many meanings to the Tale—for in writing it [...] I did not start with the idea and clothe it in form, but

began with a form and strove to make it beautiful enough to have many secrets and many answers. (*LOW*, p.218.)

Wilde said that 'all fine imaginative work is self-conscious and deliberate',[8] and his aesthetic choice to employ the fairy tale is as self-conscious and deliberate as any he made as a writer. In this respect, the fairy tales deserve to be considered as specific and important examples of those anti-realist strategies which Declan Kiberd has associated so closely with Wilde's republican and anti-imperialist sympathies.[9]

Kiberd notwithstanding, postcolonial criticism—perhaps the dominant force in contemporary Irish Studies—has not given Wilde a uniformly good press. Seamus Deane, for instance, claims in *The Field Day Anthology of Irish Writing* that Wilde's poetry is vulgar in its facility of feeling and rhythmic automatism; as in all of Wilde's work, Deane continues, 'the subversive, even radical critique of society that is implicit in what he has to say, finds no release within the linguistic conventions which he mocked but by which he remained imprisoned'.[10] The rhetorical strategy is clear: metaphorical imprisonment in linguistic convention anticipates literal incarceration in Reading Gaol as Wilde's life and work are organised into a narrative of compromise and defeat. Indeed, Wilde's postcolonialist credentials, endorsed so thoroughly by Kiberd, could be called into question by a reading of the fairy tales grounded in the work of Ashis Nandy and his influential psychology of colonialism: a reading, which, as Deane argues of the poetry, would see their political commentary as compromised by the *genre* Wilde chooses to work in. Kiberd, of course, draws heavily on Nandy and his central claim that Wilde was 'an unself-aware, but more or less complete critic of the political culture which sired colonialism'.[11] (Though Kiberd clearly regards Wilde's critique as highly self-conscious.) However, Nandy also notes that one of the principal strategies of imperialism is the construction of a fantasy of hyper-masculinity on the part of the colonisers, and the projection of childishness and effeminacy onto the colonised. Poignantly enough, it is Lord Alfred Douglas who expresses this identification most succinctly in his belligerently entitled *Without Apology* (1938): 'Unless you understand that Wilde is an Irishman through and through, you will never get an idea of what his real nature is. In many ways he is as simple and innocent as a child'.[12] In utilising the fairy-tale, then, Wilde is treading a dangerous line: laying himself open to the accusation that he has internalised the child-like qualities and awareness projected onto the Irish by a Celticism as much in the service of the imperial masters as of the cultural nationalists. Indeed, Micheal MacLiammoir (an Englishman reinventing himself as Irish) speaks of *The Happy Prince and other Stories* in symptomatic terms:

> Are these stories really intended for children? To me they seem to have been written for everybody who is or has ever been a child in the complete sense of the word, and who is fortunate enough, or wise enough to have preserved something of what, in Childhood itself, is fortunate, wise and eternal.[13]

For MacLiammoir, then, being 'in touch' with the child within is not simply a measure of his ability to appreciate the tales, it is a way of self-fashioning an Irishness which is both overperformed and overdetermined. Predictably, Wilde has it both ways on the question of intended audience. He sent a copy of *The Happy Prince* to Gladstone, coupling a declaration of his own 'Celtic blood' with the shy-sounding claim that his book 'is really meant for children' (*LOW*, p.218). Indeed, Wilde anticipates MacLiammoir in a letter to G. H. Kersley, describing the stories as 'meant partly for children, and partly for those who have kept the childlike faculties of wonder and joy, and who find in simplicity a strange subtleness' (*LOW*, p.219). Elsewhere, he chooses an entirely different tack. He responded to a review of *The House of Pomegranates* in the *Pall Mall Gazette* by declaring that no 'fairly-educated' person could really believe his stories were meant for children:

> I had as much intention of pleasing the British child as I had of pleasing the British public. Mamilius is as delightful as Caliban is entirely detestable, but neither the standard of Mamilius nor the standard of Caliban is my standard. (*LOW*, p.302.)

Nandy sees Wilde's homosexuality as a politico-pathological statement against imperialism, one he shared with the likes of his fellow Irishman George Moore, and such Bloomsbury luminaries as Lytton Strachey, J. M. Keynes, Virginia Woolf, Somerset Maugham, E. M. Forster, W. H. Auden—but emphasises constantly the lack of self-awareness in these 'chaotic, individuated' protests.[15] What I want to suggest is that it is precisely the self-consciousness with which Wilde employs the fairy-tale form which allows us to defend him against the accusation that his anti-imperialism is compromised by *genre*. After all, his identification of the British public with Caliban is a sly inversion whereby the distinction between the coloniser and Prospero's colonised subject is collapsed. Wilde does not internalise childishness, he stylises it—and gets his retaliation in first.

Norbert Kohl argues that the political edge to "The Young King" is blunted by the way Wilde's descriptions of poverty and exploitation move from the realistic to the allegorical, as the eponymous hero encounters Avarice, Fever, Plague and Death. For Kohl, this stylistic slippage is redolent of a socialism more interested in aesthetic effect than political propaganda. Of course, allegory occupies a privileged place in that postcolonial criticism which when it attributes a specific aesthetic mode to a text, is convinced—erroneously, according to Kevin Barry—'that it has defined logically the politics of that text'.[16] Barry's critique of these assumptions focuses on the work of David Lloyd and Luke Gibbons. For both, Barry argues, allegory and metonymy—the trope of difference, because it leaves things casually side by side—'throw the weight of authority and influence behind insurgent social groups which oppose or have opposed the nation-state'. Opposed to allegory and metonymy are symbol and metaphor which—to put it crudely—force things together: 'metaphor and symbol erase differences, of economy, social class and gender, in the supposed interest of a higher but fully existent unity'.[17] Allegory is the aesthetic of dissent, symbolism the aesthetic of union. Barry discusses Gibbons's analysis of the allegorical oaths of secret societies, such as the Whiteboys, dedicated to agrarian violence,[18] and David Lloyd's contention that in allegorising the landscape around Coole Park, with a superb indifference to fact, Yeats expresses a recalcitrance to the homogenising impulses of the nation-state.[19] Although Owen Dudley Edwards would no doubt balk at his own methods of analysis and scholarship being described as postcolonial, such an approach is echoed in his allegorical reading of "The Selfish Giant". Patrick Pearse, Dudley Edwards tells us, drew heavily on both "The Selfish Giant" and "The Happy Prince" for his own Gaelic tales, translating them back not just into the Irish language but into an Irish setting:

> He set the stories in the Connaught where the Wildes had worked and played. "The Selfish Giant" in particular suggests not just a peasant context, where Pearse put it, but the Giant as owner of the Big House with the little children as peasants and, presumably, Catholics.[20]

In other words Wilde's political point—that repressive authority can be both subverted and transformed from below—is refracted through the allegorical mode of representation which, according to Lloyd and Gibbons, correlates to the oppressed and dissident social groupings effecting that transformation.

A less theoretically orientated, more positivist, postcolonial criticism than Lloyd's and Gibbons's, however, attempts a direct recuperation of Wilde for the native culture endangered by the colonisers. Jerusha McCormack introduces the essays collected as *Wilde the Irishman*—and which include Dudley Edwards's—by saying that they 'seek to reinstate his spirit back in its own haunting grounds: to relocate its origins and its effects in its native Ireland and in that spiritual territory that Wilde himself understood as home to the collective unconscious of his race'.[21] In this context, the most revealing essay in the collection is by Deirdre Toomey in which she argues that Wilde's fairy-tales stem from the tradition of Irish story-telling— pointing out that many of his stories were never written down but recorded by acquaintances like André Gide, Charles Ricketts, Jean Lorrain and Guillot de Saix, who were present at their improvisation but did not have the Irish context in which to appreciate them.[22] Toomey's starting-point is Yeats's contention that Wilde's fairy tales become less original and accomplished the further they go from improvisation and a sense of particular audience, an aesthetic judgement, she points out, which 'is also a mark of an Irish cultural valuing of the oral over the written'.[23] Yeats's comments, from his introduction to a 1923 edition of *The Happy Prince and Other Stories*, now read like a retrospective attempt to reclaim Wilde from his decadent context. Paul Bourget had argued, for instance, in his *Essais de psychologie contemporaine* (1883-85) that 'a decadent literature sequesters the reader from a shared reality, and the high artifice of the style deepens the divide between spoken and written language, which Mallarmé had opened'.[24] In this respect, as Peter Nicholls notes, decadent writing could be seen to perpetrate a kind of Barthesian violence against spoken language and the forms of social cohesion it should promote and embody;[25] by emphasising Wilde's 'orality', Yeats and Toomey implicitly relocate him in an organic community which has yet to succumb to the modernist fragmentation of its social structures, sense of identity and modes of representation.

Inevitably, then, such a recuperation of Wilde is undertaken not just in the name of cultural authenticity, but for an authentic culture, and its tone veers constantly toward the elegiac. Toomey, for instance, says of Wilde's much-admired oral tale "The Poet" that it is, in effect, an Irish folk tale inverted: 'a product of that dying oral culture to which Wilde was tied by what Yeats called "his half-civilised blood", the culture of those who listened to spoken tales, undivided by book culture—"friend by friend, lover by lover"'.[26] Indeed, the temptation to see Wilde as somehow tied to these origins is strong: Owen Dudley Edwards decides that Oscar Fingal O'Flahertie Wilde 'was a hostage to Irish cultural identity'.[27] Here is the crux of the problem: how can we reconcile such more or less self-consciously postcolonial readings of Wilde's fairy tales with Wilde as proto-postmodernist? How does the Irish Wilde, tapping into folklore, square with the Wilde who, according to Terry Eagleton, anticipates to a sometimes astonishing degree 'the insights of contemporary cultural theory'?[28] After all, postmodernism challenges notions of authenticity and origin, championing instead cultural hybridity—and sees national and ethnic identities as culturally produced. What I want to suggest here is the importance of Toomey's emphasis on the element of performance in Wilde's story-telling, and on her contention that the

> cardinal sins of literacy are the cardinal virtues of orality. Originality in an oral culture consists not in inventing an absolutely new story but in stitching together the familiar in a manner suitable to a certain audience, or by introducing new elements into an old story. The persistent charge of plagiarism seems oxymoronic in an oral culture.[29]

For Wilde, of course, his own work proved that the charge of plagiarism was oxymoronic in a print-culture too: 'It is only the unimaginative who ever invents. The true artist is known by the use of what he annexes, and he annexes everything.'[30] In characteristically postmodern fashion, Wilde 'samples' his pre-texts and refuses the distinction between 'high' and 'low' culture: recognising the equivalence of all objects, he was prepared to praise a buttonhole or a teacup in much the same terms as he would a painting or a sculpture. For Susan Sontag, at least, such a 'hypertrophy of appetite for culture'[31] (she is here, significantly, describing the films of Godard) lends Wilde's writing a fundamentally democratic esprit. It also, in my view, signals that for Wilde Irishness is a form of discursive play and performance: national identity becomes a theatrical 'liminal space'[32] in which Irishness and Englishness encounter and collapse into each other. Frank McGuinness writes memorably of *De Profundis* that it is a fucking of Bosie by verbal force—and goes on to identify the characteristically Wildean drama that the letter enacts:

> Whatever is written can be published, and whatever is published is performed. *De Profundis* is not the meditation of the penitent at prayer. It is the act of a penitent as performer. It is a histrionic defiance of the histrionic judgement passed against Wilde at his trial, a theatrical explosion to break the silence that his prison sentence demanded: it is a play.[33]

Such a reading not only prevents us from accepting that the 'penitent' Wilde of *De Profundis* is in some sense the authentic Wilde—cornered, finally, in the misery of the prison-cell. It also reminds us of Wilde's other theatrical performances, including his starring-role as an Irishman in late-Victorian English society. Wilde's Irishness is not a compromised position, but a wilfully *compromising* one—a dramatic posture he can adopt in order to confront the very Englishness he needs for his theatrical effects. That nationality was histrionic for Wilde is evidenced by his reaction to the banning of *Salomé*. 'I am not English. I am Irish, which is quite another thing,' he announced—simultaneously declaring his attention to take up French citizenship.[34]

What I want to establish is that Wilde's fairy-tales are cultural hybrids. Isobel Murray, for instance, sees analogues for Wilde's parables of art and industry not in Irish material but in William Morris's *News from Nowhere* and Tennyson's *The Palace of Art*, and says that he plundered Matthew Arnold's poems for the details which flesh-out the oriental exoticism of "The Fisherman and his Soul".[35] This is, then, a complex cultural exchange: Irish and non-Irish elements are transformed, as borders and boundaries blur and collapse. What Wilde produces are tales in which the transformations of *genre* parallel a fantasised transformation of material conditions, and hence a radical politics. Intriguingly, in his essay *The Rise of Historical Criticism* Wilde maps his way elegantly across some familiar Todorovean terrain as he describes the historical methods of Greek historians. According to Wilde, Herodotus accepts—indeed searches for—the supernatural; Thucydides simply ignores it; Polybius explains it away. Herodotus, he argues, is preferable to Thucydides in particular because of his emphasis on the social and economic; Wilde tires of the latter's tedious descriptions of battles which 'we would readily exchange for some notice of the condition of private society in Athens, or the influence and position of women'.[36] In effect, Wilde's fairy-tales are narratives in the manner of Herodotus: the supernatural coexists with social, economic and political critique (and is not explained away by it) in that moment of delayed recognition which Todorov identifies with the fantastic. To fully appreciate the complexity of these stories, we need to recognise the limitations of any approach which seeks to 'naturalise' them, either by denying the artfulness of Wilde's aesthetic choices, or by authenticating them—tracing them back to Celtic origins. All those in search of the authentic Wilde should remember Lady Bracknell's verdict on Jack Worthing when she learns that he can trace his descent back to Victoria Station: he is the only person she has ever met whose origin is a terminus.

NOTES

1. Richard Ellmann, ed., *Selected Writings of Oscar Wilde* (OUP 1961), p.xii.
2. Christopher Nasaar, *Into the Demon Universe: A literary exploration of Oscar Wilde* (Yale UP 1974), pp.35-36.
3. Robert K. Martin, 'Oscar Wilde and the Fairy Tale: The Happy Prince as self-dramatization', *Studies in Victorian Fiction*, vol. 16, 1979, pp.74-77. Norbert Kohl summarises the similarly biographical approaches to "The Fisherman and his Soul", "The Birthday of the Infanta" and "The Star-Child" of Léon Lemonnier and Robert Merle. See Kohl, *Oscar Wilde: The Works of a Conformist Rebel*, trans. David Henry Wilson (Cambridge UP 1989), pp.49-50. See also Michael C. Kotzin, '"The Selfish Giant" as Literary Fairy Tale', *Studies in Short Fiction*, Vol. 16 (1979), pp.301-09; Kotzin argues that "The Selfish Giant" turns out to be about a sinner who is forgiven, 'as Wilde the sinner hoped that he himself would be'.
4. George A. Woodcock, *The Paradox of Oscar Wilde* (London: T. V. Boardman 1949), pp.148-49.
5. Jerusha McCormack, 'Wilde's Fiction(s)', in Peter Raby, ed., *The Cambridge Companion to Oscar Wilde* (Cambridge UP 1997), p.102.
6. *Daily Chronicle*, 30 June, 1890.
7. *The Letters of Oscar Wilde*, ed., Rupert Hart-Davis, (London: Hart-Davis 1962), p.221. Henceforth *LOW*.
8. *The Complete Works of Oscar Wilde* [new edn.] (London: Collins 1966), p.1020.
9. See Declan Kiberd, *Inventing Ireland: The Literature of the Modern Nation* (London: Jonathan Cape 1995), pp.33-50.
10. Seamus Deane, ed., *The Field Day Anthology of Irish Writing*, Vol. II, p.721. For a discussion of how Wilde sets the anthology's editors at odds with each and with themselves, see Neil Sammells, 'Rediscovering the Irish Wilde', in George Sandulescu, ed., *Rediscovering Oscar Wilde* (Gerrards Cross: Colin Smythe 1994), pp.362-70.
11. Ashis Nandy, *The Intimate Enemy: Loss and Recovery of Self under Colonialism* (OUP 1988), p.45.
12. Lord Alfred Douglas, *Without Apology* (NY: Secker 1938), p.75.
13. Micheal MacLiammoir, *The Happy Prince and Other Stories* (London: Puffin Books 1962), p.9.
14. Nandy, op. cit. (1988), p.36.
15. Kohl, op. cit. (1989), pp.54-57.
16. Kevin Barry, 'Critical Notes on Post-colonial Aesthetics', *Irish Studies Review*, 14, Spring 1996, pp.2-3.
17. ibid., p.2.
18. See Luke Gibbons, 'Identity Without A Centre: Allegory, History and Irish Nationalism', *Cultural Studies*, Vol. VI, no. 3 (1992), pp.358-75.

19 David Lloyd, *Anomolous States: Irish Writing and the Post-Colonial Moment* (Dublin: Lilliput 1993), pp.65-79.
20 Owen Dudley Edwards, 'Impressions of an Irish Sphinx', in Jerusha McCormack, ed., *Wilde the Irishman* (Yale UP 1998), p.59.
21 Jerusha McCormack, op. cit. (1997), p.5.
22 See Deirdre Toomey, 'The Story-Teller at Fault: Oscar Wilde and Irish Orality', in McCormack, op. cit. (1997), pp.24-35.
23 ibid., p.25.
24 Quoted in Peter Nicholls, 'A Dying Fall? Nineteenth Century Decadence and its Legacies', in T. Hill, ed., *Decadence and Danger: Writing, History and the Fin de Siècle* (London: Sulis Press 1998), p.18.
25 ibid., pp.18-19.
26 Toomey, op. cit. (1997), p.35.
27 Edwards, op. cit. (1998), p.58.
28 Terry Eagleton, *Saint Oscar* (Derry: Field Day 1989), p.vii.
29 Toomey, op. cit. (1997), p.28.
30 Dramatic Review, 30 May 1885, p.278. Quoted in S. Eltis, *Revising Wilde: Society and Subversion in the Plays of Oscar Wilde* (Oxford: Clarendon Press 1996), p.55.
31 Sontag, *A Susan Sontag Reader* (Harmondsworth: Penguin 1983), p.235. For a fuller discussion of Wilde's postmodernist 'sampling' of diverse cultural pre-texts, and an apparently unlikely comparison with the work of Quentin Tarantino, see Neil Sammells, 'Oscar Wilde at Centuries End', in J. B. Bullen, ed., *Writing and Victorianism* (London: Longman 1997), pp.306-27.
32 For a discussion of 'liminality' in related contexts, see Colin Graham, '"Liminal Spaces": Post-Colonial theories and Irish Culture', in *Irish Review*, 16 (1994), p.33.
33 Frank McGuinness, 'The Spirit of Play in *De Profundis*', in Jerusha McCormack, op. cit. (1997), p.141.
34 Richard Ellmann, *Oscar Wilde* (London: Hamilton 1988), p.37.
35 See *Oscar Wilde: Complete Shorter Fiction*, ed. Isobel Murray (OUP 1980), pp.9-14.
36 *Complete Works* (1966), p.1114.

LAFCADIO HEARN AND THE IRISH HORROR TRADITION

Paul Murray

In November 1874, 'a murder so atrocious and so horrible that the soul sickens at its revolting details' was committed in Cincinnati, Ohio; a young cub reporter, Patrick Lafcadio Hearn, was assigned by his paper to cover it. The following day, under the title, 'Violent Cremation', the Cincinnati *Enquirer* splashed over its front page Hearn's graphic treatment of a sensational crime—the 'Tan-yard Murder'.

The fact that there were no eye-witnesses did not prevent young Paddy Hearn, as he then still was, from speculatively reconstructing the crime, in the most gruesome detail, which had involved a man being stuffed into a furnace, possibly while still alive. This, together with its graphic description of the charred remains being examined at the autopsy, made 'Violent Cremation' a journalistic sensation across America. The young reporter could now parade himself as 'the *Enquirer*'s Dismal Man, whose rueful countenance was flushed with the hope of hearing or seeing something more than the usually horrible'.

Hearn was only twenty-four when the 'Tan Yard Murder' was published. However, he had been describing the most loathsome subjects in terrible detail for some time before that. This description of the decay of a corpse was written several months before 'Violent Cremation':

> Dissolution has been steadily going on, the gases generated by corruption have twisted the inanimate body, rent the integuments and torn the limbs, as with piteous sounds they have freed themselves from confines now too narrow for their expansive power. All trace of life has vanished; comeliness in form has fled; there remains but the polluted cerements, handfuls of hair, teeth and bones, a mass of putrid matter, foul liquids and effluvia which is death to the living and food for the grovelling worms that gather from the dark recesses of the earth to feed and revel upon it.

Lafcadio Hearn and the Irish Horror Tradition

Who was this Patrick Lafcadio Hearn? He was born on a Greek island in 1850, the son of a Church of Ireland officer-surgeon in the British Army and a Greek woman. He came to Dublin at the age of two and, effectively abandoned by his parents at an early age, he was brought up in the township of Rathmines by a great-aunt, Mrs Brenane, who had converted to Roman Catholicism from her solidly Protestant background.

In 1863, when he was thirteen, Mrs Brenane moved to England and young Patrick Hearn, as he was then called, was sent to an austere Catholic boarding school near Durham in the North of England. He suffered an accident which destroyed the sight of one eye and left him with a permanent sense of inadequacy about his appearance. When he was seventeen, his great-aunt became bankrupt and young Patrick spent up to two years of poverty-stricken misery in London.

At nineteen he was given his fare to America and became a journalist in Cincinnati, Ohio. He remained there from 1869 until 1877, when he moved south to New Orleans. By this time the change of his first name from Patrick or Paddy to Lafcadio was complete. After a decade of immersing himself in the Creole culture of New Orleans, he went off to spend two years in the West Indies. Then, in 1890, approaching the age of forty, he arrived in Japan, where he married, settled down, and produced a dozen books on his adopted country, before dying there at the early age of 54 in 1904.

Hearn's life was clearly interesting but the vital question is whether his work is worth remembering. The answer to that, and indeed the reason why I wanted to write his biography, is that, in my opinion, he was arguably the greatest ever Western interpreter of Japan and I hope that this will be increasingly recognised in the years ahead. I would, however, argue, that there is a powerful secondary reason for commemorating him and that is for his horror writing. Few writers have been so permeated by horror in their lives and work and few horror writers have been blessed with Hearn's literary ability.

An obvious question (although it has seldom been asked) is where this appetite for horror came from. Why did a young reporter in Cincinnati have such an insatiably gruesome appetite? The answer is that he had been immersed in it for as long as he could remember. As a middle-aged man in Japan in the 1890's, he began to hark back to his childhood and to relive his childhood horrors in print.

"Vespertina Cognitio", a masterpiece of horror, published in *Exotics and Retrospectives*, one of his Tokyo books, was based on an experience which had happened to him while dozing in a West Indian siesta. As he lies asleep, the locked door opened and

> [...] the Thing entered, bending as it came,—a thing robed,—feminine,—reaching to the roof,—not to be looked at! A floor—plank creaked as It neared the bed;—and then—with a frantic effort—I woke, bathed in sweat; my heart beating as if it were going to burst.

He recognised the shape in his dream as the one which

> [...] used to vex my sleep in childhood,—a phantom created for me by the impression of a certain horrible Celtic story which ought not to have been told to any child blessed, or cursed, with an imagination.

I think, however, that it was inspired as much by the apparition of the "Bleeding Nun" in Matthew Lewis's landmark classic of Gothic horror, *The Monk*, as by the Irish folktale to which he attributed it. A lonely child and an omnivorous reader, Hearn had been allowed unsupervised access to a library of horror literature, including the work of Lewis. Support for this conjecture comes from "Nightmare and Nightmare Legends", written in New Orleans when Hearn was 28 in which he describes a state of paralysed terror, similar to the one quoted above, and says: 'But persons with sensitive imaginations, cultivated by a peculiar kind of fantastic literature, are liable to dreams of such abnormal and ghostly terrors as may actually kill.'

In "Gothic Horror", published in *Shadowings* at the turn of the century, he analysed the terror inspired by the Gothic architecture of a childhood church which he connected with his adult horrific experiences. In "Nightmare-Touch", also in *Shadowings*, he dwelt on the haunters who had visited him as a five-year-old in Dublin; they seemed to be able to prevent him from rising or moving or crying out: this again is straight from 'Monk' Lewis's apparition of the "Bleeding Nun".

Hearn did try to come to terms with his terrors, to place them in a comforting philosophic and scientific framework. He put forward a hypothesis that this 'dream-seizure' had its origins in our ancestors' fear of falling victim to predators. Over time, the development of the human brain intensified the 'dream-fear', while 'the summed experience of the life of sleep' was inherited by succeeding generations, who rationalised it by the imposition of a religious overlay. Hearn related the fundamental values of art to the supernatural in his lecture, 'The Value of the Supernatural in Fiction' and, indeed, a phrase in it, 'there is something ghostly in all great art' was considered by Yeats as possibly a definitive definition of poetry.

Lafcadio claimed that as a child the one element of religion which interested him was the Holy Ghost: he had difficulty reconciling the concept of holiness with his terror of ghosts. He decided that the Holy Ghost was a white ghost who would not make faces at him if he behaved himself! In an unpublished letter, written from Japan to his half-sister in 1893, he said that religion had never had any effect upon him, except that, as a boy, he liked stories of angels and devils, especially the latter; he particularly liked to read of devils coming in the shape of beautiful women to tempt saints. This phenomenon of fiends assuming the shape of beautiful women to lure mortals to their doom was to be a life-long theme in Hearn's horror. It is also, of course, fundamental to the vampirism of Le Fanu and Stoker.

As a child, he thought he saw real ghosts: one was a religious relative, sometimes called 'Cousin Jane', whom he fancied appeared to him as a faceless ghoul; she died shortly after, in the very room where he had seen her spectral form. It was, therefore, an extra-ordinary coincidence that Ushaw, the Catholic boarding school to which he was packed off at thirteen, was architecturally a Gothic masterpiece. Young Patrick Lafcadio had Gothic tendencies to go with the architecture and was remembered as an eccentric with, even then, a developed sense of the gruesome.

After he had been forced to leave Ushaw prematurely by his guardian's bankruptcy, Hearn wrote from London of living in an evil quarter by the Thames where nightly horrors included violent scenes of mayhem and murder, with bodies being heaved into the river with, it would seem, regularity and impunity. In other words, Hearn was thinking, and writing, horror from earliest childhood and continued doing so up to the point where he left for America; it was no wonder that he immersed himself in it from the start of his journalistic career in Cincinnati.

However, after he moved to New Orleans in 1877, his job on the *Times-Democrat* involved editorial and literary work. No longer on the police beat, he did not have the stark raw material for the realistic sensationalism of his Cincinnati journalism. He turned instead to one of the great passions of his life, French literature, and began turning out a stream of accomplished translations, many of which were published in the *Item* and *Times-Democrat* newspapers for which he worked in New Orleans.

In 1882, he published translations of six of Gautier's stories, under the title, *One of Cleopatra's Nights*. One of them, "Arria Marcella", could be straight from the pages of Sheridan Le Fanu's "Carmilla", or Bram Stokers's *Dracula*, both by Dubliners contemporaneous with Hearn. As well as the crumbling into dust of the ghoul, you have the same mingling of the non-Christian world of ghosts, vampires and prehistoric religion which is controlled by Christian ritual.

Later, in Japan, Hearn would also write of vampires: "The Story of Chugoro" in Kotto, for example, concerns a great and ugly frog who appears as a beautiful woman to drain young men of their blood. The theme of the interrelationship of the devil with the human world recurs in a number of Hearn's other translations from the French, most notably in Flaubert's *The Temptation of Saint Anthony*, which contains some marvellous descriptions of horrific, otherworldly visions, and Gautier's "Two Actors for One Role".

The fantasy of the dead continuing to live in another dimension, associating with the living, permeated many of the 'Fantastics' which Lafcadio produced in New Orleans. The interest in ancient religions, which he shared with some of his French literary idols, was very much in evidence in his *Stray Leaves* book—there is the 'tale of weirdness' about the ancient Egyptian god, Thoth, and "The Corpse-Demon", an old Indian tale of a fiend who lived within a dead body, as well as strange tales from the Finnish epic, *Kalewala*, and the Jewish *Talmud*, among other sources. The strong Oriental flavour evident in *Stray Leaves* is even more manifest in *Some Chinese Ghosts* and both books are given coherence by the familiar intertwined themes of love and death.

His fondness for the old, essentially, pre-Christian religions of the ordinary people in preindustrial societies harked back to the Irish fairy tales of his youth and the black culture of Cincinnati as well as looking forward to his sympathy for Shinto in Japan. Naturally, the West Indian belief in Zombies engaged his attention, as Voodooism had done in New Orleans.

Hearn went back briefly to the United States when he left the West Indies in 1889, before going on to Japan in 1890, as he approached his fortieth birthday. In his early Japanese books Hearn was primarily concerned with documenting his coming to terms with Japan and outlining a timeless interpretation of its unique culture.

He challenged his readers by juxtaposing alternative visions of reality with the accepted norms of nineteenth century industrial society which he so heartily despised. A religiously obsessed moralist who gave allegiance to no particular religion, he used horror to hint at spiritual realities beyond the grasp of contemporary materialism. He also cast his personal demons into art, part of a process whereby he contributed to the English language a great body of profound and enriching literature.

In discussing Lafcadio Hearn and the Irish horror tradition, I should say that, while his relationship with Irish literature has generally been overlooked, I have not set out to cast Hearn in a narrow straightjacket of a particular tradition: he was far too elusive and his genius too malleable for that. If ever a man achieved Goldsmith's ideal of being a citizen of the world, it was Patrick Lafcadio Hearn. He was not exclusively Greek, Irish, American, or Japanese but was rather a unique amalgam of a variety of influences. His relationship with Ireland, like his feelings for the United States and Japan, was ambiguous although he came to terms with it in a series of remarkable essays towards the end of his life.

While, therefore, I am not claiming Hearn exclusively for the Irish tradition, he did spend his most formative years in Ireland and no biographer can afford to ignore their impact. In other words, while I do not believe that he should be seen exclusively in an Irish context, he certainly does have an Irish dimension. There are, I think, three interrelated aspects of Hearn's relationship worth considering in the context of the Irish tradition: background, subject matter and language. I should make it clear that I am a biographer who aims to apply historiographical rather than literary critical analysis and my aim in examining Hearn's writing is to try to illuminate the intersection of his life and work rather than entering the realm of academic literary criticism *per se*.

A fundamental question which a biographer has to confront is whether Hearn's childhood in Ireland was an accident of geography or whether it exercised an important impact on his literary output. At the very least, it is surely obvious that the culture in which he grew up was rich in literary output. Hearn was in fact one of an extraordinary quartet of writers who grew up in Dublin in the decades just after the middle of the nineteenth century. Bram Stoker was just a few years older: born in 1847, he spent his youth in Clontarf and Artane, similar suburbs on the north side of Dublin to the township of Rathmines on the south side where Hearn grew up. Oscar Wilde and George Bernard Shaw were, respectively, four and six years younger than Hearn. Their families all lived within a short distance of each other: the Wilde residence in Merrion Square and the Shaw home in Synge Street are no more than a short walk from 73 Upper Leeson Street where Hearn spent some of his most formative years.

Church of Ireland middle class would describe their family background although there were, of course, gradations of individual family circumstance. While championship of the common man would later be a feature of the work of Hearn and Shaw, and folklore a basis for the literary output of Hearn, Wilde and Stoker, they were the products of what might now be termed 'drawing-room culture'. The cradle of genius in the Dublin of their era was one of gatherings around the piano to sing the often maudlin songs and ballads of the time. James Joyce would later preserve this world in aspic in *Dubliners* and John McCormack would immortalise its torch-songs on shellac. Shaw, of course, was immersed in it from an early age, courtesy of his mother and her music teacher, George Vandeleur Lee, but Hearn too remembered those gatherings around the piano in Mrs Brenane's plush drawing-room, with standards of the time, such as Father Prout's *The Bells of Shandon*, being performed. Indeed, it was memories of his beautiful aunt, Catherine Elwood, singing Thomas Moore's *Believe Me, If All Those Endearing Young Charms* which inspired one of Lafcadio's late Japanese pieces, "*Hi-mawari*".

Oscar Wilde proposed to, but Bram Stoker married, Florence Balcombe, daughter of a Lieutenant Colonel in the British Army. Both Stoker's and Hearn's grandfathers served in the same regiment; Hearn's grandfather too was a Lieutenant Colonel. Stoker was friendly with the Wildes, especially Oscar's mother, a famous collector of Irish folklore. Hearn was one of the first critics to see the sterling worth beneath the young Wilde's foppery and, as writers, they shared with Stoker an interest in fairy tales, all three of them publishing books of fairy tales within a decade of each other later in the century.

Both the Hearns and Shaws were downwardly-mobile minor gentry, attempting to maintain a semblance of respectability while the economic basis of their position was slipping away from them. Indebtedness was a feature common to both, as it was to the Stokers: indeed, Lafcadio's father, who borrowed heavily from his great-aunt, was ruined, as was Lafcadio himself, when she became bankrupt. Both Shaw and Hearn experienced the grind of poverty in London in their youth.

It is clear therefore that Hearn grew up in a small, tightly-knit, and intensely literary world in Dublin. If we look outside his immediate contemporaries, we find that Dion Boucicault, the dominant dramatist of the mid-century, was born in 47 Lower Gardiner Street while the young Patrick Lafcadio spent his first period in Dublin at number 48 in the same street. J. M. Synge attended school in Upper Leeson Street where Lafcadio lived with Mrs Brenane for some years. W. B. Yeats was born in Sandymount, a nearby suburb, shortly after Hearn left for England. On the other side of the country, George Moore, just two years younger than Hearn, grew up on his family's estate on the shores of Lough Cara in County Mayo; Lafcadio spent a good deal of time in his youth, vividly recalled in some of his best Japanese work, on the estate of his Elwood relations—with which Sir William Wilde was familiar—on the shores of Lough Corrib, also in County Mayo. Moore grew up listening to his father's tales of the East and went to Paris to study painting, as Lafcadio's uncle, Richard Hearn, had done a generation previously.

Hearn's work throughout his life was permeated by horror and he clearly has a good deal in common with the older writers of the Irish Gothic tradition, Charles Maturin and Sheridan Le Fanu. Maturin was a Church of Ireland clergyman and Le Fanu the son of one; Hearn was the great-grandson of an eminent Archdeacon of Cashel and Church of Ireland clergymen abound in his family tree. Maturin's father, like Bram Stoker's, was a civil servant in the British administration in Ireland while Hearn's father was an officer-surgeon in the British Army. All previous three generations of the Hearn family had been educated at Trinity College, Dublin, as were Stoker, Le Fanu, and Maturin. Indeed, John Melmoth, the central character in Maturin's *Melmoth the Wanderer*, is a student at Trinity College. Bearing in mind that the Church of Ireland was a State Church until 1869-71, it means that all these families occupied comfortable middle-class niches, employed either through the Church of Ireland or the armed forces by the State, then the union of Great Britain and Ireland. Yeats, too, was a product of similar background.

Hearn, however, was sharply differentiated from the other Irish Gothic writers by the fact of having been brought up as a Roman Catholic, although important elements of his consciousness-forming were Protestant rather than Roman Catholic. We know that his great aunt, Mrs Brenane, made little effort to inculcate Catholic, or even Christian, beliefs into him; a rare attempt at that was a rather hamfisted one by a religiously-obsessed young relative. When she died, she left her considerable collection of books to him, which, strangely, included nothing overtly religious, certainly nothing of a Roman Catholic or pietistic nature; the authors listed by Hearn include Pope, Locke, Byron, Scott, and Edgeworth. The other writers whom we know influenced him were also generally outside the Roman Catholic tradition: Milton, whose *Paradise Lost* impressed him both for its imagination and its otherworld vocabulary; Defoe; and, most potently, Matthew Lewis whose *Tales of Wonder*, gave him nightmares.

We know that Hearn was familiar with Charles Maturin's *Melmoth the Wanderer*. His language and the cadences of his style seem to me to anticipate uncannily Hearn's early journalism. Take, for example, this passage describing a mad-house in *Melmoth*:

> Then your hours of solitude, deliciously diversified by the yell of famine, the howl of madness, the crash of whips, and the broken hearted sob of those who, like you, are supposed, or *driven* mad by the crimes of others.[1]

and compare it with a Cincinnati tenement as seen by Hearn:

> [...] the moans of the poor sufferer, the agonized scream of the tortured child, the savage whipping and violent cursing, the broken floor pried up in drunken fury,- all seemed the sights and sounds of a hideous dream, rather than the closing scene of a poor life's melodrama.[2]

In his personality, Lafcadio exhibited the anti-Popery elements we find in Maturin, extravagantly claiming that he would be pursued to the grave by the Jesuits, who had supposedly educated him, although he had never in fact attended a Jesuit school. At the same time, his ambiguity towards Roman Catholicism mirrored that of Le Fanu—whom he particularly admired as a writer—and Stoker, who, as Protestant writers, in "Carmilla" and *Dracula* respectively, accord a positive power to Roman Catholic ritual in subduing the forces of darkness. Stoker, incidentally, makes clear the ambiguity of his narrator, Jonathan Harker, on this point. In his personal life, Hearn was friendly with a number of Roman Catholic priests. In the West Indies his imagination was impressed by the achievements of the Dominican priest, Père Labat and, in Japan, he was defensive of the Roman Catholic missionaries *vis-à-vis* their Protestant counterparts.

Part of the answer to this riddle might be that Hearn's Irish background was essentially Protestant and, despite his upbringing as a Catholic, he was a man of fundamentally Protestant consciousness, albeit it with a strong element of Catholicism. In this way Hearn was able to embody in himself the full religious ambiguity of the Irish Gothic tradition.

Hearn landed in Japan in 1890, the year that Bram Stoker is believed by some to have started work on *Dracula*. The similarities between the two men run much deeper than the coincidence of birth or geography. Horror pervaded the work of both writers. Stoker was not just the author of *Dracula*: in his first novel, *The Snake's Pass*, set in Ireland, the gombeen man, the moneylender, is the very embodiment of evil; the horror of his last novel, *The Lair of the White Worm*, is positively hallucinogenic and he showed an extraordinary range of horrific invention in his short stories. it is interesting that he should have begun Dracula, in its early pages overtly a journey to the Orient— Jonathan Harker in the very first paragraph states that he feels he is entering the East at Budapest—just as Hearn was beginning his Oriental sojourn in Japan. Hearn translated vampire material from the French and in his person, by drinking blood and eating bugs, reflected the proclivities of Dracula and his assistant, Renfield.

Stoker based his story "The Burial of the Rats" among the *chiffonniers*, the rag-pickers of the Paris dumps. One of Hearn's best Cincinnati pieces was "*Les Chiffonniers*", set in the dumps of that city. The declaration of Stoker's narrator, that he 'determined to investigate philosophically the *chiffonnier*—his habitat, his life, and his means of life', was very similar to Hearn's posture of being a scientific observer of horrific landscapes.

Lafcadio's translations from French were part of a complex interrelationship with French culture, the importance of which extended far beyond these translations themselves and profoundly influenced his interpretation of Japan. This relationship should be viewed in the context, not alone of his family background, but of the wider cultural links between Ireland and France. These were symbolised by the Napoleonic vogue for the ancient figure of Oisin or Ossian, and the influence of Thomas Moore, whom Hearn admired, on such French cultural luminaries as Berlioz. Bram Stoker's father moved to France as a result of his debts, as Oscar Wilde would flee there after his release from prison and Hearn took refuge there mentally by claiming a French education and immersing himself in French literature. Indeed, as you know, Oscar Wilde took the name 'Sebastian Melmoth' when he went in disgrace to France in 1897, emblematic of his outcast role, knowing that the French would understand a reference to Charles Maturin's Irish exile who had so influenced Baudelaire and Balzac.

Hearn's grandfather, a hero of the Napoleonic wars, prided himself on his fluent French. His uncle, Richard, was one of the first Irish artists to go to France to study art, blazing a trail which many others would follow in the mid-nineteenth century. Wilde composed original works in French, as Samuel Beckett would do in our own century, while Lafcadio translated extensively from it. Lafcadio claimed to have been educated in France; even if there is no evidence to substantiate the claim, the fact that he wanted to have been there is significant, as was his very deliberate immersion in French language and culture during his years in America.

Lafcadio's devotion to folk material links him, not alone with his contemporaries, but also to the younger figures of the Irish literary revival—Yeats, Lady Gregory, Synge—as well as backwards to the earlier Irish poets of the nineteenth century. In tracing the line of Irish Protestant supernatural fiction through Maturin, Le Fanu, Stoker, W. B. Yeats, and Elizabeth Bowen, Professor Roy Foster has linked an interest in the occult with folklore. Hearn believed that folk tales were of priceless value to the true artist, which the uneducated peasant was fully capable of being; indeed, education was likely to destroy the source of his poetry. To him, the Celtic belief in fairies resulted in an imagination that was 'romantic, poetic and also terrible'. His view of peasant life in Ireland was, in turn, remarkably similar to the Shinto-based ethos of pre-Meiji Japan:

> Anciently woods and streams were peopled for him [the peasant] with invisible beings; angels and demons walked at his side; the woods had their fairies, the mountains their goblins, the marches their flitting spirits, and the dead came back to him at times to bear a message or to rebuke a fault. Also the ground that he trod upon, the plants growing in the field, the cloud above him, the lights of heaven all were full of mystery and ghastliness.[3]

Compare this with Yeats' vision of the survival of the supernatural in the Irish countryside:

> Once every people in the world believed that trees were divine, and could take a human or grotesque shape and dance among the shadows of the woods; and deer, and ravens and foxes, and wolves and bears, and clouds and pools, almost all things under the sun and moon, and the sun and moon, not less divine and changeable; they saw in the rainbow the still bent bow of a god thrown down in his negligence; they heard in the thunder the sound of his beaten water-jar, or the

tumult of his chariot wheels; and when a sudden flight of wild duck, or of crows, passed over their heads, they thought were gazing at the dead hastening to their rest; while they dreamed of so great a mystery in little things that they believed the waving of a hand, or of a sacred bough, enough to trouble far-off hearts, or hood the moon with darkness.[4]

What we have here is the same concept, being expressed in such similar language that the authors could almost be interchangeable. Both men believed in the fundamental importance of folk material to their respective art. In Yeats's case, it was some of the greatest poetry in the English language; in Hearn's a great body of work, culminating in the mastery *Kwaidan*, or Japanese ghost stories of his later years. Hearn posited the fundamental importance to art of the supernatural in his lecture, 'The Value of the Supernatural in Fiction' and, indeed, a phrase in it, 'there is something ghostly in all great art' was considered by Yeats as possibly a definitive definition of poetry.[5]

Hearn understood the grounding of Yeats' poetry in the myths and legends of Ireland. He connected romanticism, folklore and horror and maintained that the Celtic belief in fairies had created an imagination that was 'romantic, poetic and also terrible'. He believed that it had produced one 'representative' poet, W. B. Yeats, 'who himself collected a great number of stories and legends about fairies from the peasantry of Southern Ireland'. Yeats' poem, "The Host of the Air", he regarded as the outstanding contemporary fairy poem, unsurpassable in its *genre*, especially in its ability to communicate 'the pleasure of fear', an art Hearn greatly admired. Not only did he appreciate the 'rare excellence' of the early Yeats—the poet was thirty-nine when Lafcadio died in 1904—he also understood that ancient Celtic literature had inspired much of his poetry.[6]

Indeed, so passionate did he feel about this excellence that he wrote a letter of violent protest to Yeats in June 1901 when "The Host of the Air" appeared in *The Wind Among the Reeds* revised from its earlier form, telling the poet that 'this wonderful thing [...] must have been blown into you and through you as by the Wind of the Holy Ghost'.[7] On the other hand, not alone was the hero of Yeats's unfinished novel called *Hearne* but he wrote of a real-life 'Hearne', a witch doctor who lived on the border of Clare and Galway![8]

Both men were attracted by similar material. It is clear from a satire which he wrote in his Cincinnati days that Lafcadio was familiar, to some extent at least, with the Fianna Cycle of early Irish legend and, more specifically, that he was aware of the story of Oisin in this lore.

Oisin was said to have accompanied a beautiful woman to the Land of Youth. After what seemed like a short time, he asks to go back to his homeland; the lady allows him but enjoins him not to set foot on the soil of Ireland. He finds when he gets back that he has actually been away for three hundred years and that the Fianna are long dead and gone. Unthinkingly he comes into contact with the ground and is instantly changed into an old man.

This story parallels the Japanese legend of Urashima Taro that Hearn uses as the backbone for "The Dream of a Summer Day" where he entwines it with glorious memories of his youth in Ireland. Yeats was attracted by the Oisin theme: his dramatic dialogue, *The Wanderings of Oisin*, was published in 1889, the year before Hearn went to Japan and, in its language and subject matter, mirrored many of his preoccupations.

Hearn's awareness of Irish myth and legend also found an outlet in New Orleans, where he wrote the story of "St Brandan's Christmas" for the *Times-Democrat*. It ends with the 'horrid and frightful deformity' alone upon an ice cliff, the vision of Judas, on day-release from hell, seen by the ancient Irish saint, Brendan, on a Christmas morning. There is, incidentally, a passage in this tale which anticipates a vision of rural Ireland which found expression in Irish literature and politics earlier this century:

> But now and again an Irish fisherboy, gentle and loving to an old mother spinning by the peat fire at home, pure of heart and careful of his duty, rocked as ever on the great waves that dash high up the iron-bound coast of Western Ireland, and dreaming of the lost glories of the green land, has seen the gold and purple curtains of the sunset lift for a moment over the shining sea [...].[9]

There are other links between Hearn and the Irish literary tradition. For example, he appreciated the work of the older nineteenth-century Irish poets who influenced the Celtic revival, particularly William Allingham and Sir Samuel Ferguson; the latter's 'extraordinary power in arousing the sensation of the weird' he particularly admired.[10] Ferguson had, of course, used ancient Irish saga material and it is noticeable that it was the elements of the ghostly and the weird in this tradition to which Hearn related. His use of the phrase, 'terrible beauty', later immortalised by Yeats, is an indication of his probable familiarity with the work of Standish O'Grady, who is credited by Professor Roy Foster with having originated it. We know from his

Lafcadio Hearn and the Irish Horror Tradition 251

lectures that he was also familiar with the work of Burke, Congreve, Farquhar, Goldsmith, Lever, Sheridan and Swift.

As a young journalist in Cincinnati in the 1870s, his main local interest was in the music and lore of the black inhabitants of the levee quarter on the banks of the Mississippi. I believe that the traditional music he would have heard in Ireland, and the value placed on folk culture in general by the Anglo-Irish elite, may well have conditioned Hearn to accept African-American culture without the prejudice which clouded the approach of so many of his contemporaries. He embodied in himself therefore two of the fundamental impulses in Irish nineteenth-century culture, the aristocratic and the popular. Both of these were evident in his American and West Indian work on the coloured races, at once enlightened and sometimes condescending. It was only when he got to Japan that both elements fused into a coherent, unified, vision of another culture with which he could comfortably identify.

In addition to common subject matter, Hearn shared some fundamental intellectual and philosophical influences with his Irish contemporaries. Both Hearn and Shaw went through youthful periods of anarchism before converting to one of the grand, all-encompassing, evolutionary philosophical structures of the time. Together with Wilde, they were profoundly influenced by the philosophy of Herbert Spencer who, if largely forgotten nowadays, nevertheless wielded enormous influence on intellectuals both in the West and Japan around the end of the last century. All three were concerned with socialism, albeit it different ways: Hearn and Wilde as critics, while Shaw adhered to Fabianism. Indeed, Hearn was deeply concerned with political issues all his life, as evidenced by his private correspondence and his newspaper editorials, including those in the *Kobe Chronicle*. He saw Japan's wars with China and Russia in terms of a wider geopolitical historical perspective. One finds evidence of a similar political engagement in the work of Yeats and, currently, in that of Seamus Heaney. An important intellectual influence on Hearn was the work of the Irish philosopher, George Berkeley, whose core argument that the material exists only in the subjective consciousness of the observer also interested Joyce and Beckett.

Hearn's use of language is an area where I believe that traces of Irish influence can be discerned. Lafcadio set out his approach to language in his correspondence with Basil Hall Chamberlain. He pointed out that his approach to language was entirely different to that of his friend:

> For me words have colour, form, character; they have faces, ports, manners, eccentricities;—they have tints, tones, personalities. That they are unintelligible makes no difference at all.[12]

On another occasion, when Chamberlain admonished Hearn over the correct use of 'shall' and 'will', Lafcadio responded that tone to him was everything; the word nothing. He was guided by euphony and felt

> [...] angry with conventional forms of language of which I cannot understand the real spirit [...]. I am 'colour-blind' to the values you assert; and I suspect that the majority of the English-speaking races—the raw people—are also blind thereunto. It is the people, after all, who make the language in the end, and in the direction of least resistance.[12]

The fact that the technically correct use of 'shall' and 'will' is part of the linguistic divide between Ireland and England is, I think relevant here. So too was his rejection of Chamberlain's plea that he write with 'justice and temperateness'; he was far too passionate and anarchic in his approach to language for that.

Chamberlain may, somewhat unintentionally, have penetrated to the core of their difference when he suggested that Lafcadio's linguistic waywardness could be attributed to the 'Irish invasion' of the United States, a mass movement of which Lafcadio had been a part a generation before. Indeed, when Lafcadio had lived in the United States he had maintained that he 'hated' English and hoped to re-shape it to serve his specific literary ends. He continued doing this to some extent for the rest of his life. Run a modern spell-check computer programme through Hearn and you will realise by its rejections how much Hearn manipulated the language out of the rules and regulations beloved of Chamberlain.

In his anarchic, creative, individualistic use of language Hearn is clearly related to the Irish tradition, Joyce in particular. His refusal to be bound by grammatical correctness is representative of the process which Joyce brought to such a triumphant culmination in *Ulysses* and *Finnegans Wake*. There are, of course, other parallels with Joyce. As a young man in New Orleans, in correspondence with an American friend on the subject of the Irish keening wail (part of the 'wake' for the dead which is, of course, celebrated in the title of Joyce's last work) Lafcadio wrote of the strong similarities between the Mongolian and certain Irish faces, while Joyce in *Stephen Hero* describes the Irish peasantry as 'Mongolian types'. In his draft autobiography, Hearn describes an outburst from a sombre young girl of strong religious bent who had taken it on herself to instruct him in morality, which is very clearly similar to the celebrated sermon on hell which Joyce would later pen in *A Portrait of the Artist as a Young Man*. While Lafcadio's autobiography was never finished or published, its picture of an unwilling young intellectual being force-fed with muscular Irish Catholicism anticipates not just Joyce, but later writers such as Patrick Kavanagh, John McGahern and Colm Tóibín.

The final rubric under which I would like to consider Lafcadio's relationship with the Irish tradition is that of Orientalism. Elements of Orientalism are recognised in Maria Edgeworth's writing as they are in the work of the earlier eighteenth-century Irish writer, Frances Sheridan, whose *The History of Nourjahad* in turn has Gothic as well as Oriental aspects to it. A recent critic, Robert L. Mack, has described the character of Nourjahad as 'a kind of Faustus figure'—the Faustian legend being, of course, central to the Gothic *genre*—stating that his 'misplaced desire for immortality, too, recalls Gulliver's account of the Struldbrugs in Swift's *Gulliver's Travels*'.[14] It also recalls Maturin's Melmoth and the vampires of Le Fanu and Stoker. The same critic states that 'Nourjahad possesses a lush physicality—a delight in the voluptuous descriptions of sensuous excess [...]' and places it in a *genre* of English-language fiction which is able to 'present readers with a range of alternative cultural possibilities [...]'.[15]

The parallels here with Hearn's American and Japanese work are too striking to be missed. The subject-matter and language of *Stray Leaves from Strange Literature* and *Some Chinese Ghosts*, as well as his translations from the French in his American period, possess lush physicality and delight in voluptuous descriptions of sensuous excess, and his Japanese work, above all, presents readers with alternative cultural possibilities.

Maria Edgeworth's *Murad the Unlucky* has been described by the same critic as 'a corrective oriental tale', the clear implication of which 'is that the spoils of colonialism [...] are the results of misguided avarice and ambition' and 'exposing beneath the lush romanticism of eighteenth-century orientalism the harsh realities of life in the "gorgeous East" [...], Edgeworth tells us that we shall have to rethink the Arabian Nights if we are ever to understand the East'.[16] Hearn's Japanese work, with its rejection of colonialism and its insistence that Japan and even the Occident be viewed from a Japanese perspective has therefore much the same message for the Occidental reader as Edgeworth.

In dealing with the work of Frances Sheridan and Maria Edgeworth we have come full circle, linking some of the earliest Irish literary influences with the final phase of Lafcadio's life. I should like to leave the last word to Hearn himself, writing to Yeats of his Dublin childhood towards the end of his life in Japan:

> But I hope you will not think me unsympathetic in regard to Irish matters [...] forty-five years ago, I was a horrid little boy, 'with never a crack in his heart', who lived in Upper Leeson Street, Dublin [...]. So I *ought* to love Irish Things, and do.[17]

NOTES

1 Matthew Lewis, *The Monk* [1820] (OUP [World Classics] 1973), p.156.
2 Lafcadio Hearn, "Some Pictures of Poverty", in *The Selected Writings of Lafcadio Hearn*, ed. Henry Goodman (NY 1949; rep. 1971), p.257.
3 Lafcadio Hearn, R. Tanabe, T. Ochiai, and I. Nishizaki, eds., *On Poetry* [3rd rev. edn.] (Tokyo: Hokuseido Press 1941), p.13.
4 W. B. Yeats, *Writings on Irish Folklore, Legend and Myth*, ed. Robert Welch (Harmondsworth: Penguin 1993), pp.190-91.
5 *Confessions of an Uncommon Attorney*, Reginald Leslie Hine, (London 1945), p.152.
6 Hearn, *On Poetry* (1941), p.253.
7 Hearn to W. B. Yeats, MS letter (Tokyo, 22 June, 1901).
8 *Writings on Irish Folklore, Legend and Myth*, W. B. Yeats, p.280.
9 New Orleans *Times-Democrat* (24 December, 1889).
10 *On Poetry* (1941), p.257.
11 *Shadowings* (Vermont & Tokyo: Charles E. Tuttle Company Inc. 1971), p.218. First published in Boston in 1900.
12 Elizabeth Bisland Wetmore, ed., *The Japanese Letters of Lafcadio Hearn* (Boston & NY: Houghton Mifflin Co./Riverside Press 1910), p.430.
13 Elizabeth Bisland, ed., *The Life and Letters of Lafcadio Hearn*, [Koizumi Edition of *The Writings of Lafcadio Hearn*, Vol. XIV] (Boston & NY: Houghton Mifflin Co./Riverside Press 1923), pp.336-37.
14 Robert L. Mack, ed., *Oriental Tales* (OUP 1992), Introduction, p.xxx.
15 ibid., p.xxxiii
16 ibid., p.xlviii
17 Hearn to W. B. Yeats, MS letter (Tokyo, 24 September, 1901).

READING AND DREAMING IN *MORGANTE THE LESSER* (1890): A PLEA FOR RECLAIMING AN ABANDONED TEXT

Jerry C. M. Nolan

In 1890 Edward Martyn (1859-1923) published his satiric romance *Morgante the Lesser* under the sign and name of Sirius. In the opening pages, we find Sirius claiming to have undertaken the task of exposing the historical figure of Morgante, in spite of feeling unsafe at the prospect of being called an amateur by the academe of the historians. Thus did Martyn mask his identity as landlord in Tulira Castle, the intensely personal nature of the ambitious work and his own lack of confidence as a young aspiring writer.[1] Martyn had come back to Co. Galway from Christ Church Oxford in 1879 where he was expected by his mother to progress from being a good hunt horseman to becoming the Deputy Lieutenant of the County and Commissioner of the Peace during the Land War; and above all else, to marry to produce heirs for the estate. Increasingly, Martyn disobediently retreated to the old Norman Tower at Tulira where a decade of reading and dreaming climaxed in *Morgante the Lesser*.

At first sight, to his few contemporary readers, the work must have seemed little more than an extended extravaganza concocted from a curious brew of satire and romance, with probably too many archaic trappings for late Victorian taste. *Morgante the Lesser*, as a title, was a deft variation on Luigi Pulci's *Morgante Maggiore*, a long medieval poem about giants, knightly adventures, battles, magic and burlesques.[2] Martyn's interest was not in medieval *pastiche* but in the loose structure for telling the tale of a giant philosopher Morgante who travelled the world (including Hell) in search of converts to the world religion to end all world religions. Sirius' pseudo-learned appeals to authority, practical jokes and satirical juxtapositions of events all mirrored Pulci's pervasive sense of parody. But the satirical giant to whom Martyn became most indebted was François Rabelais. The unfolding story of Morgante's rise and fall from birth and death was fashioned to mirror the events in the tale of Rabelais' Gargantua such as prologue, genealogy and fabulous birth, antics of the pedagogues, visit to Paris among the sophists, campaign to save the world, establishment of the great abbey of Theleme, the Riddle in bronze dug up from the foundations of the abbey.[3] Thus was Gargantua reborn in Morgante. The imaginative thrust in *Morgante the Lesser* also owed a debt to the Carlyle of *Sartor Resartus*.[4] As a salute to the highly respected senior traveller, Martyn placed two apocalyptic epigraphs from Carlyle's novel at the beginning of the work. Like *Sartor Resartus*, Martyn's only prose work was partly a satirical extravaganza of things in general, and partly a Bildungroman or allegorised autobiography in the Germanic tradition, an unconventional work for an Irish landlord with agrarian agitators threatening beyond the Tower.[5]

Martyn's general approach was to give alternative interpretations of his well thumbed writers. He began by being very sarcastic about Pulci when he wrote that *Morgante Maggiore* was the favourite book of Morgante's mother, Amentia, whose fantasies were well fed by what she read. 'She never tired of fancying the world peopled by a race of such glorious beings who might move about knocking down ordinary mortals and existing institutions. This queen of women received the most sublime poetical inspirations and fore-knowledge of her son's exalted greatness.'[6] Martyn distanced himself from Rabelais, too. A direct comparison of the extraordinary births of Gargantua and Morgante provides a good example of how Martyn worked out an alternative reading. Rabelais showed little interest in the mother Gargamelle beyond the fact that she ate great quantities of tripe when she was pregnant with Gargantua whose delivery was then through the left ear. Rabelais' target was the medieval belief that the Virgin Mary miraculously gave birth to Christ through the ear.[7] The whole idea of faith as the need to believe incredible things was being ridiculed. Martyn's version of Morgante's birth was delivery down the nose. The setting for the fantastical birth was mock-Gothic, doubtless a parody of George Ashlin's neo-Gothic Tulira. Father (Fitz Ego) and Mother (Amentia) were sitting in a large drawing-room. A violent gale destroyed all windows and doors, scattered the furniture and ruined all conversation to the point where the expectant couple had to shout at each other through large speaking trumpets. Amentia's great capacity to swallow air enabled her to survive in the storm. As her labour began, she blew her nose. At the eleventh blow, Morgante slipped down his mother's nose and came to rest on her red cotton handkerchief 'like a well-grown toad'. Within Amentia's imagination, the toad in the red handkerchief was already her giant-son. For Martyn, the grotesque beginnings of the unholy founder of the future great religion had begun. Morgante's romance of the fantastical island of Agathopolis also arose from an alternative reading of Rabelais' Abbey of Theleme. The name of Theleme recalled the Greek word for 'will' and, in Rabelais, stood for the human will refusing bounds to the natural self. Rabelais described the Abbey as an elite community of healthy and beautiful men and women who, protected by exclusiveness, could celebrate the pleasures of the body: hunting, hawking, games and conversation. 'Do as you will' was the Abbey's motto.[8] The Abbey was, in miniature, a humanist Renaissance court set up in direct defiance of the deadening spirit of medieval monasticism. Rabelais' Abbey was really an anti-Abbey in its critique of all such institutions less free and less enlightened, and a kind of prelude to marriages back in the outside world: 'If at Theleme they had lived in devotion and friendship, they lived in still greater devotion and friendship when they were married.' Martyn's Agathopolis became an anti-Theleme designed to exalt the ideal of male celibacy as the sign of self-development among men who chose to educate themselves in all that was noble in the arts and sciences. 'Harmony in body and mind' could have been the motto of Martyn's island.

Alternative readings of Swift occurred in the details of the rites of Morgante's world religion. In Sect. 3 of Swift's *A Tale of a Tub*, Swift describes the worshippers of the deity of the Tailor who held the Universe to be a suit of clothes and who worshipped their god in the posture of a Persian emperor sitting with his legs interwoven under him under the ensign of the goose. The sartoristic idol was placed in the highest parts of the house on an altar erected about three feet high. The cult was described as very popular 'especially in the *grand monde* and among everybody of good fashion'.[9] In Sect. 8 of the tale, Swift introduced the Aeolists about whom he wrote 'The learned Aeolists maintain the origin of all things to be wind [...]. This is what the Adepti understand by their *anima mundi*; that is to say, the spirit or breath or wind of the world.'[10] As we shall see later, the followers of Morgante, or Enterists, were largely born out of rewritings of Swift's Sartorists and Aeolists. Swift's satire was mainly aimed against the degeneration of religious practice into magical cults. Martyn's satire was set to expose ways in which the trappings of the Christian religion were being used in the late nineteenth century to disguise the grim realities of hypocrisy, atheism and sensuality named in one of the Carlyle epigraphs as 'Phantoms and Gowls'.

Martyn's readings of Walter Pater, J. J. Winckelman and John Chrysostom helped to fashion the detail of Agathopolis. Martyn probably first discovered Winckelman in Pater's famous essay.[11] Then, during a visit to Rome in 1881, Martyn visited the Villa Albani where Winckelman had worked as Cardinal Albani's curator of antiquities.[12] The love of art on Agathopolis was to be characterised by serenity or *Heiterkeit*, the quality which Pater most admired in Winckelman who fingered 'pagan marbles with unsinged hands, with no sense of shame or loss'. The sculpture described on Agathopolis all conformed to Winckelman's classical taste. (*ML*, pp.227-28.) During the mid 1880s—probably before Martyn embarked on *Morgante*—he seems to have had a crisis of conscience which stemmed from a perceived conflict between the pleasures of ancient Greek art and the sense-denying demands of the Christian religion. While Pater was satisfied with the beauty of Greek art being able to be transformed by the likes of Winckelman into a sublime aesthetic ideal, Martyn imagined on Agathopolis the transformation of the Hellenic ideal into the beauties of Catholic Orthodox forms of religious art. The readings of Chrysostom provided a moral perspective for the Christian behaviour on the island.

Chrysostom's treatise *De Virginitate* can only have provided consolation at the height of Martyn's crisis. In the treatise, Chrysostom distinguished between celibacy which was the work of the devil and celibacy freely chosen as a more perfect way of life. Chrysostom associated the negative form of celibacy with the Manichaeans who viewed all created matter as evil. The other form of celibacy was the spirituality of voluntarily keeping the soul in silence and peace and was strongly advocated for those who felt a vocation to the monastic life where 'silence rules in the heart, as in a quiet harbour, and a still greater peace in the soul'.[13] Inspired by the vision of Chrysostom's idealistic celibacy, Martyn imagined 'uncloistered monkhood' on Agathopolis for those ready to develop the talents given to them by God. Martyn shared Chrysostom's profound mistrust of women. The figure who opposed and finally destroyed the Saint's power as Patriarch of Constantinople was the Empress Eudoxia who erected a great statue of her in 403 A.D. in front of the Santa Sophia Cathedral, wherein Chrysostom preached and presided amid the splendour of

Byzantine liturgy. The Empress used her life of extravagance and worldly ornament as a forceful assertion of her role as woman in the male-dominated Byzantine culture.[14] Amentia, Morgante's mother, likewise asserted the sublimity of the material world on an Eudoxian scale. So did Martyn's mother in her love of the life of the country gentry.

A strong central theme was needed by Martyn to order the fruits of his reading into a coherent whole. The theme chosen was the conflict between materialism and idealism, projected onto a fantastical world scale. The bulk of the work would be concerned with the history of the nineteenth century prophet of materialism, Morgante, with his genealogy, birth, education, missionary travels, decline and death all chronicled in abundant detail. The idealist response would be strong in its flow of ideas but its operations would be described in an extended lecture by a former inhabitant of Agathopolis, Theophilus, on board the steamer for Brazil with Morgante and his enthusiasts bound for missionary activities on the South American continent. The whole book would absorb all of Martyn's readings into the realisation of a fantastical world consisting of a relentless dialectic between nightmares of despair and dreams of utopia as the millennium approached.

After his strange birth, a dissection of the infant Morgante revealed the full physiological and philosophical anatomy of the Great Wind-Prophet, in whose brain 'admiration stimulates and nourishes the faculty of self-esteem [...] creates such gorgeous fancies [...] the modern method of acquiring true happiness' (*ML*, pp.54-55). After some extraordinarily absurd education in the modern manner, Morgante arrived on a camel in Oxford and in due course submitted his doctoral thesis 'A Critical Enquiry Concerning the Use and Advantages of the Abdomen as a Vehicle of Emotions'; then he graduated under the ensign of the ostrich. Morgante's academic dress caused the most excitement: 'Up his coat [...] representations of balloons, bubbles and bellows; down the legs of his trousers marvellously natural chains of sausages [...] charmed to see worked with inimitable art upon the posterior portions of the same garments the twelve signs of the zodiac' (*ML*, pp.86-87). The Oxford Manifesto was a Call to Mischief as the ultimate form of revolution.

> I am a genius [...] the champion of Humanity [...]. I assert humanity by gratifying [...] your whims and instincts [...]. The more notorious your deeds, the more will admiration be accorded to you: with which

rapture-giving commodity you may easily fill your bowels. (*ML*, pp.88-89.)

To launch the Age of Notoriety as the Oxford Movement, Morgante called on his followers to produce a great newsworthy event, by encouraging them to pull the nose of the Bishop of Oxford in the street. The poor Bishop was soon inundated by a swarm of neophytes, striving with each other to do so soonest.

Soon afterwards, Morgante's happy followers began to be known as 'Enterists', from the Greek word for 'bowels' (*ML*, p.90). Enterism spread quickly to London, especially among women. The fashionable cult blossomed as a beautiful devotion among all classes, rich and poor. 'Each individual [...] set up in his or her bed-chamber or private chambers an especial mirror upon a small altar, which was tastefully adorned with flowers and lighted candles, and before which he or she might kneel at pleasure and pray lovingly to the dearest of all objects mirrored therein' (*ML*, p.138). Morgante preached the revolution in France and Spain, amid many adventures. After a very brief unsuccessful attempt to establish a South American base in Brazil, Morgante returned to London and began to experience the process of slow physical disintegration, the inevitable price of excessive wind-swallowing. When Morgante literally stripped at a Socialist Rally in Trafalgar Square, he exploded in the midst of the rioting protesters. All that was left of the Great Wind-Prophet were his hip-bones for relics, which left Sirius wondering about the future: 'But Enterism proper, or the art of obtaining *ecstasy* from *wonder*, will [...] die very hard' (*ML*, p.326).

When Theophilus lectured Morgante and his followers onboard ship he emphasised that the dream of Agathopolis was 'recognisable in the roar of the world' as the possibility of a golden city 'that the sages have longed to reach.' (*ML*, p.246ff.) Some of the men listened so responsively that 'the seeds of yearning' took silent root within their breasts. All women in the audience reacted with 'signs of ill-disguised anger, hatred and contempt' (*ML*, p.293). So Enterism became a women's movement and Agathopolis became a men's movement, by definition. Just as Morgante the boy had been the creation of his mother, Amentia, the self-admiring and all powerful matriarch, so Morgante the giant became the massive projection of women who found satisfaction only in the emotionalism of the new liberated religion and in the utter overthrow of the iceberg beauty of Agathopolis. One of the sublime high points of aesthetic and religious beauty in Agathopolis was in the splendour of the great cathedral and, above all, in its art of liturgical music. 'Unspoiled by any instrumental accompaniment, the choristers chant in thrilling tone those plaintive old harmonies of our Greek hymns and responses, which even linger among the mosaic in the cupola when silence has settled upon the lips that gave them birth.' (*ML*, pp.279.) The contrast with the private altars could not have been more extreme. Theophilus advised the men to be strong when challenged by female Enterists. 'When men are to be found strong, wise and steadfast, women are never a power [...] I do not mean that women deliberately cause all this humiliation and disaster, but I do assert that their power is always a sign of degeneracy in men.' (*ML*, pp.301-02.)

The links between the power of women and the degeneracy in men, in the battle between materialism and idealism, was much developed in the book's most original section which described Morgante's visit to a fantastical Hell. Morgante's Hell was a place where government was firmly set in the hands of women, so much so that polyandry was an established institution among the dominant race of the Feather-Heads. Hell proved to be the polar opposite to Agathopolis: an 'absolute material civilisation [...] no sense of the beautiful, no imagination, no purely intellectual interests, no literature, no art' (*ML*, p.197). Three episodes in Hell encapsulated what followed absolute female triumph in the battle of the two civilisations in the underworld. There was the Beauty Contest where male judges used as stooges were made to wear a 'badge in the shape of a hen triumphing over the prostrate remains of a prostrate cock, worked in execrable machine modelled pinchbeck'. (*ML*, pp.207-09.) There was the fate of the effete band of Scholiaddlepates, or 'passers of examinations', where male emasculation resulted from the double castration-machine of success in public examination and ridicule from women. 'Their heads [...] wrenched round with their faces towards their backs, they were always obliged to move in a manner opposite to other folk [...] The females [...] would occasionally knock with their knuckles on the heads of those sages, and then fall into raptures at the hollow sounds.' (*ML*, pp.313-14.) There was the women-only club 'The Clattergang', uninterested in all ideas but ever eager to acquire 'such a fund of information about the private affairs of everyone else as will be sufficient to entertain those who may be in the club'. (*ML*, pp.215-16.)

Technology, often associated with the masculine domain, became an extension of feminine domination in Martyn's Hell. The emergence of the Machine in the forms of flying machines and dominant factories was linked with the modernising tendencies of women. The rule of women was celebrated by the fact that a woman was always seated in the box-seat of the flying-machines. Many practical aids to daily living were made in the dense gloom of the huge factories.[15] Newspapers were confined to cover only scandals about private persons to achieve massive circulation (*ML*, pp.197-205). The overriding plan of government by women was to eliminate once and for all the opportunities for a free inner life. In sharp contrast, the Dictator on Agathopolis was a believer in a meritocracy where individual effort and worth was valued highly. Education for the uncloistered monks had to be life-long and was based on Plato's idea that education was not about facts but about the latent qualities of human beings. (*ML*, p.271.) Government existed to foster arts and sciences among the laity. Clergy were restricted by law from holding secular appointments other than the management of hospitals and had to be content with directing 'all their energies and time to piety, good work, study and the interests of the church' (*ML*, p.270). The elected Dictator lived alone in a palace amid sculptures, frescoes, tapestries, pictures and books. The Dictator as Patron involved himself giving hospitality to gifted men, rather like the patronage given by Frederic the Great at Sans Souci. The Dictator slept in a 'prison-like cell with a marble bath and a narrow plank-bed of ebony' (*ML*, pp.288-89). The Dictator's interest was great in the progress within the two great boys' boarding-schools where the boys were trained for future service in the military, agricultural trades, law, medicine, the church, handicrafts, literature, the fine arts, philosophy and statesmanship (*ML*, p.272). A life after Agathopolis was expected as happened in the case of Theophilus, even though he was restricted to being a lonely prophetic voice in the world.

Martyn's Agathopolis served as an image of an enclave in a timeless zone of light and wonder, beyond the reach of materialists, a clarion call for spiritual reawakening in a thoroughly secularised world.[16] When seen as a kind of all male university (pledged to celibacy, study and harmony) the symbol of Agathopolis takes on the appearance of being a successor to the great ecclesiastical monasteries where learning and holiness were the ideals to be followed. Martyn's Byzantium may have been supremely beautiful in its material civilisation, but the aestheticism was never more than a splendid setting for a kind of city-state whose great purpose was a full education.

The sheer fury against women can now seriously distort the sympathetic understanding of Martyn's otherwise considerable subtlety. Readers have to remember the facts of Mrs Martyn's forms of materialism which existed in the neo-Gothic mansion while Martyn was writing the book in the old Tower. The genre of the work allowed Martyn to write with spleen about personal grudges under the cover of the fantastical. The Beauty Contest was a burlesque on the procession of young ladies who were summoned to Tulira in Mrs Martyn's quest for her son's bride.[17] The Scholiaddlepates were parodies of his own academic failures at Beaumont College and Oxford where Mrs Martyn had sent her first son for an English aristocratic education.[18] The Clattergang Club, all dedicated followers of gossip, was a lampoon of social manners in Tulira outside of the Tower—heaven for the mother but hell for the son![19] Martyn saw himself not as a married landlord with children but as a lonely, idealist dreamer. Dedicated to celibacy, he sought for off-spring in his writings. Exclusion of all women connected with his mother and the realisation of the impossibility of having real children of his own, constituted the main psychological trigger of the confident, if secret, individual stand which he took in writing and publishing *Morgante the Lesser*.[20]

There was a class dimension to Martyn's rejection of women. He was a good club man, of the Kildare Street in Dublin and of the Reform in London. Club men adopted thoughtlessly a certain style of misogyny. Members were often bachelors, or married men who spent a large part of their lives as if they were bachelors. Often, certainly in London, the gentlemen would look out of club windows on the unruly street campaigners for social justice, women's suffrage and other social and political reforms.[21] In 1886 twenty thousand dockers and building workers, supported by the women's movement, rallied in Trafalgar Square. The rally on 13 November, 1887, was violent and the troops were called out to restore law and order. The climax of *Morgante the Lesser*, with the unholy prophet as a self-exploding bomb at a socialist rally in Trafalgar Square, must surely have been inspired by that rally.[22]

Much has been written in recent years about Victorian Oxford's Hellenism as an aesthetic mask for homosexuals who lacked the courage of a Wilde to express masculine desire, not just homosocially but sexually.[23] Worlds removed from Wilde's witty sexual rebellion in *The Picture of Dorian Gray*, the impulse in Martyn's Agathopolis was predominantly a plea for cultural revival. The exclusion of ugliness and corruption from the fantastical island was profoundly undramatic on the level of character and events. But then there are no rounded characters or ordinary events in this genre of satiric romance. The great interest in the Agathopolis section now seems to be its poetic character rather like the image of the beautiful voyage to Itacha in Cavafy's poetry of 1911.[24]

During his two years at Oxford, what Martyn must have felt most deeply was the sense of impending catastrophe when the religious liberalism associated with T. H. Green was in favour with Benjamin Jowett, Master of Balliol—Morgante's college. One who satirised the liberal intelligentsia was the controversialist W. H. Mallock in the satire *The New Republic*. In Martyn's high fantastical nightmares about world domination by Enterist priestesses and hostesses, there seems to be echoes of Mallock's conservative view of English society.

At the age of thirty, Martyn was not sufficiently mature to imagine how dreams might ever become reforms. He gives very few hints of how Agathopolis might take root anywhere, least of all in Ireland, or if the dream would ever be developed to include women. Doubtless Martyn shared George Moore's feeling c.1890 that Ireland was barren ground for ideals of any kind. There was only one reference to Irish affairs in the book in the episode where evangelical female marines failed in Ireland because they held out 'no hopes to the crafty people in that country, of obtaining possession of land for next to nothing, they were laughed at ignominiously and put to flight' (*ML*, pp.132-33). The reading and dreaming landlord saw the Irish, from the seclusion of his seat, as mere grabbers for material advantage—here Martyn was still close to his mother's view of all threats to the established landlord system. Only after Mrs Martyn's death in 1898 did Martyn seek to transform his landlordism into forms of national and local patronage. As an Irish cultural nationalist, Martyn's career sprouted in many new directions as a reformer: patron of church decoration and music, playwright, journalist, philanthropist, public man, and theatre director.

Virtually all of Martyn's later reforms, with the exception of what he absorbed from Ibsen's psychology and Palestrina's polyphony, can be found potentially in *Morgante the Lesser*. The late plays like *Grangecolman* and *Regina Eyre* show the extent of the transformation of Martyn from misogynist to champion of the 'new woman'.[25] He welcomed support from strong women like Lady Gregory, Maud Gonne, Sarah Purser, Constance Markievicz and Máire Nic Shiubhlaigh. Again the foundation of the Palestrina Choir in Dublin's Pro-Cathedral shows a later preference for a choir, not like that in the great Agathopolis Cathedral but in the style of the Gothic Cathedral of Cologne.

Morgante the Lesser marked Martyn's beginnings as a writer, before he began to move towards becoming the Irish playwright still being discussed in all the Histories of the Irish Theatre. As a writer he abandoned the approaches of his satiric romance. Why his post-Morgante writings tended to droop rather than to blossom, in the light of his early promise, continues to be something of a riddle in his literary legacy.

NOTES

1. Martyn admitted to the authorship of *Morgante the Lesser* on the title page of *The Heather Field and Maeve* (London: Duckworth 1899).
2. See Louis Einstein, *Luigi Pulci and the Morgante Maggiore* (Berlin: Emil Ferber 1902). Einstein's account of Pulci's poem includes translated extracts.
3. François Rabelais, *The Histories of Gargantua and Pantagruel*, trans., and intro. J. M. Cohen (Harmondsworth: Penguin 1955); henceforth *HGP*. Rabelais' structure is discussed fully in T. M. Greene, *Rabelais: A Study of Comic Courage* (NY: Prentice-Hall 1970), pp.34-56.
4. See Thomas Carlyle, *Sartor Resartus* (Oxford: World Classics 1987), especially for Introduction by K. MacSweeney and P. Sabor, pp.vii-xxxiii.
5. For a discussion of *Sartor Resartus* as an autobiography initiated in the act of reading, see Linda Peterson, *Victorian Autobiography* (Yale UP 1986).
6. Edward Martyn, *Morgante the Lesser* (London: Swan Sonnenschein 1890); henceforth *ML*. The section dealing with Amentia's readings, dreams and child-birth falls on *ML*, pp.24-31.
7. *HGP*, pp.47-52. For comment on Rabelais' work as spiritual autobiography, see M. A. Screech, *Rabelais' Christian Comedy* (London: H. K. Lewis 1967).
8. For chapters on Theleme, see *HGP*, pp.151-63.
9. See the Introduction by A. Ross and D. Wooley in Jonathan Swift, *A Tale of a Tub* [World Classics] (OUP 1986).
10. ibid. pp.72-77. For a discussion of the nuances of Swift's satire, see M. K. Starkman, *Swift's Satire on Learning in* A Tale of a Tub (Princeton UP 1950).
11. Pater's seminal essay on Winckelman was first published in *Westminster Review* (1867) and included in *Studies in the History of the Renaissance* (1873) and revised for inclusion in *The Renaissance* (1877). Martyn arrived as an undergraduate in Christ Church Oxford in 1877.
12. Winckelman is invoked as Master in Martyn's sonnet 'The Genius of the Villa Albani', probably written in 1881 but published in *The Leader*, 29 April 1911.
13. For a discussion of *De Virginitate*, see W. R. W. Stephens, *St. John Chrysostom* (London: Murray 1883), pp.95-99.
14. See Dom Baur, *John Chrysostom* (London: Sands 1959), pp.112-15.
15. Martyn drew some inspiration for his ideas of Hell as a place of many useful inventions from Chaps. 5 and 6 of Swift's 'A Voyage to Laputa'.

There are also parallels to Martyn's technological Hell in Samuel Butler's 'The Book of Machines' (*Erewhon*, 1872, Chaps. 23 & 25).
16 Hermann Hesse, *The Glass Bead Game* (Harmondsworth: Penguin 1972), contains the all-male celibate monastery of Castalia. Unlike Martyn, Hesse depicts the complexities and ironies of the celibate relationships between individually characterised intellectuals.
17 Denis Gwynn, *Edward Martyn and the Irish Revival* (London: Jonathan Cape 1930) for further on Mrs Martyn's impatience with her son, see pp.49-52.
18 Martyn's academic achievements at Beaumont College and Christ Church were very modest, as revealed by Beaumont College Records in the Jesuit Archive Mount Street London and Christ Church Collections-Censor's Secretary Office, 1887. He used to describe himself as 'self-educated' in *Who's Who*.
19 See *Lady Gregory's Journals* ed., D. J. Murphy (Gerrards Cross: Colin Smythe 1978) for comment (7 December, 1923) on Mrs Martyn's neo-Gothic mansion. Lady Gregory recalled her husband's advice to Martyn while at Oxford 'not to build that large addition to his old castle, until at least his own taste and opinion were formed'. She goes on, 'and though the forces were too strong, his mother and her surroundings, he often regretted that he had not the strength to take that advice.' (p.494.)
20 See Elaine Showalter's fascinating essay on the theme of male flight from marriage, 'The Apocalyptic Fables of H. G. Wells' in John Stokes, ed., *Fin-de-Siècle/Fin-de-Globe* (London: Macmillan 1992), pp.69-84.
21 See Showalter's discussion of the historical background to the sexual politics of Women's suffrage in 'Borderlines', *Sexual Anarchy: Gender and Culture at the Fin-de-Siècle* (London: Bloomsbury 1990) [Chap. 1].
22 W. Von Eckardt and J. E. Chamberlain, ed., *Oscar Wilde's London* (London: O'Mara Books 1988) gives an account of the rally, with drawings reproduced from *The Illustrated News*, one showing the poor and the unemployed on the march and the other showing a few rioters looting a Trafalgar Square wine shop. (p.91.)
23 On the vexed question of the ambiguities of Oxford Hellenism, see in particular Richard Jenkins, *The Victorians and Ancient Greece* (Yale UP 1980); Richard Dellamore, *Masculine Desire* (N. Carolina UP 1990); Linda Dowling, *Hellenism and Homosexuality in Victorian Oxford* (Cornell UP 1994); Alex Potts, *Flesh and the Ideal* (Yale UP 1994); Denis Donoghue, *Walter Pater: Lover of Strange Souls* (NY: Knopf 1995). See also John Lucas, 'Introduction' to W. H. Mallock, *The New Republic*, (Leicester UP 1975) and Mallock's own *Memoirs of Life and Literature* (London: Chapman 1920) for a version of the Oxford debates about the rise of religious liberalism.
24 The full text of 'Itacha', translated by Rae Dalven is to be found in *Complete Poems of C. P. Cavafy* (London: Chatto & Windus 1961), pp.36-37.
25 See *Grangecolman* (Dublin: Maunsel 1912). For a summary of the reactions to the unpublished *Regina Eyre*, see W. J. Feeney, *Drama in Hardwicke Street* (London/Toronto: AUP 1984), pp.232-38.

MAKING THE FAMILIAR UNFAMILIAR: THE FANTASTIC IN FOUR TWENTIETH-CENTURY IRISH NOVELS

Donald E. Morse

> Twentieth-century thought [...] has been characterised by this recognition that the realms of man and nature are stranger than we had thought, along with the unceasing attempt to find out the laws of this strangeness and so make the unfamiliar familiar.
>
> —Hillis Miller[1]

Defining the fantastic in general is notoriously difficult and, since Matthew Arnold, discussing the Irish fantastic is often simply notorious. One of the few points of agreement about the nature of the fantastic among contemporary critics is that the fantastic has a symbiotic relationship with whatever is defined as reality. George P. Landow, for instance, contends that 'fantasy and our conception of what is fantastic depend upon our view of reality: what we find improbable and unexpected follows from what we find probable and likely, and the fantastic will therefore necessarily vary with the individual and the age'.[2] (The opposite is also true that our conception of what is reality depends upon our view of what is fantastic.)[3] Kathryn Hume, after surveying various critical approaches to the theory of the fantastic, offers as a useful 'working definition': *'Fantasy is any departure from consensus reality*, an impulse native to literature and manifested in innumerable variations, from monster to metaphor.'[4] Such definitions avoid that pitfall (or, rather, pratfall) *cliché* opposition enunciated by critics following Arnold—viz., that the Celts were the 'dreamers of dreams' with a 'natural' affinity for fantasy as opposed to the Anglo-Saxons who were the thinkers of thought.[5] Typical of the Irish fantastic are four Irish novels which, when taken together, span most of the twentieth century: James Stephens, *The Crock of Gold* (1912), Benedict Kiely, *The Cards of the Gambler* (1953), Seán

O'Faolain, *And Again?* (1979), and Flann O'Brien, *The Third Policeman* (1967).

Contemporary readers bring to Irish fantastic fiction expectations based upon fantasy in general. Since the 1950s prose fantasy has been read, especially in England and America, in light of the popular success of Tolkien's trilogy, *The Lord of the Rings* (1954-55) which created a kind of "mental template" against which to measure new works. Brian Attebery, for example, rightly maintains:

> With the publication and popular acceptance of Tolkien's version of the fantastic, new coherence was given to the genre. Tolkien's form of the fantasy, for readers in English, is our mental template [...]. One way to characterise the genre of fantasy is the set of texts that in some way or other resemble *The Lord of the Rings*.[6]

Three of these novels—O'Brien's as usual is the odd man out—may be accommodated within *The Lord of the Rings* template, while two of them anticipate it—Stephens' novel by some forty and Kiely's novel by a few years. Attebery's template with its three criteria for the *genre* of modern prose fantasy derived from *The Lord of the Rings* could have been obtained equally well from Stephens' or Kiely's earlier novels— perhaps because Irish fiction retained its folk and mythic roots far longer than English fiction. Rather than rediscovering such roots, as Tolkien did through his study of Anglo-Saxon and early English literature, Stephens and Kiely—having never lost theirs—could simply acknowledge them. All of which may suggest that this template does not so much derive from *The Lord of the Rings* as that *The Lord of the Rings* derives from this template. For example, both *The Crock of Gold* and *Cards of the Gambler* meet Attebery's first criterion for all fantasy that 'the essential content is the impossible'.[7] In *The Crock of Gold* readers encounter events and characters which are clearly impossible. There are the comic suicides of the first philosopher and the Grey Woman of Dun Goftin, the activities of the leprechauns of Gort na Cloca Mora, and finally the magnificent climatic scene of the hosting of the Sidhe with which the novel ends.

Given the essentially comic structure of *The Crock of Gold*, its outcome—the return to the country of the gods—is never in doubt, thus illustrating Attebery's second criterion for fantasy.

> Its characteristic structure [...] is comic. It begins with a problem and ends with resolution. Death, despair, horror, and betrayal may enter into a fantasy, but they must not be the final word.[8]

Making the Familiar Unfamiliar 269

John Cronin, in an otherwise laudatory appreciation of *The Crock of Gold* describes at some length what he terms the 'distressing lapse from his [Stephens'] masterly control of his complex narrative.' That lapse, Cronin believes, occurs 'at the very beginning of Chapter XIII, the opening passage of Book IV' and from which 'the novel [...] [never] fully recovers its first fine careless rapture'.[9] But, when seen in context, the passage referred to sounds not so much like hectoring as it does the necessary presentation of the darker side of life without which the fantasy would be in danger of either collapsing in on itself or floating off into the empyrean. Only after this dark side is acknowledged, through the several stories of illness, destitution, death, betrayal, and despair, may love, joy, and wonder prevail. Without the former the triumph of the latter would be hollow for *The Crock of Gold's* ringing affirmation of the essential goodness of life does include tragedy. Perhaps this underpinning of the fantastic accounts, in part, for the enormous appeal of the book. Writing on the occasion of the fiftieth anniversary of its publication, Augustine Martin noted that it 'is one of the few Irish prose works—perhaps the only one—to survive in print long enough to celebrate its golden jubilee'.[10]

In part, because of this confrontation with the dark side, the final effect of the book conforms to Attebery's third and last criterion for the fantastic: '[T]he effect in the reader is what Tolkien calls 'joy or consolation, but he does not mean by these terms that it is a simple emotional payoff [...]. A better word might be "wonder".'[11] Rather than approving the results of rational calculation of those in authority or the gombeen men, readers of Stephens' 'remarkable fantasy'[12] share in the ecstatic celebration—the wonder, joy, and consolation—of the return of intellect to imagination, the country of the gods.

> They swept through the goat tracks and the little boreens and the curving roads [...]. And they took the Philosopher from his prison, even the Intellect of Man they took from the hands of the doctors and lawyers, from the sly priests, from the professors whose mouths are gorged with sawdust, and the merchants who sell blades of grass—the awful people of the Fomor [...] and then they returned again, dancing and singing, to the country of the gods [...].[13]

Martin wrote of this conclusion that '[t]he book's last flourish comes through the narrative voice where Blakean rhetoric, Irish myth, and a wry note of comedy is blended into the pattern, and the allegory enacts its last gesture'.[14] Clearly, the novel's ending exemplifies Stephens' own view of the nature and worth of what he called "Pure Poetry" but which we today might term the fantastic: 'Unless delight is behind the writer of even a sad tale, his very sadness will be untrue; for it is the function of the artist to transform all that is sad, all that is ugly, all that is "real" into the one quality which reconciles the diversities that trouble us; into pure Poetry'.[15] '*The Crock of Gold* is one of those rare occurrences in literature,' asserts Martin, 'a pure or radical fantasy: the sort of book that calls into being an entire world where the rules of this world no longer apply, a world sufficient in itself, possessing its own laws or its own indigenous anarchy'.[16]

Kiely's *Cards of the Gambler* also meets Attebery's three criteria for the fantastic. That novel retells an ancient Irish oral folktale in which a gambler loses everything in an all-night card game the night of his third child's birth, meets God from whom he receives three favours, and Death with whom he strikes a bargain. The fantasy interleaves a post-World War II Irish realistic setting with the fantastic world of the older tale so God now appears in a lounge bar. Although few Irish settings are as ordinary and mundane as a lounge bar, there is something out of the ordinary in meeting God as a handsome, young, golden-haired cleric while twelve old sun-tanned men with 'oriental faces' dance in a "Ring Around the Rosie" ring.[17] The gambler also encounters 'always [...] misunderstood' Death who 'borrows' various contemporary corpses in order to be seen as well as have his presence felt in the world of the ubiquitous pub setting (*CGm*, p.126). Memorable and appropriately ironic, Death presents himself as a much harassed employee with a disagreeable job to do, with rules he must obey, bargains he must keep: 'I've an awkward job,' he complains, but quickly adds: 'I do my best for all concerned' (*CGm*, p.157). A voracious reader, he reads out to the gambler a scene from *Crime and Punishment* that eerily parallels the events and mood of the gambler's own experience of the morning (*CGm*, pp.43-44). Unlike in Stephens' novel, events in Kiely's often take a seriously ironic turn as when the gambler, attempting to thwart Death, actually aids him in his work.

'Death, despair, horror and betrayal [do] enter into [this] fantasy',[18] often in particularly painful or bitterly ironic ways. The woman, whose husband the gambler-doctor cures miraculously and at the cost of breaking his bargain with death, dies tragically without learning of her husband's recovery. The husband, in his turn, finds his wife dead in bed with his also dead brother and thereby erroneously assumes both betrayed him rather than perceiving the truth that she sacrificed herself for him. At about the same time the doctor's son dies. The gambling doctor is left asking if these events reflect the order of an indifferent, amoral, or, perhaps, malicious universe or are they 'merely' coincidental?

In an obscene parody of his compulsive gambling, the doctor meets and gambles with Satan, 'the dark horse' from whom he barely escapes and with whom he experiences deep, bone-chilling horror as the very cards themselves prove diabolical. 'Never in all his days of card-playing had the gambler seen such a king of diamonds. Looking down at those sharp, red angles was like looking into a rusted pit at all the evil things ever done for the sake of land, jewels, money, or rank in the world' (*CGm*, p.183). Finally, death does indeed come for him when least looked for. Yet that is not the last incident, for the story—like its predecessor the folktale—follows the gambler as he descends into hell, to have his life judged. The novel's ultimate word proves, however, to be neither one of earth nor of hell but of heaven to which the gambler gains admittance not for his great public deeds but for his good private ones.

What Attebery calls 'the essential content' of a work of fantasy, in this instance the bargain with death, the gifts of God, the descent into hell and subsequent rescue, 'is the impossible' and the novel's structure is comic. The novel begins with a problem and ends with resolution',[19] but while the resolution is immediately clear, the 'problem' in this novel is not. Only gradually does a reader perceive that the doctor has no significant relationships. Through his compulsive gambling, he has cut himself off from family, friends, and even his best self. Without realising it, he has grown reconciled to death-in-life. His once thriving medical practice now in shambles mirrors both his negligence and ineffectiveness. Gambling away everything he has in an all-night card game proves merely the outward and visible sign of his inward condition. Having lost everything, he is ready to strike his bargain with death—a moment which reflects a common assumption and theme of much ancient and modern fantasy, 'that man begins to live when he knows he must die'.[20]

Daniel Casey rightly claims in *The Cards of the Gambler* that 'Kiely manages to blend simplicity of design and psychological intensity to effect fiction that succeeds as *sean-sgéal* and modern novel'.[21] The folktale upon whose structure Kiely erects his contemporary story, affirms the essential goodness of the universe, the forgiveness of a loving if inscrutable deity and these are retained in the novel. The novel itself affirms the mysterious nature of a loving, forgiving god who welcomes the shriven sinner, even the gambler, to the eternal feast in heaven—a place where no mere mortal novelist, 'no storyteller with corruption in his tongue could follow' (*CGm*, p.242). This contemporary fantasy ends as does the much older folktale in wonder that defeats rational calculation before the very gates of heaven where 'from that day to this' the cards of the gambler 'may be seen by any person who goes that road' (*CGm*, p.241). Kiely clearly disagrees with the contemporary critic of the fantastic who concluded that 'The consolation that comes from fantasy is not a vision of grace from on high but a suggestion of the grace that is inherent in life, potential in man, ready to be actualised'.[22] The Grace present in *Cards of the Gambler* clearly comes 'from on high' a fact that may point once more to the oral folktale source as well as to Kiely's Irish background and/or beliefs.

Published some twenty years after *The Lord of the Rings*, Seán O'Faolain's highly original late novel, *And Again?*, ends not with gods and humans singing and dancing together in celebration nor before the very gates of heaven, but with that most mundane of artefacts, a shopping list:

Stamps
Margarine
The London Library
Elastic for knickers.[23]

And Again?, like Kiely's *Cards of the Gambler*, involves a fantastic bargain with a deity. This time the agreement is struck between the gods on Mount Olympus and Mr Younger, a nondescript, worn-out human who is about to meet a timely end at age sixty-five. In the last hour he is offered an additional sixty-five years of life if he will take part in a little experiment of the gods to see if 'what you humans call Experience teaches you a damned thing' (*AA*, p.6). The resulting manipulation of time in *And Again?* typifies the fantastic, since 'fantasy allows for a number of different, even contradictory conceptions of the nature and meaning of time, no one of which is privileged above the others'.[24] The price of Younger's entering into this experiment of the gods appears small: he 'will live backwards for sixty-five years, growing younger, and younger, until [...] the ripe age of zero' (*AA*, p.8). His memory will be severely limited to his professional skills and small details of his previous life but he will have no recollection of any intimate relationships (*AA*, p.8). (A tragically poignant version of this younging may be found in Dan Simmons's novel *Hyperion,* 1989.)[25] These conditions set by the gods eliminate two of the *clichés* that appear as staples of many such fantastic plots. First, Younger will not have the opportunity to solve the same set of problems 'all over again' and second, he will not he relive his life 'all over again' since the rest of the world will not relive it with him. Like most such Faustian bargains with the gods, however, the price of agreeing proves slightly higher than anticipated by the mortal involved.

As Younger grows physically younger, his present often appears as part of a cruel joke. For example, for several years he must live in another country apart from his wife whom he deeply loves because his 'younging' is becoming an embarrassment: How can he who appears to be a twenty-year-old husband of a forty-eight year old woman have a sixteen year old daughter? In two years the father and daughter will appear the same age! Other times, however, his present, this gift from the gods, appears most attractive as when he approaches his end and grows physically smaller and smaller but without the pain or suffering that the flesh is usually heir to. As his wife Nana describes:

> He dwindled and dwindled until he became as tiny as a clothes moth, though still talking like a man. I had long before that stopped feeding him with a spoon as small as a snuff spoon or with milk from a rubber teat. At the last I was cultivating him like a silkworm in its pupal stage, except that he was not moving onwards from larva to imago but, as all his life he had been, backwards towards his final condition of becoming his own spectre. The last night I saw him, a ghost in a padded matchbox, he was as beautiful as a scarab. [...] When I came back the next morning, his birthday, to look at his beauty again the box was empty. (*AA*, p.285.)

Mortality and death are very much present in *And Again?*, especially in Younger's lovers who all age while he 'youngs' and who all but the last, Nana, his beloved wife, predecease him. Because of his bargain with the gods, Younger will live until a time certain, his one hundred and thirtieth birthday. This privileged knowledge sets him apart from other humans who, in their omnipresent uncertainty about when the end will occur, experience death's fearful hold over their imagination and awareness. Younger alone is able to boast that 'I know what no other living creature knows about himself, that I have exactly twenty more years to live!' Humans, exemplified by the doctor in Kiely's *Cards of the Gambler,* always anticipate but never expect death. Having 'chanced life-at-any-price' (*AA*, p.282), Younger's reward is a full life—a life come full circle to fulfilment and completion, and his last words are those of thanks to his wife. 'Thank you for all you have given me, [...] for feeling with me, for opening my past to me, for being a fool with me, for being one with me in love' (*AA*, p.285).

One positive result of this experiment is that Younger's second life demonstrates how a life may be lived in full awareness of its time, yet with a sense of leisure and calm. By accepting his lot, strange as it is, and by entering fully into the gods' experiment, as fantastic as it is, Younger discovers that a human life becomes complete not simply by filling the present but also by consciously reworking or re-mapping the past through memory.[26] As Jorge Luis Borges asserts in his poem, "Cambridge":

> We are our memory,
> we are this chimerical museum of shifting forms,
> this heap of broken mirrors.[27]

In Greek mythology, Mnemosyne or memory was the mother of all nine muses. Because of memory humans have the arts, civilisation, communities. Individually, humans enjoy the possibility of continually overcoming, what Stephen Hawking calls, the second or psychological arrow of time which reflects 'the direction in which we feel time passes, the direction in which we remember the past but not the future' (145). We recall the past thanks to the mysterious workings of memory. As Saint Augustine concluded in the tenth chapter of *The Confessions*, 'I remember that I was happy when I am not happy now, and I recall my past sadness when I am not sad now; [...] I can recall a desire I had once, when I have it no longer' (10.13).[28] One could argue forcefully—with Oliver Sachs—that memory is also the basis of our humanity since it provides us with the capacity (and necessity) of creating our own histories, our lives. In his significant study, *The Importance of Memory: A New View of the Brain*, Israel Rosenfield argues that: 'Each person [...] is unique: his or her perceptions are to some degree creations, and his or her memories are part of an ongoing process of imagination'.[29] The process of imagination rooted in memory creates individuals, societies, and nations.

The narrator of *And Again?* begins his tale with the confession: 'I am writing this for myself. *I need to remember*. Only the immortals can live forgetting. Without cherished memories a man's imagination must fly wild; lose touch with common life; go off its chump' (*AA*, p.5; my emphasis). Once he does experience true happiness this second time around, he carefully holds it in memory 'and anybody who wanted to make me forget it now after it is gone for ever would have to cut a lump out of my brain and halve my heart' (*AA*, p.125). In the very last months of his life, he realises that he has spent his second life re-acquiring what he had lost of his first—although like everything else he did it backwards. At the last, as an infant he finds the joy of having and retaining memories of childhood and babyhood rather than guesses, suppositions, or gossip: 'what a [...] joy it was for me [...] to recapture after my lifelong thirst this vast gulp of infancy' (*AA*, p.284), he writes four months before his end. Without complaint or objection this second time he accepts his end as fitting for a life in which 'I have lived, loved and learned' (*AA*, p.283). If, in his first sixty-five years, Younger lived unaware of any continuity in his life, in his second sixty-five years, thanks to this fantastic gift from the gods, he discovers the joy of love and the sense of completion about life that memory helps him achieve. That sense of completion, in turn, becomes reflected in the equanimity with which he faces the certain prospect of being whisked 'back into the womb of Mother Time [...] at the ripe age of zero' (*AA*, p.8).[30]

And Again? shares with most fantastic literature the assumption that true living begins with the acceptance of mortality. This novel, as is typical of late twentieth-century fantasy, 'does not dwell on the possibility of death, but on the actuality of life'.[31] Unlike the transcendent consolation found in *The Cards of the Gambler* or *The Crock of Gold*, which stems at least in part from their roots in communal, oral, folk traditions, *And Again?*'s consolation of 'a suggestion of the grace that is inherent in life, potential in man, ready to be actualised'[32] is more typical of individually imagined modern and contemporary fantasy.

In contrast to these three novels, Flann O'Brien's wonderfully fantastic *The Third Policeman*—written in 1939 well before *The Lord of the Rings* but published posthumously in 1967 after Tolkien's trilogy had gone through several printings and reprintings—does not fit comfortably within Attebery's 'mental template.' Although the novel does meet his first criterion of the impossible content and it does appear to satisfy his second criterion of an essentially comic nature (if the structure itself is not strictly comic, it nevertheless does partake of comedy's resolution in that justice is done, evil is punished, and the moral order of the world is affirmed), it fails to meet his third criterion. Noticeably absent are the required elements of joy and consolation.

Still, *The Third Policeman* remains clearly fantastic whether fitting the Tolkien mold or not. Yet many critics, while clearly describing, for instance, the radical disorientation in space and time experienced in reading *The Third Policeman*, fail to link this disorientation to the fantastic nature of this unique fictional universe. One argues, for example, that

> The hell of *The Third Policeman* [...] is not one temporal and spatial system but many systems, some historically held, others never a part of any known philosophy of time or space [...] the fact that the narrator and the reader are unable to grasp any basis for temporal or spatial stability in this queer universe adds to the intellectual, emotional, and even physical disorientation that this novel produces.[33]

The source of this spatial and temporal instability in *The Third Policeman*, however, derives directly from O'Brien's use of techniques typical of the fantastic—techniques that 'confound and confuse the marvelous and the mimetic [...] creating a dialectic which refuses synthesis'.[34] *The Third Policeman's* setting, for example, consists of a unique, special hell constructed out of, among other things, various physical elements prominent in the commission of the earthly crime. These include Old Mathers, the narrator's now-dead victim, the box of money which was the object of the crime, the box containing the explosives hidden within another box formed by the floorboards in Old Mathers' house, and the omnipresent bicycles. Beginning with the brilliant reincarnation of Old Mathers that occurs immediately after 'something happened [...] some change [...] came upon me',[35] each of these items reappear, but in radically distorted forms as the mimetic and the marvellous join.[36] O'Brien's hellish setting, like all such fantastic settings, 'circumvents automatic responses'[37] by, in this instance, distorting the basic coordinates of space and time. Several critics believe that readers will not recognise this setting nor realise that the narrator is dead until told so at the very end of the novel,[38] but O'Brien provides numerous clues for the alert reader. Most prominent of all, the narrator makes clear that time ended for him when 'something happened', some

> alternation in everything, just as if it had held the universe standstill for an instant, suspending the planets in their courses, halting the sun and holding in mid-air any falling thing the earth was pulling towards it. (*TP*, p.23.).

In a very real sense, the narrator gets his wish to have 'my time again'

(*TP*, p.9) and, as he predicted, he does 'the same' actions again but in a radically distorted way.[39] The endless repetition occurs in an appropriately timeless world. The setting thus 'replace[s] familiarity [...] with estrangement, unease'[40] in much the same way as do the settings of Samuel Beckett's plays or James Joyce's Nighttown setting for the Circe chapter of *Ulysses*.[41]

Besides these physical items now transmogrified in the setting, O'Brien draws on a long list of non-physical particulars that figure prominently in the action. There is the secular justice that the murderers eluded but which is now about to be enacted, if in a fantastical way. '*You are going to be hung for murdering a man you did not murder and now you will be shot for not finding a tiny thing that probably does not exist at all and which in any event you did not lose*,' observes the narrator's newly discovered conscience, Joe (*TP*, p.113). A gallows is then constructed especially to hang him for a crime he did not commit. The narrator's and Divney's reliance on lies before, during, and after committing the crime recurs in various surreal scenes with the policemen beginning with the narrator's claim on a non-existent American gold watch. The greed and pride, which led the two to commit murder, returns in several incidents. Greed, perhaps most obviously, occurs when the narrator packs a suitcase to over-flowing with omnium-generated material including among other things fifty solid cubes of gold, a bottle of whiskey, and a small lethal weapon (*TP*, p.119). The *Oxford English Dictionary* defines *omnium* as 'the whole sum of what one values or is interested in; one's all' (def. 2). Pride, on the other hand, appears in the warped mirror of the pretentious parody of scholasticism represented by the narrator's lifework devoted to the third-rate hack, De Selby. His pseudo-scholarship on unreadable and unread books replete with unnecessary, extraneous, redundant parodies of scholastic footnotes culminates in the 'definitive "De Selby Index"' (*TP*, p.14)! One critic mistakenly asserts that 'the action of the book is set in motion by the narrator's desire to publish an edition of the collected works of a certain de Selby',[42] but the narrator is much less ambitious. His work is a collation of 'the views of all known commentators' (*TP*, p.14), 'my definitive "De Selby Index"' (*TP*, p.14). In other words, the book becomes a commentary on commentators—a non-book of quotations from others, rather than an original work. No doubt 'It is useful [...] and badly wanted' (*TP*, p.14)—although wanted exactly by whom and for what purpose may be best left unsaid.

The Third Policeman thus proves a very untraditional representation of a very traditional, moral tale of divine retribution and eternal damnation and punishment. If the murderers believe they actually got away with something then that, too, becomes part of their eternal hell. Evil remains its own worst punishment as seen at the novel's end when the unnamed narrator drags his confederate, Divney, back with him to hell so both can undergo its torments endlessly in the repetitious round implied in the reiterated concluding sequence. Rather than *The Crock of Gold's* exuberant celebration of a new era in an ending that opens up new possibilities, *The Third Policeman* ends somberly with the closing off of all possibility. Instead of reconstituting a life from the creation of new memories, as happens in *And Again?*, Flann O'Brien's ingenious novel constructs a hell for its protagonist out of his distorted memories. Unlike *The Cards of the Gambler*, *The Third Policeman* has no folktale base though it certainly has its roots deep in Dante's *Inferno* and catholic theology. José Lanters' description of the characters as 'mechanical puppets' (p.275) is precise and correct for how else might those behave who have neither will nor hope? 'Abandon all hope ye who enter here' reads Dante's welcome sign over the maw of hell. O'Brien, following Dante, symbolically represents the loss of hope and will by a circle. 'Hell goes round and round in shape it is circular and by nature it is interminable and repetitious and very nearly unbearable,' remarks a character in *At Swim Two Birds*.[43] 'Hell Goes Round and Round' was O'Brien's original title for the novel.[44]

All four novels, *The Third Policeman*, *The Crock of Gold*, *Cards of the Gambler*, and *And Again?*, illustrate various strengths of the fantastic generally, such as 'novelty, intensity, relationship, condensation, and transcendence of the material and the materialistic'.[45] 'Without these qualities,' Hume asserts, 'literature would only be able to affect our sense of meaning in limited, rational ways—and ultimately, meaning is not a rational matter. Reason can only deal with the material universe'.[46] Examining the uses of the fantastic in these four Irish novels 'helps us envision possibilities that transcend the purely material world which we accept as quotidian reality'.[47] The fantastic may lead, therefore, to an appreciation of both the limits and strengths of the material and the immaterial worlds with an insistence on the necessity of both. As Mikhail Bakhtin has written: '[*T*]*he fantastic here serves not for the positive embodiment of truth*, but as a mode for searching after truth, provoking it, and most important, testing it.'[48]

Making the Familiar Unfamiliar

All four novels invite readers to participate in what Harvey Cox terms 'antic play' and the free use of imagination. Cox maintains that: 'We have terribly damaged the inner experience of Western man. We have pressed him so hard toward useful work and rational calculation he has all but forgotten the joy of ecstatic celebration, antic play, and free imagination'[49]—as seen in the narrator of O'Brien's novel together with the savant de Selby, Younger in his first sixty-five years in *And Again?*, the doctor in *The Cards of the Gambler*, and the gombeen men in *the Crock of Gold*. Each fell into Matthew Arnold's trap of segregating the rational from the imaginative, thinking from dreaming. Henry James, although speaking of another subject, described the impulse behind all good fantastic literature including the Irish, when he wrote: 'Our minds are not here simply to copy a reality that is already complete. They are here to complete it, to add to its importance by their remodeling of it' (quoted in Delbanco 8). This attempt at completion and remodelling is clearly demonstrated in *The Crock of Gold*, *Cards of the Gambler*, *And Again?*, and *The Third Policeman*.

NOTES

1. Hillis Miller, *Fiction and Repetition: Seven English Novels* (Harvard UP 1982), pp.18-19.
2. George P. Landow, 'And the World Became Strange: Realms of Literary Fantasy', in Roger C. Schlobin, ed., *The Aesthetics of Fantasy Literature and Art* (Notre Dame UP 1982), p.107.
3. See Harvey Cox, *The Feast of Fools: A Theological Essay on Festivity and Fantasy* (Harvard UP 1969), p.79.
4. Kathryn Hume, *Fantasy and Mimesis: Responses to Reality in Western Literature* (NY: Methuen 1984), p.21.
5. For discussions, see Richard Kearney, *Postnationalist Ireland: Politics, Culture, Philosophy* (London: Routledge 1997), pp.172ff and my essay "Revolutionizing Reality': The Irish Fantastic', in *Journal of the Fantastic in the Arts*, 8 (1997).
6. Brian Attebery, *Strategies of Fantasy* (Indiana UP 1991), p.14.
7. idem.
8. ibid., p.15.
9. 'James Stephens (?1890-1950): *The Crock of Gold*' *Irish Fiction: 1890-1940* [1990] (Belfast: Appletree Press 1992), p.59.
10. Augustine Martin, '*The Crock of Gold*: Fifty Years After', in *Colby Library Quarterly*, 6, 4 (1962), pp.148-49. *The Crock of Gold* having fallen out of print in America, its record has been surpassed by *Ulysses*.
11. Attebery, op. cit. (1991), pp.15-16.
12. Martin, op. cit. (1962), p.148.
13. Stephens, *The Crock of Gold* [1912] (NY: Collier 1967), p.228.
14. Augustine Martin, *James Stephens: A Critical Study* (Totowa, NJ: Rowman & Littlefield 1977), p.54.
15. *On Prose and Verse* (NY: Bowling Green Press 1928), p.41.
16. Martin, op. cit. (1962), p.149.

17 Benedict Kiely, *The Cards of the Gambler* [1953] (Dublin: Millington 1973), pp.27-29; henceforth *CGm*.
18 Attebery, op. cit. (1991), p.15.
19 ibid., p.16.
20 Jane Mobley, 'Fantasy in the College Classroom', in *The CEA Critic*, 40: Special 'Fantasy' Issue, ed., Donald E. Morse (January 1978), p.4. She continues: 'Still it does not dwell on the possibility of death, but on the actuality of life' (idem.).
21 Daniel J. Casey, *Benedict Kiely* (Bucknell UP 1974), p.73.
22 Mobley, op. cit. (1978), p.5.
23 Seán O'Faolain, *And Again?* [1979] (NY: Carol 1989), p.286; henceforth *AA*.
24 Attebery, op. cit. (1991), p.61.
25 For further remarks on *And Again?* in relation to the time and memory, see my essay 'Overcoming Time: "The Present of Things Past" in History and Fiction', in *The Delegated Intellect: Emersonian Essays in Literature, Science and Art*, ed., Donald E. Morse (NY & Bern: Peter Lang 1995), pp.205-08, 218-19.
26 He also comes to realise 'that no present joy is ever quite the same thing as memory will later make it' (*AA*, p.74).
27 Jorge-Luis Borges, *In Praise of Darkness*, trans. Norman Thomas di Giovanni (NY: E. P. Dutton 1974), "Memory" [pp.20-23], ll.45-47.
28 *The Confessions of St. Augustine*, trans. Rex Warner (NY: Mentor, 1963), p.223.
29 *The Invention of Memory: A New View of the Brain* (NY: Basic Books 1988), p.197.
30 Clearly, I disagree with both O'Faolain's off-hand assessment of his hero and with Maurice Harmon's, his distinguished biographer who reports that O'Faolain 'reread *And Again?* with the "warmest" of feelings and found therein a "remarkably endearing personality" by which he meant that his hero was "a total shit and loved by all and sundry"' (*Sean O'Faolain: A Life*, London: Constable 1994, p.267). Elsewhere Harmon himself that '[l]ike anyone else, like Everyman, [Younger] is beset by ignorance of his own self and learns almost nothing from experience' (*Sean O'Faolain: A Critical Introduction* [1966], Dublin: Wolfhound, 1984, p.186). True as far as it goes; but what Younger does learn about love, life, and memory is of paramount importance for him, as it would be for Everyman.
31 Mobley, op. cit. (1978), p.4.
32 ibid., p.5.
33 Mary O'Toole, 'The Theory of Serialism in *The Third Policeman*', in *Irish University Review*, 18, 2 (Autumn 1988), p.225.
34 Lance Olsen, *Ellipse of Uncertainty: An Introduction to Postmodern Fantasy* (Conn.: Greenwood Press 1987), p.19.
35 Flann O'Brien, *The Third Policeman* [1967] (NY: New American Library 1976), p.23; henceforth *TP*.
36 For the improbable conjecture that '[w]hat has occurred is the explosion of the atomic bomb', see Charles Kemnitz, 'Beyond the Zone of Middle Dimensions: A Relativistic Reading of *The Third Policeman*', in *Irish University Review*, 15 (Spring 1985), p.61.
37 Hume, op. cit. (1984), p.196.
38 See, for instance, M. Keith Hopper, *Flann O'Brien, Bakhtin, and Menippean Satire* (Syracuse UP 1995), p.49, and Hunt, Roy L. '"Hell Goes

Round and Round": Flann O'Brien', in *Canadian Journal of Irish Studies*, 14 (1989), p.65.
39 Compare with Younger who repeats and repeats his actions but learns from the repetition. O'Brien's nameless narrator only repeats without learning.
40 Jackson, op. cit. (1981), p.179.
41 For an extensive discussion of the uses of the fantastic in the early plays of Beckett and in the 'Circe' chapter of *Ulysses*, see my essay 'Starting from the Earth, Starting from the Stars: The Fantastic in Samuel Beckett's Plays and James Joyce's *Ulysses*', in *A Small Nation's Contribution to the World: Essays on Anglo-Irish Literature and Language*, eds., Morse, et al. (Gerrards Cross: Colin Smythe; Kossuth UP 1993; NY: Barnes & Noble 1994), pp.6-18.
42 Hopper, op. cit. (1995), p.48.
43 Flann O'Brien, *At Swim-Two-Birds* [1939] (Harmondsworth: Penguin 1977).
44 Rüdiger Imhof, 'Chinese Box: Flann O'Brien in the Metafiction of Alasdair Gray, John Fowles, and Robert Coover', in *Éire-Ireland*, 25, 1, p.71.
45 Hume op. cit. (1984), p.196.
46 idem.
47 idem.
48 *Problems of Dostoevsky's Poetics*, trans., Caryl Emerson (Minnesota UP 1984), p.114; original emphasis.
49 op. cit. (1969), p.12.

YEATS AND ASTROLOGY: "SUPERNATURAL SONGS"

Elizabeth Heine

The twelve poems of Yeats's "Supernatural Songs" were first published as a complete series with his play, *A Full Moon in March*, in 1935, when he was seventy. The volume took its title from the play, linked to Easter and all supernatural rites of spring by its timing. It is also supernatural in its action, for the severed head of the swineherd sings to the queen who dances in his blood. Earlier, when the queen demands his death, he horrifies her by his tale of a woman who conceives from a drop of blood, but the idea takes effect. Yeats makes the severed head sing 'a song of Jack and Jill'. Jill murders Jack but hangs 'his heart on high', 'A-twinkle in the sky'. In the stage directions the queen's sensual dance reaches climax as *'she presses her lips to the lips of the head'*. This passionate embrace of death is also a celebration of life; Yeats's note terms the dance 'part of the old ritual of the year: the mother goddess and the slain god'.[1]

Yeats's dramatic evocation of a supernaturally solitary, ecstatic, divine union at full moon epitomises his familiar visionary system of cyclical development characterised by the phases of the moon; his choice of the full moon in March expands the monthly cycle of sun and moon to the annual measure of earth and equinox, when vernal sacrifice recurrently brings life out of death. But in *A Vision*, his prose account of his fully developed symbolic system of cyclical repetitions, and in the concluding poems of the "Supernatural Songs", Yeats also uses the 'Great Year', the 26,000-year cycle of the equinoctial points themselves. The seasonal path of the sun is the familiar one, from March to April and May, or in current zodiacal terms from Pisces to Aries and Taurus, but the point of the ecliptic at which the sun moves across the equator into the northern hemisphere, bringing spring, gradually 'precesses', moving in the reverse direction, from Taurus to Aries to Pisces to Aquarius, at a rate of about one degree every seventy years.

The precession of the equinoxes is dependent on the very slow 'wobble' of the earth's axis, which causes our earthbound relation to our circle of pole stars to change along with the ecliptic constellations by which we orient ourselves. Spring is always spring, but the full moons of March which define the diametrically opposite place of the sun now occur toward the western end of the constellation Virgo, nearer and nearer to the tail of Leo as the point of the vernal equinox also moves westward, from Pisces into Aquarius. Within the system of twelve divisions of the ecliptic that we have inherited, the constellations marking the equinoxes and solstices gradually change in sets of four, so that the same set guards the cardinal points every six thousand years or so. In *Ancient Calendars and Constellations*, a work Yeats refers to in both the earlier and later editions of *A Vision*, Emmeline Plunket points out that Aries marked the winter solstice rather than the vernal equinox some six thousand years before the birth of Christ; if the year was taken then to begin near the time of the winter solstice, as we now begin ours in January rather than March, Aries could have been regarded as first in the series even so long ago.[2]

More familiar in ancient iconography is the equinoctial pairing of Taurus and Scorpio, with the corresponding solstitial pair of Leo and Aquarius. Plunket argues that the composite beasts of Persepolis, uniting features of Bull, Lion, Scorpion and Eagle, and conquered by a young man, represent the year itself (*ACC*, p.70). Perhaps Oedipus, solving the riddle of time posed by the Sphinx, descends from a similar tradition. As Plunket shows [see her Plate VIII], the westward moving vernal point would have been precessing slowly through Taurus while the summer solstice point made its way from Leo's tail to his front paws, taking centuries to reach Leo's alpha star, Regulus; this dominant ecliptic star marked the summer solstice, the time of the Nile floods, five thousand years ago, when Thuban, in Draco, was the pole star. Regulus would have been within five degrees of the rising solstitial sun for seven centuries; the leonine form of the Egyptian Sphinx has long been regarded as a representative of those times, its human head perhaps associated with adjacent Virgo, or with Leo's opposite, the water-bearer Aquarius, rather than the eagle which often substituted for Aquarius.[3]

Over the last two thousand years, most western astrologers, following Ptolemy, have come to define the location of the vernal equinox as the 'first point of Aries', using the twelve 'signs' of the zodiac as thirty-degree divisions of the sun's annual course without adjusting them to the varying borders of the traditional constellations. Yeats deals with these differences in the first edition of *A Vision* (1925) when he uses an older and more symbolic measure of precession to consider the relationship of Virgil's prophecy of a coming saviour, and thus Christ's birth, to the transition of the equinoctial point from Aries to Pisces, or Ram to Fish. In the process he also describes the full moon in Virgo:

> The Constellations being of varying lengths and sometimes overlapping have but a vague connection either with the Twelve Divisions of the Solar Great Year, or with the Twelve Divisions of the ordinary year, but they must have dominated the ancient imagination much more than any abstract division of the ecliptic. When I find the position of the vernal equinox at the birth of Christ upon the only star map within my reach that has the ancient mythological Zodiacal creatures—Plate 3 in E. M. Plunkett's 'Ancient Calendars' [see her Plate III]—it falls exactly upon the line dividing the Horn of the Ram from the Side of the Fish. Probably the Zodiacal creatures were never drawn precisely alike on any two maps but the difference was not great, the stars of Ram and Fish are packed particularly close to one another, and neither Virgil nor his Sybil, if they knew anything of the Great Year, could have failed to find the position of the precessional Sun significant. Three hundred years, two degrees of the Great Year, would but correspond to two days of the Sun's annual journey, and his [seasonal] transition from Pisces to Aries had for generations been associated with the ceremonial death and resurrection of Dionysus. Near that transition the women wailed him, and night showed the full moon separating from the constellation Virgo, with the star [Spica] in the wheatsheaf, or in the child, for in the old maps she is represented carrying now one now the other. It may be that instead of a vague line, the Sibyl knew some star that fixed the exact moment of transition.[4]

Yeats goes on to explain his sense of the incredibility of any human agency in 'Christ being born at or near the moment of transition'; his acceptance of an astronomical objectivity for the precessional 'moment' anchors the historical cycles he shapes in *A Vision*, where he takes the two thousand years of Christianity as roughly one-twelfth of a precessionary cycle in which civilisations yield to their antithetical successors at the change of the equinoctial signs. Yet he also accepts the malleable nature of the seasonal traditions, and it is difficult to know whether he is redefining Christianity for past, present, or future civilisations when he animates and mythologises the virgin queen and her alpha star anew in *A Full Moon in March*, implying a child as the gift of Jack's head and heart, 'A-twinkle in the sky'.

Yeats's familiarity with symbolic interpretations of cycles and star-forms may have influenced his placing of Sphinx and Buddha on either side of the dancing girl who embodies the full moon in 'The Double Vision of Michael Robartes', a poem which he wrote in 1918, soon after his marriage to Georgie Hyde-Lees in October 1917, and early in the development of the visionary system which grew from her automatic writing. It certainly influenced "Conjunctions", the tenth of the "Supernatural Songs" and the most obviously astrological of all Yeats's poems:

> If Jupiter and Saturn meet,
> What a crop of mummy wheat!
> The sword's a cross; thereon He died:
> On breast of Mars the goddess sighed.

"Conjunctions" takes its title from the astrological term for the meeting of planets, seen from our geocentric perspective. In approaching the poem a recognition that Yeats wants us to think of gods and planets together is helpful, but neither recognition of the orbits that bring Mars and Venus together at least annually, and Jupiter and Saturn every twenty years, will suffice, nor will familiarity with the analogical patterns of astrological interpretation, where the 'mummy' in its age and restriction reflects Saturn, and the new growth from ancient seed suggests Jupiter's beneficent generational power. Venus and Mars represent love and war in western astrology as in Greco-Roman mythology, but to explain how Yeats associates the planetary gods with Christ, the 'He' who died on the cross rather than the sword, what is essential is knowledge of his theories of contrasting historical cycles. The gnostic definitions of Christian mysticism in the preceding "Supernatural Songs" lay some of the groundwork for the difficult conjunction of love and war with Christ, but Yeats makes the planetary symbolism explicit in the later edition of *A Vision*.

In particular, the Saturn-Jupiter couplet, with a slightly more exclamatory second line—'O what a crop of mummy wheat!'—appears also in "The End of the Cycle", the brief final section of the heavily revised second edition of *A Vision*, published in 1937. In January 1934 Yeats wrote in a letter that he had 'faced at last and finish[ed] the prophecy of the next hundred years', but nothing of this is known to remain.[5] Instead, as Yeats regrets his inability to prophesy as he would like from his fully-developed symbolism of the Great Year and its subsidiary cycles, he contents himself by presenting the couplet as an equivalent to 'the *antithetical* multiform influx' that he expects to follow the decay of Europe he sees around him (*AV[B]*, p.302). He can quote the first couplet without the contextual support of the second because he provides an explanation earlier in the book, in section XI of 'The Completed Symbol'. There he links both the Saturn-Jupiter and the Mars-Venus conjunctions to the planetary rulerships of the signs on either side of the symbolic first point of Aries; Aquarius and Pisces are in the ancient tradition ruled by Saturn and Jupiter, respectively, while Mars rules Aries and Venus rules Taurus. But these "Conjunctions" are symbolic rather than actual; the planets rule these signs no matter where they themselves are transiting in their orbits.

In the same passage, Yeats also defines the symbolism of these conjoined rulers when the full moon, always the 'fifteenth phase' in his 28-phase system, is positioned at the first point of Aries, between the two pairs of signs:

> These two conjunctions which express so many things are certainly, upon occasion, the outward-looking mind, love and its lure, contrasted with introspective knowledge of the mind's self-begotten unity, an intellectual excitement. They stand, so to speak, like heraldic supporters guarding the mystery of the fifteenth phase. (*AV[B]*, p.207)

In context, the two mental qualities characterise 'Will' and 'Creative Mind', two of the four 'Faculties' Yeats attributes to individuals. 'Will', drawn by 'love and its lure', cycles through the phases and the zodiacal signs from west to east, like the seasonal sun and monthly moon; 'Creative Mind', more purely intellectual, circles in the opposite direction, like the precession of the equinoxes.[6] But Yeats then expands the range of reference by revising "The Double Vision of Michael Robartes" without changing a word, quoting his earlier descriptions of Sphinx and Buddha after stating his own change of view: 'In certain lines written years ago in the first excitement of discovery I compared one to the Sphinx and one to Buddha. I should have put Christ instead of Buddha, for according to my instructors Buddha was a Jupiter-Saturn influence' (*AV[B]*, pp.207-08). The Sphinx remains a representative of the Saturn-Jupiter force, 'an intellectual excitement', but Christ replaces Buddha, taking over the original lines—'Yet little peace he had/For those that love are sad'—as he becomes the Mars-Venus 'influence' of "Conjunctions".

There is also a related, more personal dimension involved in Yeats's definitions, as he suggests in his introduction to what he footnotes as 'these dry astrological bones' of rulerships and 'heraldic supporters': 'I must now explain a detail of the symbolism which has come into my poetry and, in ways I am not yet ready to discuss, into my life' (*AV*[*B*], p.207). The 'poetry' must be "Conjunctions", but the actual planetary conjunctions hidden behind the facade of the symbolic rulerships are those present in the horoscopes of his two children. Yeats's marriage brought the beginnings of *A Vision* through his wife's automatic writing; in the records of the original question and answer sessions there are occasional horoscopes drawn up for the times of the question sessions themselves, and also multiple references to planets beyond sun, moon, and earth, to whose relative motions the system of *A Vision* is limited. Moreover, it is apparent in the manuscripts that transiting phases of the sun and moon were also important to spousal conjunctions and questions of conception, as well as to the power of the automatic writing itself.[7] As a result of these influences, so far as the parents were concerned, their daughter was born at a moment when transiting Mars and Venus were just past conjunction, and their son during the time of the transit of the longer-lasting Saturn-Jupiter conjunction. In his introduction to the first edition of *A Vision*, Yeats regrets that he had 'not even dealt with the whole of my subject, perhaps not even with what is most important, writing nothing about the Beatific Vision, little of sexual love [...]'. (*AVA*, p.xii). The later edition is even drier and more formal; by contrast, Yeats's poems and plays become more vividly sexual as *A Vision* is revised, and the "Supernatural Songs" celebrate beatific visions rooted in sexual love and parenthood.

In *A Vision* and in the poetry most closely related to it, personal astrological knowledge and practice lie behind what appears in public as a relatively impersonal symbolic structure. Yeats makes the relation of "Conjunctions" to his children's horoscopes explicit in a long letter of 25 August 1934 to Olivia Shakespear, in which he includes not only "Conjunctions" but also "He and She"; the latter poem encapsulates the cyclical phases of sun and moon that he calls in the letter 'my centric myth', and becomes the sixth of the "Supernatural Songs". Yeats writes openly, for in the 1890s Mrs Shakespear had been his first lover, becoming also his lifelong friend, and in 1910 her brother's marriage to Georgie Hyde-Lees' widowed mother had brought the future Mrs Yeats into her family. Yeats presents "Conjunctions" with the recollection that through the automatic writing he had been told that his two children:

> would develop so that I could study in them the alternating dispensations, the Christian or objective, then the Antithetical or subjective. The Christian is the Mars-Venus—it is democratic. The

Jupiter-Saturn civilisation is born free among the most cultivated, out of tradition, out of rule. (*L*, p.828.)

Adding that his wife had recently observed that their fifteen-year-old daughter was fascinated by death, their son by life, he sees in his daughter's studies of skeletons and Shakespearean tragedy 'the old association of love and death'. "He and She" then intervenes, to be followed by a postscript returning to his wife's comment, so reflective of his own concerns. Perhaps thinking also of *A Full Moon in March*, Yeats wonders whether 'she may have subconsciously remembered that her spirits once spoke of the centric movement of phase 1 as the kiss of Life and the centric movement of phase 15 (full moon) as the kiss of Death' (*L*, p.829). That is, life begins at phase 1, and at phase 15 the cycle rounds toward the death that comes as phase 28 becomes phase 1 again. Both phase 1 and 15 are ultimate, offering timeless moments of mystic experience which are opposite in kind but equivalent gateways to eternity.

Probably the roots of Yeats's symbolic uses of the sun-moon phases lie in the fact that Maud Gonne, the ideal love of his youth and middle age, was born at a full moon positioned in near conjunction with his own birthday sun.[8] Nonetheless, he was, as with his children, very careful to keep individual horoscopes out of *A Vision*, where the phases represent not only historical cycles but also incarnations and reincarnations within a soul's multi-generational odyssey, proceeding from the first to the twenty-eighth phase over perhaps 2,000 years. When Yeats chooses people to illustrate the characteristics of his phases there is almost no correlation with the moon's actual position on their birthdays. For example, Yeats places his old friend George Russell ("AE") in Phase 25, but at Russell's birth the moon was not relatively old but relatively new, not even at first quarter; it was also in a striking astrological position, conjunct Uranus at the 'midheaven', the highest point of the ecliptic for the time and place of his birth. Yeats knew Russell's horoscope, but mentions it only in the last sentence, with no analysis, simply implying its fateful role in a given incarnation: '[Russell's] simulated intuition is arrayed in ideal conventional images of sense, instead of in some form of abstract opinion, because of the character of his horoscope' (*AV[B]*, p.176). Further astrological comment could have drawn on the youthful nature of Russell's natal moon, conjunct Uranus in water-sensitive, moon-ruled Cancer, but Yeats keeps the geometrical mysteries of *A Vision* free of such 'dry astrological bones'.[9]

Yeats and Astrology: "Supernatural Songs"

In Yeats's late poems metaphysical uses also dominate astrological appearances; moving on in his August letter from his explanation of the association of "Conjunctions" with his children, Yeats introduces "He and She" as the most recently written of 'a lot of poetry of a personal metaphysical sort', an example 'on the soul' (*L*, p.828). This view fits its place in the sequence of "Supernatural Songs", where it follows "Ribh Considers Christian Love Insufficient". Here the medieval Irish Christian monk who is the titular speaker of the series declares that 'Hatred of God may bring the soul to God'. In not seeking, and in hating common definitions of what is sought, the purified soul becomes 'a bride/That cannot in that trash and tinsel hide':

> At stroke of midnight soul cannot endure
> A bodily or mental furniture.
> What can she take until her Master give!
> Where can she look until He make the show!
> What can she know until He bid her know!
> How can she live till in her blood He live!

The final exclamations affirm rather than query, unlike 'Did she put on his knowledge with his power?' at the conclusion of "Leda and the Swan", Yeats's visionary sonnet of a dozen years earlier; in his mythology of the Great Year the birth of Helen from this conjunction of mortal woman and God in the guise of a swan begins the classical age, as the Christian era begins with the birth of Christ from God's annunciation, in dove-like form, to Mary. The sonnet introduces the historical section, called 'Dove or Swan', in both editions of *A Vision*.

However, Ribh's cry is less historical than individual, and the easy, colloquial language of "He and She" immediately shifts the tone from mystic vision to daily life. This tiny, charming lyric, if it stood alone, would be the simplest of all Yeats's many descriptions of the egoistic subjectivity he associates with the full moon, overcome in the objectivity of the sun at the moment it becomes new once more:

> As the moon sidles up
> Must she sidle up,
> As trips the scared moon
> Away must she trip:
> 'His light had struck me blind
> Dared I stop'.

She sings as the moon sings:

> 'I am I, am I;
> The greater grows my light

The further that I fly'.
All creation shivers
With that sweet cry.

Without the context of "Supernatural Songs", the 'He' of the poem's title is like the sun, inescapable in its gravity but god-like only in religious myth. Yeats's developments of sun-moon oppositions and conjunctions in male-female terms fall well within the analogical traditions of astrological interpretation, as does his use of the cycle of the moon's phases for measures of life cycles and seasonal cycles. The supernatural and metaphysical enter as we hope to move beyond the natural cycles, wondering what powers beyond human control may govern our actions.

Yeats's astrological experience becomes a necessary but not always visible groundwork for his metaphysical cosmology. The opposite paths of the two ultimate phases take effect in Yeats's poetry without the naming of the moon; in "A Dialogue of Self and Soul", written in 1927-28, day and night serve as well. Yeats's 'Soul' argues for an ascent to the forgiveness of Heaven by way of the winding stair in the tower, leading to the broken battlement and on, 'Upon the breathless starlit air,/Upon the star that marks the hidden pole'. The 'Self' chooses the daylight way represented by the samurai sword 'bound and wound' in a fragment of a woman's robe, things 'Emblematical of love and war'; it creates its own forgiveness in a moment of self-acceptance so full of 'sweetness' that 'We are blest by everything,/Everything we look upon is blest'. Or the moon can be present with little of the metaphysics, although Yeats's mythology so pervades his poetry that in the posthumous *Collected Poems* of 1950 the 'scared' moon of "He and She" mistakenly became 'sacred', not without reason in the light of his 'centric myth'. But 'scared' suits this youthful moon, abandoning its 'sidling' for a free 'tripping' on its way to the ecstasy correlative with but very much sweeter than that of *A Full Moon in March*.

The relatively colloquial language and the short lines of "He and She" may also reflect the reading that Yeats had been doing for his edition of *The Oxford Book of Modern Verse*, which appeared to much controversy in 1936. These are elements he praises in the poetry of Dorothy Wellesley, whose work he met in an anthology before he sought her out as a kindred thinker. When he sent her a copy of *A Full Moon in March* late in 1935, he referred to "Fire", the poem he chose to open her group in his Oxford collection, as he remarked that he did not like his own book: 'it is a fragment of the past I had to get rid of. The swift rhythm of "Fire", and the study of rhythm my work for the anthology entailed, have opened my door. [...] Once I am through the door I can face the storm'.[10] The moon in fact disappears from Yeats's later poems, where he confronts his own place among the historical cycles in a more directly personal way. The "Supernatural Songs" revisit old themes from a late point of view, but not in the undisguised voice of "The Circus Animals' Desertion", for example, composed three or four years later and first printed just before Yeats's death in January 1939. Instead there is the monk first described in a letter written to Olivia Shakespear on 24 July 1934, and later in Yeats's notes to *A Full Moon in March*: 'The hermit Ribh in "Supernatural Songs" is an imaginary critic of St Patrick. His Christianity, come perhaps from Egypt like much early Irish Christianity, echoes pre-Christian thought' (*VP*, p.857).

In Yeats's first major poem, "The Wanderings of Oisin", published in 1889, the warrior-poet Oisin's love of the immortal Niamh and the isles of her paradise is not enough to keep him from falling back into a mortal Ireland converted in his absence by St Patrick. Suddenly aged, Oisin tells his stories of the Celtic paradise to the disapproving Patrick, whose ways he refuses to adopt; he would rather be with his fellow pagans in St Patrick's Hell. Ribh, however, is Christian, a gnostic follower of the Egyptian Hermes Trismegistus, whose 'Great Smaragdine Tablet' he cites in the second of the "Supernatural Songs", "Ribh Denounces Patrick", when he declares that 'Natural and supernatural with the self-same ring are wed'. In the first poem, "Ribh at the Tomb of Baile and Aillinn", the tonsured, ninety-year-old monk explains to a 'you' who has found him 'in the pitch-dark night/With open book' that he reads by the light of the unearthly love of Baile and Aillinn, Celtic forms of Romeo and Juliet whose story Yeats told in a poem published in 1903. Ribh reads with eyes 'By water, herb and solitary prayer/Made aquiline'; he seems more magician than Christian, although Yeats in his commentary focuses on Christianity before the ninth-century split between its western and eastern forms, and explains that he also 'associated early Christian Ireland with India' (*VP*, p.837).

Taken as speaker of the whole sequence, Ribh is a medieval astrologer and philosopher of history, denouncing Patrick for having accepted the 'abstract Greek absurdity' of a 'masculine Trinity'. Yeats notes that he himself 'would consider Ribh an orthodox man were it not for his view of the Trinity' (*VP*, p.837), which is gnostic: 'Man, woman, child (a daughter or a son),/That's how all natural and supernatural stories run'. In the later songs Ribh wonders about the conception of 'world-transforming Charlemagne', then precedes "Conjunctions" with "The Four Ages of Man", four couplets that match the conflicts in a man's life to the quarters of Yeats's mythic cycle of the moon; the successive struggles with body, heart, and mind end in soul: 'Now his wars on God begin;/At stroke of midnight God shall win'. "A Needle's Eye" follows "Conjunctions", symbolising the pole star and its axis as a needle-like pathway between eternity and earth; the same axis is implicit in the last poem, "Meru". Mount Meru, or Kailas, is a kind of Himalayan Olympus, home of the gods, but it is also 'the central peak of the world, the main pin of the universe, the vertical axis'.[11] In "Meru" the speaker bleakly contrasts man's illusion of civilisation with the reality of its continual destruction—'Egypt and Greece, good-bye, and good-bye, Rome!'—and concludes with a recognition that snow-bound Himalayan hermits share his cyclic view of history, knowing 'That day brings round the night, that before dawn/His glory and his monuments are gone'. The possibilities of creative joy both in destruction and in building anew, central to Yeats's later poem, "Lapis Lazuli", are only implications here.

Both the Egyptian and Indian elements of Ribh's thought can be traced back to Yeats's theosophical studies with Mme Blavatsky, whose Esoteric Section he joined in London in 1888, when he was twenty-three. She presents the statements of Hermes' Emerald Tablet in *Isis Unveiled* (1877); the first and third are particularly familiar to astrologers, as to Ribh: 'What is below is like that which is above, and what is above is similar to that which is below to accomplish the wonders of one thing. [...] Its father is the sun, its mother is the moon.'[12] Meru too is mentioned both in *Isis Unveiled* and in Mme Blavatsky's more Indian work, *The Secret Doctrine* (1888), but Yeats had also returned to his Indian studies early in the 1930s. Late in May 1934 he finished the proofs of his introduction to *The Holy Mountain*, by Bhagwan Shri Hamsa, an autobiography he thought of as a sequel to *An Indian Monk*, which Hamsa's student and translator, Shri Purohit Swami, had written and published in 1932 with Yeats's encouragement (*L*, p.823). In the commentary for the "Supernatural Songs", Yeats provides the Indian background for "Meru" through specific comparisons of Indian and Irish beliefs and still current practices:

> Shri Purohit Swami, protected during his pilgrimage to a remote Himalayan shrine by a strange great dog that disappeared when danger

was past, might have been that blessed Cellach who sang upon his deathbed of bird and beast; Bagwan Shri Hamsa's pilgrimage to Mount Kailas, the legendary Meru, and to lake Manas Sarowa, suggested pilgrimages to Croagh Patrick and to Lough Derg. (*VP*, p.837.)

Yeats and the Swami were also planning to translate some of the Upanishads; in 1935 Yeats published an introduction, 'The Mandukya Upanishad', in which he provides a variant of the mystic marriage when he suggests a link between the ideal of romantic love developed in twelfth-century Europe and Tantric sexual meditation, 'wherein the man seeks the divine Self as present in his wife, the wife the divine Self as present in the man'.[13]

Ribh's study of the love of Baile and Aillinn, perfected only in eternity, can also be matched to another early work through Forgael's answer to his steersman in the acting version of *The Shadowy Waters*, an early verse play Yeats revised for the stage in 1906. In essence Forgael's goal resembles Ribh's vision of the ideal lovers; Yeats's Rosicrucian knowledge, gained after he joined the Hermetic Order of the Golden Dawn in 1890, appears when Forgael links mystic marriage and the cross. The steersman demands to know why Forgael insists on sailing onward in search of a love not meant for mortals:

> *Forgael.* I cannot answer.
> I can see nothing plain; all's mystery.
> Yet sometimes there's a torch inside my head
> That makes all clear, but when the light is gone
> I have but images, analogies,
> The mystic bread, the sacramental wine,
> The red rose where the two shafts of the cross,
> Body and soul, waking and sleep, death, life,
> Whatever meaning ancient allegorists
> Have settled on, are mixed into one joy.
> For what's the rose but that? miraculous cries,
> Old stories about mystic marriages,
> Impossible truths? But when the torch is lit
> All that is impossible is certain,
> I plunge into the abyss. (*VPl*, p.323)

Forgael's abyss is Ribh's supernatural certainty, the difference of age and Yeats's experience as husband and father rather than ever-pursuing lover. His familiarity with the joining of opposites in the cross and rose of mystic marriage explains much of his association of Christ with Mars and Venus in "Conjunctions". His concern with the related question of why an immortal might be drawn to birth and death in the world of time, or why a soul might choose reincarnation rather than nirvana, is addressed in his letters to Olivia Shakespear in 1933 and 1934; he also published some contemporary commentary on the nature of the choice in *Wheels and Butterflies* (1934), a collection of four of his plays with accompanying essays and a preface dated 4 August 1934, in the midst of the composition of "Supernatural Songs".

In *Wheels and Butterflies* Yeats explains the metaphysical aims of his dance-plays and returns again to his 'centric myth' in the new commentary he wrote for an earlier play, *The Cat and the Moon*. The play and the accompanying poem which provides its title were both written early in the development of *A Vision*; the dramatic fable about the blind man who carries the lame man to the holy well and chooses sight, while the lame man chooses the holiness of the saint rather than a cure, and is then cured, was to Yeats a tale of body and soul:

> But as the populace might well alter out of all recognition, deprive of all apparent meaning, some philosophical thought or verse, I wrote a little poem where a cat is disturbed by the moon, and in the changing pupils of its eyes seems to repeat the movement of the moon's changes, and allowed myself as I wrote to think of the cat as the normal man and of the moon as the opposite he seeks perpetually, or as having any meaning I have conferred upon the moon elsewhere. Doubtless, too, when the lame man takes the saint upon his back, the normal man has become one with that opposite, but I had to bear in mind that I was among dreams and proverbs, that though I might discover what had been and might be again an abstract idea, no abstract idea must be present. (*VPl*, p.807)

Yeats seems somewhat weary of explanation when he writes of 'any meaning I have conferred upon the moon elsewhere'. Nonetheless, in the poem about the cat, 'The sacred moon overhead/Has taken a new phase', and as he continues his commentary the opposite choices of the lame man and the blind are like those he associates with the completion of the human cycle. As he proceeds he uses some of his earlier astrological terminology and introduces an historical analogue for Ribh; Bardaisan or Bardasanes, half a century older than Plotinus, was an early Syriac convert to Christianity who was known, like Yeats, for his poetry and his astrological cosmology:

> Perhaps some early Christian—Bardaisan had speculations about the sun and moon nobody seems to have investigated—thought as I do, saw in the changes of the moon all the cycles: the soul realising its separate being in the full moon, then, as the moon seems to approach the sun and dwindle away, all but realising its absorption in God, only to whirl away once more: the mind of a man, separating itself from the common matrix, through childish imaginations, through struggle— Vico's heroic age—to roundness, completeness, and then externalising,

> intellectualising, systematising, until at last it lies dead, a spider smothered in its own web: the choice offered by the sages, either with the soul from the myth to union with the source of all, the breaking of the circle, or from the myth to reflection and the circle renewed for better or worse. For better or worse according to one's life, but never progress as we understand it, never the straight line, always a necessity to break away and destroy, or to sink in and forget. (*VPl*, p.807)

The elements of both "He and She" and "The Four Ages of Man" are apparent, as is Yeats's belief in historical cycles of destruction rather than in any infinite linear 'progress'. Less clear is the Buddhistic choice between nirvana or a return to the world of time. The difficult word is 'reflection', which Yeats also uses in his "Seven Propositions", a little known and abstruse document of 1930 or so, entitled "Astrology and the Nature of Reality" in manuscript. There he defines reality as 'a timeless and spaceless community of Spirits which perceive each other' and 'determine' each other through their perceptions. These Spirits can 'reflect themselves in time and space', where perceptions continue to be the reality: 'Time and space are unreal'. But the natal horoscope marks the 'reflection' of a 'Spirit' into the world of time and space, the moment when 'the destiny receives its character' for that incarnation: 'The horoscope is a set of geometrical relations between the Spirit's reflection and the principal masses in the universe and defines that character.'[14] Thus are we caught within the cycles of the moon and stars.

Yeats gave Olivia Shakespear a less abstract definition of the soul's choice: 'One might say the love of the beloved seeks eternity, that of the child seeks time' (*L*, p.817). He was commenting in November 1933 on the 'inner ideas' of *The King of the Great Clock Tower*, the play which is the precursor of *A Full Moon in March*. In the later play he drops the third character of the king, puzzled by his silent queen and her demanding wooer; in the earlier the critical moment comes at 'stroke of midnight', as in the "Supernatural Songs", but any midnight can be taken as the completion of a cycle. When Yeats compares the two plays late in 1934, he prefers the later one, remarking, 'I don't like *The Clock Tower* which is theatrically coherent, spiritually incoherent' (*L*, p.830). His decision to change the time from the indefinite anniversary night of *The Clock Tower* to the equinoctial *Full Moon in March* roots the later play in all the larger cycles of months, seasons, year and Great Year; the limitation to two characters emphasises the man-woman pair. The possibility of children is unmentioned in the completed *Clock Tower*, but is explicit in the drafts of the opening songs that Yeats included in his November letter to Olivia Shakespear. The first of the early songs prefers the timeless love of disembodied spirits, for 'Time/Comes from the torture of our flesh'. The second insists that 'All love is shackled to mortality, [...] It dreams of the unborn' (*L*, p.817).

When Yeats sends the middle stanzas of "Ribh Denounces Patrick" to Olivia Shakespear late in July 1934, he again associates children with time and mortality, in opposition to the perfection of eternity: 'The point of the poem is that we beget and bear because of the incompleteness of our love' (*L*, p.824). Ribh himself seems ambivalent. Mrs Shakespear could see Ribh's insistence in the second stanza that 'As man, as beast, as an ephemeral fly begets, God-head begets God-head'; in the third that 'copies' are engendered 'When the conflagration of [...] passion sinks' and 'juggling Nature mounts'; and in the first line of the fourth and last stanza that 'The mirror scaled serpent' of time brings the 'multiplicity' of increase. The last two lines of the poem were not included; in them Ribh returns to a kind of Yeatsian orthodoxy:

> But all that run in couples, on earth, or flood or air,
>   shares God that is but three,
> And could beget or bear themselves could they but love as He.

In Yeats's poetry the sense of being 'self-begotten' can come in a flash of beatific joy like that in "Stream and Sun at Glendalough", written in June 1932, when he felt 'Self-born, born anew', if only for a moment. Or it can be the 'introspective knowledge of the mind's self-begotten unity' that he associated with the Saturn-Jupiter Sphinx in "The Double Vision of Michael Robartes" (*AV*[*B*], p.207). The self-forgiveness in "The Dialogue of Self and Soul" is similar. However, all of these relate to the visionary timelessness of the fifteenth phase rather than 'the spider smothered in its own web' of the last; full moon seems always most triumphant.

The King of the Great Clock Tower was produced at the Abbey Theatre in Dublin at the end of July 1934 with *Resurrection*, another of the earlier plays included in *Wheels and Butterflies*. The new play was a success; the eight poems of the first sequence of "Supernatural Songs" were added to the proofs of *The King of the Great Clock Tower* and published late in 1934. Yeats added four poems to complete the sequence and included both a verse and a prose version of *The King of the Great Clock Tower* with *A Full Moon in March* in the 1935 volume.

"Ribh in Ecstasy" and "There" now follow "Ribh Denounces Patrick". 'What matter that you understood no word!' is Ribh's opening exclamation in the first, which retreats not at all from an insistence on the sexual qualities of enlightenment; Ribh insists that as he was caught up in his soul's happiness in itself, 'Godhead on Godhead in sexual spasm begot/Godhead'. The second poem, "There", is a four-line description of the end of time, completing all cycles in the ultimate return to origins; I take it to be an equivalent of Ribh's ecstatic mystic experience as well as a gathering of Yeats's geometric symbols:

> There all the barrel-hoops are knit,
> There all the serpent-tails are bit,
> There all the gyres converge in one,
> There all the planets drop in the Sun.

In the opening line of "Meru", 'Civilisation is hooped together' in a temporal illusion of orderly history. The serpent biting its tail is Ouroboros, the Orphic symbol of the endless cycles of time. The gyres are spirals, extended cycles of change which can outline the shape of cones like those formed by dust-devils or rising smoke or the shadows we perceive as eclipses, or by the earth's pole as it slowly makes its circuit among the stars. In *A Vision* the gyres Yeats uses to measure historical change can pair off in double helix form, like the entwined snakes of Aesculapius' staff, or any other Tree of Knowledge that connects eternity with time. The fate of the planets as they slowly spiral closer to the sun reflects the theosophical view of evolution, ending all cycles in the eventual return of everything to its divine origin.

The other two late poems follow "He and She". In its first three-line triplet "What Magic Drum?" creates a powerful amalgam of fatherhood, child, and 'Primordial Motherhood' as child rests on father's breast. In the second triplet the 'magic drum' resounds through 'light-obliterating garden foliage' as mouth and tongue move down limb and breast or belly. Natural and supernatural seem to merge in a wild, primeval garden; the final question assures progeny: 'What from the forest came? What beast has licked its young?' The last of the additions, "Whence Had They Come?", develops a metaphor of 'Dramatis Personae' in which unknown forces seem to speak through those who are caught in the throes of passion; the metaphor suits the playwright Yeats better than the hermit Ribh, although the poem returns to Rome before its final question, 'What sacred drama through her body heaved/When world-transforming Charlemagne was conceived?'

The last four poems remain in their original sequence: "The Four Ages of Man", "Conjunctions", "A Needle's Eye", and "Meru". All draw on Yeats's symbolic cycles, but "A Needle's Eye" least obviously:

> All the stream that's roaring by
> Came out of a needle's eye;
> Things unborn, things that are gone,
> From needle's eye still goad it on.

Here the eye of the needle is generative, a gateway for life pouring to earth from a rich eternity of old souls and new, inverting the Biblical suggestion of a needle's eye as a heavenly gateway too narrow for a rich man to enter. But the needle is also cosmological, comparable to the earth's axis and its circle of pole stars, like the 'Tent-pole of Eden' that centres the heavens in Yeats's earlier poem of 1929, "Veronica's Napkin". There he contemplates 'The Heavenly Circuit', its historic constellations, and a Dantean vision: 'The Father and His angelic hierarchy/ [...] Stood in the circuit of a needle's eye'. The direct association with Christ, whose image is still believed to be imprinted on the cloth said to have been offered to him by Veronica as he carried the cross on which he died, comes in the separate final couplet:

> Some found a different pole, and where it stood
> A pattern on a napkin dipped in blood.

Thus the sword and cross of "Conjunctions" conjoin also with the world axis and the procreative stream of "A Needle's Eye"; both poems draw on the precessional cycle of Yeats's Great Year. The role of Christ as the divine child who is born to die evokes and challenges the order of time; even the gods have their generations. Saturn and Jupiter will guard their Egyptian crop of 'mummy wheat', and with the coming of spring Christ is suitably linked with Mars and Venus, man and woman, love and death, as in some painterly figure of the love of the two gods, echoed in a Pieta.[15]

NOTES
1   *The Variorum Edition of the Plays of W. B. Yeats*, ed., Russell K. Alspach assisted by Catharine C. Alspach (NY: Macmillan 1966), p.1311; henceforth *VPl*. Yeats's notes will also be quoted from *The Variorum Edition of the Poems of W. B. Yeats*, ed. Peter Allt and Russell K. Alspach (NY: Macmillan 1957), henceforth *VP*. Dates of composition and

publication of the poems, as well as their texts, are taken from *Yeats's Poems*, ed., A. Norman Jeffares with an appendix by Warwick Gould (Dublin: Gill & Macmillan 1989).

2 Emmeline M. Plunket, *Ancient Calendars and Constellations* (London: John Murray 1903), p.13; henceforth *ACC*. The reference in the later edition of *A Vision*, which does not have this passage, is a footnote in Section IX of 'The Great Year of the Ancients', giving Plunket's book as the source for a quotation from Syncellus. Yeats consistently spells her surname Plunkett.

3 Richard Hinckley Allen, *Star Names: Their Lore and Meaning* (NY: Dover 1963), p.253. Allen's work originally appeared in 1899 as *Star Names and Their Meanings*. Constellations vary across cultures. Plunket uses Ganymede, cup-bearer to the gods, to link Aquarius to Aquila, the Eagle: 'in Grecian mythology the Eagle is sent by Zeus to carry Ganymede up to heaven, and in Grecian astronomy Ganymede is placed in Aquarius' (*ACC*, p.70).

4 *A Critical Edition of Yeats's "A Vision"* [1925], ed., George Mills Harper and Walter Kelly Hood (London: Macmillan 1978), pp.156-57. The facsimile paging is that of the first edition, henceforth *AVA*. The 1937 edition is quoted from *A Vision: A Reissue with the Author's Final Revisions* (NY: Collier 1966), henceforth *AV[B]*.

5 *The Letters of W. B. Yeats*, ed., Allan Wade (London: Rupert Hart-Davis 1954; NY: Macmillan 1955), p.819; henceforth *L*.

6 In this passage Yeats also writes that Creative Mind moves from Aries to Taurus, seasonally, rather than precessionally, from Taurus to Aries. This makes no difference to the 'conjunction' of Venus and Mars, but the inconsistencies of directions and signs cause confusion for readers struggling with the many technicalities of *A Vision*. Yeats is particularly clear about the different directions of the cycling 'Faculties' in one of his *Vision* notebooks now in the National Library of Ireland (MS 13, f.576).

7 *Yeats's "Vision Papers"*, eds., George Mills Harper et al., 3 vols. (London: Macmillan 1992), Vol. 2, p.487, et passim.

8 For more information about the two horoscopes, see Elizabeth Heine, 'Yeats and Maud Gonne: Marriage and the Astrological Record 1908-09', in *Yeats Annual*, No. 13 (London: Macmillan 1998), pp.3-33.

9 Russell's horoscope was drawn up by Yeats's uncle, George Pollexfen, in the 1890s, and remains among the Yeats papers in the library of Michael Butler Yeats. Most of these can also be studied as photocopies in the William Butler Yeats Microfilmed Manuscripts Collection, Special Collections Department, Melville Library, State University of NY at Stony Brook. To calculate rough horoscopes for those named in *A Vision*, I used birthplaces and dates given in the *Encyclopaedia Britannica* and a computer program set for noon for the given place and date. Times of birth were not necessary; if Yeats's 28 phases are taken literally they equate to slightly more than a day in the moon's usual 30- to 31-day cycle from New to New, or Full to Full. (The moon returns to the same star in about 28 days, but is in a different phase because of the sun's apparent monthly progression.) Lady Gregory, Yeats's patron, friend and partner in the creation of the Abbey Theatre, is one of those whose birth phase is close to that given in *A Vision*; her birthdate, 14 March 1852, used in horoscopes Yeats cast for her, is wrongly given as 4 March in the *Encyclopaedia*.

10 *Letters on Poetry from W. B. Yeats to Dorothy Wellesley*, ed., Dorothy Wellesley (OUP 1940), p.44.

11 Heinrich Zimmer, *Myths and Symbols in Indian Art and Civilisation*, ed. Joseph Campbell [Bollingen Series VI] (Princeton UP 1946), p.52.
12 H. P. Blavatsky, *Isis Unveiled: A Master-Key to the Mysteries of Ancient and Modern Science and Theology*, 2 vols. [unabridged edn.] (Pasadena: Theosophical UP 1988), Vol. 1, p.507.
13 *Essays and Introductions* (London: Macmillan 1961), p.484.
14 "Seven Propositions" can be found in Virginia Moore's *The Unicorn: William Butler Yeats' Search for Reality* (NY: Macmillan 1954), pp.378-79; Richard Ellmann's *The Identity of Yeats* [1954] (Oxford UP 1970), pp.236-36; and also my essay, 'W. B. Yeats: Poet and Astrologer', in *Culture and Cosmos: Journal of the History of Astrology and Cultural Astronomy*, 1, 2 (1997), pp.65-66.
15 I am indebted to Deirdre Toomey for her suggestion of Botticelli's '*Venus and Mars*', in the National Gallery (London).

Yeats and Astrology: "Supernatural Songs" 301

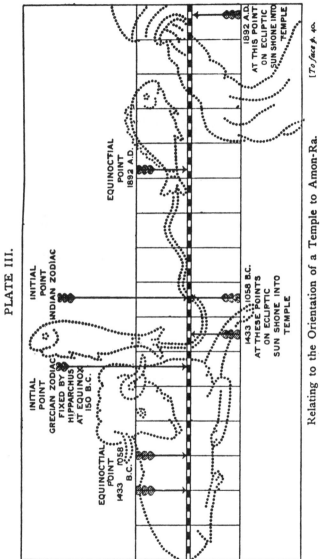

PLATE III.

Relating to the Orientation of a Temple to Amon-Ra.

PLATE VIII.

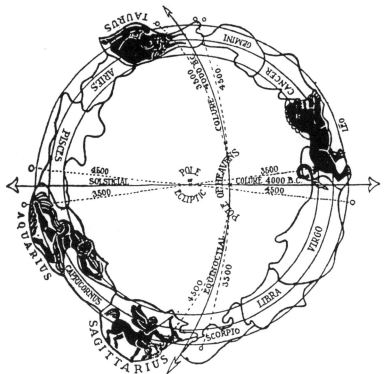

Position of Colures amongst the Constellations at the dates 4,500–4,000 and 3,500 B.C.

[*To face p.* 80.

STRANGE EXPERIENCES IN PEMBROKE ROAD

Deirdre Toomey

In *The Celtic Twilight* (1893), Yeats claimed that

> In Ireland we hear but little of the darker powers, and come across any who have seen them even more rarely, for the imagination of the people dwells rather upon the fantastic and capricious, and fantasy and caprice would lose their freedom which is their breath of life were they to unite them either with evil or with good.

By 1902 he was to qualify this statement darkly with 'I know better now'.[1] The sentence opens the most anomalous of the narratives which make up the volume, "The Sorcerers", an account of black magic in Dublin and never separately published, was probably based on an experience of October 1891, written up shortly afterwards. It was vehemently disliked by most reviewers of *The Celtic Twilight*—indeed rejected by some as being 'uncanonical'.

In October 1891 Yeats was staying at 3, Ely Place with the Hermetic Group of Theosophists which had formed around George Russell, a stay which—although brief—had a powerful effect on Yeats's sense of himself, of a certain phase of Dublin life, and of the supernatural.[2] In the same house were D. N. Dunlop, Frederick Dick and his wife, and, 'a strange red-haired girl' discovered by Frederick Dick starving in a Dublin attic, Althea Gyles, later the designer of the covers of *The Secret Rose, The Wind Among the Reeds, Poems* (1899) and of the second edition of *The Celtic Twilight*. No meat was eaten in the house and most of its inhabitants thought of themselves as *chelas* dedicated to a life of celibacy—although both Dunlop and Russell later qualified this by contracting shot-gun marriages. Russell's influence on Yeats was at its greatest at this time:

> I used to listen to him at that time, mostly walking through the streets at night, for the sake of some stray sentence, beautiful and profound [...] and there were others, too, who walked and listened, for he had

become, I think, to his fellow-students, sacred, as the fool is sacred in the East [3]

In *Autobiographies* Yeats presents an experience of 1889 as if it were of 1891:

> Russell has just come in from a long walk on the Two Rock mountain, very full of his conversation with an old religious beggar, who kept repeating, 'God possesses the heavens, but He covets the earth—He covets the earth'.[4]

Yeats then moves—achronologically—from this fragment of the 'great Celtic phantasmagoria' to something very different.

> I get in talk with a young man [...]. He is a stranger, but explains that he has inherited magical art from his father, and asks me to his rooms to see it in operation. He and a friend of his kill a black cock, and burn herbs in a big bowl, but nothing happens except that the friends repeats again and again, 'O, my God,' and when I ask him why he has said that, does not know he has spoken; and I feel that there is something very evil, in the room

In the *Autobiographies* account of this experiment, Yeats is presented as a marginal witness, not an active participant.[5] The same picture is given in "The Sorcerers":

> I have indeed come across very few persons in Ireland who try to communicate with evil powers, and the few I have met keep their purpose and practice wholly hidden from the inhabitants of the remote town where they live [...]. They are mainly small clerks and the like, and meet for the purpose of their art in a room hung with black hangings. They would not admit me into this room, but finding me not altogether ignorant of the arcane science, showed gladly elsewhere what they would do. 'Come to us,' said their leader, a clerk in a large flour-mill, 'and we will show you spirits who will talk to you face to face, and in shapes as solid and heavy as our own.'
>
> I had been talking of the power of communicating in states of trance with the angelical and faery beings,—the children of the day and of the twilight,—and he had been contending that we should only believe in what we can see and feel when in our ordinary everyday state of mind. 'Yes,' I said, 'I will come to you,' or some such words; 'but I will not permit myself to become entranced, and will therefore know whether these shapes you talk of are any the more to be touched and felt by the ordinary senses than are those I talk of.' I was not denying the power of other beings to take upon themselves a clothing of mortal substance, but only that simple invocations, such as he spoke of, seemed unlikely to do more than cast the mind into trance and thereby bring it into the presence of the powers of day, twilight, and darkness.
>
> 'But,' he said, we have seen them move the furniture hither and thither, and they go at our bidding, and help or harm people who know

nothing of them.' I am not giving the exact words, but as accurately as I can the substance of our talk.

On the night arranged I turned up about eight, and found the leader sitting alone in almost total darkness in a small back room. He was dressed in a black gown, like an inquisitor's dress in an old drawing, that left nothing of him visible except his eyes, which peered out through two small round holes. Upon the table in front of him was a brass dish of burning herbs, a large bowl, a skull covered with painted symbols, two crossed daggers, and certain implements shaped like quern stones, which were used to control the elemental powers in some fashion I did not discover. I also put on a black gown, and remember that it did not fit perfectly, and that it impeded my movements considerably. The sorcerer then took a black cock out of a basket, and cut its throat with one of the daggers, letting the blood fall into the large bowl. He opened a book and began an invocation, which was certainly not English, and had a deep guttural sound. Before he had finished, another of the sorcerers [...] came in, and having put on a black gown also, seated himself at my left hand. I had the invoker directly in front of me, and soon began to find his eyes, which glittered through the small holes in his hood, affecting me in a curious way. I struggled hard against their influence, and my head began to ache. The invocation continued, and nothing happened for the first few minutes. Then the invoker got up and extinguished the light in the hall, so that no glimmer might come through the slit under the door. There was now no light except from the herbs on the brass dish, and no sound except from the deep guttural murmur of the invocation.

Presently the man at my left swayed himself about, and cried out, 'O god! O god !' I asked him what ailed him, but he did not know he had spoken. A moment after he said he could see a great serpent moving about the room, and became considerably excited. I saw nothing with any definite shape, but thought that black clouds were forming about me. I felt I must fall into a trance if I did not struggle against it, and that the influence which was causing this trance was out of harmony with itself, in other words, evil. After a struggle I got rid of the black clouds, and was able to observe with my ordinary senses again. The two sorcerers now began to see black and white columns moving about the room, and finally a man in a monk's habit, and they became greatly puzzled because I did not see these things also, for to them they were as solid as the table before them. The invoker appeared to be gradually increasing in power, and I began to feel as if a tide of darkness was pouring from him and concentrating itself about me; and now too I noticed that the man on my left hand had passed into a death-like trance. With a last great effort I drove off the black clouds; but feeling them to be the only shapes I should see without passing into a trance, and having no great love for them, I asked for lights, and after the needful exorcism returned to the ordinary world.

I said to the more powerful of the two sorcerers—'What would happen if one of your spirits had overpowered me?' 'You would go out of this room,' he answered, 'with his character added to your own.' I asked about the origin of his sorcery, but got little of importance, except that he had learned it from his father. He would not tell me more, for he had, it appeared, taken a vow of secrecy.

> For some days I could not get over the feeling of having a number of deformed and grotesque figures lingering about me. The Bright powers are always beautiful and desirable, and the Dim Powers are now beautiful, now quaintly grotesque, but the Dark Powers express their unbalanced natures in shapes of ugliness and horror.[6]

In the manuscript draft of this version of "The Sorcerers" there is a cancelled coda:

> ~~So at any rate I have come to think after many talks with some studying these things talking much with men & women who see them continually.~~[7]

This passage was presumably cancelled because it indicated something more than a brief engagement with sorcery. George Russell told the young Austin Clarke that he had once met Yeats staggering out of a session with the magician, '[...] hurrying along Pembroke Road, his olive complexion turned to a bilious green. He had just been present in a nearby house where an Englishman, adept in the Black Art, had sacrificed a cock. The sensitive poet rushed out into the street, horror-stricken by the bloody rite, and never again had anything to do with this ancient cult'.[8] However D. N. Dunlop's daughter Edith Young recalled a story told by her father which suggests that Yeats went a little further in life than he admitted in "The Sorcerers":

> Father [...] gave an account of Willy trying his hand at magic. In a fine old Georgian house a staircase took him to a bare back room in which he was to join the privileged few chosen by Yeats to witness the rite. An opulent marble mantelpiece stood in the stead of an altarpiece. Wine bottles acted as sconces for the candles by whose light Yeats was to chalk a pentagram on the floorboards. The stage thus set, the audience squatted cross-legged against the wall. Into their midst strode Yeats, garbed in black, like the priest of some forgotten cult, a raven lock sweeping his brow, to chant a mantrum designed to call into being apparitions from the nether world. Into his hand a participant placed a slaughtered cock; and in accordance with the instructions of those versed in the black arts, Yeats, holding the sacrificial bird at arm's length, whilst droning an incantation, sprinkled blood from its matted feathers into the middle of the mystical five pointed star.
> 'What happened? Did you see anything?' I eagerly enquired.
> 'All I saw,' father confessed, 'was Willy turning away in disgust from the dead bird at his feet. But if nothing came of his tricks, it was well worth my while to have been there. To hear him expound the mysteries of the Caballa or recite one of his early lyrics over a bottle of wine afterwards was an experience I'm not likely to forget'.[9]

There were thus possibly at least two episodes, not—as "The Sorcerers" suggests—one, and Yeats evidently participated in a little animal sacrifice on his own behalf. This all seems to sit oddly with Yeats's account of his sensitivity towards the killing of animals in *Reveries Over Childhood and Youth*:

> I fished for pike at Castle Dargan and shot at birds with a muzzle-loading pistol until somebody shot a rabbit and I heard it squeal. From that on I would kill nothing but the dumb fish.[10]

The magical ceremony which W. B. Yeats witnessed probably derives from grimoires and from other written summaries of magical processes rather than from any secret tradition tapped by the Sorcerer's father. In most ceremonies of black (and white) magic, the sacrifice of an animal is not the central element in the ritual, but is the means of obtaining virgin parchment upon which words of power can later be transcribed; the animal killed is typically a goat or kid. However the best-known grimoire, *The Grimoire of Pope Honorius*, also recommended that a black cock be killed at sunrise and the first feather of the left wing be reserved. At sunrise the eyes, tongue and heart of the bird were to be pulled out and reduced to powder and the rest of the bird buried in a secret place. Later the cock feather was to be used during a 'Mass of the Angels' to write cabbalistic formulae using consecrated communion wine.[11]

Eliphas Levi's descriptions of instruments necessary for a magical rite might be the local source for the Sorcerer's apparatus; he lists as necessary for the ritual 'une robe noire sans coutures et sans manches [...] un vase de cuivre contenant le sang de la victime [...] la tête d'un chat noir nourri de chair humaine pendant cinq jours [...] le crâne d'un parricide'. In all such ceremonies herbs are burnt in a bowl or chafing dish and two knives or daggers, one black-handled and one white are also universally used. Invocations are given in all grimoires, and Levi points out that the more unintelligible the invocation, the more effective; he gives as a 'suprême appellation' the following formula:

> '*Hemen-Étan! Hemen-Étan! Hemen-Étan!* EL* ATI* TITEIP* AZIA* HYN* TEU* MINOSEL* ACHADON* vay* vaa* Eye* Aaa* Eie* Exe* A EL EL EL A Hy! HAU! HAU! HAU! HAU! VA! VA! VA! VA! *CHAVAJOTH* Aie Saraye, aie Saraye, aie Saraye! Per Eloym, Archima, Rabur, BATHAS super ABRAC ruens superveniens ABEOR SUPER ABERER *Chavajoth! Chavajoth! Chavajoth!* impero tibu per clavem SALOMONIS et nomen magnum SEMHAMPHORAS'[12]

The mysterious Englishman who introduced Yeats to black magic was a certain Captain Roberts.[13] Maud Gonne thought Captain Roberts was the model for Michael Robartes in 'Rosa Alchemica'.[14] In fact Yeats used George Russell as the physical model for Robartes, and MacGregor Mathers, the founder of the Golden Dawn, as the general model for Robartes's personality, yet certainly Captain Roberts contributed to the name and perhaps to the element of diabolism and cruelty in Robartes. MacGregor Mathers, Yeats recalled, was 'gentle, and perhaps even a little timid [...] once when he was left in a mouse-infested flat with some live traps, he collected his captives into a large birdcage, and, to avoid the necessity of their drowning, fed them there for a couple of weeks'.[15]

Why did Yeats involve himself in these strange experiences in Pembroke Road? His desire for practical magic had led him to join the Esoteric Section of the Theosophical Society in 1888: this Theosophical group was devoted to 'practical occultism'. Yeats was thrown out in 1890 and was not forced to decide whether he could take the inner group's programme of celibacy, teetotalism and vegetarianism. He had joined the Order of the Golden Dawn in March 1890, but until the end of 1891 the Order was without magic, although ritual magic subsequently became a key element. What Yeats got from the Order in his first two years was a spiritual philosophy, symbols, robes, an Order motto, the experience of initiation and of some impressive non-magical rituals, but not much else—as MacGregor Mathers was still trying to write the rituals for an Inner, Rosicrucian, magical Order. It might be that by October 1891 Yeats was frustrated by the lack of magic—white or black—in the Outer Order of the Golden Dawn and so was easy game for the mysterious Captain Roberts and the 'dark powers'.

Indeed, evidence of Yeats's desire for direct supernatural experience in c.1890-1891 is found in a powerful reminiscence in his essay 'Magic'. Yeats recalls going with an acquaintance to witness a magical operation being performed by 'an evoker of spirits and his beautiful wife'—in fact Moina and MacGregor Mathers. (This was not part of a Golden Dawn ceremony but, as it were, a private performance.) Yeats saw a series of images purporting to be the past life of his friend: these culminated in a Gothic vision of a man in black engaging in an attempt to create life by animating a 'thing wrapped in numberless clothes'.[16] This activity had attracted evil spirits and the image was partly alive. The magician poured blood into the image's mouth but eventually tried to destroy it by cutting off its head. This was of course white magic—clairvoyance combined with invocation—but the grisly content of the vision does not seem remote from the experiments of Captain Roberts. Later, in early 1893, Yeats was to defend practical experience of magic—whether black or white. In a remarkable letter to Lionel Johnson of February 1893, he argued that

> an idealism or spiritualism which denies magic, and evil spirits even, and sneers at magicians and even mediums [...] is an academical imposture. Your church has in this matter been far more thorough than the Protestant. It has never denied *Ars Magica* though it has denounced it.[17]

Autumn 1891 was also a nodal point in Yeats's early adult life. Parnell was buried in Dublin on 11 October 1891 and in his commentary on 'Parnell's Funeral' Yeats wrote, 'I did not go to the funeral, because, being in my sensitive and timid youth, I hated crowds, and what crowds implied, but my friend went. She told me that evening of the star that fell in broad daylight as Parnell's body was lowered into the grave'.[18] Maud Gonne had accompanied Parnell's coffin to Dublin, wearing deep mourning for her own son who had died of meningitis on 31 August. She had written Yeats a letter of 'wild sorrow' telling him that an 'adopted' child had died and asked him whether the child could be reincarnated in the same family. The unsuspecting Yeats asked the advice of George Russell and was told that this could be achieved, if there were only a short interval between death and rebirth. In the grip of grief Maud Gonne was happy to cling to any supernatural support; evidently pressed by Yeats she also agreed to join the Order of the Golden Dawn.[19] They also seem to have briefly become engaged and Yeats presented her with a vellum manuscript book containing two of his most celebrated love lyrics, "When You Are Old" and "The Sorrow of Love".

Maud Gonne, however, subsequently took Russell's advice in the most literal manner: in 1894 she and her French lover Lucien Millevoye 'reincarnated' her lost child at dead of winter in the crypt of the massive classical tomb which she had constructed at the cemetery of Samois-sur-Seine, in the forest of Fontainebleau. Yeats's venture into black magic in 1891 cannot be separated from this extraordinary period of personal and political crisis.

Yeats included "The Sorcerers" in all versions of *The Celtic Twilight* despite its anomalous character, although it was cut severely for the 1925 *Early Poems and Stories*; this cutting, which reduced the penumbra of meditations on the nature of the 'dark powers', thus threw into even bolder relief the central episode, which reviewers had disliked from the outset. Andrew Lang, in a highly informed review of *The Celtic Twilight*, which questioned Yeats's assumption that the Irish supernatural was free of terror, concluded

> It is [...] rather odd that there are sorcerers in Ireland who sacrifice black cocks, sit in the dark over smouldering herbs, play all the old, old games, and let Mr Yeats view the performance. One wonders how these men vote.[20]

Perhaps the most striking response is that of John M'Grath in the radical *United Ireland*. M'Grath was a friend of Yeats and a fellow member of the IRB. M'Grath's long review is eulogistic:

> Mr Yeats is a symbolist and a poet. He is no compiler of mere idle tales, made for an idle hour; and though this latest volume is composed of what a Philistine might dub shreds and patches, there is a vein of philosophy, of speculation, but above all of poetry running through it from beginning to end which makes it One—one in its subtle mystical suggestiveness, and one in the personality—Mr Yeats himself—which the reader sees behind the book, by the moral pointed with his own pen, sometimes by the moral purposely unwritten, dimly, and like a distant echo. There are three elements which go to make up the fascination which is in these morsels: their writer believes in them, they are told in the simplest language, and behind them all the time is the great unknown of Ghostland and of Fairyland.

M'Grath quotes lavishly from the volume and praises "A Visionary", "The Man and His Boots", "The Three O'Byrnes and the Evil Faeries", "The Golden Age"; however he completely withdraws from "The Sorcerers":

> I have said that most of the things in 'The Celtic Twilight' are more or less founded on fact; and that Mr Yeats himself is the authority for the statement. Still it must be confessed that it is sometimes hard to know whether or not one should treat Mr Yeats seriously. The story of 'The Sorcerers'—to adopt an expression I once heard used by a county Down fisherman—rather 'hits me on the mouth'. It has to do with what Mr Yeats calls 'the dark powers'. Now Mr Yeats, as he confesses, does not like the 'dark powers'; but on the occasion dealt with in this tale, he accepted the invitation of a leader of them 'to see what might be seen'. And here is what he writes, quite gravely, and meaning that the reader should take it seriously.

M'Grath then quotes in full the central episode of the narrative, the sacrifice of the cock and the subsequent hallucinations of evil, concluding, 'As a bit of sensationalism, to be sure, this may be very good; but it no more belongs to the Celtic Twilight than does Mr Stead's Julia.' ('Julia' was a spirit guide who communicated with

Strange Experiences in Pembroke Road 311

the journalist W. T. Stead.) M'Grath identified the 'true' Celtic Twilight as being depicted in "The Golden Age":

> That is the genuine Celtic twilight, for it is of the Celt's belief and imagination. Here Mr Yeats is close to himself and to his art; here he is at home. Over the dark river of 'The Sorcerers' no one who hopes for his future will care to see him wander, for often there is no return, even for such as he, from that Plutonian shore.

M'Grath was prepared to reject part of *The Celtic Twilight* as uncanonical because, like most reviewers of the volume, he had immediately assumed ownership of the concept embodied in the title.[21] Yeats was moved to respond to M'Grath's criticism at the end of a long letter to *United Ireland* on another matter:

> P.S. While thanking you for your kind review of 'The Celtic Twilight', I take this opportunity of saying it is not 'founded on fact,' as your review says, but, with the exception of one or two changes of name and place, literally true (*CL1*, p.373).

Yeats's experience with Captain Roberts concluded his practical engagement with black magic, unless we are to take seriously Aleister Crowley's "At the Fork of the Roads". In Crowley's tale of black magic, the noble hero Count Swanoff (who conceals his 'royal Celtic descent' under this pseudonym) represents Crowley, the evil 'lank melancholy unwashed poet' Will Bute is transparently Yeats and the artist Hypatia Gay, Althea Gyles. Bute is consumed with envy of Swanoff's poetic and magical powers: 'Will Bute was not only a poetaster but a dabbler in magic [...] black jealousy of a younger man and a far finer poet gnawed at his petty heart.' Will Bute decides to use the innocent Hypatia to destroy Swanoff by stealing a drop of his blood to be used as a vehicle for destructive forces. However the black magic rebounds on Hypatia and she finds herself having intercourse with a blood and slime covered skeleton in Swanoff's flat and—worse—is reduced to having an affair with an evil publisher, patently modelled upon Leonard Smithers, the publisher of the *Savoy*: 'bloated with disease and drink; his loose lips hung in an eternal leer; his fat eyes shed venom [...] He saw the leprous light of utter degradation in her eyes; a dull flush came to his face; he licked his lips'.[22] This florid concoction might seem to proceed wholly from Crowley's frank detestation of Yeats, who had thrown him out of the Golden Dawn in early 1900; but Yeats's occult diary for November 1899 and his letters in early 1900 suggest that some vestige of these events occurred.

Althea Gyles was indeed having an affair with Smithers at this time—something of a shock to Yeats and her other old friends: Yeats told Lady Gregory:

> A very unpleasant thing has happened but it is so notorious that there is no use in hiding it. Althea Gyles, after despising Symons & Moore for years because of their morals has ostentatiously taken up with Smithers, a person of so immoral a life that people like Symons & Moore despise him. She gave an at home the other day & poured out tea with his arm round her waist & even kissed him at intervals.[23]

At the same time Aleister Crowley was progressing at breakneck speed through the various grades of the Outer Order of the Golden Dawn. In his *Visions Notebook*, Yeats wrote that his life had been disturbed on many levels: 'I was ill [...] & sleepless [...] & met certain very sensual persons, & heard observed certain disagreable things of this kind in connection with a friend. This may only be that a high sexual symbol cannot appear without an accompanying excitement among the lower powers that correspond to it.'[24] Crowley gave his own version of these events to Richard Ellmann, telling him of an evening he spent at Woburn Buildings with Althea Gyles, of her attempting to obtain a drop of Crowley's blood for Yeats's demonic schemes and of ten nights of vampirism ended by his strangling his visitant.[25] Finally, in April 1900, Yeats was to use magical means to attempt to free a mistress of Crowley's from a regime of tantric sex, and torture—she had been hung up naked by hooks in a cupboard—a regime which Yeats informed George Russell was more than worthy of Captain Roberts:

> We found out that [Mathers's] unspeakable mad person [Crowley] had a victim, a lady who was his mistress & from whom he extorted large sums of money. Two or three of our thaumaturgists after, I think, consulting their master, called her up astrally, & told her to leave him. Two days ago (and about two days after the evocation) she came to one of our members (she did not know he was a member) & told a tale of perfectly medeaval iniquity -- of positive torture & agreed to go to Scotland Yard & there have her evidence taken down. Our thaumaturgists had never seen her, nor had she any link with us of any kind. It & much else that has happened lately is a clear proof of the value of systematic training even in these subtle things. The unspeakable mad person is a much worse Captain Roberts (*CL2*, pp.523-4).

Arthur Machen, recalled Yeats's telling him a

> queer tale of the manner in which his life was in daily jeopardy [from a] monster [... [who] had, for some reason I do not recollect,

taken a dislike to my dark young friend. In consequence, so I was assured, he had hired a gang in Lambeth, who were grievously to maim or preferably to slaughter the dark young man; each member of the gang receiving a retaining fee of eight shillings and sixpence a day.[26]

In fact Crowley typically resorted to the magical (and less expensive) expedient of making a wax image of an enemy and then throwing it into a fire.

Although Yeats was finished with black magic, he became, in the late 'nineties, increasingly obsessed with the 'dark' side of Irish folk belief. From 1896 to mid-1898, Yeats and Lady Gregory did the bulk of the folklore collecting which resulted in six long folklore articles published between 1897 and 1902; these were to have been the basis of what he called 'a big book about the commonwealth of faery'.[27] The primary material, which was gathered in Aran, on the Coole estate, in the Burren, in Sligo and in Doneraile, Co. Cork, was from the outset dominated by those aspects of Irish folk belief and practice which Yeats had largely denied in the 1893 *The Celtic Twilight*. That collection's largely innocent world of enchanted rabbits and snipe, of water-horses, leprechauns, ballad-mongers, fiddlers, Homeric tramps and village ghosts, contributed to a construction of folkloric Ireland so powerful and enduring that it has separated itself from Yeats and become a cultural *cliché*.

In the six folklore essays Yeats deals with unpicturesque and unpalatable subjects, all described with brutal economy in the actual words of the informants. The essays are dominated by the theme of 'away', that is of those who are stolen by the fairies, usually because they are young and strong—children, young men and women and young mothers being the most popular victims. Sometimes those abducted seem to die (i.e., they are 'taken') in other cases they appear to become paralysed or demented, affected by the 'fairy stroke' [*poc sidhe*]. A young healthy woman or girl would be magically replaced by 'an old woman with long teeth, that you'd be frightened, and the face wrinkled and the hands'.[28] The country people asserted that death, disease and substitution were part of the supernatural illusion, the 'real' person being elsewhere. This motif predominates in "The Prisoners of the Gods", "The Broken Gates of Death", "Ireland Bewitched", "Irish Witch Doctors" and, of course, "Away", the climax of the series. Yeats had, in 1895, been deeply disturbed by the Clonmel witch burning—a young man called Cleary had burnt his wife Bridget to death under the delusion that she was a substitution and that his real wife had been stolen by the fairies.[29] Yeats discussed the matter with his uncle's second-sighted servant, Mary Battle. The case must have been shocking to him, presenting the dark side of peasant belief and it was some years before he could face this ugly problem, reporting Mary Battle's wisdom 'it is a sin against the traditional wisdom to really ill-treat the dead person [...] you should only threaten'.[30] "Away" is the ruling motif of the essays, and unlike the consciously playful and fantastic anecdotes illustrating this belief collected in *The Celtic Twilight*, the material is sombre, focusing on disease, madness and premature death. The *Celtic Twilight's* vision of the Golden Age—

> that still the kindly and perfect world existed, but buried like a mass of roses under many spadefuls of earth. The faeries and the more innocent of the spirits dwelt within it, and lamented over our fallen world in the lamentation of the wind-tossed reeds, in the song of the birds, in the moan of the waves, and in the sweet cry of the fiddle [...].[31]

—is replaced by oral accounts of blood scattered around cottages and small children dead. These tales are ridden with what Yeats later identified as, 'the pathos of many doubts'.[32] Needless to say, Yeats found it much more difficult to place these articles in periodicals than the original material from *The Celtic Twilight*: editors knew what they wanted from Yeats—and it was not this dark world of disease and death.[33] The *sidhe*—in *The Celtic Twilight* idealised and benevolent—here are seen as darker and crueller, stealing children and young men and women to serve them in the other world. When Yeats used material from these essays in the second edition of *The Celtic Twilight* it was severely cut and softened and idealised by the addition of visions experienced by George Russell. The motif of "Away" is the most obsessive element in the six folklore essays, but there is also abundance of material on witches and wizards, many of whom Yeats and Lady Gregory interviewed. Indeed in summer 1897 Yeats took the advice of one wizard—a natural healer like all those so termed—and tried violets boiled in milk as a cure for his eye problems.[34] However the most important Irish witch had been dead for more than twenty years and Yeats relied on a mass of oral accounts of her. This was Biddy Early (1798-1874) who possessed a magical bottle variously described as black, blue or green. With this she was able to effect magical cures for which she would accept presents, typically whiskey for which she had a 'soft palate', but not money. The empty bottle would sometimes fill with a cloud in which she would discern portents. (Biddy Early occasionally provided racing tips as well as cures from her bottle.)

However, as Yeats was told in 1897, her power was not exclusively benevolent; when her landlord tried to evict her 'she cursed him & presently a house he was in caught fire & fell on him & burnt him'. Lady Gregory also collected a version of this story in which the landlord's house 'caught fire and was burned down, and all that was left of him was one foot that was found in a corner of the walls'.[35] A shepherd in Doneraile told Yeats in 1897 that Biddy Early, when consulted by a man who sought some buried treasure, sacrificed a black cock in order to obtain the treasure.[36] The sacrifice of a black cock was not alien to Irish peasant culture and in Rosses Point (and elsewhere) on St. Martin's day a black cock was killed in honour of the Saint and its blood sprinkled around the house.

One might dismiss Yeats's concern with figures such as Biddy Early as a fixation of a folklore-haunted youth, but in 1937, he spoke at length and in terms of 'warm approval' about her to D. A. MacManus, a writer on folklore, calling her 'the wisest of wise women' and regretting that he had not collected the stories about her into a book. When Yeats repeatedly intoned her name, MacManus recalled: 'she seemed a vibrant reality, alive and potent still'.[37]

Yeats never assembled from these materials the 'big book of folklore' which he had planned as early as December 1898. Eventually Lady Gregory's *Visions and Beliefs in the West of Ireland* with Yeats's two long essays, 'Swedenborg Mediums and the Desolate Places' and 'Witches and Wizards and Irish Folklore' became a substitute for it. However his exploration of the darker side of Irish peasant belief coincided with his return to spiritualism after a ten year gap. Yeats had had a terrifying experience at a London seance in January 1888:

> a Catholic friend brought me to a spiritualistic seance at the house of a young man lately arrested under a suspicion of Fenianism, but released for lack of evidence [...] there were some half-dozen of us, and our host began by making passes until the medium fell asleep [...] then the lights were turned out, and we sat waiting in the dim light of a fire. Presently my shoulders began to twitch and my hands. I could easily have stopped them, but I had never heard of such a thing and I was curious. After a few minutes the movement became violent and I stopped it. I sat motionless for a while and then my whole body moved like a suddenly unrolled watch-spring, and I was thrown backward on the wall. I again stilled the movement and sat at the table [...] presently my right hand banged the knuckles of the woman next to me [...]. I was now struggling vainly with this force which compelled me to movements which I had not willed, and my movements became so violent that the table was broken. I tried to pray [...]. Presently all became still and so dark that I could not see anybody [...] Then I saw

shapes appearing in the darkness and thought they are spirits [...]. For years afterwards I would not go to a seance [...] and would often ask myself what violent impulse had run through my nerves. Was it a part of myself—something always to be a danger perhaps; or had it come from without, as it seemed?[38]

In many ways Yeats's reaction is comparable to his sensations at the sacrifice of the black cock—the sense of struggling against overwhelming forces—save that at the seance he went into the hysteric's arc, something generally experienced—in the nineteenth century—by women rather than by men.

In early 1899, after Yeats and Lady Gregory had completed the greater part of their folklore collecting, he consulted a London medium, the notoriously crooked Charles Williams, seeking to supplement the beliefs and experiences of Irish peasants with direct encounters with spirits and the dead, a process which was to conclude with the syncretic presentation of spiritualism, magic and folklore in "Swedenborg, Mediums and the Desolate Places". At this seance he heard a voice whispering faintly in his ear and connected this experience with one which had been with him since childhood.[39] It is as if Yeats, stimulated by contact with the darker side of Irish peasant belief, were in search of increasingly direct and powerful experiences—stronger meat. Whatever the precipitating force, from this point on spiritualism was to take over the energies once invested in folklore researches, visionary experiments and—to some extent—magic. Although Yeats's most powerful statement of his magical beliefs, "Magic", was not published until 1901, it is, in terms of the date of the magical experiences recorded and analysed, for the most part markedly retrospective. After the departure of MacGregor Mathers in 1900, Yeats continued to be a responsible member of the Order of the Golden Dawn, but Ritual Magic no longer satisfied the urge he was developing to 'touch the phantom's beating heart', to have direct contact with the Dead.

NOTES
1. *The Celtic Twilight* (London: Lawrence & Bullen 1893); p.55 [henceforth *CT* 1893]; *Do.* (London: A. H. Bullen 1902) p.61 [henceforth *CT* 1902]
2. 3, Ely Place was the Dublin Theosophical Lodge and the headquarters of the Theosophical Society in Ireland.
3. *Autobiographies* (London: Macmillan 1955) p.240. Henceforth *Au*.
4. *Au*, p.249.
5. *Au*, pp.249-50.
6. *CT* 1893, pp.56-63.
7. Manuscript of "The Sorcerers", National Library of Ireland.
8. *A Penny in the Clouds* (London: Routledge & Kegan Paul 1968) p.56.

9 Edith Young, *Inside Out* (London: Routledge & Kegan Paul 1971) p.7.
10 *Au*, p.55.
11 *Grimoire of Pope Honorius* (Paris 1760), p.8. The 'Devils Book' of the Red Hanrahan story published under that title in 1892 is the *Grimoire*, in which Red Hanrahan reads: 'how to destroy your enemies in divers sudden fashions . . . [his] eyes lit on a receipt for making the spirits appears by writing certain words with the blood of a bat . . a bat fluttered in through the half-closed door, and beat itself against the white-washed canvas that hid the thatch and the rafters. He struck it down with the shovel and killed it, and wrote the names on the back of a reading-book used by him in his hedge school' (*The Secret Rose, Stories by W. B. Yeats: A Variorum Edition*, eds., Warwick Gould, Phillip L. Marcus and Michael J. Sidnell, London: Macmillan 1992, p.189).
12 *Dogme et Rituel de la Haute Magie* (Paris: Germer Balliere 1861), Vol. II, pp.227-28; 230-31. Yeats was probably well aware of this celebrated study; he would also have had some knowledge of the Rites of White Magic from MacGregor Mathers's *The Key of Solomon the King* (London: George Redway 1889).
13 'The Chief of "The Sorcerers" is a certain Captain Roberts, slightly disguised.' (Lionel Johnson to Edmund Gosse, 29 December, 1893 [BL].) Johnson had undoubtedly been told this by Yeats.
14 Richard Ellmann to Rev. Raymond Roseliep, 14 July, 1953 (Loras College).
15 *Au*, p.339.
16 The episode described in 'Magic' took place between June 1890 and c. March 1891, when MacGregor Mathers was working as a curator and living with his wife Moina at the Horniman Museum in Forest Hill, South London.
17 *Collected Letters of W. B. Yeats*, Vol. I: 1865-1895, eds., John Kelly and Eric Domville (Oxford: Clarendon 1986), p.355. Hereafter *CL1*.
18 *Variorum Edition of the Poems of W. B. Yeats*, eds., Peter Allt and Russell K. Alspach (NY: Macmillan 1966) p.834.
19 *Memoirs*, ed., Denis Donoghue (NY: Macmillan 1972), pp.47-48. Maud Gonne joined in November 1891 on her return to London from Dublin; her motto was "Per Ignem ad Lucem".
20 *Illustrated London News*, 23 December 1893.
21 *United Ireland*, 23 December 1893, p.5. Yeats retained the story in subsequent editions, but the reviewers' animosity remained undiminished: the *Saturday Review* opined that the 'unpleasant picture of "The Black Art"' was 'a solitary exception to the excellence of the revised version'. ('Legends and Erin', *Saturday Review*, 8 August, 1903, p.174.)
22 Equinox, Vol. 1, No 1, 21 March, 1909, pp.101-08.
23 *Collected Letters of W. B. Yeats*, Vol. II: 1896-1900, eds., Warwick Gould, John Kelly and Deirdre Toomey (Oxford: Clarendon, 1997), p.473; hereafter *CL2*. The poet's misspellings have been retained.
24 Retrospective entry for 25, November 1899 (Private Collection).
25 Richard Ellmann papers, University of Tulsa.
26 *Things Near and Far* (London: Secker 1923) p.148.
27 *CT* (1902) p.3; *CL2*, pp.323-24.
28 *Uncollected Prose by W. B. Yeats*, Vol. 2, eds., John P. Frayne and Colton Johnson (London: Macmillan 1975; NY: Columbia UP, 1976) p.103. [Henceforth *UPr2*.]

29 See Genevieve Brennan, 'Yeats, Clodd, *Scatalogic Rites* and the Clonmel Witch Burning', *Yeats Annual*, No 4 (1986), pp.207-15.
30 *UPr2*, pp 277.
31 *The Celtic Twilight* (London: Lawrence and Bullen 1893) pp.184-85.
32 *UPr2*, p.95
33 Yeats took four years to place "Away", unsuccessfully offered to *Blackwood's Magazine* in the summer of 1898, but not published until April 1902 (*CL2*, p.246).
34 *UPr2*, pp.221-22.
35 *CL2*, pp.137-38.
36 *UPr2*, p.182; *Au*, p.401.
37 D. A. MacManus, *The Middle Kingdom* (London: Max Parrish 1960), pp.154-55.
38 *Au*, p.103-104.
39 This experience is recalled in "Leo Africanus", but is dateable by Yeats's indicating that it followed shortly after a trance vision of Bessy Sigerson's, which had occurred on 12 December, 1898; see 'The Manuscript of "Leo Africanus"' ed., Steve L. Adams and George Mills Harper (*Yeats Annual*, No. 1, London: Macmillan 1982, pp.23-24).

THE OTHERWORLDLY DEBTS OF
W. B. YEATS'S *A VISION* (1937)

Matthew M. DeForrest

William Butler Yeats is one of the great masters of poetry in English and an innovative playwright. Yeats is less well remembered, however, for his prose work and metaphysical thought, which has achieved a certain infamy among scholars. Yet this body of work, of which *A Vision* is the most important, is necessary for a full understanding of the rest of his work. From 1917 on, Yeats's creative works call upon the unfolding system of *A Vision* as both a subject and a source of 'metaphors for poetry'.[1]

Although created out of the automatic writing and trance states of his wife, George, *A Vision* is deeply indebted to several philosophical and metaphysical traditions, as is indicated by Richard Ellmann: 'Reading the *Vision* we are conscious of many echoes of Yeats's previous work and interests. The mixture has a different taste but the ingredients have been used before.'[2] Yet, the depth of the influence many of these sources had on *A Vision* has not been fully explored. It is in the examination of how Yeats employed these sources that we can come to a fuller understanding of Yeats's 'arbitrary, harsh, difficult symbolism'. (*AV[B]*, p.23.)

Any examination of its metaphysical influences must begin with the disclaimer Yeats placed in the 'Introduction to "*A Vision*"'.

> Apart from two or three of the principal Platonic Dialogues I knew no philosophy. Arguments with my father, whose conviction had been formed by John Stuart Mill's attack upon Sir William Hamilton, had destroyed my confidence and driven me from speculation to the direct experience of the Mystics. I had once known Blake as thoroughly as his unfinished confused Prophetic Books permitted, and I had read Swedenborg and Boehme, and my initiation into the 'Hermetic Students' had filled my head with Cabbalistic imagery, but there was nothing in Blake, Swedenborg, Boehme or the Cabbala to help me now. (*AV[B]*, p.12.)

While Yeats's claims to ignorance about the fine points of philosophy is a subject for a different time, his statement that 'there was nothing in

Blake, Swedenborg, Boehme or the Cabala to help' his understanding of the unfolding system is patently untrue. Yeats refers to these sources repeatedly in the text of *A Vision*. Indeed, in 'To Vestigia', the introduction to the 1925 version of *A Vision*, he boldly states that these men and their systems of belief contain the same material as his.

> What I have found indeed is nothing new, for I will show presently that Swedenborg and Blake and many before them that knew all things had their gyres; but Swedenborg and Blake preferred to explain them figuratively, and so I am the first to substitute for Biblical or mythological figures, historical movements and actual men and women.[3]

Even without precedent in the previous edition's introduction, however, there are numerous indications of the influence these sources had upon *A Vision*.

Before beginning my examination of these and other sources, it is necessary to briefly address the system itself.[4] *A Vision* is an extremely complicated world view which attempts to give metaphysical explanation of the universe at the micro- and macrocosmic levels. Unlike most metaphysical systems, however, *A Vision's* focus is on the personal cycle inherent in this world rather than the process of becoming one with the divine. This focus on the mundane world allowed Yeats to continue his creative work within its bounds of his system which, unlike the Cabalistic system of the Golden Dawn, strove towards a greater union with the Godhead at the sacrifice of the phenomenal world, permitted metaphysical progress while maintaining a grounding in everyday life. Since Yeats chose to write of both his personal passions and his metaphysical experiences, the freedom to exist and equally function in both realms was important.

Finally, the question must be addressed, 'why would Yeats purposely lie to his readers about the assistance these sources gave him in the interpretation of the automatic script?' The accidental inclusion of these parallels, especially in light of his citation of this material throughout *A Vision*, is implausible. While it is possible that, in covering the same topics, he came to similar but independent conclusions, Yeats could then have indicated that these sources were of help to him in his codification of George's automatic writing and sleep expositions. In denying that he received help from these traditions, however, he calls the initiated reader's attention to the material, rendering parallels more obvious. This technique also serves to direct readers who recognise the presence of one mystical tradition in

A Vision to others, much as a bibliography serves to direct scholars to texts utilised in the preparation of a scholarly work.

Emanuel Swedenborg's influence is most keenly felt in Yeats's examination of the *Principles* and the mechanics of the afterlife in Books II and III of *A Vision*. The states which follow death in Swedenborg and Yeats are remarkably similar. According to Yeats, 'consciousness passes from *Husk* to *Spirit*' and '*Husk* and *Passionate Body* are said to *disappear*' at the moment of death (*AV*[*B*], p.188). The '*Husk* is symbolically the human body' while the *Spirit* is the 'mind' of the individual which survives death (*AV*[*B*], pp.187-88). This corresponds to Swedenborg's description of what occurs at the death of the physical body:

> I was brought into a condition of unconsciousness as far as my physical senses were concerned—practically, that is, into the condition of people who are dying. However, my more inward life, including thought, remained unimpaired so that I perceived and remembered the things that happened, things that do happen to people who are awakened from the dead.[5]
>
> The angels who sat by my head were silent, only their thoughts communicating with mine. When these thoughts are accepted, the angels know that the person's spirits in a state to be led out of his body. (*H&H*, p.346.)

While the parallel is not exact, Swedenborg's angels, in their assistance to the dying individual, fulfil a role similar to that of Yeats's *Teaching Spirits*, who both guide, assist, and 'conduct the *Spirit* through its past acts' (*AV*[*B*], p.229).

The most direct parallel drawn by Yeats comes in a footnote to his examination of the *Dreaming Back* and *Return*. In these states, the soul is 'compelled to live over and over again the events that had most moved it' in both 'the order of their intensity' and 'the order of their occurrence', respectively.

> Compare the account of the *Dreaming Back* in Swedenborg's *Heaven and Hell*. My account differs from his mainly because he denied or ignored rebirth. Somebody has suggested that he kept silent deliberately, that it was amongst those subjects he thought forbidden. It is more likely that his instructors were silent. They spoke to the Christian churches, explaining the 'linen clothes folded up', and even what they said or sought to say was half transformed into an opium dream by the faith of those churches in the literal interpretation of the Bible. (*AV*[*B*], pp.226-28.)

This passage refers to the judgement that, in Swedenborg, each soul goes through following their death.

> As to the retention of people from the world of their whole memory, this has been shown me by many things. I have seen and heard quite a few things worth relating, and should like to tell some of them in a sequence.
>
> There were people who denied crimes and disgraceful things they had committed in the world. So lest people believe them innocent, all things were uncovered and reviewed out of their memory, in sequence, from their earliest age to the end. Foremost were matters of adultery and whoredom.
>
> In short, each evil spirit is shown clearly all his evil deeds, his crimes, thefts, deceits, and devices. These are brought out of his own memory and proven; there is no room left for denial, since all the attendant circumstances are visible at once. (*H&H*, pp.361-62.)

This examination of the sins of the individual under the supervision of angels (*H&H*, p.362) comes, as in *A Vision*, early in the soul's movement through the afterlife. The difference between Swedenborg's state and the *Dreaming Back* which, as stated above, is conducted under the guidance of the *Teaching Spirits*, is that the former is done primarily for the edification and protection of other souls while the latter is done for the edification of only the individual spirit in order that it might understand its life in preparation of its rebirth into the material world.

Boehme, of those authorities named who Yeats asserted could provide no help, appears by name in *A Vision* the least often of his metaphysical sources.[6] This may be partly due to the inability or unwillingness of the Communicators to comment on Boehme.

> 2. Do you know Boehmes [sic.] symbolism?
> 2. No, I do not know any symbolism from book and I cannot get it from your minds because I am here only to create[7]

And later, in a description of 'the primary memory', which is available to the spirit following the death of the body.

> 25. How do you distinguish?[8]
> 25. You would [remember] all details of your life but would not remember your knowledge of Blake or Boehme.
> 26. Do you mean that my memory to do daily dinner is deeper than my knowledge of Boehme.
> 26. Yes
>
> (*TMYV*, Vol. 1, p.333.)

Boehme's influence upon the system, however, should not be underestimated. It was from Boehme that Yeats drew the term *tincture* to apply to the *primary* and *antithetical* extremes of the Great Wheel (*AV*[*B*], p.72). Tincture is described in *The 'Key' of Jacob Boehme* as being that which has 'pierced through all the Properties', 'pierced through the Earth and through all Elements, and tinctured all'.[9] From these descriptions, and others like them, the properties which attracted Yeats to the term *tincture* to describe the *primary* and *antithetical* extremes of the Great Wheel are readily apparent. It is a force which penetrates and permeates an object without being limited by that specific object as the *primary* and *antithetical* infuse all phases without being limited to or by them.

Additional parallels between Boehme's and Yeats's cosmologies are fundamentally due to their shared interest in the Kabbalah.[10] Yeats's knowledge came, primarily, from S. L. MacGregor Mathers's *The Kabbalah Unveiled*.

> The 'Book of Concealed Mystery' opens with these words: 'The Book of Concealed Mystery is the book of equilibrium of balance.' What is here meant by the terms 'equilibrium of balance'? Equilibrium is that harmony which results from the analogy of contraries, it is the dead centre where, the opposition of opposing forces being equal in strength, rest succeeds motion. It is the central point. It is the 'point within the circle' of ancient symbolism [...] The term balance is applied to the two opposite natures in each triad of the Sephiroth [...] This doctrine of equilibrium and balance is a fundamental qabalistic idea.[11]

This passage, which stresses balance and an 'equilibrium between contraries' as being a basic tenant of Kabbalistic systems, provides a sound basis for comparison with Yeats's *antinomies* and the geometric balance maintained by the *Faculties* and *Principles* on the Great Wheel.

The magical system of the Golden Dawn had more influence upon Yeats's work than any other single occult system.[12] Its presence permeates the entirety of *A Vision*, as is hinted at in the above quotations from the 'Dedication' to *A Vision* (1925). Indeed, Yeats linked the creation of his system to his work in the Golden Dawn.

> Perhaps this book has been written because a number of young men and women, you and I among their number, met nearly forty years ago in London and in Paris to discuss mystical philosophy. (*AV*[*A*], p.ix).

This predominance of material is, perhaps, to be expected considering that both of the Yeatses were members of the Order and involved deeply in its mysteries and politics.[13] There is more than a simple acknowledgement of a source in this sentence, however. The Golden Dawn not only provided a bank of material for their system, it was an occult experience shared intimately by the Yeatses prior to their marriage—he had sponsored her membership[14]—and provided George with the basic training necessary for her to take up her role as medium and interpreter.[15]

The Yeatses and their communicators called repeatedly upon the terminology and teachings of the Order in their unfolding system, although many terms were changed or discarded before *A Vision* was published in 1925. The Evil Persona, described in the 'Fifth Knowledge Lecture' as the dark projection of an adept's personality through the Qlippoth,[16] was a part of Yeats's system in the early script but, as George Mills Harper points out, was a concept for which Yeats 'found no use in *VA*' (*TMYV*, Vol. 1, p.513). In addition, the Lightning Flash, which appears in the script linking the various important moments of an individual's life, was tied to both the Yeats's experiences in the Golden Dawn and the path of divine emanation on the Tree of Life (*TGD*, pp.61, 162).

A more telling example of Yeats's debt to the magical knowledge of the Golden Dawn is his placement of the Fool at Phase 28. This phase rests on the verge of the entity's loss of individuality as it returns to Phase 1. At Phase 1, beings become plastic and 'the instrument of supernatural manifestation, the final link between the living and more powerful beings [...] . All plasticies do not obey all masters [...]' (*AV[B]*, p.183). As an individual may pass 'many times through the twenty-eight phases' (*AV[B]*, p.118), Phase 28 may be seen as Phase 0.

Zero, of course, is the number of the Fool in the Tarot deck. This card, in the Golden Dawn system of meditation, is placed on path 11, which leads from Chokmah, the Sephirah called Wisdom, to Kether, the Sephirah called the Crown (*TGD*, p.71). Kether is the final step on the Cabalistic Tree from which the initiate either moves onto the next Elemental Tree or, after passing through the Tree in the Element of Fire, merges with the Godhead or, in Yeatsian terminology, passes into the Thirteenth Cone. When moving between these elemental states, the Golden Dawn initiate passes through a plastic state and is subject to control by higher forces (*TGD*, pp.613-15).

Another parallel with between *A Vision* and the Golden Dawn can be found in Yeats's own words. In 'Is the Order of R.R. & A.C. to remain a Magical Order', we find Yeats beginning to explore the mechanics behind being in or out of phase:

If indeed we must make this change, this transference of influence from Degrees, which are like wheels turning upon a single pivot, to 'groups' which will be like wheels turning upon different pivots,[17] like toothed wheels working one against the other, this surrender of ancient unity to anarchic diversity, let us make it as complete as possible. Let us re-shape the Order, Inner and Outer alike, destroying that symbolic Organisation which, so long as it exists, must evoke a being into continuous strife with these alien bodies within its spiritual substance.[18]

The central image of wheels within a wheel is remarkably similar to the symbol of the Great Wheel, which symbolises 'every completed movement of thought or life, twenty-eight incarnations, a single incarnation, a single judgement or act of thought' (*AV[B]*, p.81). If the Great Wheel can be seen as both a single incarnation or a series of incarnations, there is, symbolically, a Great Wheel at every phase of the Great Wheel being observed. Thus, when an individual remains in phase, the movement of the Great Wheel, which represents his twenty-eight incarnations would move, in the terms Yeats used to describe the Golden Dawn under a system of degrees, as a set of wheels 'turning upon a single pivot'. Should the individual try to live out of phase, trying to live counter to the direction of the gyres,[19] the difficulties experienced by the individual would be symbolised on the Great Wheel as being 'like wheels turning upon different pivots, like toothed wheels working one against the other' (*YGD*, p.264).

Yeats also took inspiration for *A Vision* from Sir Walter Scott's translation of the *Hermetica*, the ancient writings attributed to Hermes Trismagistus, as can be seen in the notations Yeats made in his copy of Scott and his scattered references to the text in *A Vision*.[20] As with the other systems from which he draws material from, Yeats does not shy away from disagreeing with his source, as is seen in his discussion of the difference between Fate, Necessity, and Destiny.

> [...] when *Passionate Body* predominates[,] all is *Destiny*; the man dominated by his *Daimon* acts in spite of reason; whereas the man finds through reason or through the direct vision of the *Spirit* Fate or Necessity, which lies outside himself in *Body of Fate* or *Celestial Body*.[1]
>
> [1] The Hermetic Fragments draw somewhat the same distinction. Necessity comes, they say, upon us through the events of life and must be obeyed. Destiny sows the seeds of those events and impels evil men. On fragment adds 'Order' connecting 'Necessity' and 'Destiny' and identifies it with the Cosmos. The three seem to constitute a Hegelian triad. I am summarising from Scott's *Hermetics (sic.)* Exc. vii. Exc. viii. and Aeslepius iii. Section 39. The difference between their point of view and mine is that I cannot consider that Destiny inspires only evil men. The Hermetic Fragments are full of

Platonic Intellectualism. Destiny becomes evil when the *Passionate Body* is subject to Necessity. (*AV[B]*, p.190.)

The passages in Aeslepius and the Excerpts of Stobaeus' anthology of Hermetic writing which Yeats refers to primarily concern themselves with the seven celestial spheres of the Ptolemean Cosmos, their astrological and, in its distinctions between Fate, Destiny, and Necessity, metaphysical influence upon the development of an individual. Each, however, covers the material slightly differently. In Aeslepius, there is little with which Yeats would have quarrelled. Both posit a force external to the control of the individual which determines the course of an individual's life. They even agree that, despite the highly ordered systems which they posit, there is an element of 'chance or contingency [... which] also exists in the Kosmos, being intermingled with all material things'.[21] Indeed, Yeats quotes other segments of this passage throughout *A Vision* to support both his theories of the *Principles* and the Great Year.[22]

In Excerpts VII and VIII from Stobaeus', however, Yeats and Hermes begin to diverge:

> *Hermes.* For there is a mighty deity, my son, who is posted in the midst of the universe, and watches over all things done on earth by men. For as Necessity has been set over the divine order, even so has Penal Justice been set over men. For Necessity holds in her grasp the order of those above, inasmuch as they are divine, and do not wish to err, and cannot err; [...] but Penal Justice has been appointed to punish those who err on earth. For the human race is apt to err, because it is mortal, and is composed of evil matter; [...] and men are subject to Destiny by reason of the forces at work in their birth, but are subject to Penal Justice by reason of their errors in the conduct of their life. (*Herm*, pp.419-21.)

> Now the ineligible substance, if it is drawn near to God, has power over itself, and in saving itself, it also saves the other part. As long as it is by itself, it is not subject to Necessity, and its choice is in accordance with Providence. But if it falls away from God, it chooses the corporeal world, and in that way it becomes subject to Necessity, which rules over the Kosmos. (*Herm*, p.423.)

Here, as Yeats indicates in his note, Hermes[23] begins to refer to Necessity in judgmental terms. Necessity is no longer simply the force which enforces Destiny but, instead, has taken on the role of punishing those not enlightened enough to follow God's plan. As noticed by Yeats in his copy of the *Hermetica*,[24] 'Necessity is subservient to providence', that is, 'God's ordering' (*Herm*, p.433). By extension, if you are acting outside of God's will, your actions must be evil. Yeats's system does not contain such a moral divide. In Yeats's system, Destiny is when an individual is acting under the direction of his *Daimon*, a source of supernatural guidance. Necessity, on the other hand, is the description of what happens when an individual solely reacts to his surroundings, as represented by his *Body of Fate* or *Celestial Body* (*AV*[*B*], p.190). In addition, such a moralistic division conflicts with the phrase which became Yeats's motto in the Golden Dawn: *Demon est Deus Inversus*—translated as either 'The Devil is God Inverted' or 'As above, so below'. This Kabbalistic concept is in opposition with Stobaeus: 'Forces do not work upward form below, but downward from above' (*Herm*, p.433).

Nor would have Yeats agreed with the final passage he cited in the inside back cover of his copy of the *Hermetica*, which cautioned against struggling against Necessity and Destiny.

> He who has learnt to know himself ought not to set right by means of magic anything that is thought to be amiss, nor to use force to overcome necessity, but rather to let necessity go its own way according to nature. A man ought to seek to know himself and God and hold his passions in subjection, and to let Destiny deal as she wills with the clay which belongs to her, that is, with his body. (*Herm*, p.541.)

Here, the Hermetic fragment demands a complete surrender to God's will, as advocated by such divergent religious and mystical traditions as the Golden Dawn, Buddhism, and Roman Catholicism, and summarised in the phrase 'Thy will be done'. Yet Yeats separates the cause of the higher powers, defined as *Destiny*, with the simple cause and effect of the mundane world, *Necessity*, even though the latter may be caused by the former. In a way, Yeats advocates a greater level of personal responsibility for the direction of an individual's life by positing that the direction of a life is, ultimately, as much the choice of the individual as it is the direction of the supernatural.

In addition to the mystical and magical, Yeats calls upon his knowledge of Irish folklore and mythology to help frame and support the system of *A Vision*. The most obvious of these comes in the poem "All Souls' Night: An Epilogue". The night of the poem's setting, Halloween, is the night of the year in Irish folklore when the barrier between this world and the Otherworld is so weak that spirits and *Sidhe* may cross it at will. This is significant in relation to the placement of the poem. Yeats arranged the twenty-six roman numeraled sections and two poems of the introductory material of *A Vision* to parallel the Phases of the Moon on the Great Wheel, with Section I of "Rapallo" paralleling Phase 2. This places "All Soul's Night" at Phase 1, which is the phase at which the soul may escape the cycle of rebirth and move into the Thirteenth Cone or, more importantly, from which spirits are sent into the mundane world at the command of higher powers (*AV[B]*, p.183).

Most other references Yeats makes to Irish folklore are employed to illustrate or support points made in his system. He refers to a fairy woman who climbs into the air in a gyring motion, similar to that of Blake's *Jacob's Dream*,[25] which he used in *The Celtic Twilight* to parallel the use of Gyres by St. Thomas Aquinas (*AV[B]*, p.69), the inversion of seasons in Celtic Mythology between the mundane world and the lands of the *Sidhe* to illustrate the arrangement of the Great Wheel of the Faculties and the Great Wheel of the Principles (*AV[B]*, p.210), and a ghost story from Leap Castle to illustrate one of the states of the soul after death (*AV[B]*, p.224).

> In the third discarnate state, a state I shall presently describe, it may renounce the form of man and take some shape from the social or religious tradition of its past life, symbolical of its condition. Leap Castle [...] is haunted by what is called an evil spirit which appears as a sheep with short legs and decaying human head. I suggest some man with the *Husk* exaggerated and familiar with religious symbolism, torn at the moment of death between two passions, terror of the body's decay with which he identified himself, and an abject religious humility, projected himself in this image. (*AV[B]*, p.224.)

Yeats called upon these mythological references, as he did with his mystical source material, to validate his system. By showing that these traditions and his system 'draw upon some unknown [...] source' (*AV[B]*, p.189) of common, archetypal images, he could justify the placement of his system alongside 'those hard, symbolic bones' (*AV[B]*, p.24) called on by Dante, Blake, and others in the creation of their great works.

NOTES

1. *A Vision [B]* (London: Macmillan 1937), p.8. Henceforth *AV[B]*.
2. Richard Ellmann, *Yeats: The Man and the Masks* (London: Penguin Books 1988), p.230.
3. *A Vision [A]* (London: T. Werner Laurie, Ltd. 1925), pp.xi-xii. Henceforth *AV[A]*.
4. Due to constraints of space, I will be unable to cover Blake here.
5. Emanuel Swedenborg, *Heaven and Hell*, trans. George F. Dole (West Chester: Swedenborg Foundation 1979), p.345. Henceforth *H&H*.

6 Boehme appears, by name, three times. See Craig Wallace Barrow, 'Comprehensive Index to Yeats's *A Vision*', *Bulletin of the New York Public Library*, Vol. 77 (Autumn 1973), p.53.
7 George Mills Harper, *The Making of Yeats's A Vision: A Study of the Automatic Script*, Vol. 1 (Southern Illinois UP 1987), p.325. Henceforth *TMYV*.
8 The Communicators are explaining that with the death of the physical body, specific memory (i.e., a knowledge of Boehme and Blake) dies with it. Instinctual or repetitive memory, however, the spirit 'gets [...] from every living or written source—the spirit knows its details of life but no acquired intellectual learning' (*TMYV*, Vol. 1, p.333).
9 Jacob Boehme, *The 'Key' of Jacob Boehme*, trans., William Law (Grand Rapids: Phanes Press 1991), p.44.
10 According to Adam Maclean's 'Introduction' to William Law's translation of *The 'Key' of Jacob Boehme*, Boehme's mysticism was influenced by both the Kabbalah and Paracelsian alchemy. (Boehme, op. cit., 1991, p.9.)
11 McGregor Mathers, *The Kabbalah Unveiled*. (York Beach: Samuel Weiser, Inc. 1989), p.16.
12 Excluding, of course, his own.
13 For a discussion of their involvement, albeit with a focus more on W. B. Yeats than Georgie Hyde-Lees, see George Mills Harper, *Yeats's Golden Dawn* (London: Macmillan 1966), and Ellic Howe, *The Magicians of the Golden Dawn: A Documentary History of a Magical Order, 1887-1923* (York Beach, Maine: Samuel Weiser, Inc. 1984; Wellingborough: Aquarian 1985).
14 R. F. Foster, *W. B. Yeats: A Life. Volume I: The Apprentice Mage 1865-1914* (Oxford & NY: OUP 1997), p.525
15 Among other things, Initiates of the Golden Dawn were trained to be receptive to higher powers and to be able to distinguish true from false when having a metaphysical experience.
16 Israel Regardie, *The Golden Dawn* [6th edn.] (St. Paul: Llewellyn Publications 1986), p.107. Henceforth *TGD*.
17 According to George Mills Harper, this image of the monstrous factories of the Industrial Revolution may have been taken from 'Blake's *Jerusalem* of "'wheels without wheel, with cogs tyrannic" which drive the "Loom of Locke".' See *Yeats's Golden Dawn* (London: Macmillan 1966), p.182.
18 ibid., p.264. Henceforth *YGD*.
19 This statement is a summation of the mechanics behind the "RULES FOR DISCOVERING TRUE AND FALSE MASKS" and the "RULES FOR FINDING THE TRUE AND FALSE CREATIVE MIND" in *A Vision[B]*, pp.90-92.
20 Edward O'Shea, *A Descriptive Catalog of W. B. Yeats's Library* (New York: Garland 1985), pp.124-25.
21 Sir Walter Scott, trans. and ed., *Hermetica: The Ancient Greek and Latin Writings which Contain Religious or Philosophical Teachings Ascribed to Hermes Trismegistus*. (Boston: Shambala 1993), p.365.
22 See *AV[B]*, pp.211, 253; and *Hermetica*, pp.351-53, henceforth *Herm*.
23 This, of course, is an illusion created by the nature of Scott's compilation. These texts, as he states in his 'Introduction', were written by men who 'gave out as taught by Hermes what was really their own teachings'. Scott draws parallels with this to the books of the Hebrew Bible, in which he explores that which 'made a Jew write a Book of Daniel [...] instead of a book of his own'. *Herm*, pp.3-5.
24 O'Shea, op. cit. (1985), p.125.

25 Kathleen Raine, *Yeats the Initiate: Essays on Certain Themes in the Work of W. B. Yeats* (Mountrath: Dolmen Press 1986), p.241.

STRANGER THAN FICTION: YEATS AND THE *VISIONS* NOTEBOOK, 1898-1901

Warwick Gould

I

Yeats himself—not Tzvetan Todorov—described "Rosa Alchemica", "The Tables of the Law" and "The Adoration of the Magi" as 'fantastic romance'.[1] The stories were 'preliminary studies'[2] studies for *The Speckled Bird*, a novel which Yeats never finished. Their publication began in *The Savoy* in April 1896. When Yeats looked back on them, he saw them as but one of the many ways in which he had sought to embody his own 'myth that was itself a reply to' the Victorian public myth of 'progress'.[3]

In their own mode of the fantastic, however, the stories are perfectly finished. To that mode Yeats never returned. He nevertheless revised this tight unit of tales from time to time so that they remained a moving image of his aesthetic and symbolical preoccupations.[4] The stories are Yeats's only 'genre' fiction, and they are usually thought of as an 'apocalyptic' triptych, but the definition is limited and opportunistic.[5] It eschews their close affinities with comparable fiction of contemporary occult experience, including work by Joris-Karl Huysmans, Villiers de l'Isle Adam, Oscar Wilde, and three Arthurs—Symons, Quiller-Couch and Machen. Particularly, it overlooks Yeats's use of what Linda Dowling has called the 'central Decadent *topos*, the fatal book'.[6] These stories are Yeats's greatest contribution in prose upon the European *symboliste* tradition. They reveal that his debts to previous writers of short fiction are consciously incurred.

A 'style found by sedentary toil | And by the imitation of great masters'.[7] But which? 'He wrote of me in that extravagant style | He had learnt from Pater' averred Michael Robartes *redivivus*.[8] Pater is a profound influence on the young Yeats because he validates a model for aesthetic subjectivity. Numerous of his books (including his essay on 'Style') remain sacred texts and his name a talisman for Yeats, but Paterian style does not distinguish the "Rosa Alchemica" triptych from (say) the prose of *Ideas of Good and Evil*.[9] Michael Robartes is in fact a notoriously unreliable witness, and his words have been unreflectingly reiterated as though the matter were a simple one. While various of Yeats's prose styles have Paterian affinities, the authentic signature of the three tales of the Order of the Alchemical Rose is the fantastic, not the Paterian.[10] More particularly, what is distinctive about the style of the stories is Yeats's use of that 'formula of alternate possibilities' Yvor Winters' discerned in Hawthorne and in other works of 'American obscurantism', notably those of Edgar Allan Poe.[11]

In Yeats's narratives of failed initiation the 'fantastic' set pieces cluster most thickly in "Rosa Alchemica", in Robartes' temptation of the narrator in his house in Dublin, and the narrator's entry into the temple of the Alchemical Rose.[12] Incense possibly acts on the narrator as a drug, as does the gum in the torches in the hands of companies of immortal beings which pervade the ending of the second story (they are also the immortal demons of the third story). Attempted domination is resisted by mental fight;[13] but the method of domination—human (by Robartes) or supernatural (through Robartes, or independently of him) is questioningly to be read as *either* the narrator's visions, *or* as mesmerism caused by evocation, *or* as spiritual irruption by immortals. Thus, in "The Tables of the Law" a perfume with mysterious effects seems to return to the narrator's consciousness as he examines what purports to be the lost manuscript of the *Liber Inducens in Evangelium Aeternum*. He asks Owen Aherne if he is lighting incense.

> 'No,' he replied, and pointed where the thurible lay rusty and empty on one of the benches; as he spoke the faint perfume seemed to vanish, and I was persuaded I had imagined it. (*VSR*, p.162.)[14]

The formula of alternate possibilities insists upon the deferral, rather than the solution (or closure) of a problem of perception. It says, in effect, to the reader 'it's your choice'.

> Suddenly I saw, or imagined that I saw, the room darken, and faint figures robed in purple, and lifting faint torches with arms that gleamed like silver, bending, above Owen Aherne; and I saw, or imagined that I saw, drops, as of burning gum, fall from the torches, and a heavy purple smoke, as of incense, come pouring from the flames and sweeping about us. Owen Aherne, more happy than I who have been half initiated into the Order of the Alchemical Rose, and protected

perhaps by his great piety, had sunk again into dejection and listlessness, and saw none of these things; but my knees shook under me, for the purple-robed figures were less faint every moment, and now I could hear the hissing of the gum in the torches. They did not appear to see me, for their eyes were upon Owen Aherne; and now and again I could hear them sigh as though with sorrow for his sorrow, and presently I heard words which I could not understand except that they were words of sorrow, and sweet as though immortal was talking to immortal. Then one of them waved her torch, and all the torches waved, and for a moment it was as though some great bird made of flames had fluttered its plumage, and a voice cried as from far up in the air: 'He has charged even his angels with folly, and they also bow and obey; but let your heart mingle with our hearts, which are wrought of divine ecstasy, and your body with our bodies which are wrought of divine intellect.' And at that cry I understood that the Order of the Alchemical Rose was not of this earth, and that it was still seeking over this earth for whatever souls it could gather within its glittering net; and when all the faces turned towards me, and I saw the mild eyes and the unshaken eyelids. I was full of terror, and thought they were about to fling their torches upon me, so that all I held dear, all that held me to spiritual and social order would be burnt up and my soul left naked and shivering among the winds that blow from beyond this world and from beyond the stars; and a faint voice cried, 'Why do you fly from our torches that were made our of sweet wood, after it had perished from the world and come to us who made it of old times with our breath?' (*VSR*, p.163-64).[15]

For Tzvetan Todorov 'the fantastic' is that mode in which the reader hesitates between alternate possibilities of the unprecedented but explicable—in these fictions, drug-induced hallucination—and the supernatural but hitherto unencountered.

> *Ainsi se trouve-t-on au coeur du fantastique. Dans un monde qui est bien le nôtre, celui que nous connaissons, sans diables, sylphides, ni vampires, se produit un événement qui ne peut s'expliquer par les lois de ce même monde familier. Celui qui perçoit l'événement doit opter pour l'une des deux solutions possibles: ou bien il s'agit d'une illusion des sens, d'un produit de l'imagination et les lois du monde restent alors ce qu'elles sont; ou bien l'événement a véritablement eu lieu, il est partie intégrante de la réalité, mais alors cette réalité est régie par des lois inconnues de nous. Ou bien le diable est une illusion, un être imaginaire, ou bien il existe réellement, tout comme les autres êtres vivants: avec cette réserve qu'on le rencontre rarement.*
>
> *Le fantastique occupe le temps de cette incertitude; dès qu'on choisit l'une ou l'autre réponse, on quitte le fantastique pour entrer dans un genre voisin, l'étrange ou le merveilleux. Le fantastique, c'est l'hésitation éprouvée par un être qui ne connaît que les lois naturelles, face à un événement en apparence surnaturel.*
>
> *Le concept de fantastique se définit donc par rapport à ceux de réel et d'imaginaire: et ces derniers méritent plus qu'une simple mention.*[16]

Todorov denies that his formulation is original, finding predecessor definitions for his unstable genre postulated by Vladimir Solovyov, and by M. R. James. Readerly hesitation between the strange and the marvellous which for Todorov is the essence of the matter is exactly the effect Winters finds in the 'formula of alternate possibilities'.

Todorov, like Yeats (and Hawthorne himself), is working in a tradition of generic self-consciousness.[17] In his back-formation of 'moods' for the doctrines of the Order of the Alchemical Rose, Yeats alluded to his own tradition as

> that mood which Edgar Poe found in a wine-cup, and how it passed into France and took possession of Baudelaire, and from Baudelaire passed to England and the Pre-Raphaelites, and then again returned to France, and still wanders the world, enlarging its power as it goes, awaiting the time when it shall be, perhaps, alone, or with other moods, master over a great new religion, and an awakener of the fanatical wars which hovered in the gray surges, and forget the wine-cup where it was born. (*VSR*, pp.143-44vv.)

Poe provided Yeats with an aesthetic so strongly held that he habitually forgot both its origins and the means whereby he had absorbed it. On the first page of "Ligeia" he found an adage from Bacon's essay "Of Beauty": "'There is no excellent [sic; 'exquisite' in Poe] *Beauty* that hath not some strangeness in the proportion'."[18] The adage exactly fitted Yeats's 'mood'. It had also filtered through Pater in the Postscript to *Appreciations* (1889) and via Baudelaire's '*Le Beau est toujours bizarre*';[19] and, between them, Poe and Hawthorne provided Yeats's 'very phantastic' style for his 'phantastic stories'.[20] Julian Hawthorne, Nathaniel Hawthorne's son was a neighbour of John Butler Yeats's in Bedford Park.[21] Lionel Johnson's poem "Hawthorne" (1889) attributed the knowledge of 'fatal sorrows binding life and death' to the American writer whose 'music' was 'sorrow's perfect breath'.[22] In fact, there was something of a cult of Hawthorne in the Bedford Park of the 1880s and 1890s. Most of Yeats's recorded comments on Hawthorne are occasioned by the production of John Todhunter's *The Poison Flower*, a play adapted from "Rappaccini's Daughter". Reviewing the play, Yeats was driven back to the story in *Mosses from an Old Manse*

> [...] beautiful as it is, [it] has always seemed to me a little fanciful and arbitrary. I could never get it out of my head that Hawthorne wanted to make one's flesh creep [...] and did not care how he managed it.[23]

Todhunter's play was 'a much more solid thing'.

> One finds it quite easy to believe that this worn-looking Kabalist [...]
> has in mind some wild dream for the regeneration of men [...] [t]he
> copy of the Kabala that lies on my desk pleads for him, and tells that
> such men lived, and may well have dreamed such a dream, in the
> mystic Middle Ages. In becoming a thinker of a particular school, he
> has obtained the historical reality lacked by the Rappaccini of
> Hawthorne . . [e]ven in our own age men dream of 'the poison that
> drives out poison' (*LNI*, pp.51-52.)

Rappaccini was more 'completely realised than was possible in Hawthorne's dreamy little story, and the garden is made more significant with hints of allegory', Yeats told another American paper.[24]

Yeats's criticisms in fact focus on the very dilemma descried by Yvor Winters in Hawthorne's lesser work and in the work of other writers who employ the formula of alternate possibilities for symbolical, rather than allegorical effects. For Winters, this unstable mode shows the descent from the 'pure allegory' of *The Scarlet Letter* (1850) to the 'impure' forms of Hawthorne's (to him) lesser prose, 'with unassimilated allegorical elements'. Where Hawthorne went wrong, Winters averred, was in 'following the advice of Poe and other well-wishers', and in throwing 'his allegorising out of the window'.[25] At his best, as in the ninth chapter of *The Scarlet Letter*, Hawthorne uses the formula of alternate possibilities such that 'the idea conveyed is clear enough, but the embodiment of the idea appears far-fetched, professing to let you take it or leave it'.[26] If we reverse the formula, however, so as to make the physical representation perfectly clear but the meaning uncertain, we have a very serious situation, a state of affairs which, in Winters' view, spoils *The Blithedale Romance* (1852) and the four unfinished romances.[27]

The fantastic, then, from Poe and Hawthorne to Yeats and M. R. James and onwards to critics such as Winters and structuralist theorists such as Todorov, remains a stable concept for dealing with unstable experience. We all know what we are talking about. While Todorov considers reader-response, Winters allows for the writer's intention by looking at the effects of style. It is merely that Yeats was far from sure whether the mode he could handle so assuredly was the right one for what he wanted to do.

II

Why? I suggest that to Yeats the mode came to seem false to experience. His own early visionary experiences and early drug experiences (if he had any) are largely unrecorded. His first recorded hashish experience is a recreational experiment in Paris in December 1896, which took him on a singular adventure among the Martinists.[28] Havelock Ellis first experimented with mescal, that 'some stray cactus, mother of as many dreams' which, with hashish, 'keeps alone [...] immemorial impartiality', on both Yeats and Symons in April 1897.[29] The fantastic is a mode of fiction which (bluntly) Yeats forswore forever as unsatisfactory as he embarked on (to him) real visionary experience and further drug experiences in the quest for vision.

If *'le temps de cette incertitude'* is Todorov's concern, the narrator of the triptych begins the "The Adoration of the Magi" (written in November 1896) by letting

> some years go by before writing out this story, for I am always in dread of the illusions which come of that *inquiétude* of the veil of the temple, which M. Mallarmé considers a characteristic of our times; and only write it now because I have grown to believe that there is no dangerous idea which does not become less dangerous when written out in sincere and careful English. (*VSR*, p.165, my emphasis).

John Wilson Foster rather solemnly terms this a 'literary counter-ceremony' or 'exorcism'[30] of the style of the first two tales, but it is of course only an apparent *demarché* from the fantastic and a deft prelude to what is in many ways the most antinomian and bizarre of the stories.[31] Nevertheless, Yeats did become unhappy with the 'elaborate style' of the "Rosa Alchemica" stories even as he wrote them, and the Poe passage quoted above from *The Savoy* version of "Rosa Alchemica" did not even survive into *The Secret Rose* (1897).

Dissatisfaction led him to seek, with the help of Olivia Shakespear's mediumship, the advice of a 'symbolic personality' called Megarithma, who advised him to 'live near waters and avoid woods because they concentrate the solar ray'. Yeats interpreted 'solar' influence in terms of that growing artifice of style he detected in the 'goldsmith'-like elaboration of "Rosa Alchemica". Water was 'lunar', referring to 'all that is simple, popular, traditional, emotional'.[32]

This 'enigmatic sentence', Yeats came to believe, 'came from my own Daimon, my own buried self, speaking through my friend's mind'.[33] It certainly was thereafter associated with the 'Archer Vision'. In his bedroom at Tulira Castle on the night of 14 August, 1896, Yeats invoked a 'vision of Diana', or the 'lunar power' which he saw as 'the chief source of my inspiration'. He 'saw first a centaur and then a marvellous naked woman shooting an arrow at a star. She stood like a statue upon a stone pedestal, and the flesh tints of her body seemed to make all human flesh in the contrast look unhealthy. Like the centaur she moved amid brilliant light'.[34]

The event remained enigmatic for Yeats, and together with the 'Megarithma' experience, constitutes almost all that we know of Yeats's visionary life before the two-volume *Visions Notebook*.[35] This records dreams (some drug-induced), visions (some drug-suppressed), and occult experiences from 11 July, 1898 until March 1901. Yeats returned to it for evidence of wisdom that had come to him, as he came to believe (and to try to interpret) directly from *Anima Mundi*. Its self-grounded personal witness provides the authority for *Per Amica Silentia Lunae* (1918). Once we had deciphered it, it was apparent that much material scattered throughout his published prose and verse depended upon it. Annotating it and editing it, we are trying to recover some sense of its use at various points in Yeats's life thereafter.

> It was at Coole that the first few simple thoughts that now, grown complex through their contact with other thoughts, explain the world, came to me from beyond my own mind. I practised meditations, and these, as I think, so affected my sleep that I began to have dreams that differed from ordinary dreams in seeming to take place amid brilliant light, and by their invariable coherence, and certain half-dreams, if I can call them so, between sleep and waking [...] such experiences come to me most often amid distraction, at some time that seems of all times the least fitting, as though it were necessary for the exterior mind to be engaged elsewhere, and it was during 1897 and 1898, when I was always just arriving from or just setting out to some political meeting, that the first dreams came.[36]

The *Notebook* became also a record of his relationship with Maud Gonne, including their 'spiritual marriage' in December 1898, his emotional *rapprochement* with Olivia Shakespear in 1900, and her dream-parable of the destructiveness of his passion for Maud Gonne.

At the same time he worked on a Celtic Mystical Order. The ultimate source of the idea is Nora Hopper's "The Gifts of Aodh and Una", in *Ballads in Prose* (1894), with its 'Temple of Heroes' on an island in the Shannon. Yeats was obsessed by the story in early 1895;[37] and, while staying with Douglas Hyde in April that year at Frenchpark, Co. Roscommon, he wondered whether Castle Island, Lough Key, might not become his 'temple of heroes', the centre of 'mysteries like those of Eleusis and Samothrace'.[38] For the next 'ten years', his

> most impassioned thought was a vain attempt to find philosophy and to create ritual for that Order. I had an unshakable conviction [...] that invisible gates would open as they opened for Blake, as they opened for Swedenborg, as they opened for Boehme [...].' (*Au*, p.254.)

There was a wider ambition at work here:

> I must find a tradition, that was a part of actual history that had associations in the scenery of my own country, and so bring my speech closer to that of daily life. Prompted as I believed by certain dreams and premonitions I returned to Ireland, & with a friends help began a study of the supernatural belief of the Galway and Arran cottages. Could I not found an Eleusinian Rite, which would bind into a common symbolism, a common meditation a school of poets & men of letters, so that poetry & drama, would find the religious weight they have lacked since the middle ages perhaps since ancient Greece. I did not intend it, to be a revival of the pagan world, how could one ignore so many centuries, but a reconciliation, where there would be no preaching, no public argument.[39]

The Celtic Order was not to be part of the Golden Dawn, but it was to have a similar structure and rites. Mathers on behalf of the 'Chiefs of R.R. & A.C [...]. promise[ed] recognition and help'.[40] In November 1897 Yeats began magical work towards the creation of the Order, with a group of GD Second Order members of whom only Dorothea Hunter and George Pollexfen were Irish. From the outset Yeats seems to have kept discrete cells working on symbolism for the Order. He drew regularly on visions experienced by Maud Gonne, George Russell—who had visions 'perhaps more continually than any modern man since Swedenborg'[41]—William Sharp (and 'Fiona Macleod'), occasionally using acquaintances such as Nora Hopper and Susan Mitchell. Papers in the National Library of Ireland record these activities and contain draft Rituals for the Order.[42]

Dorothea Hunter recalled that '[h]e could not himself get the visions he so desired; he said his mind was too analytical & questioning'.[43] The *Visions Notebook* contains his own 'private' work on proposed Outer Order Rituals to be structured on the Tuatha de Danaan talismans of Sword, Stone, Cauldron and Spear.[44] From 12 September onwards, he evoked Irish gods and goddesses daily, summoning Aengus, Boann, Bobh Derg and An Dagda. In this endeavour, the *Notebook* carries on the kind of exploration hinted at in the symbolism of the first version of "The Adoration of the Magi" and later dropped from the story. Yeats told Fiona Macleod that the story was 'a half prophesy of a very veiled kind';[45] the prophecy was of the return of the pagan gods—a very Paterian vision, though with an Irish habitation.[46] The dying prostitute

> told them the secret names of the immortals of many lands, and of the colours, and odours, and weapons, and instruments of music and

instruments of handicraft they held dearest; but most about the immortals of Ireland and of their love for the cauldron, and the whetstone, and the sword, and the spear, and the hills of the Shee, and the horns of the moon, and the Grey Wind, and the Yellow Wind, and the Black Wind, and the Red Wind. (*VSR*, p.170vv.)

The dreams recorded in the *Notebook* are partly controlled by the dreamer and include hypnagogic visions before sleep and 'concurrent dreams' later analysed in *Per Amica Silentia Lunae*. There are also waking hallucinations superimposed upon the ordinary, non-hallucinatory environment. In all these experiences Yeats became more and more conscious of the relative weakness of his own visionary powers. He tried hashish and mescal (which 'certainly in my case interferes with inner vision'). Actual experience of drugs seems to have shown him that their effects were in fact quite distinct from those obtained by meditation or evocation. Drugs complicated the matter, and Yeats's record of his use of them could easily be overstated. Mainly, he used standard Golden Dawn evocations to induce visions, tattwa cards—symbols of the elements—typically to direct clairvoyance in others but used also to banish evil or negative visions. These are what the Golden Dawn classified as 'etheric' experiences, i.e., three dimensional, with the visionary at times a participant.

An early draft of *Per Amica Silentia Lunae* acknowledges 'The world of spirits became & still is the great preoccupation of my life [...] a study, that even more than poetry has absorbed my life'.[47] That preoccupation needed to be externalised: actual experience in all its complexity showed that the fantastic, or quasi-gothic fiction was not the way forward. For the moment there was no obvious way of putting such experience before the public.

The published *Notebook* will demonstrate particular sources for later poems, and it should be possible to point out just how and when rereadings of the *Notebook* helped Yeats forward. More important today, is the matter of Yeats's rare mystical experiences, which occur amid much evidence of what we must agree to call the failure of thaumaturgy, in which the magus cannot control visions which, as it were, turn against him.[48] "A Dream of the World's End" appeared in Pamela Colman Smith's *The Green Sheaf* (1903),[49] offering a phantasmagoric condensation of the events—private and public—of 1898. While Yeats worked on *The Shadowy Waters* at Coole, and decided to evoke with apple blossom:

I had no true vision but a visionary dream. I dreamed that I was going through a great city—it had some likeness to Paris about Auteuil—at night. Presently I saw a wild windy light in the sky and knew that dawn was coming in the middle of the night and that it was the last day.

The published text has an introductory paragraph:

I have a way of giving myself long meaning dreams, by meditating on a symbol when I go to sleep. Sometimes I use traditional symbols, and sometimes I meditate on some image which is only a symbol to myself. A while ago I began to think of apple-blossom as an image of the East and breaking day, and one night it brought me, not as I expected a charming dream full of the mythology of sun-rise, but this grotesque dream about the breaking of an eternal city.[50]

The 1899 note to "The Cap and Bells" is more detailed:

I dreamed this story exactly as I have written it, and dreamed another long dream after it, trying to make out its meaning, and whether I was to write it in prose or verse. The first dream was more a vision than a dream, for it was beautiful and coherent, and gave me the sense of illumination and exaltation that one gets from visions, while the second dream was confused and meaningless. The poem has always meant a great deal to me, though, as is the way with symbolic poems, it has not always meant quite the same thing. Blake would have said 'The authors are in eternity' and I am quite sure they can only be questioned in dreams. (*VP*, p.808.)

Per Amica Silentia Lunae ascribes to the poet a liminality which is the condition that distinguishes him from the saint: he 'may not stand within the sacred house but lives amid the whirlwinds that beset its threshold'.[51] Yeats lacked Russell's saintly capacity for mystical vision; conversely Russell was—in Yeats's view—a secondary poet. That marginality also distinguishes the poet from the magician: Yeats, unlike Mathers had no talent for constructing rituals for his Celtic Order.[52]

The poet's liminality is central to *The Wind Among the Reeds*, by nature a secondary creation, a De Quinceyan involute of earlier works. Its composition depended upon obsessive and recurrent imbrication of redreamt dreams. A taxonomy of visionary experiences was to be expected from a writer who redreamt materials from his own writing and re-read his own record of visions and dreams.[53] Failure of vision was as central to the writer's creative economy as was delay. In 1908, reflecting on certain poems in *The Wind Among the Reeds* Yeats had recalled:

When I wrote these poems, I had so meditated over the images that came to me in writing 'Ballads and Lyrics', 'The Rose', and 'The Wanderings of Oisin', and other images from Irish folk-lore, that they

Yeats and The Visions Notebook, 1898-1901

had become true symbols. I had sometimes when awake, but more often in sleep, moments of vision, a state very unlike dreaming, when these images took upon themselves what seemed an independent life and became part of a mystic language, which seemed as if it would bring me some strange revelation. (*VP*, p.800.)

Once composition was completed by first volume publication, Yeats seems to have been able to distance himself somewhat from obsessive dream-patterns.[54] He could therefore contemplate a somewhat disvested volume rather differently:

Being troubled at what was thought a reckless obscurity, I tried to explain myself in lengthy notes, into which I put all the little learning I had, and more wilful phantasy than I now think admirable, though what is most mystical still seems to me the most true. I quote in what follows the better or the more necessary passages. (*VP*, p.800.)

Amid the failures of vision there were also unexpected and wholly personal blessings. In mid-July 1898 while crossing a stream in Inchy Wood he had 'suddenly felt a sense of dependence of the divine will and had passed for a moment into a state of passive mysticism unusual with my nature, which has been shaped by thaumaturgy'. The following night he had a dream:

I awoke slowly and could not remember what I had seen but knew that I had been told that the love of God was infinite for every human being, because every human being is unique and God's love can find no other capable of satisfying the same need [...]. I was not in a true trance but perhaps had been.

'[T]his thought came to be, as I believe, supernaturally', he later recalled, and the experience was alluded to in many places in his prose, published and unpublished.[55] Such direct experience of the numinous was believed by Yeats to be 'the root of Christian mysticism'.[56] Blessedness was *no* mere 'metaphor for poetry'. Its rarity guaranteed the poet's place in the scheme of things, below the saint or the magus. "A Voice", in the *Speaker* (19 April, 1902), one of the 'New Chapters in the Celtic Twilight', is an adjusted account of an experience of 20 September, 1898, now attached to this mystical experience of July 1898—again taken very directly from the *Notebook*.

Self-reading was often the way forward for Yeats, and re-reading the Notebook for the draft Autobiography seems to have provided a stimulus for Per Amica Silentia Lunae, which is really a meditation upon the extraordinary spiritual experiences of 1898-1900.[57] 'I am writing out these thoughts to escape from their obsession', Yeats announces at the outset of its ur-draft, "Spiritus Mundi" (which will also be included in our edition),[58] linking the themes and material of 'Swedenborg, Mediums and the Desolate Places' to the mystical experience of July 1898.[59] In *'Anima Mundi'* he summed up this great period of vision and dream:

> I had found that after evocation my sleep became at moments full of light and form, all that I had failed to find while awake; and I elaborated a symbolism of natural objects that I might give myself dreams during sleep, or rather visions, for they had none of the confusions of dreams, by laying upon my pillow or beside my bed certain flowers or leaves. Even today, after twenty years, the exhalations and the messages that came to me from bits of hawthorn or some other plant seem, of all moments of my life, the happiest and the wisest. (*Myth*, p.345.)

The Stirring of the Bones concludes with a magnificent realisation of the shaping power of the period of intense visionary activity in the light of the revelations of the Automatic Script. Recalling yet again the mystical experience in Inchy Wood of July 1898, Yeats indicates the way in which such experiences were still, after more than twenty years, part of his daily thought as well as an essential element in his philosophy:

> I woke one night to find myself lying on my back with all my limbs rigid, and to hear a ceremonial measured voice, which did not seem to be mine, speaking through my lips. 'We make an image of him who sleeps', it said, 'and it is not he who sleeps, and we call it Emmanuel.'[60] After many years that thought, others often found as strangely being added to it, became the thought of the Mask, which I have used in these memoirs to explains men's characters. A few months ago at Oxford I was asking myself why it should be 'an image of him who sleeps', and took down from the shelf, not knowing what I did, Burkitt's *Early Eastern Christianity*, and opened it at random. I opened it at a Gnostic Hymn that told of a certain King's son, who, being exiled, slept in Egypt—a symbol of the natural state—and how an Angel while he slept brought him a royal mantle; and at the bottom of the page I found a footnote saying that the word mantle did not represent the meaning properly, for that which the Angel gave had the exile's own form and likeness. (*Au*, pp.378-79.)

III

Why did Yeats give up the *Notebook* record at the end of March 1901? The quarrel in the Order of the Golden Dawn had estranged Yeats from Florence Farr and Dorothea Hunter—the latter a key figure in visionary work for the Celtic Mystical Order, and women's vision was crucial. The theatre increasingly consumed him and, his own great period of visionary activity over, there might have seemed little point in seeking from others what he could not achieve himself.

Yet it remained as the book of evidence—to himself—that he had undergone a period of vision however fragmented, and was not simply dependent on the powers of others.[61] In "Spiritus Mundi", a draft of *Per Amica*, he wrote that the *Notebook* contained

> much recorded at the moment it happened, & while the memory was clear, that once I thought to publish but I am no longer of that mind. Why should I hope to convince when notably accurate and careful men have failed? I am an imaginative writer & so must appear to be of those who lose themselves in the fancy [...]. I will but say like the twelve year old boy in the Arabian Nights 'O brother I have taken stock in the desert sand and of the sayings of antiquity'.[62]

The problem for Yeats's belief in visionary experience, then, was that he was a writer. Representing experience of the supernatural to unbelievers is difficult. Affirmation by declaration proves the best accommodation of the supernatural.

I see the trajectory of Yeats's prose, then as something like this. In so far as visionary experience was concerned, "Rosa Alchemica" and the fantastic had to be written off as surely as Michael Robartes had to be killed off, and Owen Aherne's fatal book had to be burnt and its box 'flung [...] into the sea'.[63] Fantastic style was compelling but 'too elaborate, too ornamental' and embodying 'little actual circumstance, nothing natural, but always an artificial splendour'.[64] After the experience of 'The Archer Vision' in Tulira in August 1896 the triptych had to be completed, and perhaps inevitably there is some diminution of the fantastic in 'The Tables of the Law' (published in the November issue of *The Savoy*) and 'The Adoration of the Magi'.[65]

Other acts of critical judgement followed. After *The Secret Rose* and *The Tables of the Law*. |*The Adoration of the Magi* were published in 1897, Yeats sought the advice of various friends such as Robert Bridges (who disliked "Rosa Alchemica" and was 'glad that Michael Robartes is dead'),[66] and William Sharp.[67] W. T. Horton sent Yeats a copy of Edgar Allan Poe's *The Raven. The Pit and the Pendulum* with seven illustrations and a cover design by Horton.[68] On 3 September, 1899 Yeats wrote,

> I do not know why you, or indeed any body should want to illustrate Poe however. His fame always puzzles me. I have to acknowledge that, even after one allows for the difficulties of a critic who speaks a

> foregne [for 'foreign'] language, a writer who has had so much influence on Boudeleire & Villiers De L'Isle Adam must hav[e] some great merit. I admire a few lyrics of his extremely & a few pages of his prose, chiefly in his critical essays which are sometimes profound. The rest of him seems to me vulgar & commonplace, & the Pit & the Pendulum & the Raven do not seem to me to have permanent literary value of any kind. Analyse the Raven & you find that its subject is a commonplace & its execution a rythmical trick. Its rythm never lives for a moment, never once moves with an emotional life. The whole thing seems to me insincere & vulgar. Analyse the Pit & the Pendulum & you find an appeal to the nerves by taudry phisical affrightments, at least so it seems to me who am yet puzzled at the fame of such things.[69]

The stories were rewritten for *The Collected Works in Verse and Prose* (1908), after which Yeats made several notes towards the improvement of the latter two before again rewriting "The Adoration of the Magi" for *Early Poems and Stories* in 1925.[70] By the time of *Stories of Michael Robartes* (1931), Yeats has John Aherne report the views of Robartes, now restored to life.

> Robartes makes no complaint about your description of his death and says nobody would have thought the Aherne and Robartes of such fantastic stories real men but for Owen's outcry. He is however (and this I confirm from my own knowledge) bitter about your style in these stories and says that you substituted sound for sense and ornament for thought[...]. I said that you wrote in those tales, as many good writers wrote at the time over half Europe, that such prose was the equivalent of what somebody had called 'absolute poetry' and somebody else 'pure poetry'; that though it lacked speed and variety, it would have acquired both, as Elizabethan prose did after the *Arcadia*, but for the surrender everywhere to the sensational & the topical; that romance driven to its last ditch had a right to swagger. He answered that when the candle was burnt out an honest man did not pretend that grease was flame.[71]

Experience had to find a way to prevail over literary convention, especially over anything so conventionally literary as the fantastic. Yeats went much further. Speculative prose took over, even from more 'realistic' and satirical modes of fiction. *The Speckled Bird*, on which he had worked from 1896 until 1902, was strangled before it had flown. Yeats's first published reference to the *Notebook* is in 'Magic', drafted in December 1900, offered as a lecture on 4 May 1901 and published in *The Monthly Review* in September 1901. Though it includes one episode from the *Notebook* Yeats wrote, 'I have written of these breakings forth, these loosenings of the deep, with some care and some detail, but I shall keep my record shut';[72] and also, 'We who write, we who bear witness, must often hear our hearts cry out against us, complaining because of their hidden things'.[73]

Garnered folklore, the witness of others (first tried out in the six faery lore essays), became the accompaniment to self-revelation as passages of the diary were impressed into the revised *Celtic Twilight* of 1902. Learned in written testament from Swedenborg and the Cambridge Platonists, Yeats could supplement such witness in 'Swedenborg, Mediums, and the Desolate Places' and other (unpublished) occult essays before similarly buttressing his own great pre-marital testament to vision, *Per Amica Silentia Lunae*, where the evidences of the *Notebook* offered Yeats his escape from fantastic fiction into the 'mythic method' of *Per Amica Silentia Lunae*.[74] But throughout his career, experience of the supernatural remained less the irruption of the past into the present, than the present adumbrating an expanded future consciousness. For Yeats, Celtic spirituality was neither Ernest Renan's remnant culture nor a revenant disturbance. It remained an experience available only to a few, who would write a literature of—and for—the future.

NOTES

1 *The Variorum Edition of the Plays of W. B. Yeats*, ed., Russell K. Alspach assisted by Catherine C. Alspach (London &NY: Macmillan 1966), p.932. Cited from the corrected second printing of 1966. Henceforth *VPl*.
2 *The Collected Letters of W. B. Yeats, Vol. II: 1896-1900*, eds., Warwick Gould, John Kelly and Deirdre Toomey (Oxford: Clarendon Press 1997), p.63. Henceforth *CL2*.
3 *VPl*, p.932.
4 The history of the changing texts can be studied in *The Secret Rose, Stories by W. B. Yeats: A Variorum Edition*, eds., Warwick Gould, Phillip L. Marcus and Michael J. Sidnell (London: Macmillan Academic & Professional 1992) [2nd edn., rev. and enl.]. Henceforth *VSR*.
5 See Augustine Martin's two articles, '*The Secret Rose* and Yeats's Dialogue with History', *ARIEL: A Review of International English Literature*, 3:3 (July 1972), pp.91-103 and 'Apocalyptic Structure in Yeats's *Secret Rose*', *Studies* [Dublin], LXVI (Spring 1975), pp.24-34. See also John Wilson Foster, *Fictions of the Irish Literary Renaissance: A Changeling Art* (Syracuse UP 1987), pp.73-4.
6 See Linda Dowling, *Language and Decadence in the Victorian Fin de Siècle* (Princeton UP 1986), pp.20, 154-60, 169-74, and, on Yeats's stories, pp.248, 262 & ff. Michael Fixler first explored 'The Affinities between J.-K. Huysmans and the "Rosicrucian Stories" of W. B. Yeats' in *PMLA*, 74 (1959), pp.464-69; see also Marjorie Reeves and Warwick Gould, *Joachim of Fiore and the Myth of the Eternal Evangel in the Nineteenth Century* (Oxford: Clarendon Press 1987), pp.186-271.

7   *The Variorum Edition of the Poems of W. B. Yeats*, eds., Peter Allt and Russell K. Alspach (NY: Macmillan 1957), p.370. Cited from the corrected third printing of 1966. Henceforth *VP*.
8   *VP*, p.373
9   See *Autobiographies* (London: Macmillan 1955), pp.130, 302. Henceforth *Au*. See also *Letters to the New Island: A New Edition* edited by George Bornstein and Hugh Witemeyer (London: Macmillan 1989), p.53. Henceforth *LNI*.
10 Yeats himself elsewhere claimed that Villiers de l'Isle Adam 'had shaped whatever in my *Rosa Alchemica* Pater had not shaped' (*Au*, pp.320-21). For a Paterian advocate, see F. C. McGrath, '"Rosa Alchemica": Pater Scrutinized and Alchemized', *Yeats-Eliot Review*, 5 (1978), pp.13-20.
11 Winters, 'Maule's Curse, or Hawthorne and the Problem of Allegory', first collected in *Maule's Curse: Seven Studies in the History of American Obscurantism* (Norfolk, Conn.: New Directions 1938) and subsequently collected in *In Defence of Reason* (London: Routledge 1960; Denver UP 1947), pp.157-175; pp.170-2.
12 *VSR*, pp.132-36vv, 144-48vv.
13 Here Yeats is probably drawing on the experiences collected as 'The Sorcerers' in *The Celtic Twilight* (1893). See Deirdre Toomey, 'Strange Experiences in Pembroke Road', elsewhere in this volume.
14 The version quoted is that of 1897.
15 Do.
16 Todorov, *Introduction à la littérature fantastique* (Paris: Editions du Seuil 1970), p.29.
17 The famous distinction between the novel and the romance propounded by Hawthorne in the preface to *The House of the Seven Gables* (1851) draws on a tradition which reaches back to Scott and beyond.
18 For Yeats's usages of the adage see *Uncollected Prose by W. B. Yeats*, Vol. 2, eds., John P. Frayne and Colton Johnson (London: Macmillan 1975; NY: Columbia UP 1976), p.412; Henceforth *UP2*. In *Samhain* (1905) the remark is attributed to Ben Jonson: see *Explorations*, sel. Mrs W. B. Yeats (London: Macmillan 1962; NY: Macmillan 1963), p.181.
19 'It is the addition of strangeness to beauty, that constitutes the romantic character in art; and the desire of beauty being a fixed element in every artistic organisation, it is the addition of curiosity to this desire of beauty, that constitutes the romantic temper'. See *Appreciations, with an Essay on Style* (London: Macmillan 1901), p.246. Baudelaire's remark can be found in 'Exposition Universelle de 1855', in *Oeuvres Complètes* (Paris 1923), *Curiosités Esthétiques*, p.224. Yeats's admiration for Poe's essay 'The Poetic Principle' (1850) centred on Poe's notion that the poet is inspired by an 'ecstatic prescience of the glories beyond the grave' (*Collected Works* ed., J. A. Harrison [New York 1902], XIV 273-4): see *VSR*, pp.157-58; *UP 2*, p.131 and *The Speckled Bird, With Variant Versions*, ed., William H. O'Donnell (Toronto: McLelland & Stewart 1976), p.247. Henceforth *SB*. See also *CL2*, p.448 n. 6.
20 *CL2*, pp.15, 45.
21 See Ian Fletcher, 'Bedford Park, Aesthete's Elysium' in Fletcher, ed, *Romantic Mythologies* (London: Routledge & Kegan Paul 1967), pp.169-208; p.192.
22 *The Collected Poems of Lionel Johnson* ed., Ian Fletcher (New York & London: Garland Publishing, Inc. 1982), pp.34-35.

23 The review was published in *The Boston Pilot*, 1 August, 1891. See *LNI*, pp.51-22.
24 Review for the *Providence Sunday Journal*, 26 July, 1891 (*LNI*, pp.113-14).
25 Winters, *In Defence of Reason*, pp.153-54.
26 ibid., p.171.
27 ibid., p.172.
28 *CL2*, p.66, see also 'Concerning Saints and Artists', in *Essays and Introductions* (London & NY: Macmillan 1961), p.281. Henceforth *E&I*.
29 *E&I*, p.283. Ellis wrote up these experiments in a number of places including 'Phenomena of Mescal Intoxication', *The Lancet*, 5 June, 1897, 1540 & ff., and in 'Mescal: A New Artificial Paradise' (*Contemporary Review* January 1898, 130-41) in which Yeats though unnamed is described as 'interested in mystical matters, an excellent subject for visions, and very familiar with various vision-producing drugs and processes. His heart, however, is not very strong. While he obtained the visions, he found the effects of mescal on his breathing somewhat unpleasant; he much prefers hashish, though recognising that its effects are much more difficult to obtain' (p.139). A different account, however is found in 'Mescal: A Study of a Divine Plant' (*Popular Science* Monthly [May 1902] pp.52-71). See also *CL2*, 95n.
30 *Fictions of the Irish Literary Renaissance: A Changeling Art* (Syracuse UP 1987), p.78.
31 Linda Dowling also thinks that there is a thematic and stylistic *diminuendo* in the triptych which shows the narrator's increasing power over the fatality of books. 'Paterian Euphuism' would simply not have served the purposes of the last tale in the triptych which marks a return to orthodox piety on the part of the narrator. 'I no longer live an elaborate and haughty life, but seek to lose myself among the prayers and sorrows of the multitude. I pray best in poor chapels, where frieze coats brush against me as I kneel' (*VSR*, p.172). See *Language and Decadence* (Princeton UP 1986), pp.267-68. However, she is incorrect in thinking that in prose Yeats 'returned to the speaking voice of the Irish peasant' as a 'belated [...] reaction against Paterian Euphuism' (p.268). Yeats's prose style remains Paterian (e.g., in the essays of *Ideas of Good and Evil*, 1903). What he abandons is the fantastic.
32 *Au*, p.371, *Memoirs: Autobiography—First Draft* [&] *Journal* ed., Denis Donoghue (London: Macmillan 1972; NY: Macmillan 1973), p.100. Henceforth *Mem*. Sometime before mid-August 1896, Olivia Shakespear—not a member of the Golden Dawn—passed 'into a condition between meditation and trance' and 'obtained [...] sentences, unintelligible to herself' under the influence of Yeats's 'cabalistic symbols'.
33 *Au*, p.371.
34 *Mem*, pp.100-01. See also *Au*, pp.372-75 and the appendix on the Archer Vision in *CL2*, pp.658-63, from which this basic description of the event is drawn.
35 Private collection. Deirdre Toomey and I are editing it for publication, and I am very grateful to Ms Toomey for her contribution to this paper.
36 *Au*, p.378. Yeats had arrived at Coole from Dublin on 20 June, 1898 in the summer of the 1798 Centennial Celebrations. He was President of the organisation in Great Britain and had been working since February 1897, travelling, addressing large crowds, negotiating with small revolutionary factions, quelling explosive quarrels which were part of the movement,

addressing committees, political in-fighting which spanned 'some of the worst months of my life' (*Au*, p.355). He also planned the Irish Literary Theatre with Lady Gregory and Edward Martyn, successfully pressing for the change in Irish law which allowed them to mount a first season in May 1899.

37 *Ballads in Prose* (London: John Lane/The Bodley Head; Boston: Roberts Brothers 1894), pp.123-44. To end a plague and famine caused by blight, Aodh, a Prince of the O'Rourkes and Una, 'of the royal blood of Ullad', journey to the 'temple builded to the heroes of the Fianna' and the 'temples of Crom [...] the Thunderer' (p.132) on a 'shadowy island' in the Shannon (pp.132, 36). Aodh pledges to the Fianna and their gods his youth (to Diarmuid), his knowledge (to Grania), and his death (to Oisin). He pledges to other gods his hope, faith, courage, dreams, and heart (to Maive), love (to Angus), and soul (to Finn). Una gives her life to Crom, while Aodh lies 'as one who is dead' for seventy years before returning to the Temple and joining the Heroes: 'She gave: and I gave; and who shall reckon up our gifts?' (p.142).

38 See *CL2*, pp.176, 663-69; *Au*, p.254.

39 'Spiritus Mundi', National Library of Ireland (henceforth NLI) MS 3052. I am grateful to A. P. Watt on behalf of the Yeats Estate for permission to quote from this manuscript.

40 *CL2*, p. 665.

41 *Au*, p.242.

42 NLI MS 13568-9.

43 See Warwick Gould, '—The Music of Heaven—: Dorothea Hunter' in Deirdre Toomey, ed., *Yeats and Women* (London: Macmillan 1997), pp.73-134; p.98.

44 George Pollexfen also kept a *Visions* notebook (now in the collection of Mr Michael Yeats), which records his own work for the proposed Order: Yeats added some genealogies of Irish gods to it.

45 *CL2*, p.75.

46 See *The Renaissance: Studies in Art and Poetry: The 1893 Text*, ed., Donald L. Hill (California UP 1980), p.19.

47 'Spiritus Mundi', NLI, MS 3052.

48 Much of the darker personal material is expressed in this way.

49 *The Green Sheaf* (London: Elkin Mathews 1903), pp.6-7.

50 It concludes with a rhetorical question, 'Was this some echo of what the Bible has said about 'one who shall come as a thief in the night?'

51 *Mythologies* (London & New York: Macmillan 1959), p.333. Henceforth *Myth*.

52 *A Vision* (London: Macmillan 1962), p.8. Henceforth *AV*[*B*]. In 'Magic' Yeats outlined not only his belief in the 'Great Memory', but his belief that 'invisible beings, far-wandering influences, shapes that may have floated from a hermit of the wilderness' determine history and that imaginative writers once chose to act directly on the minds of others, rather than by 'paper and [...] pen', that once poetry was 'enchantment', magic (*E&I*, pp.41-43). In their use of symbols, poets and other artists are the 'successors' of magicians (*E&I*, p.49).

53 As in a vision of 27 December, 1898 which 'celticises' the vision of Eros in "Rosa Alchemica" (ll.532-88; *VSR*, pp.145-47).

54 External reasons for delay of publication (between 1893 to 1899) included the troubled love affair with Olivia Shakespear, a disorganised designer, mean and quarrelsome publishers, transatlantic printing, and the fire in the

Boston Bookbinding Company. The poems of *The Wind Among the Reeds* met with comparatively little by way of rewriting or improvement after 1899, which is not to say they were not significantly changed and reordered.
55 'Spiritus Mundi' MS (NLI MS 3052); *Au*, p.379; *Mem*, p.126; *Myth*, p.347, and *Interviews and Recollections*, ed., by E. H. Mikhail [2 vols.] (London: Macmillan 1977), p.142.
56 *Myth*, p.68.
57 Other, much later, segments of *Autobiographies* are rich in references. *Hodos Chameliontos* contains Russell's visions of 1897 as well as the Sligo visions of winter 1898-9 shared by Yeats with George Pollexfen and Mary Battle.
58 'Spiritus Mundi', NLI MS 3052.
59 '[...] and this thought came to me, as I believe, supernaturally "The love of God for every human soul is infinite for every human soul is unique; no other can satisfy the same need in God"' (*Visions* Notebook). The moment is returned to in 'Anima Mundi' section V of *Per Amica Silentia Lunae* (*Myth*, pp.347-48), clearly written with the *Notebook* beside him.
60 Cf., *Myth*, p.366. Yeats also gave this experience to Michael Hearne, the hero of *The Speckled Bird* his own experiences of summer 1898, including that the voice which spoke through his lips saying '"We make an image of him who sleeps and it is not him who sleeps, though it is like him who sleeps, and we call it Emmanuel".' (William H. O'Donnell, ed., *The Speckled Bird, with Variant Versions*, Toronto: McClelland & Stewart 1976, p.30.
61 The republication of a part of *The Stirring of the Bones* (first privately printed by T. Werner Laurie in *The Trembling of the Veil* as 'A Biographical Fragment with some notes' in October 1922) in *The Criterion* and *The Dial* in July 1923 comes at the close of George Yeats's work as a medium.
62 'Spiritus Mundi', NLI MS 3052; cf., *Myth*, p.343.
63 *VSR*, p.162v.
64 'Spiritus Mundi', NLI MS 3052. The passage prefigures Robartes' revulsion from the 'extravagant style | He had learned from Pater' in 'The Phases of the Moon' (*VP*, p.373). By 1925, Yeats was ready broadly to denounce 'that artificial, elaborate English so many of us played with in the 'nineties' which encouraged him to 'come to hate' the stories (*VSR*, p.173).
65 Bullen 'disliked' the last two stories, and 'made me leave them out' as Yeats recalled in 1925 (*VSR*, p.269), and then printed them privately. His reasons remain obscure.
66 *CL2*, p.111 & n.3.
67 'I send you [...] the little book with two stories left out of "The Secret Rose". The first story at any rate will have to be altogether rewritten. It has no atmosphere & the central argument about morels is overweighed with circumstance' (*CL2*, p.118).
68 *The Raven. The Pit and the Pendulum* (London: Leonard Smithers 1899). Yeats's copy is inscribed 'W. T. Horton | to his friend W. B. Yeats | with best wishes. | Saty. 22. 7. 99'. See Edward O'Shea, *A Descriptive Catalog of W. B. Yeats's Library* (NY & London: Garland Publishing 1985), No. 1600.
69 *CL2*, p.447. Such judgements were informed: one of Horton's drawings was 'a really admirable grotesque' (ibid). When Yeats used such terms as 'fantastic', 'allegory' or 'grotesque' he spoke as one who knew the genres

in which Poe and Hawthorne and, after them, Horton, were consciously working.
70 *VSR*, p.267.
71 *Stories of Michael Robartes and His Friends: an Extract from a Record made by his Pupils: and a Play in Prose* (Dublin: Cuala 1931), pp.25-26; cf. *AV[B]*, p.55.
72 *E&I*, p.38. The episode is 'I find in my diary of magical events for 1899 that I awoke at 3 A.M. out of a nightmare, and imagined one symbol to prevent its recurrence, and imagined another, a simple geometrical form, which calls up dreams of luxuriant vegetable life, that I might have pleasant dreams. I imagined it faintly, being very sleepy, and went to sleep. I had confused dreams which seemed to have no relation with the symbol. I awoke about eight, having for the time forgotten both nightmare and symbol. Presently I dozed off again and began half to dream and half to see, as one does between sleep and waking, enormous flowers and grapes. I awoke and recognised that what I had dreamed or seen was the kind of thing appropriate to the symbol before I remembered having used it (*E&I*, p.47). In *Memoirs* he recalled his inhibition 'I tried to describe some vision to Lady Gregory, and to my great surprise could not. I felt a difficulty in articulation and became confused. I had wanted to tell her of some beautiful sight, and could see no reason for this. I remembered then what I had read of mystics not being always [able] to speak [...].' (*Mem*, p.128.)
73 *E&I*, pp.51-52.
74 See Warwick Gould, '"A Lesson for the Circumspect": W. B. Yeats's 'Two Versions of *A Vision* and the *Arabian Nights*' in Peter L. Caracciolo, ed., *The Arabian Nights in English Literature* (London: Macmillan 1988), pp.244-80; p.245.

NIAMH: A SYMBOL OF DESIRE IN THE POETRY OF WILLIAM BUTLER YEATS

Stan Galloway

In his early poem, "The Wanderings of Oisin", William Butler Yeats borrowed the character of Niamh, the faery bride, from Irish folklore, developing her into a humanised faery character. In later poems he disregarded her humanisation, changing her into a symbol of desire. As Yeats's poetry matured, the symbol underwent a transformation, in what may be Yeats's attempt to reflect, for him, the growing impotency of the symbol.[1]

Yeats used Niamh in seven poems after "The Wanderings of Oisin". In early poems such as "The Hosting of the Sidhe" and "The Danaan Quicken Tree" she represents escape to faeryland. In "The Lover asks Forgiveness because of his Many Moods", the escape has been intellectualised to a kind of disembodied desire. Shortly after, in "Under the Moon", her character blends both physical and formless desire. Much later, "Alternative Song for the Severed Head in The King of the Great Clock Tower" provides a transition to a more detached appeal to 'heroic wantonness'.[2] The late poems, "The Circus Animals' Desertion" and "News for the Delphic Oracle", use her to represent a type of frustrated desire.

Following hard on the fervour of his first two books, Yeats's long narrative poem, "The Wanderings of Oisin", appeared in his third collection as a kind of capstone to his faery studies to that point. With the poem he included several other poems about faeries, some previously published, such as "The Stolen Child". In Yeats's poetic version of the Oisin-Niamh tale, Oisin confronts Saint Patrick with the delight of pre-Christian Ireland, a land that Oisin has missed because of, as Saint Patrick calls it, Oisin's three century 'dalliance with a demon thing' (*VP*2).[3] Oisin in relating his story, shows his great regret at having lost both Fenian Ireland and Niamh's faeryland and at being burdened with the restrictive, unmanly creeds of Saint Patrick, which leave him 'All emptied of purple hours as a beggar's cloak in the rain' (*VP*63).

In "The Wanderings of Oisin" (1889), Niamh originally enters the poem as [4]

> [...] more mild and fair
> Than doves that moaned round Eman's hall
>
> Her eyes were soft as dewdrops hanging
> Upon the grass-blades' bending tips,
> And like a sunset were her lips. (*WO*, pp.2-3)

In the 1895 edition, she enters the same scene as:

> A pearl-pale, high-born lady who rode
> On a horse with bridle of findrinny;
> And like a sunset were her lips. (p.3)

Oisin's description of her shows his attraction from the very first. Yeats takes the tale from folklore, adapting it as he sees fit, especially in framing the tale in the dialogue between Oisin and St. Patrick, but essentially following the traditional roles set for each character.

As in the folklore, Niamh interrupts the unsuccessful hunt of the Fenians to ask Oisin, one of the most noble and famous of the group, to escape with her in marriage. Oisin further describes her:

> Her hair was of a citron tincture,
> And gathered in a silver cincture;
> Down to her feet white vesture flowed
> And with the woven crimson glowed
> Of many a figured creature strange,
> And birds that on the seven seas range.
> For brooch 'twas bound with a bright sea-shell,
> And wavered like a summer rill,
> As her soft bosom rose and fell. (*WO*, p.3.)

Oisin is obviously pleased with what he sees. She offers eternal youth to him in the faeryland of Tir nan Og—though Yeats changes this from one island to a series of three islands—and together they ride her horse 'across the oily sea, / For the sparkling hooves they sank not in' (*WO*, p.6). Oisin is sad at leaving his companions, but quickly loses track of time because

> faery songs continually
> Sang Niam, and their dewy showers
> Of pensive laughter—unhuman sound –
> Lulled weariness. (*WO*, p.7.)

Niamh: A Symbol of Desire in the Poetry of William Butler Yeats

Oisin is startled then by phantom images passing them. Niamh soothes him:

> 'Fret not with speech the phantoms dread',
> Said Niam, as she laid the tip
> Of one long finger on my lip. (*WO*, p.8.)

One understands at this point that Niamh has the ability to make Oisin forget any torment and live only in pleasure, as Oisin reports they rode on 'full of loving phantasy' (*WO*, p.8).

When they reach the first island, Niamh blows upon a trumpet and they are greeted by troops of singing faeries. After a hundred years of laughter, dancing and hunting, Oisin finds a part of 'some dead warrior's broken lance' (*VP*, p.24) and pines to be away. Niamh, sensing his need, leads him to the second island.

Book 2 of the poem begins with their second ride across the sea where Oisin is again concerned by phantom images racing around them. Niamh salves his concern with singing 'of faery and man' (*VP*, p.29) from before time. Likewise she soothes the horse which is frightened as they approach the Isle of Many Fears. In *The Myth Against Myth: A Study of Imagination in Yeats's Old Age* (1972), Daniel Albright remarks on the development of Niamh's character at this point: 'It is important that Niamh sings about the coupling of mortals and immortals immediately after they see the phantoms' he says, because these images 'show the sterile consequences of trying to imitate the immortals; so Niamh must try to comfort Oisin by retreating from strict immortality into a half-human, more possible love-affair.'[5] It must have been this same kind of retreat, though, that led her to meet Oisin at the Fenian shores in the beginning.

On the second island, Oisin enters into a four-day cycle of battle and feasting. To save a chained maiden, he fights her guard-demon for a day then feasts with Niamh and the maiden for three more. After the battle, they bring him food to refresh him then they sleep together. On the first day of celebrating, Oisin describes the end of the feast:

> and on the skins supine
> Of wolves, of boreal bears, we quaffed the wine
> Brewed of the sea-gods, from huge cups that lay
> Upon the lips of sea-gods in their day,
> And on the skins of wolves and bears we slept. (*WO*, p.29.)

After the three days of feasting, the demon rises from the sea and the cycle renews. After a hundred years of this cycle, Oisin finds a beech bough, which reminds him of his father. Niamh immediately is prepared, 'Holding that horse, long not seen' (*WO*, p.32), and they depart for the Island of Forgetfulness with Niamh weeping because of her inability to satisfy Oisin's human needs.

When Book 3 begins, Niamh's remorse, by the contrast to earlier rides, is evident.

> And never a song sang Niamh, and over my finger-tips
> Came now the sliding of tears and sweeping of mist-cold hair,
> And now the warmth of sighs, and after the quiver of lips.
> (*VP*, p.47.)

When they reach the next island, they discover a squadron of giant warriors sleeping under the trees. There the supernatural bell-branch brings forgetfulness and slumber, with Niamh's head pillowed on Oisin's chest for a hundred years. A starling and the unnamed horse rouse Oisin after a century has passed. Oisin rouses Niamh and begs to return to his own people. Niamh grants him permission with one stipulation, knowing he will not abide by it. She tells him:

> Then go through the lands in the saddle and see what the mortals do,
> And softly come to your Niamh, O Oisin, weep; for if only your shoe
> Brush lightly as haymouse earth's pebbles, you will come no more to my side.
> I would die like a small withered leaf in the autumn, for breast upon breast
> We shall mingle no more. (*VP*, p.55-56)

Oisin rides away to his Ireland. There he finds no Fenians and finds himself 'shivering and lonely, and longing for Niam' (*WO*, p.49), his heart 'longing to leap like a grasshopper into her heart' (*VP*, p.60). After inadvertently touching the soil, the centuries collapse on him, leaving him 'A creeping old man, full of sleep, with the spittle on his beard never dry' (*VP*, p.60), his only pastime discussing theology with St. Patrick. Oisin's misery grows as he realises, as A. G. Stock said, that 'instead of his ever-living bride there was nothing for him but the insubstantial Christian heaven'.[6]

Some critics claim Niamh's development in the poem is sketchy. For example, Frank Kinahan thinks, 'Yeats describes her at length at the start of the poem, but after that is plainly at a loss as to what precisely to do with her'.[7] Others regard her as a stock figure of menace. Albright calls her 'a Celtic Helen of Troy',[8] dooming not ships but men. Allen R. Grossman labels her as a solitary faery 'of the Leanhuan Shee' a vampire-like creature who draws her strength from mortals,[9] much like Keats's supernatural woman in "La Belle Dame sans Merci" or the woman in the apple tree in Dante Gabriel Rossetti's "The Orchard-Pit". Some regard her as simply 'a pre-Raphaelite goddess clothed in melancholy languor'[10] or 'a fairy-lady, of enchanting loveliness [...] who happens to conceive a violent passion for the mortal hero and lures him on to the faery kingdom'.[11] Few scholars concede that Niamh is humanised.[12]

But Yeats is clear. In the poem, Niamh is the fantasy wife who makes every effort to please her husband, never nagging nor contradicting him when he is set in his way, as when Oisin wants to return to his native Ireland. She pleases Oisin's every desire, when she is able. It is her struggle with her inability, as she becomes more human in characterisation, which makes her character live in this poem. After Book 1 of the poem, Albright notes, 'Niamh is a much more tearful, feminine creature'.[13] Hazard Adams supports Albright, claiming 'the only really sentient being among the faery is Niamh'.[14] The other faeries are static. Adams contends that 'we are able to grasp the faery Niamh's feelings through Oisin's narrative. It is she who is abandoned. She is projected not as a wicked goddess but as a sensitive lover'.[15] The appeal to this is clear; Niamh is changed by the beginning of Book 3: 'her music and her laughter, the faery qualities which made her a fit princess [...] on the first island, have vanished, and she is to all intents a mortal woman',[16] Albright says. When Oisin leaves her on the Island of Forgetfulness, Niamh 'wishes to die like any mortal woman who has lost her lover'.[17]

Yeats tried to humanise other faeries in *The Wanderings of Oisin and Other Poems*, but was apparently dissatisfied with the development, for he left those poems uncollected.[18] Thuente believes 'Yeats tried unsuccessfully to impose human passions on his fairy characters' in these poems and left them behind as failures.[19] Abandoning Niamh's humanised image, Yeats uses her fantasy-fulfilment role in later poems to develop a new poetic outlook on desire.

After "The Wanderings of Oisin", Niamh returns to Yeats's poetry not as a solitary lover on a nuptial quest but as leader of, or at least spokeswoman for, the faeries. In "The Hosting of the Sidhe", she entices anyone who can hear her faery cry—'Away, come away'—to escape from his 'mortal dream' and to separate himself from 'the deed of his hand' and 'the hope of his heart' (*VP*, p.140-41). This cry is nearly identical to Niamh's earlier plea to Oisin, 'Away, away with me', (*WO*, p.5). In "Hosting", though, the plea is generalised.

The poem is not Yeats's first to develop the theme of escape to faeryland. In his first anthology, "The Stolen Child" gives much the same plea from the fairy host: 'Come away, O human child!', this time called 'To the waters and the wild / With a faery, hand in hand [...]' (*VP*, p.87). This earlier call, is quieter, lacking the energy of the faeries 'rushing 'twixt night and day' (*VP*, p.141). "The Stolen Child" is an anonymous plea like the whisper of a breeze at a twilight windowsill. "The Hosting of the Sidhe" names Caoilte and Niamh in the host and places the call in Niamh's mouth; the breeze has become an overpowering gale, catching up anyone not strong enough to actively resist. Wayne E. Hall notes that '"The Hosting of the Sidhe" opens the volume [*The Wind Among the Reeds*] with a compelling anapestic rhythm and the imagery of passion and sexual energy'.[20] Such a vivacious escape tugs at the listener with the sound of supernatural hoofbeats calling for participation. The promise of escape that she makes is not new—in addition to "The Stolen Child", the poems "To an Isle in the Water" and "The Lake Isle of Innisfree" have articulated such a departure—but this is the first time Yeats uses Niamh to symbolise that escape.

In a kind of sequel to "The Lake Isle of Innisfree", Yeats uses an enchanted berry-bearing tree as a mythic Tree of the Knowledge of Good and Evil, the first temptation mankind had to face in Eden. The quicken tree, or mountain ash, is, in folklore associated with the faeries. In one Celtic romance, Finn, Oisin's father, discovers a spectacular palace:

> As Finn and his party came nigh to the palace, they were amazed at its size and splendour; and they wondered greatly that they had never seen it before. It stood on a level green, which was surrounded by a light plantation of quicken trees, all covered with clusters of scarlet berries.[21]

Of course, the quicken trees signal that this is an area of supernatural activity, and Finn soon discovers that the palace is an illusion.

In Yeats's poem "The Danaan Quicken Tree", a first-person narrator has been caught up in

> A murmuring faery multitude,
> When flying to the heart of light
> From playing hurley in the wood. (*VP*, p.742-43.)

The faery host has carried away this mortal to Innisfree 'Where Niam heads the revelry' (*VP*, p.743). While Yeats did not actually name her as leading the faeries in "Hosting", here he names her, epitomises her as the strongest image of escape into the world of the faeries. The narrator implies that such an escape is not pure bliss, though, with his parenthetical lament, 'Ah, mournful Danaan quicken tree!' at the end of each stanza. The narrator is disappointed to realise that his tasting of the faery fruit has separated him from his beloved. Though the fruit is not so sinister as to make one pine away and die for the lack of it, as in Christina Rossetti's "Goblin Market", the berries have somehow caused a permanent separation from the human realm for the narrator. Perhaps the tree is 'mournful' because of that separation. As does Eve after tasting the forbidden Edenic fruit, the narrator implores his beloved:

> And taste with me the faeries' meat,
> For while I blamed them I could hear
> Dark Joan call the berries sweet,
> Where Niam heads the revelry. (*VP*, p.743)[22]

Niamh then becomes the image of pleasures found through eternal revelry, escape through pleasure.

The image of riotous escape associated with Niamh in "The Hosting of the Sidhe" and "The Danaan Quicken Tree" is only slightly removed from the character he developed in "The Wanderings of Oisin" a few years before. He has merely broadened her love from one mortal to all mortals. She still retains much of the character's image from the long narrative poem. In "The Lover asks Forgiveness because of his Many Moods", though, Niamh becomes a shadow of the character she had been. The Niamh of this poem, on which the critics are silent, is portrayed as hovering over the sea. It is obvious Yeats did not intend this reference to Niamh to be a physical character but rather to a symbolic image, for in these 'dove-grey faery lands' 'Queens [are] wrought with glimmering hands' (*VP*, p.162). Here the Lover 'saw young Niamh hover with love-lorn face / Above the wandering tide' as if she were the spirit of his 'words lighter than air' (*VP*, p.162). She becomes an ethereal image in the same way that his 'hopes [...] in mere hoping flicker and cease' (*VP*, p.162). The Lover, in the same context as the invocation of Niamh's image, addresses 'Winds, older than changing of night and day' (*VP*, p.162) and 'Piteous Hearts, changing till change be dead' (*VP*, p.163). The Lover in asking excuse for his changeability claims that nothing is constant because desire cannot be solidified into a constant form. Later Yeats made the comment in a letter to T. Sturge Moore: 'Sexual desire dies because every touch consumes the Myth, and yet a Myth that cannot be so consumed becomes a spectre.'[23] Though he had not yet articulated it, Niamh becomes a spectre of desire for the very reason that she can no more be consumed than the wind. This use of Niamh as an image of incorporeal desire is a shift for Yeats, a shift which once accomplished he incorporates into her role. In later poems she is symbolic of desire, a physical character unattainable.

Niamh's appeal, in Yeats's poetry, fades after the turn of the century. In "Under the Moon" the narrator begins: 'I have no happiness in dreaming of Brycelinde' (*VP*, p.209), the traditional home of Merlin, the Celtic wizard. In effect, he says that the magic is gone. The beauty is still there in 'queens like Branwen and Guinevere; / And Niamh and Laban and Fand, who could change to an otter or fawn' (*VP*, p.209); but such legendary beauty lacks the pull of reality: 'To dream of women whose beauty was folded in dismay, / Even in an old story, is a burden not to be borne' (*VP*, p.210). Yeats uses Niamh as the literal queen of Tir nan Og in his catalogue of beautiful women; he also provides an image of incorporeal deception through the shape-shifting ability he gives these queens. Though Yeats did not use a shape-shifting character in the Niamh of "The Wanderings of Oisin"— he reserved that for the demon of Book 2—he did acknowledge 'a Galway tale that tells how Niamh [...] came to Oisin as a deer'.[24]

The ability for beauty to change leaves the narrator 'no happiness' (*VP*, p.209). Peter Alderson Smith concludes that 'the dreams of fairyland that have sustained Yeats's poetry hitherto have now betrayed him'.[25] The poem seems to say he is done with all the unfulfilled expectations of these fantasies.

As if in resolve not to enter that dangerously disappointing realm, Yeats left Niamh out of his new poetry for the next thirty years. Though he obviously considered her role during his copious revisions, it was not until his retrospective poetry, what Albright calls 'a genre which is almost uniquely Yeatsian [...] the summing-up poem',[26] that her image returned. The 'summing-up poem' 'revives the *dramatis personae*, the situations and themes of the poet's previous works, as the poet continually tries to redefine, clarify, and reinterpret his own mythology, tries to subsume his myths into more inclusive frameworks'.[27] In the reinterpretation, Yeats's conception of Niamh has faded with a loss of power and clarity.

Niamh: A Symbol of Desire in the Poetry of William Butler Yeats

"Alternative Song for the Severed Head in The King of the Great Clock Tower" is the earliest of these summing-up poems to include Niamh. Yeats gives a 'roll call' of characters which he has previously borrowed from Irish folklore.[28] Niamh is placed between Cuchulain who 'fought night long with the foam' (*VP*, p.549) in "Cuchulain's Fight with the Sea" and an unnamed 'lad and lass', most likely representing Naoise and Deirdre in Yeats's play *Deirdre*.[29] Eight characters meet 'Out of [...] Knocknarea' and 'turn from Rosses' crawling tide' to meet 'upon the mountain-side' (*VP*, p.549). This meeting is reminiscent geographically of two early poems, "The Hosting of the Sidhe" where 'The host is riding from Knocknarea' (*VP*, p.140) and "The Stolen Child" where the faeries' revelry is placed near Rosses (*VP*, p.87). Though Niamh is the only faery, the entire scene places the folklore characters into the faery realm as well.

While the early short poems of faeryland invite or compel the reader to join the faeries, "Alternative Song for the Severed Head in The King of the Great Clock Tower" makes no such invitation. The narrator is compelled only to ask, 'What brought them there so far from their home?' (*VP*, p.549). His answer, 'heroic wantonness' (*VP*, p.550), marks a quality of life that Yeats yearned to have, to be able to boldly act without regard to circumstances, but was unable to attain. Yeats prayed, in "A Prayer for Old Age", that he would have the 'heroic wantonness' to 'seem, though [he] die old, / A foolish, passionate man' (*VP*, p.553). Niamh represents for him the 'heroic wantonness' that is now, and has been always, just beyond his grasp.[30]

It seems more than coincidental that in the first of "Two Songs Rewritten for the Tune's Sake", which immediately follows "Alternative Song", the narrator cries out in distress: 'My Paistin Finn is my sole desire, / And I am shrunken to skin and bone' (*VP*, p.550). One critic points out that 'Paistin Finn' 'may be a popularised version of a song from the Ossianic cycle',[31] a collection of stories related to Oisin and Niamh. This becomes even more probable when observing one revised version, which begins, 'That blonde girl there is my heart's desire'.[32] Niamh is, according to legend, blonde, calling herself 'Golden-headed Niamh', 'Niamh of the Golden Head', or 'Niam of the Golden Hair', in various translations.[33] The 'heroic wantonness' of the preceding poem, then, is here, by the inferred Niamh, his 'sole desire' (*VP*, p.550). One begins to detect resentment building between Yeats and all that Niamh represents, a grudge that builds in the final two poems under consideration.

In "The Circus Animals' Desertion" Yeats summarises his early work, beginning with "The Wanderings of Oisin", calling the islands of the faeryland allegories of 'Vain gaiety, vain battle, vain repose' (*VP*, p.629). Though he does not name Niamh in the poem, she is implied in the description of 'that sea-rider Oisin led by the nose' and the later references to 'his faery bride' (*VP*, p.629). Oisin's willingness to follow Niamh in "The Wanderings of Oisin" is clear enough. He does not follow her like some barnyard animal. Oisin admits to Patrick, 'There was no limb of mine but fell / Into a desperate gulph of love!' (*VP*, p.7), and after his declarations of love for her he mounted the horse, sitting in front of her, refusing to hear his comrades' plea for him to stay.[34] A few years later, Yeats continued to portray such a bond of love for them in his play, *The Countess Cathleen*. In some versions of the play, old Oona recounts:

> See you where Oisin and young Niamh ride
> Wrapped in each other's arms, and where the Fenians
> Follow their hounds along the fields of tapestry.[35]

The change in Niamh's image, then, seems to come from the narrator of the later poem who admits to an 'embittered heart' (*VP*, p.629). He views the cruel entrapment as a snare because he himself was 'starved for the bosom of [Oisin's] faery bride' (*VP*, p.629). The ethereal quality established in "The Lover asks Forgiveness because of his Many Moods" cannot be ignored. The dictum at the end of "Under the Moon" must be reinterpreted: the 'burden not to be borne' (*VP*, p.210) is no longer an insubstantial annoyance that can be ignored—the burden is still firmly in place, too heavy to carry. Albright makes the biographical assertion: 'The gaiety, the battle, and the repose were vain, soured, because Yeats the man could not attain the supernatural consummation he longed for, the consummation which he tried in vain to project onto Oisin' (*VP*, p.160). This is further demonstrated in "News for the Delphic Oracle".

Yeats had commented, in the notes to his play, *The Resurrection*, that early in his career he found it difficult 'to refrain from pointing out that Oisin after old age, its illumination half accepted, half rejected, would pass in death over another sea to another island' (*Plays*, p.932). "News for the Delphic Oracle" seems to take the early impulse and, for Yeats, shape the proper end for Oisin.

In "News for the Delphic Oracle" Yeats paints a word picture illustrating the reason the burden of illicit desire cannot be carried.

Here, with the same bitterness shown in "The Circus Animals' Desertion", Niamh is named 'Man-picker' (*VP*, p.611). While the term can be construed neutrally, after all she did come to the Fenian shore to choose Oisin above all others, the negative connotation as in 'fruit picker' is more likely. In the folktale, Niamh has picked the jewel of Fenian society—he represents:

> [...] all that wisdom and the fame
> Of battles broken by his hands,
> Of stories builded by his words
> That are like coloured Asian birds
> At evening in their rainless lands (*VP*, p.7)

— and removed him from mortal circles. In "News for the Delphic Oracle", too, Niamh has kept him from human interaction in a kind of pagan paradise.

Yeats has finally gotten his physical and incorporeal role to work together. He portrays her, here, as a physical being but as incapable of action as if she were simply the spirit of desire. In this place:

> [...] the great water sighed for love,
> And the wind sighed too.
> Man-picker Niamh leant and sighed
> By Oisin on the grass. (VP, p.611)

This sighing has caused varied critical impressions. Contrary to Richard Ellmann's thought that these are 'too pure lovers, caught up in mutual contemplation when they might have embraced' and thus become 'fitting companions for the thoughtful philosophers and fitting denizens of a heaven of such rarefied love',[36] contrary to F. A. C. Wilson's claim that they are sighing in Platonic contentment,[37] contrary to John Unterecker's discussion which says the sighing is but a prelude to joining the 'nymphs and satyrs [who] / Copulate in the foam' (*VP*, p.612),[38] Niamh and Oisin are suspended in frustrated desire, like the characters imaged on Keats's Grecian Urn. This is neither intellectual heaven nor prelude to pagan orgy. This is a pagan hell as Bosch would have painted it. From the beginning of his poetry, Yeats equated: 'God is joy and joy is God' (*VP*, p.20). Here the two are separated from joy and thus from God. The sigh should be seen as destructive, as in the end of Book 1 of "The Wanderings of Oisin" when God's sigh signals the end of the world (*VP*, p.28). On the first island, the Isle of Dancing, Niamh and Oisin lived in a state of continual gratification, a state that, by its very nature, cannot produce desire. There, Oisin received a kind of satisfaction that the narrator of "The Circus Animals' Desertion" begrudges him. The narrator, here, reverses Oisin's position to align him with the image of the never-satisfying Niamh he had come to see. Now as Pan's 'intolerable music falls' all around them and as 'nymphs and satyrs / Copulate in the foam' (*VP*, p.612), Niamh and Oisin are held in stasis, ever desiring gratification, seeing others in abandoned fulfilment, never reducing their own pent desire. Albright may have understood this when he made the paradoxical claim that 'the codgers are in a state of post-coital depression associated with no act of coitus'.[39] He further explains 'that the paradise [in "News for the Delphic Oracle"] is Oisin's first island turned inside-out, a prolongated satiation instead of a prolongated coitus which never satiates'.[40] On the contrary, the poem seems to be filled not with sighs of satiation but of frustration, the frustrated desire foisted on the scene by a narrator who seems set on punishing Niamh for not fulfilling his own desire after her earlier invitation, 'Away, come away' (*VP*, p.140).

Albright, one of few critics to note Niamh's crucial role, saw these final poems, "The Circus Animals' Desertion" and "News for the Delphic Oracle" as Yeats's final synthesis of Niamh's character. He gives scope to Yeats's poetry: 'Yeats does not make anything of Niamh's humanisation in "The Wanderings of Oisin"; it is only a minor theme which required decades of imaginative thought to find its resolution' (*VP*, p.88). That Yeats did not abandon Niamh to the early poetry shows that her image remained powerful for him. The fantasy woman of "The Wanderings of Oisin", he discovered was not real, no matter how hard he tried to make her so. Adams shows this: 'the land of faery is escapist, passive, and artificial in its expressions of desire, therefore negating the real' (*VP*, p.35). He claims that Niamh, though, transcends this negation in Yeats's own life: 'The true object of desire, Niamh, exceeds her false world and threatens [...] to break into real life as the beloved of later poems, finally named Maud Gonne' (Adams 35).[41] Though Yeats's portrayal of Niamh bears a long silence beginning nearly with Maud Gonne's marriage, equating Niamh and Maud Gonne may be hasty.

Regardless—whether a pleasant fantasy, a call to escape, an incorporeal beckoning, a beauty 'not to be borne' (*VP*, p.210), or the inverted desire-in-limbo—Niamh's image as a woman of desire never died in Yeats's poetry. Though he may have tried to punish her in the end, he could not outlive her haunting call.

NOTES

1. Yeats's frequent revisions left many spelling variants; I have adopted that of *The Variorum Edition of the Poems of W. B. Yeats* in most cases. For a discussion of Yeats's erratic spelling, see Hugh Kenner, *A Colder Eye: The Modern Irish Writers* (NY: Knopf 1983), p.86.
2. Peter Allt and Russell K. Alspach, eds., *The Variorum Edition of the Poems of W. B. Yeats* (NY: Macmillan 1965), p.550. Henceforth *VP*. When quoting from texts noted as variants in this edition, I have gone to the original to provide a clearer source for reading. This is especially so for *The Wanderings of Oisin*, which underwent its most radical changes between 1889 and 1895.
3. In the first edition, Saint Patrick accused Oisin of having been 'Trapped of an amorous demon thing' (*The Wanderings of Oisin and Other Poems*, 1889, p.1), coinciding with the full title which Yeats abandoned after the first edition: 'The Wanderings of Oisin / and / How a Demon Trapped Him'; the revision, of course, places the responsibility more fully on Oisin than Niamh.
4. *The Wanderings of Oisin and Other Poems* (London: Macmillan 1889); all further references to this edition marked *WO*.
5. Daniel Albright, *The Myth Against Myth: A Study of Yeats's Imagination in Old Age* (OUP 1972), p.80.
6. Stock, *W. B. Yeats: His Poetry and Thought* (Cambridge UP 1961), p.18.
7. Kinahan, *Yeats, Folklore, and Occultism: Contexts of the Early Work and Thought* (Boston: Unwin Hyman 1988), p.220.
8. Albright, op. cit. (1972)
9. Grossman, *Poetic Knowledge in the Early Years: A Study of "The Wind Among the Reeds"* (Virginia of 1969), p.38.
10. Kinahan, op. cit. (1988), p.20.
11. Rama Nand Rai, *W. B. Yeats: Poetic Theory and Practice* (Salzburg, Austria: Institut fur Anglistik und Amerikanistik 1983), p.52.
12. Notable exceptions are Hazard Adams in *The Book of Yeats's Poems* (Florida State UP 1990), and Daniel Albright (op. cit., 1988).
13. Albright, op. cit. (1988), p.87.
14. Adams, op. cit. (1990), p.33.
15. idem.
16. ibid., p.88.
17. Albright, op. cit. (1988), p.88.
18. See, in particular, "The Fairy Pedant", "A Lover's Quarrel among the Fairies", and "The Priest and the Fairy" (poems l, v, and w in the *Variorum* edition).
19. Mary Helen Thuente, *W. B. Yeats and Irish Folklore* (Totowa, NJ: Barnes & Noble 1981), p.102.
20. Hall, *Shadow Heroes: Irish Literature of the 1890s* (Syracuse UP 1980), p.190.
21. P. W. Joyce, trans., *Old Celtic Romances* [2nd edn.] (NY: Longmans, Green 1901), p.190.
22. Yeats notes, 'The Dark Joan mentioned in the last verse is a famous faery who often goes about the roads disguised as a clutch of chickens. Niam is the famous and beautiful faery who carried Oisin into Faeryland.' (*VP*, p.742n).

23 See Ursula Bridge, ed., *W. B. Yeats and T. Sturge Moore, Their Correspondence 1901-37* (OUP 1953), p.154.
24 *Essays and Introductions* (NY: Macmillan 1961), p.90.
25 Peter Alderson Smith, *W. B. Yeats and the Tribes of Danu: Three Views of Ireland's Fairies* (Totowa, NJ: Barnes & Noble 1987), p.269.
26 Albright, op. cit. (1972), p.59.
27 idem.
28 Richard F. Peterson, *William Butler Yeats* (Boston: Twayne 1982), p.160; John Unterecker, *A Reader's Guide to William Butler Yeats* (NY: Octagon 1977), p.245.
29 Another possible identity for this couple might be the witch and 'Father Wrinkles' (*VP*, p.721) who also play chess in preparation for death in "Time and the Witch Vivien", which immediately follows "The Wanderings of Oisin" in *The Wanderings of Oisin and Other Poems* (1889).
30 This 'heroic wantonness' is given additional importance from the chess players who follow Niamh in the catalogue of characters. Naoise and Deirdre attempt to play chess as if nothing were amiss as they wait their coming doom. Naoise recounts how 'Lugaidh Redstripe and that wife of his / [...] Played at the chess upon the night they died'. (*Variorum Edition of the Plays of W. B. Yeats*, 1966, p.356.) Naoise later amplifies his reference:

> They knew that there was nothing that could save them,
> And so played chess as they had any night
> For years, and waited for the stroke of sword. (ibid., p.373.)

Such nonchalance in the face of death seems the epitome of 'heroic wantonness' for Yeats.
31 A. Norman Jeffares, *A New Commentary on the Poems of W.B. Yeats* (Stanford UP 1984), p.348.
32 Yeats, *A Full Moon in March* (London: Macmillan 1935), p.54
33 Respectively in John O'Daly, ed., *Transactions of the Ossianic Society* [Vol. 4] (Dublin 1859; rep. NY: Johnson 1972), p.239; Lady Augusta Gregory, *Gods and Fighting Men* (London: John Murray 1901; rep. 1926), p.431; and P. W. Joyce, op. cit. (1901), p.386.
34 How else could they ride with her 'triumphing arms' wound around him (9)?
35 Russell K. Alspach, ed., *The Variorum Edition of the Plays of W. B. Yeats* (NY: Macmillan 1966), p.53n.
36 Ellmann, *The Identity of Yeats* (OUP 1964), p.284.
37 F. A. C. Wilson, *W. B. Yeats and Tradition* (London: Gollancz 1958), p.219.
38 Unterecker, op. cit. (1977), pp.281-82
39 Albright, op. cit. (1972), p.118.
40 idem.
41 John Unterecker and Peter Ure also identify Niamh with Maud Gonne. See Unterecker op. cit. (1977), pp.288-89, and Ure, *Yeats* (Totowa, NJ: Barnes & Noble 1963), pp.24-25.

adjective was probably intended by Yeats to denote the natively fecund kind of darkness peculiar to the Irish Heroic d as distinct from a kind which is merely 'formless' and uctive associated with the Dark Ages.

or Yeats, Irish life had a psychic and a literary value somewhat at ngent to the experience of the majority: he could celebrate things they were generally inclined to feel ashamed of at that period, as *Playboy* riot of 1907 tended to show. To him it did not matter ch, perhaps, that the existence of a rich reservoir of myth and klore such as the literary *élite* could draw on for their own creative rposes might simultaneously spell a perpetuation of superstitious rrors for the ordinary population of what James Joyce—in youthful isparagement of his own country—called a 'benighted island' and 'an after-thought of Europe.'[6] On one occasion, Yeats was confronted by a *Cork Examiner* editorial drawing attention to the discrepancy between the fairy faith cultivated by his followers in the Celtic Twilight and the tragic ignorance that caused a peasant woman to be burnt to death by her husband in the belief she was a fairy changeling.[7] In *Finnegans Wake* Joyce was eventually to satirise the hermetic bent of Yeats's brand of folklore as 'cultic twalette' in a memorable pun;[8] yet, from earliest days in Dublin, he had always been apt to see the superstitious inclinations of that movement as ancillary to the work of religion in repressing intellectual freedom and deferring the moment when the 'soul is born' in Ireland—a 'batlike soul waking to the consciousness of itself in darkness and secrecy and loneliness,' as the *Portrait* tells us.[9] In an attitude pointedly at odds with Yeats's folkloric attachment to the peasant, Joyce makes Stephen say, 'I fear him. I fear his redrimmed horny eyes', and, 'It is with him I must struggle all through this night till day come, till he or I lie dead, gripping him by the sinewy throat [...].'[10]

For Yeats the Irish peasant was a vehicle, however unlikely, of a brand of transcendent thought in some relation to the highest traditions of Aryan philosophy: 'If Lady Gregory had not said when we passed an old man in the woods, "That man may know the secret of the ages", I might never have talked with Shri Purohit Swāmi or made him translate his Master's travels in Tibet'.[11] For Joyce, he was the helot of Irish Catholicism—the worst case of the supine intellectual culture exemplified by his fellow-student at the Royal University amongst whom he himself stood out as a self-confessed agnostic. Joyce was in some regards deeply superstitious and not devoid of mystical concerns;

'We Irish' is a proprietary-sounding phrase borrowed, of course, fr[om] the Anglo-Irish philosopher George Berkeley—a connection unlike[ly] to endear it boundlessly to a modern Irish audience.[3] In Yeats's lexico[n] it collocates with 'Irishry', a haughty term likewise derived from Anglo-Irish usage and used by him to describe that in Irish tradition which he loved but which the majority were apt to regard as a mark of colonial subjection.[4] Nor is 'filthy modern tide' much in favour as a popular epithet in these days of Celtic Tigerism—though the leaders of pre-Whitaker Ireland might have found a way to relish it as fending off invidious comparisons with neighbouring Britain (or even neighbouring Ulster), little as they liked the poet in his own person.[5] Nor, finally, are Irish people of today apt to respond very warmly to the well-made phrase about 'our proper dark', with its dubious allusion to the native capacity for ratiocination. Yeats was certainly in earnest in preferring the supernatural after-glow of pagan Ireland (*aka* 'the Celtic Twilight') to the banalities of industrialism and democracy, but it is hard to avoid detecting a hint of a malice in his choice of adjective. Nobly archaic as it may sound, 'proper' seems to strike an ambiguous note as signifying *all that we are fit for* as well as *what is intrinsically our own*. In fact yet whether his conception of the 'soul'—which so much preoccupies Stephen Dedalus—refers to a supernatural entity or a purely formal one remains (oddly enough), a largely unexamined question. Although a decided Aristotelian, Joyce has never yet been called a materialist, cultural or otherwise. Perhaps, he ought to be, since *A Portrait of the Artist as a Young Man* (1916), was carefully constructed to chart the growth of what he insistently calls his 'soul'—some one-hundred-and-sixty times in the course of the novel—in terms of its structural rather than its conventionally moral development.[12] What is notable about its use in Chapter Five of *A Portrait* is that it is purged of the confessional significance attaching to it in the paranoiac 'hell-fire' section of the novel, thus marking a liberation from the less sophisticated and more oppressive meaning inherited from Catholicism. Stephen's parting (and best-known) allusion to the 'smithy of [his] soul' deploys an utterly secular sense of the word, corresponding to the term 'entelechy' that features so prominently among his 'rare thoughts' in *Ulysses*.[13] Thenceforth 'soul', for Joyce, meant the 'whatness' or 'formulable essence' of any 'ensouled' thing, to quote the terms that he inscribed in his 1904 'Paris Notebook'.[14]

These are ingenious and perhaps fanciful metaphysics and certainly remote from the ordinary conception of Joyce as a realist author, yet there is little room for doubting that he intended his early reflections on 'aesthetics' to serve both as an epistemological platform for his subsequent writing and as the foundation of a secular psychology for his countrymen—replacing the confessional psychology that enslaved them.[15] In this way he meant to intervene in the social and cultural life of the Irish majority, bringing spiritual enlightenment as he understood it in terms of the literary tradition—while contesting the right of the Catholic clergy to do so. Yet even if Joyce is closer to the real temper of modern Ireland than Yeats (as Seamus Deane and others have averred),[16] Yeats's anomalous reference to 'our proper dark' gives a name to something that is nevertheless central to the identity of the modern nation. By the same token, it happens to be the case that Yeats contributed more to the cultural formation of that nation through the revivalist project that he sponsored—a project aiming to make the country not merely a 'Nation Once Again' but a nation reinvested with its ancient myths and legends together with the anti-modern spirit deemed intrinsic to them. Of course he did not succeed as he would have wished. Yeats came to believe that Irish Catholicism—which he saw as having 'sprung from the aspidistra and not from the root of

Jesse'[17]—had hampered that kind of reappropriation, but he also chose to believe that Pearse, MacDonagh, and Connolly would have attempted it in full measure had they not been executed in 1916.[18] They, after all, were part of 'our proper dark' in his mythology. For Joyce, somewhat to the contrary, the atavistic inclination of the Irish revolutionaries was all part of what he called 'the old pap of racial hatred'.[19]

It was the astonishing persistence of supernatural and fantastic *mythemes* in late nineteenth-century rural Ireland that made possible the literary revival and seemed, indeed, to confer on the island its distinctive character as the last bastion in Europe where the rule of merchantilism and mass society might be thought to have made no headway. Irish historians have of course no trouble nowadays in showing that the tenant farmer—who appeared to the Anglo-Irish landlord in the guise of 'Irish peasant'—was perfectly pragmatic and even innovative in his relation to land-usage, market adaptation, and so forth; yet the culture remained by British and continental standards perceptibly backward, especially in its adherence to what Lady Wilde characterised in her famous title as *Ancient Legends, Mystic Charms and Superstitions of Ireland* (1887). In the 1860s the persistence of such a legacy had provided Matthew Arnold with grounds for his famous assertion that the Celtic imagination chafes against the 'despotism of fact'—by which, perhaps, he meant the world defined by the Protestant Reformation.[20] In our own day Irish critics have strenuously repudiated this formulation, however well-intentioned it may have been on Arnold's part: the conception of Ireland as an emotional rather than a thinking being is clearly the prologue to its feminisation and hence an adjunct of colonial domination—and Arnold, in fact, explicitly proclaimed the Celtic spirit to be feminine.[21] The 'Union of Hearts', so conceived was, of course, a political marriage under the old rules which made a chattel of the woman.[22] On this point post-colonialism and feminism perfectly concur.

In some quarters postcolonial reactions to the insulting implications of a pseudo-Celtic propaganda with its romantic claim that the Irish are addicted to the irrational have gone very far indeed; so far that the occurrence of supernatural themes in works of nineteenth- and early twentieth-century Irish writers is seen as the product of colonialism in itself, whether in its character as a weapon or a wound. Thus, according to one commentator, a 'focus on the inner world' producing 'fantasy, magical thinking, superstition, and creativity' is 'associated with loss of pride and self confidence, shame, worthlessness, and self-hatred'—all being seen as symptoms of colonial oppression.[23] Yet, satisfactory as this may seem from the standpoint of the clinical psychologist, it is unlikely to meet with general assent among the large class of Irish literary critics for whom fantasy and magical thinking retain their interest as aspects of Irish culture of much more ancient origin and much greater present value than this diagnostic sketch suggests—a viewpoint that several essays in this collection such as those by Csilla Bertha and Donald Morse eminently illustrate.

Having survived the socio-political depredations of the second millennium, it is not improbable that Irish cultural holdings in the supernatural and the fantastic will persist well into the third—at least in the character of a recurrent *topos* if not actually a corpus of beliefs. Recent plays by Brian Friel, Vincent Woods, Sebastian Barry and Conor MacPherson, as well as novels by Patrick McCabe and others all suggest that the supernatural motifs are not about to be dispensed with in Irish writing, even if their secular status as psychological phenomena is clearly indicated also. Where else, in modern European drama, has the stage been visited so frequently by ghosts and revenants as in Barry's *Steward of Christendom* and MacPherson's play *The Weir?*— whether these be regarding as expressions of true credulity or astute recyclings of supernatural ingredients in the spirit of theatrical post-modernism. (The apparently vacuous allusion to a phrase from Lucky's speech in *Waiting for Godot* as a title for Martin McDonagh's *Skull in Connemara* provides a test-case of this phenomenon.)

How far the persistence of the supernatural and the fantastic in such writings is an imaginative necessity or a self-conscious ploy is of course related to the thorny question of the progress of modernism and post-modernism in the intellectual life of Ireland. Have we genuinely participated in either of these movements to date, or shared in the climate of religious apostasy and agnosticism that underpins them (even when they are in reaction to it)? Some think not—though the Irish modernism of Thomas MacGreevy and Denis Devlin has its proponents.[24] Joyce is of course a modernist, but it may be that he arrived there accidentally by postcolonial routes; and in any case he is so much the Irish artist in exile that he barely impinged upon his Irish contemporaries. Yeats's tacit involvement with modernism is of course a hypothetical question since he would be the last to admit any such affinities, though we are entitled to ask it nevertheless.[25]

The grand historical narrative of Irish literary supernaturalism is plain enough. It is not only that Ireland was never conquered by the Romans and that St. Patrick in the fifth was obliged to reach an accommodation with the highly-institutionalised culture of the Druids, nor even that the eighteenth-century *Aufklarung* gave Ireland something of a go-by; we laboured strenuously during much of the nineteenth and twentieth centuries to build up a distinctive self-image of our national culture that takes these intellectual *lacunae* as defining elements—or, rather, fills them with the stuff of myth and folklore which fully-romanised, duly reformed and ultimately enlightened European cultures have tended to *dis*claim as parts of their national heritage, and to extirpate from their social life as far as possible. To a great extent Irish literature in the English language—almost to the extent that it is distinct from any other—is all about the inherence of supernatural and fantastic elements in an imaginative repertoire derived from an earlier written and oral 'literature', and brought forward from thence as viable material for cultural production under the aegis of two great periods of revivalism.

Whether we look to the eighteenth-century Celtic revival instigated by indignant reactions to the fraudulent pretensions of James MacPherson, or to the late-nineteenth century Gaelic revival which so readily combined with the movement for political separation from Britain, we appreciate that the presence of the fantastic and the intrusion of the supernatural are just those things which mark out the intellectual project of the authors as characteristically Irish. In the twentieth-century revolutionary period it was perhaps inevitable that the strengthening of national identity should have been accompanied by a confirmation of the intellectual habits of fideism—belief both in the cathetical doctrines of Irish Roman Catholicism (seen as a defining mark of Irishness by the great majority)[26] and in the non-cathetical and folkloric lore of native Ireland (often seen as a form of cultural patriotism). That Patrick Pearse could enact in his own person both the sacrifice of the Christian saviour on Golgotha and the last fight of Cuchulain involves a synthesis of literary themes and imaginative ideals that could only have been effected in the white heat of enthusiastic credence. As Yeats put it, 'in the imagination of Pearse and his fellow soldiers[,] the Sacrifice of the Mass had found the Red Branch in the tapestry.'[27] Perhaps, then, the intellectual fact of greatest importance in twentieth-century Ireland has not been this or that partisan conviction so much as the universal habit of believing.

"Our Proper Dark": A Chapter of Conclusions

Whether or not Irish history has been a nightmare, it is certainly one from which we have recently awoken. Probably no one could sleep through the amount of noise now percolating through the airwaves—a surprising amount of it currently about Ireland. Urgings to *deconstruct*, or at least *reconstruct* Irish fideism have now been heard in every fissure of Irish society, even if some elements seem unwilling or unable to abandon ancient loyalties of one kind or another (sometimes with tragic consequences for themselves and others). In such a climate, it would take a very special degree of inconscience to sustain the earlier degree of militant insularity so characteristic of Irish cultural nationalism in its hey-day, without toppling over into fakery and narcissism. It is likely, in any case, that the patterns of belief required to moor a culture that has traditionally made so much use of the supernatural and the fantastic have been fatally disrupted by the depopulation of rural and the growth of urban areas—or only subsist patchily as simulacra self-consciously enacted in interstices between international media events and the work-world agendas of the late-capitalist society.

To what extent that revival was itself imbued with an atmosphere of fakery and wishful thinking is an difficult question, involving a specialised—perhaps too specialised—brand of criticism taking the linguistic traces of religious and mythopoeic *epistemes* as its primary subject-matter. Yeats's radically sceptical conception that

> Death and life were not
> Till man made up the whole,
> Made lock, stock and barrel
> Out of his bitter soul [...][28]

—in a sense quite neighbourly to Joyce's post-Catholic thoughts on standing of a Church 'ineluctably constructed upon the incertitude of the void'[29]—requires some acknowledgement of the premises of agnosticism for its most effective reading. Indeed, the 'proper dark' of "The Statues", instead of referring finally to the nacreous illuminations of druidical lore may signify a climate of mind in which the clouds of unknowing gather ever closer 'among the deepening shades'.[30] To this subject we must inevitably return since it concerns the question, what share had the Irish intelligentsia in modern critical thought down to our own time.

Nineteenth-century Irish and Anglo-Irish writers knew that, in regard to the literary marketplace, the hallmark of their island culture was its contiguity to the primitive sources of folkloric culture as well as the comic resources of life on a colonial periphery marked by imperfect assimilation of the metropolitan language. Yeats knew it also, and though he was glad to escape the humorous burden of Irish nineteenth-century writing,[31] there is an undeniable element of truth in John Frayne's assertion that, while the poet 'did not have to use these [Irish] myths in his poetry' since they were not in fact 'an essential part of his culture or upbringing', he *did* however need them as 'an independent body of undeveloped myth close to English and Irish experience yet sufficiently strange to his contemporary readers so as to seem novel and original'.[32] In other words, he needed them to play the game of English poetry most effectively at the period in which he played it. Yeats himself may have intended to concede as much when he said, in his "General Introduction", 'I am no Nationalist, except in Ireland for passing reasons'—though he also spoke therein of the way in which the English and the Irish components in his personality created a dynamic tension of the most intimate emotional kind: 'my hatred tortures me with love, my love with hatred.'[33] This represents a complex state of postcolonial self-knowledge, and in the midst of it one of the things he seemed to know was that the separatism in culture as in politics did not necessarily preclude the attainment of great distinction in English letters precisely by annexing what he called 'the great tapestry' of Irish history and legend and using it as a vehicle for the most advanced philosophical poetry in the English language.[34]

Something of the same sort of knowledge, shorn of irredentist wishes, subsisted in the minds of other Anglo-Irish writers. For the most part they recognised that the very outlandishness of Irish material provided them with their market-niche, though often with misgivings coloured by the equal recognition that they were thereby prone to sequestration in a severely restricted quarter of the literary globe. Charles Robert Maturin prefaced his *Milesian Chief* (1812) with the remark:

> I have chosen my own country for the scene, because I believe it is the only country on earth, where [...] the extremes of refinement and barbarism are united, and the most wild and incredible situations of romantic story are hourly passing before modern eyes.[35]

—and it is reasonable to infer that he knew the value of these things in a culture with an appetite for the sensational, but also that he was genuinely affected by the un-English scenes and passions he attested to.

There is room here to ask why an English yard-stick was in use and certainly the answer has to do with contemporary British rule in Ireland; but it should be noted that his express comparison is not with England so much as *every* country and that the possessive adjective leaves no doubt as to where he thought that he was actually living.

Maturin's mental character was marked by strong religious belief, Calvinist in tendency and markedly anti-Catholic in temper. There is an account of him in the footnotes of Hardiman's *Irish Minstrelsy* (1831) to the effect that he

> died with a broken heart, after having been made the dupe of a party of religious bigots in Dublin, who, with all the bitterness of sectarian zeal, prevailed on him to preach a series of shallow 'Sermons against popery', for which he was laughed at by many, and pitied by all.[36]

Hardiman's purpose is uncertain, but probably he means at once to shame the Protestants and to rescue Maturin's fame as an Irish writer. In the following remarks he narrates that Walter Scott was horrified to find how Maturin's widow was neglected by his supposed friends—a further blot on the social record of the Protestant community. As to his account of Maturin's motivation in writing the *Five Sermons on the Errors of the Roman Catholic Church* (1824)—which incidentally went to a second edition in 1826—this has neither been asserted nor contested by other commentators. Strongly partisan religious convictions, at any rate, make an unsurprising ingredient in the *recipé* of Irish Protestant Gothic, or indeed contemporary Anglo-Irish letters in the period of Catholic Emancipation.

When Sheridan Le Fanu embarks on a profession about the fundamentally metaphysical character of existence at the beginning of "Green Tea", it is unlikely that he is merely furnishing such ideas for the delectation of a jaded British audience: 'I may remark [that] I believe the entire natural world is but the ultimate expression of that spiritual world from which, and in which alone, it has its life.' And likewise when, in 1901 Yeats wrote out firmly, 'I believe in three doctrines, which have been handed down from early times, and been the foundations of nearly all magical practices' (going on to specific them with some precision), he was not merely bidding for the premier position in a specialist niche of the late-Victorian bookmart. Both Le Fanu and Yeats were giving voice to earnestly held ideas which they believed to be in general abeyance in contemporary Britain and knew to be comparatively widespread in contemporary Ireland—though perhaps under confusing denominational colours. Notwithstanding, the evidence is strong that Le Fanu and William Butler Yeats believed in a supernatural existence, and believed, moreover, in the interfusion of the supernatural and the natural in the world of lived experience. In writing, as he did in his "General Introduction" that he was 'convinced that in two or three generations it will become generally known that the mechanical theory has no reality',[37] Yeats might have been paraphrasing Le Fanu's profession in the metaphysical exordium to "Green Tea". Hands up, those among modern students of Irish literature who actually assent to such metaphysical propositions.

Much depends upon whether we assent or not. If we do so, then we join a dwindling band for whom it is still possible to assert that there are supernatural quiddities in Ireland, be they ghosts, demons, fairies or avatars—or rather, in the cant-phrase of the moment, concur with the old lady who is reputed to have said, 'Sure, I don't believe in them, but they exist all the same'.[38] For some in recent decades, it has been a matter of importance to assert that Irish culture is significantly aligned with the lost lore of the Aryan peoples. Books by Robert O'Driscoll and Michael Dames are susceptible to this interpretation, more or less explicitly urging that Ireland be regarded as the fountainhead of a mythopoeic mix of world-redeeming notions with convenient purchase in such fashionable fields as feminism, post-colonialism, and ecology.[39] In an enthusiastic introduction to *The Celtic Consciousness* (1982), O'Driscoll launched into this account of 'the Grail'—a recurrent theme of Celtic folklore, as he sees it:

> [T]he vessel is a symbol of inexhaustible resources of the spirit, forever renewing itself, whether it be the hidden spirit that animates all matter, or, in modern psychological terms, an energy in the depths of the mind that, if developed, can free man from dependence on the body and the tyranny of historical fact.[40]

In so doing, he inevitably harped on Matthew Arnold's formulation—thus cutting himself off from the more progressive tendency in contemporary Irish criticism which sets out precisely from a repudiation of Arnoldian Celticism; indeed, anathemises it as a colonial strategy for the subordination of Ireland in the Victorian political and cultural system.

O'Driscoll's project was belatedly revivalist in something like the spirit articulated by George Russell when he wrote that he and others in the movement were seeking to 'reflect our own ideals, and to embody that national soul which has been slowly incarnating in our race from its cloudy dawn'.[41] In some ways, the atavistic bent of *Celtic Consciousness* merely reflected the literary cult which espoused the name of 'Sense of Place' in the 1970s and trailed on sophomorphically in the 1980s. Based on the premise that modern Irish literature participates in the spirit of *dinnschencas* (or 'ancient lore of places')—a premise best suited to the poetics of Seamus Heaney[42]—it was doomed by its share in essentialism to be side-stepped by intellectuals of the coming generation whose increasingly international perspectives brought with it a crucially modified conception of the literary topography of Ireland.[43] The older, implicitly autochtonous conception of the landscape as being invested with traditional significances, often reserved in place-names, gave way to a view in which that construction was itself seen as a *discursive formation* along with everything else in the purview of cultural materialism and one no longer heard it said that Irish literature 'Antheus-like grew strong/by contact with the soil.'[44] In the light of post-modernism theory both the autochtonous and the transcendent became unfashionable resorts. In consequence there are at present very few exponents of a spiritual or even ethnological conception of Irishness teaching at present in Irish colleges or, indeed, any of the universities world-wide where Irish culture is studied and enjoyed. At the popular level, similarly, the appeal to Irish Catholic tradition and a putative substrate of Celtic sensibility as a comfortable measure of identity has been severely vitiated by ecclesiastical scandals, ethnic warfare, feminist politics, and above all else the rise of material standards of living.

What, then, is to become of 'the supernatural and the fantastic' in contemporary Ireland? Will it be perpetuated *only* as a 'discursive formation'—all question of transcendence having been abandoned? And if transformed in this manner, is it destined to serve merely as the chief exhibit in a national theme-park and the *chef d'oeuvre* at a hundred Irish summer schools? Will it be gathered up into the zone of redundant furnishings of the national ego in the naïve old days of Irish separatism along with 'humour' and 'hospitality', or even less honoured emblems such as thatch cottages, clay-pipes and crubeens? Or will it await, along with more glamorous cultural forms such as Irish Palladianism and Irish art nouveau, its return into circulation as the tastes and needs of a later modernist generation may demand? Though unpleasant to contemplate, all of this is not unthinkable. As to thinking it, Yeats entertained the notion; indeed, his poem "The Statues", for all its hermetic complexities, is essentially a plea for the perpetuation of those traits that he considered most irrecusably Irish. These he located in the 'ancient' culture of the country, with its mythopoeic resources; and when he did not meet with them he was quite prepared to moot the view that "Irishry" had passed into extinction.

In his "General Introduction", an unpublished prefatory writing composed about the same time as that poem, Yeats quoted with some chagrin Arnold Toynbee's *obiter dicta* on the country, then broaching a new existence as bourgeois national state rather than Arnoldian rebel against fact beloved by romantic adherents to its cause. In Toynbee's scheme of things, Ireland stood in the nomad-warrior tradition as opposed to the settled peoples who engender civilisation. 'Modern Ireland', he therefore wrote (as Yeats quotes it), 'has made up her mind, in our generation, to find her level as a willing inmate in our workaday world'.[45] This acquiescence in the Anglo-American status quo, so little to Yeats's taste, left the poet with but a slender hope: 'If Irish literature goes on as my generation planned it, it may do something to keep the "Irishry" living [...]. It may be indeed that certain characteristics of the "Irishry" must grow in importance.'[46] Those 'characteristics' were, of course, synonymous with the mythic forces that he calls 'our proper dark', and which he identifies with the sacrificial politics of Patrick Pearse.

In appointing Pearse to the 'ancient sect' of mythopoeic druids, as Yeats does in the poem, he was not—as some readings suggest— heralding a new Pythagorean order based on republican politics and a sculptural reverence for human proportion. In the arrangement of forces envisaged by the poet, Pearse's summoning of Cuchulain is *answered*, not in the first instance *embodied by* those Pythagorean quanta of 'calculation, number, measurement'. (That Pythagoras was an animist should not be entirely forgotten.) In "The Statues" Pearse is actually aligned with the 'vague Asiatic immensities' of pre-Hellenic despotism; he represents 'passion' as opposed to 'calculation', which therefore comes to complete his partial nature making it possible for an Irish state to come into existence. Yeats's poem speaks centrally of a new dispensation based on Irish anti-rationalism raising to the power of nationhood the mythic consciousness that lies at the centre of his imaginative approbation of the country. In this way, the pre-destined Irish contribution to history is to be made: reinvesting world history with the supernatural dimension that Locke and the continental rationalists evacuated from it in their inert versions of a spiritless democracy.

At the heart of "The Statues" stands an anomalous and—indeed—a contradictory application of the metaphoric 'darkness' which features signally in the phrase 'our proper dark'. The Druids are not kindred to the Greek philosophers, nor is their 'ancient sect' in mythological Ireland companionable with the Pythagoreans' cult of universal numbers. On the contrary, the mythological ethos of the Irish is seen as standing in diametrical opposition to the rule of reason represented by that cult. The statues of Phidias, wrought under Pythagoras's philosophical tutelage, are said to possess 'proportion' while chronically lacking 'character'—as boys and girls, 'pale from imagined love', well know. It is 'boys and girls' of this type who start revolutions in the knowledge that 'passion could bring character enough'; and it is they who enliven the geometric idea with its necessary quota of irrational energy by pressing 'live lips' against the statues—much as Pygmalion with *his* statue. For Yeats, the Irish revolution was part and parcel of that process of epochal destruction and renewal which he famously visualised, in "The Second Coming", as a 'rough beast, its hour come round at last,/Slouch[ing] towards Bethlehem to be born'.[47] Yeats's Pearse is not the agent of a rational preference for republican democracy tipped, accidentally, into revolutionary violence but—as Terence Brown has recently reminded as—'a magus who summoned a ghost out of the racial dark'.[48]

In poem after poem Yeats elaborated upon this idea. For him Pearse became the harbinger of the return of mythological forces under the form of modern violence, a Celtic avatar no less than a Fenian revolutionary.

> And yet who knows what's yet to come?
> For Patrick Pearse had said
> That in every generation
> Must Ireland's blood be shed.
> *From mountain to mountain ride the fierce horsemen.*[49]

What Yeats envisages here as spreading out from the mythic drama of the Easter Rising is something like the overthrow of the Roman empire, plunging it—as he remarks elsewhere—into 'a fabulous formless darkness'.[50] (The analogy with the British empire should not, of course be missed.) In that benighted state, he further tells us, 'we are lost amid alien intellects, near but incomprehensible, more incomprehensible than the most distant stars.'[51] Here, indeed, he might be talking of the Anglo-Irish— men such as Henry Middleton in the first 'song' of this cycle—surrounded in their social twilight by the atavistic passions in nationalist Ireland.⁵² Of course, the 'we' in that last sentence is much more like the empirical subject of contemporary British life than the national community denoted as 'We Irish' in "the Statues". For that poem, by contrast with his suave metropolitan persona, Yeats adopts the mask of a latter-day Irish philosopher-bard in touch at once with the supernatural sources of poetry and spectral origins of revolutionary nationhood as well as participating in what he called the 'cold, logical intellect' of Bishop Berkeley.⁵³ At the same time he describes everything opposed to these as 'filthy' and 'formless', caricaturing them as spawning, furious *wreckers*—code the anti-aristocratic forces of democracy.⁵⁴

> We Irish thrown up this filthy modern tide
> And by its formless spawning fury wrecked,
> Climb to our proper dark [...]

Since 'formless' in those lines obviously rhymes with 'formless dark' in *Wheels and Butterflies*, the 'proper dark' attributed to the Irish is obviously a different kind of darkness from that which is merely formless. Hence we must recognise in it an antithetical kind of 'dark' instinct with passion and knowledge, as distinct from that which is purely moribund, destructive and occlusive. The identity thus ascribed by Yeats to Ireland and the Irish in "The Statues" is indeed profoundly antithetical to the tradition of Western thought deriving from Greek philosophy and culminating in the Enlightenment, yet it is also antithetical to the 'mere anarchy' that succeeds it in the vision of "The Second Coming". To be a generative kind of 'dark' it must contain some forms within itself—forms such as the emblematic person of Cuchulain in the heroic stories of the Ulster Cycle, an avatar of the kind the Yeats and Russell dreamed of. In all of this the unspoken term is therefore 'atavism', suggesting that those ancient forms of racial consciousness resurfaced in such a fashion that Cuchulain *actually* stands by Pearse side in the GPO in answer to his summons, thus giving the Volunteers an irresistible, mythopoeic impulsion towards modern nationhood. It might be that Cuchulain was present simply in the manner of a stereotype shaping Pearse's action, yet Yeats chose to imagine that he was there in 'real presence' (to employ the eucharistic term) and as such he was a supernatural revenant, an active instance of Celtic atavism.

It has always seemed necessary for Irish intellectuals to embrace the idea of atavism as one of the positive and indispensable ingredients of

Irish nationhood: after all, national independence for an ancient nation means that that world of the racial forefathers has been in some effective way recuperated. It is this syllogism that informs the complaint levelled against Conor Cruise O'Brien by Seamus Deane in taking issue with the former's disparaging attachment of the term to the activities of the Provisional IRA in the 1970s.

> But surely this very clarity of O'Brien's position is just what is most objectionable. [...] In other words, is not his humanism here being used as an excuse to rid Ireland of the atavisms which gave it life even though the life itself may be in some ways brutal?[55]

Much as Deane might later remonstrate against Yeats's élitism in *Heroic Styles* (1984), this indignant protest is little removed from the nation-making premises of "The Statues" in which a tenuous distinction is developed between the destructive and creative forms of darkness. In Yeats's phraseology, the irrationalism of Irish political action is called 'our *proper* dark' as distinct from the 'fabulous formless darkness' which wrecked the Roman empire—though perhaps they too contained within themselves the medieval 'Unity of Being' which Yeats looked to as an ideal form of social organisation.[56] In this light, we can see that 'proper' bears the sense of 'the *right kind* of dark', and that the sense 'our own'—deriving from the French pre-positional adjective '*propre*' and perhaps hinting at Sinn Féin—is secondary to the philosophical meaning. It is worth nothing that Yeats's 'dark' is strictly ungrammatical, deficient in the '-ness' suffix of the abstract noun. 'Dark' (n.) occurs in prepositional phrases such as 'in the dark', but probably the effect here is to connote such canonical adjectival uses as 'the dark night of the soul'.

In prose writings of the period, Yeats repeatedly made paradoxical allusions to 'dark' and 'darkness' as a generative notion. In this he is, of course, remote from the *lumen gentium* tradition of conventional Christian iconography and rationalist traditions stemming from it (such as, notably, the Cartesian). In his annotations to the 1929 edition of *The Winding Stair* he wrote of one poem, 'I have symbolised a woman's love as the struggle of the darkness to keep the sun from rising from its earthly bed.'[57] This was not meant pejoratively. Comparably, in the closing remarks of his profoundly undiplomatic "General Introduction", he looks upon the contemporary form of Irish statehood as it may be witnessed in the metropolitan streetscape, and remarks:

> When I stand on O'Connell Street [...] where modern heterogeneity has taken physical form, a vague hatred comes up out of *my own dark* and I am certain that wherever in Europe there are minds strong enough to lead others the same vague hatred will have issued in violence and imposed some kind of rule of kindred. I cannot know the nature of that rule, for its opposite fills the light; all I can do to bring it nearer is to intensify my hatred.[58] [My emphasis.]

'My own dark': a phrase that corresponds with some exactitude to the coinage 'our proper dark' in "The Statues". Yeats surely means that the racial consciousness of the Irish, with its promise of a dark illumination at the polar extreme from the commercial illuminations of Western (and especially Anglo-American) civilisation has failed—as Toynbee's sentence bore witness—and that he must turn to yet darker sources of irrationalism for the 'Unity of Being' that he seeks. Hence his parting assertion that he never had been an Irish nationalist except for 'passing reasons';[59] now he must look elsewhere. Yet Ireland had provided Yeats with a context in which he could experience the interfusion of the natural and the supernatural, and indeed—at one point in its political history—the domination of the social order by atavistic, supernatural forces, sustained by the 'passion' of the revolutionaries. To a great extent everyone in Ireland has experienced that in modern times—not so much through the persistence of fairy faith or the literary revival of ancient legends as through the presence and activity of Irish nationalism both in its benign and its malignant forms.

The occurrence of the fantastic in any literature is probably due to the marginalisation of social and psychological forces which find no room for representation under prevailing intellectual conditions. Analagously, the prevalence of the fantastic in modern Irish literature is probably ascribable to this cause: that the nightmare of colonial history bestowed on successive generations a traumatic memory that refused to be exorcised by the ordinary processes of modernisation.[60] Viewed thus, the supernatural is itself a representation of historical fixations subsisting in the consciousness of the community, where it arises from an awareness of killings, dispossessions, and other brutal transactions felt to be unrequited. The sum of such transactions in the memory of the colonised amounts to 'the spirit of the nation'—an entity for whom absence is in fact its highest form of presence. In a postcolonialist analysis, the supernatural and the fantastic which permeate so much of Irish writing give expression to the self-awareness of the nation under conditions where it cannot be spoken of as truly present and refuses to be wholly absent either. That, insistently, is the conclusion offered in so many of the papers at this conference.

There remains the question of Yeats's belief in the supernatural. It is generally held that he believed in the existence of an otherworld and certainly in immortality; yet he was also alert to the significance of the Kantian revolution which entrusted the subject with the making of the realm of perception (at least that part of it which was constitutive rather than regulative). His dynamic apprehension of the idea that the transcendent is a projection of the human imagination is epitomised by the oxymoronic phrase in "Sailing to Byzantium" about 'the artifice of eternity'—a phrase that might almost conduce to the conclusion that he was, in fact, a post-modernist *avant le mot*. For the conjunction of *artifice* and *eternity* bears the interpretation that eternity is not transcendent at all. Likewise, in "The Tower", he plays with the relation between imagination and reality in regard to the question of post-mortal being:

> Being dead, we rise,
> Dream and so create
> Translunar Paradise.[61]

Here he stubbornly postulates that relation as irreducibly symbiotic in such a way that we are seen to be mortal and immortal without contradiction. (To say that the grave-diggers 'but thrust their buried men/Back into the human mind again' is not to deny them immortality since the mind is the alembic where eternity is forged.)[62] The imagination in Yeats's system was not essentially mimetic and had more to do with 'creation' in the theological sense than the aesthetic. It was totally implicated in a reality that was no less real for being 'hooped together [...] by manifold illusion'.[63] In such a world, the thing that knows and the thing that is known are essentially the same being grounded in the same act of perception. In this sense, Yeats reduced knowledge to action, rendering the two indistinguishable—his drama has the corresponding epistemological valency. Not surprisingly, Berkeley's *esse est percipi* helped him with all of that, but it was nevertheless a mystical rather than a rational conception.

For this reason it is questionable how far formalism can proceed with the interpretation of the Yeatsian literary text. In a world like Yeats's where *to be perceived* as supernatural is *to be* supernatural, the 'hesitation' between the pragmatic and the marvellous which serves Tzvetan Todorov as a definition of the fantastic is less likely to be met with.[64] Granted, Todorov admits that we proceed from the perception of a given untoward phenomenon either to its recognition as *uncanny* or to its affirmation as *marvellous* (that is, supernatural); but the whole weight his theory rests on the supposition that the supernatural never really happens. Yeats and his followers believed otherwise; his predecessors in Victorian Ireland were likewise committed to a haunted conception of the world; and the antecedents of all of them in ancient Ireland were the foremost literary fantasists of Europe. In Irish literature, it may be truer to say that the uncanny rarely happens and the supernatural often does. The reason why this is so has provided the main topic of debate at this conference and will no doubt be taken up again at other conferences.

NOTES

1 "General Introduction to My Work" [1937], in *Essays and Introductions* (London: Macmillan 1961), p.518.
2 "The Statues", *Collected Poems* (London: Macmillan 1950 & Edns.), p.376.
3 Berkeley wrote in his *Philosophical Commentaries*, a notebook of 1744, 'We Irish cannot attain to these truths' (entry 392; first cited by Alexander Campbell in 1871 and published by A. A. Luce in 1944). Yeats harped on it in his Preface to Mario Rossi and Joseph Hone's biography of Berkeley (1931), making much of his sense of separation from the philosophers of the 'neighbouring nation' ('Bishop Berkeley', in *Essays and Introductions*, 1961, p.396), and also in his prefatory notes to *King of the Great Clock Tower* (1934), Sect. II.

   Luce did not think anything should be made of Berkeley's apparent nationalism, but Denis Donoghue considers that the Berkeley, like Yeats, 'believed in something called the Irish intellect'. (See Donoghue, *We Irish: Essays in Irish Literature and Society*, Brighton: Harvester Press, 1986, p.6). See also Seán O'Faolain, *The Irish* (Harmondsworth: Penguin 1944), p.87, and Harry Bracken, 'George Berkeley, the Irish Cartesian', in Richard Kearney, ed., *The Irish Mind* (Dublin: Wolfhound 1985), pp.107-18.
4 The *locus classicus* of 'Irishry' in his writing is obviously the lines in "Under Ben Bulben": 'That we in coming days may be/Still the indomitable Irishry". Its chief place in his prose is in the "General Introduction" where he speaks about that certain characteristics of the "Irishry"' that must grow in importance' if his vision of the world is to be fulfilled. (*Essays and Introductions*, 1961, p.517.)
5 Cf. de Valera's oft-quoted version of the 'Ireland that we dreamed of' in his St. Patrick Day speech of 1943: 'the home of a people who valued material wealth only as a basis of right living, of a people who were satisfied with frugal comfort and devoted their leisure to the things of the spirit.' (Quoted in Terence Brown, *Ireland, A Social and Cultural History*, London: Fontana, 1981, p.146.) For estimates of Yeats in nationalist Ireland at the time of his death, see R. F. Foster, 'When the Newspapers Have Forgotten Me ...', in *Yeats Annual*, No. 12 (1996).

6 *Stephen Hero: Part of the First Draft of A Portrait of the Artist as a Young Man* [1944] (London: Jonathan Cape; rev edn. 1956), p.52. In the Wake he jocosely called his compatriots 'the most phillohippuc theobibbous paùpulation in the world.' (*Finnegans Wake*, London: Faber & Faber 1939, p.140 [FW140.13].)
7 See Geneviève Brennan, 'Yeats, Clodd, *Scatalogic Rites* and the Clonmel Witch Burning', in *Yeats Annual*, No. 4 (1986), Hubert Butler, 'The Eggman and the Fairies' in *The Sub-prefect should have held his tongue and other essays* (Dublin: Lilliput 1990), and the fate of Bridget Cleary is the subject of the *Cure* (1995), a recent novel by Carlo Gébler.
8 *Finnegans Wake* (1939), p.344 [344.12].
9 *A Portrait of the Artist as a Young Man* [1916; Definitive Text 1964], eds., Chester G. Anderson and Richard Ellmann (London: Jonathan Cape 1991), pp.186-87. See also
10 ibid., p.256 [Stephen's diary entry for 15 April].
11 "General Introduction" (1961), p.519
12 Distributed as follows: Chapter 1: 1; Chap. 2: 7; Chap. 3: 103; Chap. 4: 50, and Chap. 5: 41. In the later chapters, the religious and confessional sense of the word as met with so insistently in the 'Hell-fire' (Chap. 3) gives way to a more strictly Aristotelian sense of the term as denoting the 'formulable essence' or 'whatness' of the individual.
13 *Ulysses* (London: Bodley Head Edn. 1963), p.24.
14 Printed in 'materials for *Stephen Hero*' in Robert Scholes and Richard Kain, eds., as *The Workshop of Daedalus* (Evanston Ill.: Northwestern UP 1965). Among others, Joyce copied out Aristotle's sentence, 'The soul is the first entelechy of a naturally organic thing.' (*De Anima*, 1, 2.)
15 See Jacques Aubert, *The Aesthetics of James Joyce* [trans.] (Johns Hopkins UP 1992).
16 See *Heroic Styles: The Tradition of an Idea* (Derry: Field Day Co. 1984), rep. in *Ireland's Field Day*, ed., Roger McHugh (Derry: Field Day Co. 1985): pp.45-59. The operative distinction in Joyce is between 'classical' and 'romantic' tempers as set out in *Stephen Hero* (1956 edn.), pp.73-74.
17 "General Introduction" (1961), p.515.
18 Idem.
19 Letter to Stanislaus Joyce (25 Sept., 1906), in Richard Ellmann, ed., *Selected Letters* (London: Faber & Faber 1975), p.111.
20 *The Study of Celtic Literature* [1867], ed. R. H. Super (Michigan UP 1962), pp.344-45).
21 See Elizabeth Butler Cullingford, 'British Romans and Irish Carthaginians: Anticolonial Metaphor in Heaney, Friel and McGuinness', *PMLA* (March 1996), pp.222-36. In common with some other commentators, Cullingford quoting Arnold's contention that 'sensibility of the Celtic nature, its nervous exaltation, have something feminine in them' (*On the Study of Celtic Literature*, 1865).
22 Key studies of Arnold's view of Ireland and—more generally—of Celticism are to be found in John V. Kelleher, 'Matthew Arnold and the Celtic Revival', in Harry Levin ed., *Perspectives in Criticism* [Harvard Studies in Comparative Literature, Vol. 20] (Harvard UP 1950), pp.197-221; W. J. McCormack, in 'Varieties of Celticism', *From Burke to Beckett* (Cambridge UP 1985), pp.224-53, and Seamus Deane, 'Arnold, Burke and the Celts', in *Celtic Revivals: Essays in Modern Irish Literature, 1880-1980* (London: Faber & Faber 1985), pp.17-27. David Cairns and Shaun Richards, *Writing Ireland* (Manchester UP 1988) and Deane, *A short*

History of Irish Literature (London: Hutchinson 1986) may also be consulted.
23 Geraldine Moane, 'A psychological analysis of colonialism in an Irish context', in *The Irish Journal of Psychology*, 'The Irish Psyche' [Special Issue], Vol. 15, Nos. 2 & 3 (Psychol. Soc. of Ireland 1994), p.259.
24 See for instance Alex Davis, '"Foreign and Credible": Denis Devlin's Modernism', in *Éire-Ireland*, 30, 2 (Summer 1995), pp.131-48; but note Michael Smith, ' Modernist Eye', *Poetry Now* column, *The Irish Times*, 25 July, 1998: '[...] not a great deal of contemporary Irish literature ... can lay claim to being Modernist.'
25 See such studies as James Longenbach, *Stone Cottage, Pound, Yeats, and Modernism* (OUP 1988) and Leonard Orr, ed., *Yeats and Postmodernism* (Syracuse, UP 1991).
26 See Terence Brown, *Ireland: A Social and Cultural History, 1922-1972* (London: Fontana 1981): 'The Church [...] offered to most Irishmen and women in the period a way to be Irish which set them apart from the rest of the inhabitants of the British Isles [...].' (pp.28-29.)
27 "General Introduction" (1961), p.515.
28 Yeats, "The Tower" (III), in *Collected Poems* (London: Macmillan 1950 & edns.), p.223.
29 *Ulysses* (1963), p.818.
30 "The Tower", *Collected Poems* (1950), p.225.
31 Yeats recorded that he was 'enraged' by writers of the 1840s and 1850s who had 'turned the country visions into a joke'. ("General Introduction", 1961, p.513.)
32 John P. Frayne, ed., *Uncollected Prose by W. B. Yeats*, Vol. 1: First Reviews and Articles, 1886-1896 (London: Macmillan 1970), p.47.
33 'General Introduction" (1961), pp.526, 519. Seamus Deane estimates this passage to be 'The pathology of literary unionism has never been better defined', p.10
34 "Behind all Irish history hangs a great tapestry, even Christianity had to accept it and be itself pictured there.' (ibid., p.513.)
35 Maturin, *The Milesian Chief* [1812] (NY: Garland Publ. 1979), p.v. Joyce may have consciously echoed this phrasing when he wrote to Grant Richards, 'My intention was to write a chapter in the moral history of my country and I chose Dublin for the scene because that city seemed to me the centre of paralysis. (Letter of 5 May, 1906; *Selected Letters*, ed., Richard Ellmann, London: Faber & Faber p.83.)
36 James Hardiman, Irish Minstrelsy, or Bardic Remains of Ireland with English poetical translations, 2 vols. [1831] (Shannon: IUP 1971), Vol. I, p.lxxvi, ftn.
37 Yeats, op. cit. (1961), p.518.
38 See Kiberd, *Inventing Ireland* (London: Jonathan Cape 1995), p.5.
39 See Robert O'Driscoll, ed., *The Celtic Consciousness* [papers of 1978 symposium at Toronto] (Dublin: Dolmen Press; Edinburgh: Canongate Publ. 1982), and Dames, *Mythic Ireland* (London: Thames & Hudson. 1992).
40 O'Driscoll, op. cit. (1982), p.xi. The author cites copious *sententiae* by Irish writers of the revival period including Patrick Pearse's contention that 'Men here saw certain gracious things more clearly and felt certain mystic things more acutely and heard certain deep music more perfectly than did men in ancient Greece.' (ibid., pp.xviii-xix.)

41 Russell, 'Literary Ideals in Ireland', in John Eglinton, ed., *Literary Ideals in Ireland* (London: Unwin; Dublin: *Daily Express* 1899; facs. rep. NY: Lemma 1973), p.18; also cited in O'Driscoll, op. cit. (1982), p.xix.
42 See Heaney's essay 'The Sense of Place', in *Preoccupations* (London: Faber & Faber 1980), pp.131-49.
43 A more testing reading of the relation between semiology and topography in Ireland can be met with in J.F. Foster, 'Topographical Tradition in Anglo-Irish Poetry [1974] and 'The Geography of Irish Fiction', essays in J. F. Foster, *Colonial Consequences: Essays in Irish Literature and Culture* (Dublin: Lilliput 1991), while Luke Gibbons's *Transformations in Irish Culture* (Cork UP 1996) takes on a full panoply of post-modernist ideas with somewhat radical consequences for the naïve conception of the subject.
44 See Yeats's "Municipal Gallery Revisited", in *Collected Poems* (1950), Stanza VI, p.369
45 Essays and Introductions (1961), p.527.
46 idem.
47 *Collected Poems* (1950), p.210.
48 Terence Brown, 'Celticism and the Occult', in Brown, ed., *Celticism* (Amsterdam; Atlanta G.A. Rodopi 1996), p.221.
49 "Three Songs to One Burden, III", *Collected Poems* (1950), p.374.
50 *Wheels and Butterflies* (London: Macmillan 1934); pp.77-78. Yeats purports to quote an anonymous philosophy living at the time.
51 Idem.
52 See "Three Songs to One Burden, II", in *Collected Poems* (1950), pp.372-73.
53 *King of the Great Clock Tower* (1934), Sect. II; cited in A. N. Jeffares, *A New Commentary on the Poems of W. B. Yeats* [1968] (London: Macmillan 1984), p.333.
54 See "Three Songs to the One Burden (I)": 'I beat the common sort/And think it is no shame'. (*Collected Poems*, 1950, p.371)
55 See Deane, 'Interview with Heaney', in *The Crane Bag*, 1, 1 (1977), pp.61-72.
56 See *Autobiographies* (London: Macmillan 1955), pp.190-95.
57 See Jeffares, op. cit. (1984), p.326.
58 "General Introduction" (1961), p.526.
59 idem.
60 This has been the theme of several writings by Luke Gibbons, 'Identity Without A Centre: Allegory, History and Irish Nationalism', *Cultural Studies*, Vol. VI, No. 3 (1992), pp.358-75.
61 Yeats, "The Tower, III", in *Collected Poems* (1950), p.223.
62 "Under Ben Bulben (II)", in *Collected Poems* (1950), p.398.
63 "Meru", in *Collected Poems* (1950), p.333.
64 For relevant citations from Todorov see papers by Csilla Bertha, Irene Eynat-Confino, Monique Gallagher, Warwick Gould, Joseph M. Hassett, Christopher Morash, and Maria Tymoczko in these transactions. Tzvetan Todorov, *The Fantastic: A Structural Approach to a Literary Genre* [1970], trans. Richard Howard (London: Case Western Reserve University 1973), p.25.

CAPTAIN HEAVEN

Medbh McGuckian

The erect flag lifts from its emptiness
like a masted boat, a pyramid balanced
on its apex, or a tie that has worked free
into a blowy sky

I fasten one to my easel, it touches the canvas
at various points, draping it in an inoffensive
light-green churning, as if a whole month's
history of Ireland were fainting into leaf.

Now it is a rose lying on his arm, that settles
into a pool of ruby rust about the back
of his head; a rose-coloured membrane
that wanders coarsely on the rim of his coat;

a little pennon of gently purled and slender
feathers where his elbows break out,
that brushes his clothes from neck to ankle;
a banner of tossed blue, that nolens volens

brings a feeling of the air to the tilt
of his arms. His left hand is casual,
as though expecting fruit, and his unemployed
hand gathers up the countryside

on the nipple of the pistol, its halfness,
in his pocket. There must be a path
up from the sea through his legs firmly apart
in the dockscape, two sets of steps

opposite each other as they rest between acts.
The day has moved on some hours,
but seems to find its horizon in moments
of yellow mauve with heather and gold

with gorse on his forehead and Bedouin instep.
Immediate as a cloud, I lay my dark dress
like a living part of a letter posted wordless
thirty years later among weapons in an imitation tomb.

INDEX

A.E. (see Russell, George)
Adams, Gerry, 8
Adams, Hazard, 355, 362
Albani, Cardinal, 258
Albee, Edward, 170
Albright, Daniel, 353-55, 358, 360, 362
Alexander II, Tsar, 42
Allingham, William, 250
Anderson, Benedict, 41
Appadurai, Arjun, 43
Aquinas, Saint Thomas, 328
Arata, Stephen, 32-33, 35
Aristotle, 11
Arnold, Matthew, 2, 235, 267, 279, 368, 374, 376
Arrabal, Fernando, 170
Ashlin, George, 256
Attebery, Brian, 268-71, 275
Auden, Wystan Hugh, 231
Auerbach, Eric, 10
Auerbach, Nina, 52
Augustine, Saint, 274

Bach, Johannes Sebastian, 192
Bacon, Francis, 158, 334
Bakhtin, Mikhail J., 188, 278
Balcombe, Florence, 18, 244
Balzac, Honoré de, 248
Banim, John, 223
Banim, Michael, 223
Barrenechea, Anna Maria, 194
Barry, Kevin, 232
Barry, Sebastian, 132-33, 369
Battle, Mary, 314
Baudelaire, Charles, 248, 334, 344
Beckett, Samuel, 79, 158, 163, 167, 170-86, 248, 251, 277
Beethoven, Ludwig van, 189
Belford, Barbara, 78, 79
Benveniste, Emile, 161

Berkeley, George, 121-22, 159, 251, 365, 378, 381
Berlioz, Hector, 247
Bertha, Csilla, 369
Bhabha, Homi, 48-49, 100, 113
Biko, Steven, 70
Blake, William, 319-20, 322, 328, 337, 340
Blavatsky, Helena Petrovna, 292
Bloom, Harold, 193
Boehme, Jacob, 319-20, 322-23, 337
Borges, Jorge-Luis, 146, 178, 191, 193-94, 274
Bork, Sidonia von, 220
Bosch, Hiëronymus, 361
Boswell, James, 159
Botting, Fred, 36
Boucicault, Dion, 245
Bourget, Paul, 233
Bowen, Elizabeth, 248
Boyce, George, 71
Brantlinger, Patrick, 40
Brenane, Mrs, 239, 244-45
Breuer, Josef, 52-53
Brod, Max, 179, 181, 185-86
Brontë family, 40
Brusati, Franco, 43
Burke, Edmund, 251
Burkitt, Francis Crawford, 342
Burleson, Donald, 93
Burne-Jones, Edward, 220
Byron, George Gordon, 246

Callois, Roger, 200
Carleton, William, 30, 222
Carlyle, Thomas, 256, 258
Carroll, Lewis, 158, 163-65, 206
Carter, Robert Brudenell, 55-58, 61
Casey, Daniel, 271
Cavafy, Constantine, 264
Chamberlain, Basil Hall, 251-52
Charcot, Jean-Martin, 53, 56, 59, 61
Chesney, George, 42
Chrysostom, John, 258
Clarke, Austin, 306
Claudel, Paul, 170
Cleary, Bridget, 313
Cocteau, Jean, 170
Cohn, Ruby, 181
Coleridge, Samuel Taylor, 12, 26

Index

Collins, Wilkie, 45
Columbus, Christopher, 121
Congreve, William, 251
Connolly, James, 3-8, 11, 217, 368
Conrad, Joseph, 43
Corkery, Daniel, 136-43
Cox, Harvey, 278
Croker, Thomas Crofton, 219
Cronin, John, 268
Crowley, Aleister, 311-13
Cullingford, Elizabeth Butler, 213

Dames, Michael, 374
Dante Alighieri, 278, 328, 355
Davis, Thomas, 221
De Palma, Brian, 45
De Valera, Eamon, 68
Deane, Seamus, 32-33, 67, 80, 104, 230, 367, 379
Defoe, Daniel, 246
Delbanco, Andrew, 279
Deleuze, Gilles, 162
Democritus, 182
Derrida, Jacques, 164
Devlin, Denis, 369
Dick, Frederick, 303
Dickens, Charles, 27, 45, 120
Donne, John, 146
Douglas, Alfred, 230
Dowling, Linda, 331
Doyle, Arthur Conan, 42
Dudley Edwards, Owen, 232-34
Dudley Edwards, Ruth, 9
Duffy, Carol Ann, 148
Duffy, Charles Gavan, 67-68
Dunlop, D. N., 303, 306
Dunne, John William, 191, 204-05
Dunsany, Lord, 84-88, 90-95

Eagleton, Terry, 40, 69, 159-60, 234
Early, Biddy, 314-15
Edgeworth, Maria, 30, 160, 246, 253-54
Einstein, Albert, 189-91, 205
Eliade, Mircea, 123
Eliot, George, 151
Ellis, Havelock, 336
Ellmann, Richard, 228-29, 312, 319, 361
Elwood, Catherine, 244-45

Engels, Friedrich, 5, 7, 125, 127-28
Epimenides, 192-93
Escher, Maurits Cornelius, 192
Eudoxia, Empress, 258-59
Everett, H. D., 42

Fanon, Franz, 4
Farquhar, George, 251
Farr, Florence, 342
Ferguson, Samuel, 250
Fitzmaurice, George, 124
Flannery, James, 170, 175
Flaubert, Gustave, 242
Forster, Edward Morgan, 231
Foster, John Wilson, 336
Foster, Roy, 9, 248, 250
Foucault, Michel Paul, 2
Frayling, Christopher, 18
Frayne, John, 372
Freud, Sigmund, 52-53, 129, 167, 184
Friel, Brian, 125, 129

Gautier, Théophile, 242
Gelder, Ken, 32-33, 52
Genette, Gérard, 204
Ghelderode, Michel de, 170
Gibbons, Luke, 74, 80, 105, 232-33
Gide, André, 233
Gillane, Peter, 14
Gilroy, Paul, 41
Gladstone, William, 66, 71, 77, 231
Godard, Jean-Luc, 234
Godwin, William, 27
Goldsmith, Oliver, 243, 251
Gonne, Maud, 210, 212-17, 264, 288, 307, 309, 337-38, 362
Goring, Charles, 73
Gray, George W., 189
Green, Thomas Hill, 264
Greene, Graham, 188
Gregory, (Lady) Isabella Augusta Persse, 14, 121, 225, 248, 264, 312-16, 366
Griffin, Gerald, 223
Grossman, Allen R., 355
Gyles, Althea, 303, 312

Hagedom, Jessica, 45
Haining, Peter, 78-79
Hall, Wayne E., 356

Hamilton, William, 319
Hamsa, Bhagwan Shri, 292-93
Hardiman, James, 373
Harper, George Mills, 324
Harrington, Timothy Charles, 65
Hawking, Stephen, 274
Hawthorne, Julian, 334
Hawthorne, Nathaniel, 332-35
Heaney, Seamus, 97-99, 106-07, 109, 111, 116-17, 154, 251, 375
Hearn, Lafcadio, 238-54
Hearn, Richard, 245
Henry VIII, King, 37
Herodotus, 235
Hillman, James, 121
Hobbes, Thomas, 158
Hofstadter, Douglas, 192
Holub, Miroslav, 146
Homer, 193
Hopper, Nora, 337-38
Horton, W. T., 343
Hume, Kathryn, 267-78
Hunter, Dorothea, 338, 342
Hutchinson, Thomas, 229
Huysmans, Joris-Karl, 331
Hyde, Douglas Montgomery, 222-24, 337
Hyndman, Henry Mayers, 5

Ibsen, Henrik, 170, 264
Ionesco, Eugène, 170

Jackson, Rosemary, 129-30, 150, 154
James, Henry, 279
James, M. R., 334-35
Jameson, Fredric, 45
Jarry, Alfred, 170
Jeffares, A. Norman, 141
Johnson, Lionel, 309, 334
Johnson, Samuel, 156, 159
Jordan, Eamon, 125
Jowett, Benjamin, 264
Joyce, James, 3, 136, 141, 161, 179, 189-91, 244, 251-53, 277, 366-69, 371

Kafka, Franz, 146-47, 149-50, 154, 156, 177-86
Kane, Father, 7
Kaun, Axel, 178

Kavanagh, Patrick, 253
Keats, John, 355, 361
Kemnitz, Charles, 205
Kennedy, Patrick, 223
Kern, Edith, 181
Kersley, G. H., 231
Keynes, John Maynard, 231
Kiberd, Declan, 3, 4, 103, 230
Kiely, Benedict, 267-68, 270-73
Kilroy, Thomas, 124, 129
Kinahan, Frank, 354
Kinevane, Pat, 125
Knowlson, James, 179
Kohl, Norbert, 232

Labat, Père, 246
Lacan, Jacques, 19, 129, 158, 160
Lalor, James Fintan, 68
Landow, George P., 267
Lanters, José, 278
Larcom, Thomas, 221
Le Fanu, Joseph Sheridan, 19, 21-22, 27-30, 36, 46, 69, 241-42, 245-46, 248, 253, 373-74
Le Guin, Ursula K., 84
Lee, George Vandeleur, 244
Leiber, Fritz, 84
Leonard, Hugh, 129
Leslie, John, 5
Lester, H. F., 42
Lever, Charles, 251
Lewis, Matthew Gregory, 240, 246
Lloyd, David, 232-33
Locke, John, 158, 163, 246, 376
Lombroso, Cesare, 73-74, 76
Lorrain, Jean, 233
Lovecraft, Howard Phillips, 84-85, 89, 91
Lover, Samuel, 222
Lynch, Thomas, 144-45

M'Grath, John, 310-11
MacDonagh, Thomas, 11, 212, 217, 368-69
MacGreevy, Thomas, 369
Machen, Arthur, 312, 331
Mack, Robert L., 253
Macleod, Fiona, 338
MacLiammóir, Mícheál, 231
MacManus, D. A., 315

Index

MacNeice, Louis, 145
MacPherson, Conor, 369
MacPherson, James, 370
Maeterlinck, Maurice, 170
Maguire, Conor, 223
Mallarmé, Stéphane, 233, 336
Mallock, William Hurrell, 264
Markievicz, Constance, 211-13, 264
Márquez, Gabriel García, 148
Martin, Augustine, 269-70
Martin, John, 68
Martin, Robert K., 228
Martyn, Edward, 255-59, 262-65
Martyn, Mrs, 263-64
Marvell, Andrew, 146
Marx, Karl, 5, 42, 125, 127-28, 228
Mathers, S. L. MacGregor, 308, 316, 323, 338, 340
Maturin, Charles Robert, 30, 69, 245-46, 248, 253, 372-73
Maugham, Somerset Maugham, 231
McCabe, Patrick, 369
McCarthy, Mary, 189
McCormack, Jerusha, 228, 233
McCormack, John, 244
McCormack, W. J., 35
McDonogh, Martin, 369
McGahern, John, 253
McGuinness, Frank, 124-26, 128-29, 234
McHale, Brian, 193
Meer, Ameena, 45
Meinhold, Johann Wilhelm, 220
Middleton, Henry, 377
Mill, John Stuart, 319
Miller, Hillis, 267
Millevoye, Lucien, 309
Milton, John, 246
Mitchell, Susan, 338
Moore, George, 76, 136, 138, 141, 231, 244-45, 247, 264
Moore, Thomas Sturge, 358
Moore, Thomas, 244
Moran, D. P., 3
Moretti, Franco, 77
Morris, William, 220, 228
Morse, Donald, 369
Moses, Michael Valdez, 69, 70-71
Moynahan, Julian, 30-31
Murphy, Patrick D., 122

Murphy, Tom, 124-25, 128-29
Murray, Christopher, 134
Murray, Isobel, 235

Nandy, Ashis, 230-31
Nasaar, Christopher, 228
Neruda, Pablo, 144, 146
Newman, Judie, 33
Ní Dhomhnaill, Nuala, 121
Ní Shiubhlaigh, Máire, 264
Nicholls, Peter, 233

O'Brien, Conor Cruise, 379
O'Brien, Flann, 178, 188-94, 196-04, 206-07, 267-68, 275-79
O'Casey, Sean, 121
O'Connor, Frank, 136
O'Donovan, John, 221
O'Driscoll, Robert, 374
O'Faolain, Sean, 136, 267, 272
O'Grady, James Standish, 67, 250
O'Kelly, Seumas, 137, 139
O'Shea, Kitty, 79

Palestrina, Giovanni Pierluigi da, 264
Parker, Stewart, 120, 129
Parkin, Andrew, 31-33
Parnell, Charles Stewart, 65, 66, 69, 70, 71, 79, 309
Pascal, Blaise, 177
Pasley, Malcolm, 179-81
Pater, Walter, 258, 331, 334
Patrick, Saint, 118, 225, 291, 351-52, 354, 360, 370
Paul, Saint, 76
Pearse, Patrick (Padraig Mac Piarais), 3, 4, 8-11, 212, 217, 232, 368, 370, 376-78
Picasso, Pablo, 189
Piggott, 71
Plato, 11
Plunket, Emeline, 283-84
Plunkett, Joseph, 11
Poe, Edgar Allan, 84, 332, 334-36, 343
Pollexfen, George, 338
Polybius, 235
Popa, Vasko, 146
Pope, Alexander, 163, 246
Porter, Peter, 148

Potter, Dennis, 149
Prout, Father, 244
Pulci, Luigi, 255-56
Purser, Sarah, 264
Pythagoras, 376-77

Quiller-Couch, Arthur, 331

Rabelais, François, 255-57
Renan, Ernest, 2, 213, 345
Richards, Thomas, 32-33
Ricketts, Charles, 229, 233
Ricks, Christopher, 182
Ricoeur, Paul, 71, 106
Ripper, Jack the, 71
Rosenfield, Isaac, 274
Rossetti, Christina, 357
Rossetti, Dante Gabriel, 355
Roth, Phyllis A., 38, 58
Russell, Charles, 71
Russell, George (A.E.), 1, 3, 11-13, 121, 288, 303-04, 306, 308-09, 312, 314, 338, 340, 374, 378

Sachs, Oliver, 274
Said, Edward, 40-41
Saix, Guillot de, 233
Salih, Tayeb, 43
Saroyan, William, 188, 202
Scott, Walter, 246, 325, 373
Shakespear, Olivia, 287-88, 291, 294-96, 336-37
Shakespeare, William, 193
Shapcott, Jo, 146
Sharp, William, 338, 343
Shelley, Mary, 19, 27
Sheridan, Frances, 253-54
Showalter, Elaine, 53
Sigerson, George, 74
Simic, Charles, 149
Smith, Clark Ashton, 84
Smith, Pamela Colman, 339
Smith, Peter Alderson, 358
Smithers, Leonard, 229, 311-12
Solovyov, Vladimir, 334
Sontag, Susan, 234
St Leger, Anthony, 37
Stead, W. T., 311
Stephens, James, 267-70
Sterne, Lawrence, 121

Stock, A. G., 354
Stoker, Bram (Abraham), 18-21, 24-25, 27-32, 34-35, 37-38, 40-43, 46, 48-49, 52-53, 65-67, 69-71, 73-80, 241-48, 253
Strachey, (Giles) Lytton, 231
Strindberg, August, 170
Swami, Shri Purohit, 292-93, 366
Swedenborg, Emanuel, 315-16, 319-22, 337, 342, 345
Sweeney, Matthew, 144-51, 153-56
Swift, Jonathan, 121, 146, 161, 251, 253, 257
Symons, Arthur, 312, 331
Synge, John Millington, 141, 214, 225, 245, 248

Thornton, Weldon, 121
Thucydides, 235
Thuente, Mary Helen, 355
Todhunter, John, 334
Todorov, Tzvetan, 1, 2, 10-12, 149, 151, 188, 192-93, 235, 331, 333-36, 381-82
Toibin, Colm, 253
Tolkien, J. R. R., 163, 268-69, 275
Toomey, Deirdre, 233-34
Toynbee, Arnold, 376, 380

Unterecker, John, 361

Victoria, Queen, 127
Villiers de l'Isle d'Adam, Auguste, 331, 344
Virgil, 284

Weil, Simone, 154
Wellesley, Dorothy, 290
Wilde, Constance, 228
Wilde, Janes Francesca "Speranza", 219-26, 368
Wilde, Oscar, 228-36, 243, 244, 247, 248, 251
Wilde, William, 219-26
Williams, Charles, 316
Williams, Tennessee, 170
Winckelman, Johann Joachim, 258
Winters, Yvor, 332-35
Woodcock, George, 228

Index

Woods, Vincent, 97-99, 102-03, 109, 111-13, 115, 117
Woolf, Virginia, 231

Yeats, Georgiana (Georgie Hyde-Lees), 285, 287
Yeats, William Butler, 1, 3, 11-14, 30, 35, 121, 124, 136, 159, 167-71, 174-75, 208-17, 219-21, 223, 226, 232-34, 241, 245, 248-51, 254, 282-98, 303-04, 306-16, 319-28, 331-32, 334-43, 351-62, 365-67, 369-82
Young, Edith, 306

Ziolkowski, Theodore, 21